MATERIALS FOR A SANTALI GRAMMAR

Vol. 2

P. O. Bodding

GYAN

MATERIALS FOR A SANTALI GRAMMAR

Vol. 2

P. O. Bodding

ISBN : 9788121297301

First Published 1929, reprint 2019 in India by

Gyan Books Pvt ltd
Gyan Avenue 12 Pragati Market
Ashok Vihar Phase-2
Delhi-110052

MATERIALS

FOR

A SANTALI GRAMMAR

II

MOSTLY MORPHOLOGICAL

By

The Rev. P. O. Bodding

DUMKA

Published by the Santal Mission of the Northern Churches

1929

FOREWORD

In the Foreword to the first part of these 'Materials for a Santali Grammar' it was remarked that the work was called so, because the writer wanted to have more latitude than would have been possible with another title such as simply 'Grammar'. This remark also applies to the present part, that should principally deal with the morphology of the language. Much syntactic matter has come in, partly because omission would make it more difficult for the student to understand the peculiar working of this agglutinating language. Some matter, more belonging to a treatise on the formation of words, has also been included. It is the writer's wish, if spared, in a third part to deal with the syntax and word formation.

The nomenclature presents many real difficulties. The working of an agglutinating language or of the mind of the speakers of such a language is, as will be seen, very different from that of an inflexional language. The ordinary grammatical terms have (with a few additions) been used; these are not, however, adequate to the needs of a language that represents a stage of development different from that of the inflexional languages. Any one who could coin terms suitable for the needs of an agglutinating language would render a real service to the student of this and similar languages.

It has often been said that a language like Santali has many expressions or words for what is concrete and special and few for what is general and abstract. This is quite so; but the writer has often wondered whether it would not be more correct to say, that the words, the ingredients of the language, are in themselves, not abstract, but rather not-applied, pre-concrete, if such an expression can be used, and that the Santal mind to use the ingredients must make concrete application. This to some extent explains why a word may be used as a noun, a verb, etc. The use depends on the immediate concrete application of the concept.

Mohulpahari,
Santal Parganas } 18th April 1929 P. O. Bodding.

——:000:——

Introductory remarks

Before entering on grammatical details it may be of some use to the advanced student of the Santali language to pay attention to some of the general principles underlying the working of the language, more especially where some difference is observable between our languages and Santali.

1. The phonetics of the Santali language have been examined in the first part of this work (Materials for a Santali Grammar I.), with results as follows, compared with our languages :—

(*a*) As regards the details of phonetical *analysis*, as might be expected, no fundamental difference has been found between Santali and other languages. Some differences are, of course, met with in minor details, but not more than may be found between any languages. Santali has a number of sounds not heard in our languages.

(*b*) When we investigate phonetial *synthesis*, that is to say, the subjects generally treated under this heading, we are met with some difference between our languages and Santali with regard to one point, apparently due to the kind of agglutinating* principle ruling the language. The agglutination affects the whole language and also its phonetics.

---

* This old name is retained here: it fits the language well.

This has to some extent been examined in the section on Stress, to which the reader is referred (see Materials I. paras 148 ss.); it is here just mentioned that it should not be lost sight of.

The peculiarities of Santali in respect of the matters here referred to may be said to be the following:-

Stress is comparatively level and dependent on vowel quantity.

Double (long) stop-consonants are not met with inside the base word, but may occur when a suffix added has the same consonant initial as the final consonant of the preceding word.

Consonant combinations requiring strong stress to be pronounced are not met with.

The spoken language is divided into what has been called stress-units.

The slurring over, or swallowing up of sounds and syllables, so common in inflexional languages, partly due to the mode of stress employed, is unknown in Santali, all sounds and syllables being fully pronounced.

2. While there is not so much difference with regard to phonetics, there is a more decided difference when we look at the language from the morphological and lexicological points of view.

Now, Santali may be said to have or, in any case, to use the same parts of speech as our languages. It uses Interjections, Conjunctions, Demonstratives, Pronouns, Numerals, Adverbs, Verbs, Adjectives and Nouns.

But while in our languages a noun is a noun, an adjective an adjective, a verb a verb, and so on, in Santali every word, that is to say, the same word may, with the same stress and intonation, stand for what we call a noun, an adjective or a verb, the context showing what part of speech we shall have to make use of to express what the word conveys to the Santal mind. As a matter of fact there is not a word in the Santal language, belonging to any of the above enumerated parts of speech to which a verbal suffix cannot be added, in other words, that cannot be used as a verb, or as what we understand by a verb, in some way or other. Even an interjection or a numeral, a personal pronoun or a demonstrative adverb may be so used.

All flexion of words, what we call declension and conjugation, is, in our sense of the terms, non-existent.

A word represents or gives expression to, or name to a concept. The further development of this concept, its relation to concrete reality, to time and to other concepts or realities, its execution or its action, and so on, all this is expressed through auxiliaries, i. e., suffixes and postpositions that specify and fix all particulars wanted and needed.

The base-word is always left untouched, the only exceptions from this last rule being, (*a*) a reduplication of the initial consonant with its following vowel, or an infixed checked consonant after the first vowel, to show that the concept is to be taken to be active, to be looked at from the point of view of the doer (this 'make up' is found in what has been called the Performative form of the verb); (*b*) the change of a final checked to a full voiced consonant in a certain verbal form; (*c*) certain infixes.

If the forms referred to under (*a*) are not to be considered as belonging to the category of new words, coming under word-formation, to express new concepts (as seems likely with all infixes), we may have to accept them as forms showing some development outside Santali agglutination.

3. We may, for the sake of convenience, in Santali grammar make use of the *termini technici* employed in the grammars of our own languages. It should, however, be distinctly understood that in many cases, perhaps one should say generally, our *termini*, when used for the purposes of the Santali grammar, do not fully express what they are wanted for in connection with Santali. They fall short of what is needed; our terms are limited.

When something is called a noun in Santali, this is necessarily only one aspect of what the word in question stands for; it may be the predominant one; but the same word may, as stated above, be used as, and consequently also be grammatically styled, something different.

We shall come back to this a little further on.

4. The Santal language may be said to be made up of two classes of words, those expressing selfcontained or independent concepts, and the auxiliaries.

The selfcontained words might, so far as Santali is concerned, be roughly divided into

(1) descriptive elements;

(2) demonstrative and pronominal elements;

(3) interjectional elements.

The auxiliaries are

(1) enclitic particles;

(2) postpositions;

(3) suffixes.

The auxiliaries do not in the present language represent any selfcontained or independent concept; they are used partly as determinatives to emphasize or fix the concrete reality of the concept, partly to show the place, time, &c., of the concept, to show or mark its position in, or in relationship to concrete reality. They may consequently roughly be divided into two classes, one class consisting of the determinatives, another of suffixes showing the relation to time or sequence of events or to action.

With reference to the auxiliaries we shall here only say that they likely are not all of them originally what they at present stand for. It seems to be possible to trace the origin of some of them. This does not, however, alter their present status, whatever their 'individual' history may be. The language demands and is in need of these subservient elements. They will be discussed in detail in the grammar itself.

5. To help the student to understand the working method of the language we shall make some detailed remarks concerning what we have called the descriptive elements.

The words representing these each give expression to a concept. They may be either primary or secondary.

A primary word may be the bare root, or a word that in the present language is the result of a formation or combination, which it may, or may not, be possible to trace now.

If it is a borrowed word (present-day Santali has a very large number of these), it is always adapted to the genius of the language of the Santals, whatever may be its status where the word originally belonged.

Whatever the history of a word may be, i. e., however a word of this kind may be formed, and whatever component parts it may really consist of, in Santali a word of the class here mentioned represents a particular concept.

While a concept as such is not naturally concretely fixed the word representing it will, when used, be concretely applied, according to need, and in accordance with the nature of the concept.

The Santal language aims at and insists on reality and on the logic of realities. It seems to be a necessity for the Santal mind, as shown in its language, to apply the concepts to concrete facts. It might perhaps be expressed in the following way: The Santal mind is naturally turned towards the concrete, and applies language to this; but, except when having become names of special objects, their words do not, so to say, reflect the concrete, until such application is made and exhibited, especially also through the use of what has been here called auxiliaries (suffixes, &c.).

A concept will by usage and intention be fixed to something concrete, and the word, the sound-expression of the concept, will become the name of the being or thing, action or quality in question, and will as such become something having a reacting power or influence on the Santal mind. In other words, the word represents something having a separate existence, with all that this includes or conveys to the mind.

The frequency of the application to some definite concrete thing, &c., may influence the character of the word and narrow its use and meaning down to one object.

According to the nature of the object to which the concept is applied the word may, by us, be counted a noun, an adjective, a verb or an adverb. The same Santal word may, according to the meaning of the concept, be any of these, consequently something more and something less, something a little different from, and not exactly the same, as what we understand by the terms mentioned.

The way in which a word, according to our terminology, is used to some extent depends on the character of the concept, whether it will stand for something having a separate existence, or is naturally an attribute to something else, needing a kind of substratum.

The use of a word may restrict its application to a certain class; in this way a word may become practically a noun or an adjective, &c., according to our terminology. It should not, however, be forgotten that this is the result of the general employment of the word. The nature of a Santal word, as here described, is never lost. The possibility of a manifold use is always there.

Above remarks refer to primary words. The same holds good for compounds, when they are a word repeated or a number of words juxtaposed, and also for base-words formed by a prefix or an infix.

6. To some limited extent the same applies also to secondary or constructed words, base-words or primary words to which suffixes have been added.

Some difference naturally occurs between the primary and the secondary words, these last ones, as distinguished from the primary received words, being momentary constructions, fixing the concept of the primary word in relation to time, place or concrete existence or in any other way.

The auxiliaries will necessarily define and restrict the use of the concept applied, i. e., eliminate the possibility of any use or application except one or a very few. The concept thus created or applied may, e. g., be used as an adjective or as a verb, but not as a noun, or vice versa.

It should not, however, be understood as if the above mentioned limitations in use were in opposition to the described nature of the language. To some extent it may be said that Santali by the constructions just alluded to approaches the formations met with in inflexional languages. There is, however, a decisive difference.

While in the inflexional languages the base and the suffixes have grown together into one word, the component parts of which are inseparable, in Santali all constructions are always and naturally dissolvable. All combinations are momentarily made, the speaker making use of the base-words and the auxiliaries placed at his disposal by the language; the constructions are only temporary and as easily dissolved.

Further: in Santali the suffixes, &c., do not alter the nature of the concept, but only define its relation to concrete reality, to place, time, action, object, or whatever it may be.

All particles of speech necessary to produce living language are more or less important separate units, never losing their identity and character. Although the auxiliaries have no independent existence they have a peculiar and decisive force, directing the concepts of the words.

7. In Santali a number of words are found that have got certain concrete meanings attached to them. Investigation shows that such words are either loan-words taken over primarily to give name to something non-Santal (perhaps when the thing or the concept was first introduced to the people), or they may represent a concept that may be demonstrated and has by usage been attached to some separate

concrete object. As has been stated elsewhere, all borrowed words are, as a condition for adoption into the language, made subject to the ordinary laws of Santal words, especially also the phonetic laws of the language.

8. In our languages we have a very large number of words (or perhaps we should say most of the words) that in their present form are the result of a long development and stand for correspondingly developed concepts, far removed from what may have been the original, concepts implying possibilities, abstractions or whatever it may be.

The state of matter is somewhat different in Santali. Here also every word must have a shorter or longer history behind itself, whether we, as in the case of loanwords, are able to trace a word's history and probable origin, or else not, as is often the case. This is not, however, the present point. We have to take account of the way in which the Santal mind makes use of the concepts, incidentally also what kind of concepts the Santal mind works with.

9. With the already stated borne in mind it is easy to understand another characteristic of the language.

A word does not in itself regularly represent a concrete object or a definable reality, although usage may let it develop into doing so. On the other hand a word may, as already pointed out, stand for several of what we call parts of speech. But this is not all.

With the lack of a defined fixity of the concepts it is obviously possible to look at certain concepts from different points of view. If we take a concept representing an action, it is possible and indeed necessary to look at it from several standpoints, or, if one likes, to look at the different stages in the development or the performance of an action. We may look at an action from the standpoint of the subject (the actor or doer), or the beginning, from the standpoint of the object (what is done), the result or conclusion of an action; we may look at the middle, more or less neutral as to beginning and end. The aspect will in all cases be different.

Whatever a concept may be to the Santal mind, in our languages we are obliged to, and also entitled to, render the same word in different ways. According to circumstances we may have to translate a word with a noun or an adjective, with the infinitive, the present participle or the *participium perfecti passivi*, in Santali in all cases the identical unaltered word.

In some words all the meanings mentioned may be in constant application, in others only a couple may be ordinarily met with.

The auxiliaries will, if at all used, show the aspect taken, otherwise the surroundings.

Some examples will show how the language works and the different ways in which a word may be used. Details will be found in the grammar itself.

The Santali word *kombṛo*, a thief, a theft, thieving, to steal, stolen, bereft, may according to the context be translated with any of the meanings given. Thus: *kombṛoko sap'kedea*, they caught the thief; *kombṛo sạbudena*, a theft was proved to have taken place; *kombṛokeṭae*, he stole; *kombṛo hoṛ*, a thieving person (might also mean, a bereft person); *kombṛo merom*, a stolen goat; *kombṛokedeako*, they have stolen it (e. g. a goat), or, they have stolen from him, robbed him (lit. made him the object of stealing), or, they made him out to be the thief. The last example shows, how the meaning may alter according to the point of view taken with regard to the primary word.

Oṛak', house; *oṛak' hoṛ*, house-person (mostly used about the wife, but may also be used about the husband); *oṛak'-keṭae*, he made a house; *oṛak'anae*, he made a house for himself; *tala oṛak'*, the middle house, or the middle (inner part) of a house; *tala oṛak' kandha*, a room in the middle of the house; *tala oṛak'kedeako*, they put him in the middle of the house, made him one of themselves; *oṛak' oṛak'*, houses; *oṛak' oṛak' ñelme*, look house house, i. e., in every house; *oṛak' ṭhenak' dare*, the tree near the house; *oṛak' ṭhenak'keṭae*, he gave it its place near the house.

Pasi, a snare; *pasi cẽṛẽ*, a snared bird; *pasikeṭae*, he made a snare; *pasikedeako*, they snared him, hanged him.

Hende, blackness; *hende gai*, a black cow; *hende horo*, black paddy; *hendeyena*, it has turned black; *hendeic'*, the black one (as distinguished from one of another colour); *hendeye rimil-akat'ae*, lit. he has 'clouded' blackly, about dark, threatening clouds overspreading.

Ak'yur, leading; *ak'yur hoṛ*, a leading man; *ak'yur kan tahẽkanae*, he was leading.

Bebenao (or *beknao*), building, making; *bebenao hoṛ*, a man who builds or makes; *bebenao kanae*, he is building.

Etohop', beginning (from *ehop'*); *etohop' kami*, the first work; *etohop'keṭae*, he made a beginning.

Mucat', end; *mucat' cando*, ending month, i. e., the end of the month; *mucaṭenae*, he ended, died; *munucat'*, end; *munucat' orak'*, the ending house, end of house.

Bapla, marriage; *bapla hoṛ*, a married person; *baplak' kanako*, they are having a marriage; *baplayenakin*, they (two) were married.

10. In our languages, or for instance, in Latin and Greek, we have a large number of word-forming terminations that in one way or another develop, modify, amplify, qualify, or to some degree alter the original concept and consequently give expression to something new, and even different, a fresh concept by degrees grown out of the old one, a peculiarity that may be said to be one of the conditions for progress and one of the causes of this; there is an interaction.

Santali has no terminations of the same kind, only suffixes, infixes and prefixes. None of these, however, modifies the concept a such. They serve to make the concrete application of the concept.

11. A result of this is that while it is possible to apply one concept to different objects, and in this way to give different meanings to the same word, the concept itself is not so liable to unconscious growth and development as is met with in our languages.

Now, the Santali words are naturally not exclusively root-words; indeed, few of them are the naked roots; they may be, and in many cases without doubt are, compositions of roots or later added or infixed characters (i. e., sounds). This does not, however, take us further than the base-words themselves, that are expressions of concepts.

In our languages the terminations are always incorporated in the words themselves; they are word-forming and may, and often do, modify the original concept by qualifying it in different ways. In Santali the words do not get an intrinsically modified meaning (because such word-forming terminations do not appear to be found in the present language), but every word is a specialized application, referring to some observable, particular, concrete existing state or action.

A direct result of this is the existence in Santali of an immense number of words giving a name to anything observed by any of the senses, when we very frequently have no corresponding word and have to be, and for that sake are, satisfied translating with something general and describing. The Santals have apparently a great faculty of coining words for the concrete existing.

The stage reached by the inflexional languages represents a decided advance, the implements of thought having been both augmented or manifolded and refined.

12. It has often been stated that Santali has few words to express abstract and general ideas, while the language, as just mentioned, has an abundance of words for the concrete and the special. This is true, and the cause is the tendency of the language, or rather of the Santal mind, to give all concepts concrete application, just the opposite of what lies in the word abstract, and the opposite of generalization.

Our languages may be said—within certain spheres—to have got more or less away from specializing by separation or multiplying words, and to attain what is wanted by combining words, by definition and description.

The Santal likes the manifold concrete names and finds possibly his own method to be the easier, as it in one way may also be. The sound-combination making up a word may to them likely often seem to be representative of realities, to have an inherent meaning. They are, so to say, nearer to the roots than we are.

13. What has been stated above will in one respect require a small qualification. Santali has naturally concepts that are the result of combination or co-ordination. In stead of one word we may have two or more, sometimes co-ordinated, sometimes standing in interdependent relation to one another. Sometimes a whole sentence may be treated as a concept, just as it may happen in our languages.

The peculiarity with Santali is that compound ideas are always naturally dissolvable into their component parts. It might be said that all Santal combinations are mechanical, not chemical compounds.*

---

*How far the peculiarities mentioned affect the mental development and consequently also the civilization of the people, might form the subject of a most interesting inquiry. Roughly taken it might seem that this concretely specializing peculiarity, and the more or less concretely fixed meaning of the words, allow less room for thought and deliberation and especially less opportunity for the play of the imagination, so immensely important for all development, and also allow less room for mistakes, because there are fewer possibilities, less to choose between. The borderland between reality and non-existence, between right and wrong, where the mind has constantly to work, and has its many possibilities for advance and development, for gaining new territories and eliminating fallacies, —this borderland is with people like the Santals and in languages like theirs much more confined than is the case with, e.g., us and our languages.

Incidentally it may be remarked that the distance from uncertainty to downright wrong or the truth or fact is much shorter with the Santals than with us. There is not that latitude naturally bound up with or given by the language which permits of uncertainty, doubt or even unconscious selfdeception. The possibilities of unwitting and unconscious erring with all that this may open a way for, are very few. According to the demands of the language a decision will have to be made or a *non liquet* declared. I suppose we have here the explanation of the often remarked truthfulness of the people (although not the only one), a characteristic which is now, more is the pity, often changed into deliberate lying. Their language does not afford so many opportunities of keeping in the borderland; it will have to be the one or the other.

When their imagination commences to play, it is liable to run into the regions of the fairy-tale.

Taking all into consideration one might be inclined to think that unaided, left to themselves, their possibilities of development are limited to certain spheres. Their history also seems to prove this. Within their own sphere and with the implements at their disposal they are good and efficient. To get further they must have help.

The question that arises and that cannot find an absolute answer, whether it concerns the Santals or others, is this: would it help, if they were taught the use of a modern language? Or, to put it in another way, will the Santals be able to develop, if they do not adopt for use a foreign language?

——————(o)——————

14. As mentioned in the Introductory remarks the Santali language does not to the same extent as our languages distinguish the different parts of speech. On the other hand it may be said, that the descriptive elements of the language may be and are used now as nouns, now as adjectives, verbs, &c. We shall in the following examine the use of these words as nouns, &c. It should, however, always be borne in mind that the bare word is something more or something less than what we understand by the terms.

Before entering on details with reference to the different uses of words mentioned, especially as nouns and adjectives, it is necessary to know, how the language is equipped with regard to Gender and Number, how these are shown, and also to know certain determinative particles and suffixes employed.

Gender.

15. Genuine, or rather original, Santali, as distinguished from what the language has borrowed from other, especially Aryan, languages, does not formally distinguish between genders. It has not the means of doing so, i. e., has no suffixes to be used for this purpose. The language, on the

other hand, distinguishes between the male and the female sexes, by adding a word denoting the sex or by using a special word indicating the male or the female of any class. Besides Santali distinguishes between the animate and the inanimate.

16. (*a*) In Santali we certainly meet with a very large number of words with separate masculine and feminine forms, the masculine forms ending in -*a*, and the feminine ones in -*i*, these last ones also often a little differentiated by an alteration in the preceding vowel of the word (nearly all these words are dissyllabic) when demanded by the laws of harmonic sequence ruling the language (see Materials I. para 24.).

(*b*) Investigation shows that practically all these words have been borrowed from Aryan sources, especially from Hindi.

In order to explain these masculine and feminine forms in Santali it is not necessary to seek further than to what has been mentioned with reference to the concrete application of every word. In each case the whole word has been adopted, without any special reference to the genus-termination. The borrowed word had this form.*

(*c*) Another matter is, that with such a large number of borrowed words, having genus-terminations, these word-endings may possibly have impressed the Santal mind, so that they sometimes instinctively combine the terminations, or rather words having such terminations, with genus, possibly not so much as regards sex, as regards

---

*It is a mistake to conclude, as has been done, that the whole is more than an adoption of foreign words in their original form, and to conclude that these forms should be an indication, that Santali has formerly formally distinguished the genders.

It might also be mentioned, that Santali has words for masculine beings ending in -*i* and for females ending in -*a* (as e. g., *mañjhi*, headman; *kuli*, a working man, as opposite *reja* a working woman; *era*, wife; *eñga*, mother, female.)

size and strength, -*a* conveying the idea of what is large and strong, and -*i* of the opposite, what is small, fine and weak, exactly as is the case in the Aryan languages of North-India.

E. g, *koṛa*, boy; *kuṛi*, girl; *bheḍa*, a ram; *bhiḍi*, a sheep, an ewe; *bạkrạ*, male young sheep; *bạkri*, do. female; *kala*, deaf, m.; *kạli*, deaf, f.; *ḍaṅgra*, a bullock; *ḍạṅgri*, a word found only in certain combinations, meaning a cow or cattle in general, possibly formed by Santals in accordance with the Aryan feminine termination; *bacha*, bull calf; *bạchi*, female calf; *ṭamna*, mattock; *ṭạmni*, do.; *hạtạuṛa*, a sledge hammer; *hạtạuṛi*, do. smaller; *ḍhakna*, an earthenware lid; *ḍhạkni*, do., but smaller (of this last word a very commonly used form is *ḍhạknic̓*, a Hindi word to which a genuine Santali word-forming 'sound' has been added, a not uncommon occurrence in the language): *ḍubhạ*, a large metal bowl; *ḍubhi*, a smaller do.; *kaṅkha*, rim of a vessel; *kạṅkhi*, do.

17. A great many of the jingles or double words occurring in Santali consist of the just mentioned masculine and feminine forms of the same word. There is little thought, if any, of gender; it is the collective completeness which is sought expressed in this way, big and small, strong and weak, coarse and fine, the opposite extremes, whether to express completeness or opposite parties or ends.

E. g., *ạuṛạ ạuṛi*, vainly; *dhara dhạri*, neighbourhood; *purạ puri*, what completes, all of it; *bara bạri*, equal(ly), *ạulạ ạuli*, disorder; *dhawa dhạvi*, chase, on the heels of; *hara hạri*, competing; *khijlạ khijli*, worry, pestering; *samna sạmni*, face to face; *sesa sisi*, what is towards the end, about to end, close up; *ṭana ṭạni*, pulling in different directions, strife, uncertainty of mind; *badu bạdi*, enmity; *aḍra ạḍri*, bellow; *khanḍa khạnḍi*, wrangle.

All examples that might be adduced are either simply borrowed or adapted from, generally, some Hindi dialect.

18. While Santali, except, as mentioned, in borrowed and adopted words, does not formally distinguish genders, the language, as a matter of course, *distinguishes between the sexes*, when reality demands such a distinction. The language distinguishes between the male and the female, where such concretely exist and are observable.

19. Like other languages Santali has, a *genus commune*, used to denote a class, including both sexes; sex is not reflected on.

Among the words denoting a *genus commune* the following may be noted :

A *genus commune* is found in connection with the names for certain relationships and also for offspring, whether human or otherwise.

Boeha (from Skr. *bhratri*, brother) is used in Santali about both brother and sister; if the sex is to be distinguished, another word has to be added, although used alone it is commonly understood as meaning brother. The list of the names of relationships will show a few more of the same kind.

Bọkọ (*-ń, -m, -t*), my, etc., younger brother or sister.

Họpọn, child, young one, small one, is used about both males and females.

Korar (*-iń, -me, -tẹt'*), my, etc., grandchild; *nạti*, do; *erwel* (*-iń, -me, -tẹt'*), my, etc., wife's younger brother or sister; *bala* (*-ń, -m, -t*), my, etc., co-parent-in-law.

Janwar, animal; *nrić*, cattle, cows or bullocks (now not often heard); *mĩhũ*, calf;

jel, deer, used about all kinds of wild deer; also used about flesh, meat (possibly the original meaning);

seta, dog; *pusi*, cat; *sukri*, pig; *sim*, fowl; *sãk*, goose; *cẹ̃rẽ*, bird;

the names of practically all animals, birds, reptiles, fishes and insects.

In a few cases the name of the female, or the male, or the name of the young ones of the class may be used, as if it were *genus commune.*

E. g., *mẹrọm*, a goat (she-goat), used also collectively about both sexes mixed. The same is the case with *gạí*, cow (*aema gạí menakkotaea*, he has a large number of cows, meaning cattle, excluding buffaloes). *Mĩhũ mẹrọm*, lit. calf goat, the most common expression for cattle, goats and sheep, in general; *bhiḍi mẹrọm*, lit. sheep goat, including both sexes. *Gạí kaḍa*, lit. cow buffalo (male), about cattle in general, including buffaloes.

20. The language distinguishes between the sexes

(*a*) by using different words for the male and the female. A large number of relatives of different sexes is distinguished in this way.

This manner of distinguishing the sexes is mainly confined to human beings, to domesticated animals and to game animals and other beings, with whom man in some way or other comes, or is, in constant contact.

E. g., (for human beings) *hẹṛẹl*, or seldom *hẹpẹl*, man; *maejiu*, woman, *qimạí*, woman (often vulgar); *

bạbu, male child, young man, also used in addressing any male younger than oneself, when a relationship-term is not used (*bạbu* is also used, by all, as a name for membrum virile, just as *mĩụi* is used about the female organ);

mĩụi, girl; *mạku*, girl (specially used of young girls and also as a term of endearment; both *mĩụi* and *mạku* are used in addressing females younger than oneself, in the same way as *bạbu* is used to males); besides *mạku* in recent years *pạku* (also pronounced *poku*) has come into use;

haṛam, old man, also husband; *buḍhi*, old woman, also wife; *buḍhiạ*, old woman, mother; *buḍhiạ ayo*, mother, grandmother.

---

* I am informed that in certain parts the expressions *sạṇḍi gate* and *kalọṭ gate* are used in the meaning of boy companion and girl companion or friend; this probably is due to influence from Muṇḍari.

(For animals) *sāṇḍ*, steer; *ḍaṅgra*, bullock; *damkom*, bull calf; *gai*, cow (also, as remarked, used as a common name for cattle); *pheṭāṛ*, heifer; *guṇḍi*, a cow used for ploughing;

kaḍa, male buffalo (sometimes also used as *genus commune*); *kaḍru*, male buffalo calf; *bitkil*, buffalo cow; *kaḍi*, buffalo calf (young, f.); *saṇḍharo*, buffalo heifer;

kuḍu, a boar; *paṭhi*, a young sow before littering; *badhia*, a castrated pig; *boda*, he-goat; *merom*, * goat; *paṭhi*, a she-kid; *khasi*, castrated he-goat or ram; *kaloṭ*, a grown hen, not yet laying; *gaya*, a capon;

jhaṅkar, the spotted deer male; *posta*, do. female; *murum*, the Nilgae male; *sosam*, do. female; *sal*, the Indian Gour, *saram*, do. female (*saram* is also used about certain other species of deer);

ṭira, the male quail (Turnix sykesii), *ghura*, the female do.; *ṭira* is also used about the male of several silkworm moths, and *patni* about the female of the same moths; *huker gunḍri* and *kasi jerak*, the male and female of a species of quail.

A few more examples will be found under (*b*); they have not been mentioned here, because the names in question as a rule do not stand alone, but are prefixed to a word denoting the *genus commune*.

(*b*) The principal words signifying relationship are the following, enumerated here to have them in one place:

Ba, *baba*, father, mostly used in addressing and in children's language; *bap*, *bapa*, *bapu*, father, ancestor (these forms with *p* are now obsolete, except in certain stereotyped expressions, in invocations and *binti*);

---

* *Merom*, although really meaning she-goat, is frequently used as if being *genus commune*, as *merom boda*, he-goat; *merom eṅga*, a full-grown she-goat; *merom khasi*, a castrated he-goat.

apa (*-t*), his, her, their father (*apa* without a following suffixed pronominal consonant (see below under personal pronouns) is used only in a very few combinations, when there is no reference to any particular relation, and never alone, *apa hor*, *apa hon*, *enga apa*) ; *apu -ñ, -ñ, -m*, my, our, thy, your father (*apuñ* is used in addressing ; *apu* without suffixed consonant is not met with) ; *apus*, relations, kindred (on father's side).

Go, *gogo*, mother (*gogo* especially in children's language) ; *go budhia*, mother ;

enga (*-ñ, -m, -t*), my, our, thy, your, his, her, their mother (for *engañ*, my, our mother, *ingañ* is frequently used, cp. Materials I. para 23 ; in the meaning of mother *enga* is used without a suffixed pronominal consonant only in a few combinations, like *apa* : *enga apa*, *enga hon*, *enga hopon*) ; *ayo* (also *ayo*), mother ; *ayo budhia*, do. ; *aia*, mother (used by small children, not common).

Hadkur, male relatives on father's side ; *mamkur*, male relatives on mother's side.

Gorom, namesake, grand-parent (also used about grand-child), *gorom ba*, *- baba*, grandfather ; *gorom* (*-iñ, -me, -tet'*), my, thy, his, her, their namesake, *- haram*, my, thy, etc., grandfather ; *-budhi*, *-budhia*, *-ayo*, *-go*, my, etc., grand-mother ; *gorom* (*-iñ, etc.,*) *kora*, *- kuri*, *- gidra*, *-hopon*, my, etc., grandson, granddaughter, grandchild (the pronominal suffixes are not necessary with *gorom*, but used when definite relationship to somebody is mentioned) ; *buda ba*, *-baba*, grandfather (now seldom used) ;

haram baba and *budi go* (*-ayo*) are also used about grandfather and grandmother ; (*gorom baba*, *gorom ayo*, may also be used addressing any elderly man or woman, when not known to speaker) ;

jae dada (*-ñ, -m, -t*), my, etc., great grandfather ; *jae tata* (*-ñ -m -t*), do. ; *jae didi* (*-ñ, - m, -t*), *jae dai*, great grand-mother ;

korar (*-iñ, -me, -tet'*), my, etc., grandchild (often with added *kora* or *kuri*, grandson or granddaughter) ;

jae korar, great grandchild (further constructed as above) ; *nati*, grandchild (*- kora, -kuri*) ; *nati puti*, grandchildren ;

aja, grandfather, father's father (used nearly exclusively in *binti*); *aja nạti*, grandfather and grandchild ; *ạji*, grandmother.

Da, elder brother (mostly in address) ; *dada* (*-ń*, *-m*, *-t*), my, etc., elder brother ;

dại, elder sister, especially in addressing ; *didi*, do. (not common), *ạji* (*-ń*, *-m*, *-t*), my, etc., elder sister (*ạji* without pronominal suffix is not used about a sister), *nạji* (*-ń*, *-m*, *-t*), do.

The Santals count cousins, any number of times removed, brothers and sisters ; the following are examples of how such relationship may be described : *kumạń hopon ạjiń*, my elder sister who is the daughter of my father's sister ; *mamoń hopon ạjiń*, do. who is the daughter of my maternal uncle ; *goṅgoń hopon ạjiń*, do. who is the daughter of my father's elder brother ; *kakań hopon ạjiń*, do. who is the daughter of my father's younger brother ; *kạkiń hopon ạjiń*, do. who is the daughter of my *kạki*, father's younger brother's wife ; *hatomiń hopon ạjiń*, do. who is the daughter of my father's sister ; *bahońhariń rinič ạjiń*, do. who is the wife of my wife's elder brother ; *ajhnariń ạjiń*, do. who is the elder sister of my wife or husband ;

bohok' bohok' boeha, *bohok' bohok' boeha hopon*, *bohok' bohok' hopon*, cousins any number of times removed, descendants in the male line ; regularly used only about males, but now females are also included, but not children of these.

Boko (*-ń*, *-m*, *-t*), my, etc., younger brother, or sister (generally, but not necessarily, *koṛa* or *kuṛi* is added to show whether it is brother or sister) ; *boko*, without the pronominal suffix, is found in a few expressions, *boko boeha*, and *boko bokoeha*, brothers and sisters.

Bhại, brother, near relative ; the word is a recent loan-word, and is constantly used about a companion, especially also in addressing any male, equivalent to 'my dear fellow' or something similar ; *dada bhại*, elder brother ; *saṅ bhại*, *soṅ bhại*, *saṅga bhại* brother, companion (mostly used about artificial brother-relationship) ;

bhạiạdi, brothers, relatives ; *bhại bhagar*, relatives.

Goṅgo (*-ń*, *-m*, *-t*), my, etc., father's elder brother, *or*, younger brother's child (whether it is uncle or nephew will be understood from the situation) ; often *baba* (father, in case of uncle), and *koṛa* or *kuṛi* (in case of nephew and niece) are added; *goṅgo* without pronominal suffix is used in certain combinations (such as *goṅgo salaka, goṅgo bala, goṅgo hoṅhar*, and some others); in address, and

goṅgo ayo, the same as *goṅgo era* aunt, father's elder brother's wife. †

Ka (in Santali in address only), *kaka* (*-ń, -m, -t*), my, etc., father's younger brother, *or*, husband of mother's younger sister; the pronominal suffix is generally used, but not necessarily always; it is omitted in addressing, and in certain combinations, *kaka* (or *kaka-ń*, etc.) *apu-ń, kaka baba*, stepfather, *kaka hoṅhar* (father in-law's younger brother), *kaka khuṛa* (cousins, sons of brothers), and *kaka goṅgo*, paternal uncles, *kaka bala*, younger brother of one's son's or daughter's father-in-law, or, husband of son's or daughter's mother-in-law's younger sister; (*kaka baba* is used as the name for a step-father, likely because in case of the father's death their father's younger brother may take the mother for his wife);

kaki (*-ń, -m, -t*), wife of my, etc. father's younger brother, *or*, mother's younger sister; *ki* (used only in address), do., *kaki go, - eṅga, - ayo, -hanhar, - gaṛhan.* *

---

† *Goṅgo* is possibly a reduplication of *go*, now used in address to wife's or husband's elder brother.

* In speaking of uncles and aunts the Santals instead of using *goṅgo, kaka*, etc., often say *maraṅ baba, tala baba, huḍiń baba*, i. e., big father, middle father, little father, *maraṅ go, tala go*, etc., big mother, middle mother, and so on. If there are more than three, they may be further distinguished by *maraṅ tala, huḍiń tala, saṅjhla* (*saṅjla*), *saṅjhli* (fem.), *maṅjhla* (m.) *maṅjhli* (f.), i. e. big middle, small middle, the one between the big and the middle one, or between the middle and the small one; *saṅjhla* (*saṅjhli*) is the third and *maṅjhla* (*maṅjhli*) the fourth one. The same way of distinguishing is used about brothers and sisters, also other relatives mentioned, when standing in similar relationship (*maraṅ jãwãe, tala kimin*, big son-in-law, husband of eldest daughter, middle daughter-in-law, wife of middle son). *Saṅjhla* is used also about females. Instead of *huḍiń* in these expressions *hopon* is also commonly used (*hopon ba*, small, young father, *hopon go*, small mother, youngest aunt). It should be further remarked, that the

Bhaca (*-ń, -m, - t*), my, etc., nephew or niece, i. e., younger brother's, or wife's elder sister's child (*kora* or *kuri* is frequently added to show sex) ; *homon* (*-iń, -me, -tet'*), my, etc., nephew or niece, girl's (elder or younger) brother's child.

Hatom (*-iń, -me, -tet'*), my, etc., father's sister ; *bonga hatom*, do. (but always full sister, only *hatom* may be father's cousin) ; *hatom hanhar*, father-in-law's sister ; *mamo hatom*, mother's brother's wife.

Mama, maternal uncle (mostly in addressing) ; *mamo (-ń, -m, -t)*, my, etc., mother's brother (as to pronominal suffixes the remarks made regarding *kaka* apply) ; *mamo hońhar*, wife's maternal uncle ;
ma masi, children of sisters.

Bhagna (*-ń, -m, -t*), my, etc., sister's child (if needed, *kora* or *kuri* is added to make it clear, whether it is a nephew or a niece) ; *deo bhagin* (used in *binti*), sister and her children ; *mamo* (or *mama*) *bhagna*, maternal uncle and nephew ; *mami*, maternal uncle's wife ; *mami hanhar*, wife's maternal uncle's wife ; *nana*, father's sister ; *nana bhagni*, do. and her nieces.

Bare (*-ń, -m, -t*), my, etc., brother (of a woman, not of a man ; the pronominal suffixes are always used when a special person is referred to ; without such it is found in a few expressions, *apa bare*, father and brothers, male relatives of a woman ; *bare itat'*, a special kind of cloth given to bride's eldest brother at the time of marriage).

Misera (*-ń, -m, -t*), my, etc., sister, elder or younger (of a man, not of a woman).

Hopon, child, offspring, son or daughter (original meaning probably, small, little, a meaning preserved in the language) ; *hopon herel*, son ; *hor hopon*, a Santal, *deko hopon*, a deko ; *herel hopon*, a man, *kora hopon*, a son, boy ; *kuri hopon*, a girl, daughter ; *hopon era*, a daughter ; *era hopon*, wife and children ; *enga hopon*, lit. mother child, the whole family ;

hon, son, child ; *apa hon*, father and child ; *enga hon*, mother and child ; *hon hopon*, children ; *hon kimin*, son and daughter-in-law ; *hon jãwãe*, daughter and son-in-law ;

---

marań, etc. refers to the relative ages of the uncles or aunts, etc., and not to whether the person referred to is a *yongo* or a *kaka*, and so on.

bạbu, boy, son (see above, para 20 (a)).

Beṭa, son, boy (especially in address); *jãwãe beṭa*, son-in-law, bridegroom; *ṭa* (in address only, shortened from *beṭa*, is now heard used for) son.

Họpọnera (*-ń, -m, -t*), my, etc., daughter; *mãi* or *mại*, girl, daughter (see above, para 20 (a)); *mạku*, girl (see above); *biṭi*, daughter (corresponding to *beṭa*); *ṭi*, do. (heard used in address only, shortened from *biṭi*);

kumạ (*-ń, -m, -t*), *kumạń*, my, etc., father's sister's husband; *kumạ họńhar*, husband of father-in-law's sister.

Jãwãe, son-in-law, bridegroom, husband; *jãwãe beṭa*, bridegroom; *jãwãe gomke* (*-ń, -m, -t*), my, etc., son-in-law; *bạhu*, daughter-in-law (so always in address), bride, wife; *bạhu jãwãe*, bride & bridegroom; *bạhu biṭi*, daughter-in-law (mostly in address);

kimin (*-iń, -me, -tẹt'*), my, etc., daughter-in-law.

Họńhar (*-iń, -me, -tẹt'*), my, etc., father-in-law; *goṅgo họńhar*, *kaka họńhar*, father-in-law's elder, or younger brother; *mamọ họńhar*, mother-in-law's brother; *kumạ họńhar*, father-in-law's sister's husband;

hanhar (*-iń, -me, -tẹt'*), my, etc., mother-in-law; *goṅgo hanhar*, father-in-law's elder brother's wife, or, mother-in-law's elder sister; *kạki hanhar*, father-in-law's younger brother's wife, or, mother in-law's younger sister; *hatọm hanhar*, father-in-law's sister, or mother-in-law's brother's wife (in these compound relationship names the pronominal suffix is added to the principal, here the last word, *họńhar* and *hanhar*); *mạmi hanhar*, wife's maternal uncle's wife;

bahọńhar (*-iń, -me, -tẹt'*), my, etc., brother-in-law, husband's or wife's elder brother; *gọ*, do. (only in address);

ajhnar (*-iń, -me, -tẹt'*), my, etc., sister-in-law, husband's or wife's elder sister;

teńa (*-ń, -m, -t, -ń*), my, etc., elder sister's husband; *teńa era*, *teńaea*, the *teńań* and his wife's younger brothers and sisters;
ḍhạuliạ, do.; *saṅga* (*-ń, -m, -t*), the same as *teńa*, but used only by men; *saṅgat* may be used also addressing;

misera (*-ń, -m, -t*) *jãwãe*, my, etc., younger sister's husband (only by men), *bọkọ* (*-ń, -m, -t*) *jãwãe*, my, etc., younger sister's husband (used by both men and women);

hili (*-ń, -m, -t*), my, etc., elder bother's wife;

ervel (*-iń, -me, -tet*), my, etc., wife's or younger brother's wife's younger brother or sister (to avoid misunderstanding, *kora* or *kuri* is often added);

ńala (*-ń, -m, -t*), my, etc., (woman's) brother-in law's wife (*era* is frequently added); *ńatea, ńatea gotop*, the wives of two or more brothers;

batki, first wife; *chutki*, second wife, last wife; *sańjhli* (*sańjli*), second wife, *mańjhli*, third wife, if more than two: *chutki* is always the last one, third, etc., if there are more than two);

hirom(*-iń, -me, -tet*), my, etc., co-wife.

Bala (*-ń, -m, -t*), my, etc., co-parent-in-law, the man, or woman, whose son, or daughter, is married to my, etc., son or daughter; *hor* or *herel* is generally added, when the man, and *era*, when the woman is meant;

gongo bala (*-ń, etc.*), *kaka bala* (*-ń, etc.*), *mamo bala* (*-ń, etc.*) *kumo bala* (*-ń, etc.*), my, etc, *bala's* (only about the man) elder or younger brother, my, etc., *bala era's* brother, or *bala herel's* sister's man, my, etc., *bala* (*herel*)'s sister's husband;

balaea, those whose children have married;

saka, the same as *bala*, and only used together with this word, *bala saka, balaea sakaea*;

gongo bala era, wife of *gongo bala*;

bala (*-ń, -m, -t*) *kuri*, the same as *bala* (*-ń, -m, -t*) *era*;

sumdhi, co-parent-in-law (mostly in address); *sumdhi saheb*, do. (only in address, to men), *bihai*, co-parent-in-law (in address to women).

Sadge (*-ń, -m, -t*), (my, etc.) wife's sister's husband;

sadgea, husbands of two (or more) sisters.

Haga, relative (mostly cousin);

hagaea, mostly about cousins (otherwise generally *kaka gongo boeha*).

(*c*) By prefixing or suffixing a word, denoting sex, to another word that denotes the *genus commune*.

Several of the words mentioned under (*a*) and (*b*) are, as will be seen, used in this way.

The words used to denote sex are principally the following:

For human beings :

herel (or very rarely *hepel*), male, man ; *haṛam*, old man ; *koṛa*, young man, boy ; *maejiu*, female, woman ; *aimai*, woman ; *era*, female, wife ; *budhi*, old woman ; *kuṛi*, young woman, girl.

For others :

aṇḍia, male, used about animals, birds, fishes, insects, dioecious trees and plants ;

saṇḍi, cock, used about certain birds ;

eṅga, mother, female, used about animals, birds, fishes and insects, also about a palm ;

jo, fruit, used about a few dioecious trees.

The sex distinction is used only when required, and when possible of observation.

The sex distinction may be prefixed or suffixed to the word to be defined.

Prefixed the word simply denotes sex ; suffixed it implies something more, existence as qualified or shaped by sex. This is more especially observable in the case of animals.

E. g., *hoṛ herel*, a Santal man, *herel hoṛ* a male (especially) Santal, a man, opposite *maejiu hoṛ*, a woman ; *deko herel*, a Hindu man, not a Santal ; *hopon herel*, child man, i. e., son ; *herel hopon*, a male, man, one belonging to the male section of humanity (significantly, *maejiu hopon*, or, *aimai hopon* are never used, only *kuṛi hopon*, as opposed to *koṛa hopon*, belonging to the girl or boy class) ;

hoṛ koṛa, a Santal boy ; *koṛa hoṛ*, a man or boy (Santal), opposite *haṛam hoṛ*, an aged man ; *hoṛ haṛam*, an aged Santal ; *musla koṛa*, a Mohammedan boy ; *hoṛ aimai*, a Santal woman ; *hoṛ kuṛi*, a Santal girl, *kuṛi hoṛ*, a young (espec. Santal) girl, opposite *budhi hoṛ*, an elderly woman ; *bokoń kuṛi*, my younger sister ;

era, female, wife ; *hoponera*, daughter ; *boeha era*, elder or younger sister (may be used also of a woman's sister) ; *mis-*

era, a man's (not about a woman's) sister; *erattẹt'*, his wife; *mañjhi era*, the village headman's wife; *paranik era*, the deputy headman's wife; *naeke era*, the village priest's wife; *jaher era*, the lady of the sacred grove, a certain goddess; *kisạṛ era*, the master's wife; *bạhu era*, daughter-in-law; *rạṇḍi era hẹmẹ era*, widows and women of ill omen, i. e., witches; *kusmbi era*, a harlot; *jhạlki era*, a licentious woman; *sạṇḍhin era*, do. *

Aṇḍiạ pusi, a male cat, opposite *eṅga pusi*, a female cat; *pusi aṇḍiạ*, a cat of the male class, opp., e. g., *seta aṇḍiạ*, a dog of the male class; *pusi eṅga*, a female cat who lives as a female. The difference in meaning according to whether the word denoting sex is prefixed or suffixed is easily grasped, when it is noted, that while, e. g. *aṇḍiạ pusi* and *eṅga pusi* may be used about a kitten, *pusi aṇḍiạ* and *pusi eṅga* are not so used. *Aṇḍiạ sãk* and *sãk aṇḍiạ*, a gander, *eṅga sãk* and *sãk eṅga*, a goose, the distinction between the two ways of expression being the same as that stated above; *eṅga gẹḍẹ* and *gẹḍẹ eṅga*, a female duck;

aṇḍiạ potam, a male dove; *aṇḍiạ gharwa*, a male sparrow;

eṅga potam, a female dove;

aṇḍiạ kakṛa, a male lizard; *eṅga kakṛa*, a female do.

Sạṇḍi sim, a cock, as opposed to *eṅga sim*, a hen; *sim sạṇḍi*, a domesticated fowl cock, as different from, e. g., *bir sim sạṇḍi*, a wild fowl cock. The use of *sạṇḍi* is restricted to fowls and related birds. The language seems to vacillate a little, some using *sạṇḍi* about most male birds, except waterbirds.

Aṇḍiạ hako, a male fish (rarely used); *aṇḍiạ dare*, a male tree; *eṅga hako*, a female fish; not, however, *hako eṅga*, *dare eṅga*, and so on.

Uru eṅga, "beetle" mother; *rọ eṅga*, a bluebottle; *aṇḍiạ biṅ*, a male snake.

Jọ dare, a tree bearing fruit, may be used of any tree bearing fruit, but also especially of the fruit bearing

---

**Era* probably originally means female, but is now, except in the words mentioned, used about a wife; generally it is used about an honourable position, but may also be used satirically; *era* is never prefixed.

dioecious trees; *dare jo*, means tree fruit.‡

As regards fishes, reptiles and insects the language does not as a rule trouble to distinguish the sexes; it is only done, when occasion arises, and is then not carried further than to state that this or that is a male or female, or "mother" (*andia* and *enga*).

In a few cases the language distinguishes males and females in insects (two examples are given above, *uru enga*, a "beetle" supposed to be the cause of a certain kind of spreading sores, and *ro enga*, where a female is meant, but no male is recognized), and in trees. The male Palmyra palm is called *andia tale*, and the fruit-bearing one *enga tale*; the same is the case with *amrit*, the Papaya tree; a never fruiting marking-nut tree is called *andia soso*, as opposed to *enga soso*. The male of dioecious trees are sometimes styled *gele* or *baha dare*, a tree with an ear or flowers.

It should further be mentioned, that a number of deer are named *sandi* (*sandi ured jel*, *selep' jel*, *potret' jel*); but as one of these is a female, it cannot well be anything else than a name. Attention might, however, be drawn to the fact, that in the related Mundari language many male animals are styled *sandi* (e. g. *sandi sadom*, a stallion).

In the same way a number of plants are named *andia* (*andia dhurup arak*, *andia kongat'*, *andia morou arak*); it is a name only; the meaning of *andia* is not reflected on.

(*d*) Besides the terms hitherto mentioned, that all have a more common application, there are a few terms of the same nature with special application, being used only about one kind of animals. They have not been mentioned under (*a*), because they are not generally used alone, but prefixed to the word denoting the *genus commune*.

Selep' jel, *kurmbi selep' jel*, *badar selep' jel*, the buck of the Ravine deer; *potret' jel*, *ghotret' jel*, *ghotra jel*, the hind of the same;

pincur marak, the peacock; *matu* or *martu marak*, the peahen.

‡ Note: *jok dare*, a fruit-bearing tree, as opposed to a barren tree; *jok kan*, or *jo jok kan dare*, a tree in fruit.

21. Except as described Santali does not show gender in any class of words. When necessary, sex is shown. Except in a number of borrowed words (see above para 16) the same form is used for masculine and feminine in all words of the classes called descriptive elements. When a word is used as (what we would call) an adjective, the form is always, except as stated, the same for both sexes. It is, e. g., always *boge,* good, whether it is *koṛa,* boy, *kuṛi,* girl, *hoṛ,* person, or *kicriċ,* cloth; *bogekedeae,* he made him or her good; but (in borrowed words) *kala koṛa,* a deaf boy, *kali kuṛi,* a deaf girl, *kalayenae,* he became deaf, *kaliyenae,* she became deaf.

The Animate and Inanimate Forms.

22. While Santali, except as stated, ignores *genera,* it distinguishes between the *animate* and the *inanimate.* This distinction to a large degree affects the grammatical construction of the language. In the demonstrative, the interrogative and partly the indefinite pronouns separate forms are used for the animate and the inanimate; the determinative and other suffixes used are different, and the verbal constructions are different for the animate and the inanimate.

This distinction is not between living and dead matter, or between spirit and matter, but between what, according to Santal ideas, has a soul and what has not.

One might be tempted to define the animate as that which has a 'substance' with something living, a living force, inside this, that makes it capable of acting and moving; a combination of 'matter' and a spirit or spirit-force is demanded.

A living tree is inanimate; *jivi,* soul, and *jiu,* spirit, are also inanimate. A Santal will distinguish between *jivianko,* those with a soul, and *bin-jivianakko,* those without a soul.

The Santal conception of animate and inanimate does not always coincide with what we may consider naturally the one or the other.

23. As *animate* the Santals count all that are capable of separate or independent action and movement, thus :

(*a*) human beings and all animals, fishes, birds, reptiles, insects and invertebratæ, all living beings ;

(*b*) the following which we would not think should come under the *genus animale* according to Santal classification : *puṭkạ*, a puff-ball, *ẽṛgoť*, ear-wax ; the complete shells of snails and molluscs, and *jạnum*, thorn, this last, however, only when one has been pricked by such.

To show the construction with the last mentioned words the following examples will serve :

puṭkạko halaṅket'koa, they collected mushrooms ; *ẽṛgoť menak'koa*, there is ear-wax ; *iṅren jhinukiṅ rapak'ket'koa*, I burnt my shells, e. g., to make lime ; but *noa jhinukte buluṅ emaṅme*, give me some salt in this shell (the single shell is constructed inanimate, being only a part of the mussel ; both shells taken together seem to represent the whole mollusc) ; *jạnumiṅ toť kedea*, I extracted the thorn.

(*c*) Also when dead, human beings and animals are treated as animate, provided the same name is used, or the person, etc., is referred to.

E. g., *gọc' hoṛko ạgukedea*, they brought a dead man ; *iṅren gọdic'*, my dead one ; *uniren gọc' ḍaṅgra*, his dead bullock ; but *lasẹť ko ạgukeť a*, they brought the dead body.

(*d*) The Supreme Being, whatever name is used. The old traditions call Him *Ṭhạkur-jiu*, and this is constructed animate, while *jiu* alone is not so treated. *

(*e*) The sun, moon and stars.

E. g., *holaren ipiliṅ ńẽl ńamkedea*, I have caught sight of the star of yesterday ; but *ipil ic'*, lit. star-excrement, as a shooting

* In analogy with this *Sẹnọt Jiu* has been constructed animate.

star is called in Santali, is, as might be expected with such a name, considered and constructed inanimate.

(*f*) Spiritual beings (angels), *bongas*, spirits, *bhut* and *curin*, spirits of a lesser kind, demons, also the Ancestors (spirits of the dead) are treated as animate beings.

E. g., *bongae botorako kana*, he is afraid of the *bongas*; *Kaliye benao akadea*, he has made a Kali idol; *curin do, kathae, carkha leka bohok ńelokǃtakoa rap rapa, ar bhut doko katić katićgea galam galam*, the *curins*, people tell, have heads like a spinning wheel standing out, and the *bhuts* are very small and indistinct.

(*g*) Figures of living beings, provided the name is used or implied, especially also idols; anything representing a living being or a *bonga*.

E. g., *pea phutol menakǃkotaea*, she has three dolls; *bhitre janwarko ol akat'koa*, they have written (i. e., drawn or painted) animals on the wall; *janwar muthanko ol akat'a* (or *-akat'koa*), they have drawn animal figures (*muthan* may be constructed animate, especially when the name of the being it represents is mentioned, as *orakǃ bonga muthan parkomreye dohokedea*, or *dohoket'a*, he placed the house-godling-figure on the bedstead); *ńel akat'koale la tot' bongako do*, we have seen bongas that have been dug out (refers to a stone painted with sindur and with hair wound round it, or similar objects, supposed to be buried by witches, and to represent a bonga).

(*h*) In cases where the same word is used about animates and the inanimate, the construction is according to the meaning. Thus *jel*, deer, is constructed animate, but *jel* in the meaning of meat is not. *Buru* (*maraṅ buru*) is treated as animate when used about spirits, but is inanimate when standing for mountain.

Babu and *mai*, when used about the private parts, seem to be able to take both constructions.

(*i*) Anything supposed to act as an animate being is constructed accordingly.

E. g., *matkom darebon bicar ocoyea* we shall get the mahua tree to judge; *lebraren ses*, one who is the limit of covetousness; *ere reakǃ ses*, the limit of falsehood.

24. The differences in form and construction between the animate and the inanimate are mainly the following, the reader being referred to the details given where the different classes are described :

(*a*) Certain classes of words have different forms when used about the animate and the inanimate.

Certain pronouns are different for the two classes.

In the demonstrative pronouns, when there is any difference, the animate pronouns end in *-i*, and the inanimate ones in *-a* (e. g.. *uni*, *nui*, *huni*, this or that one, animate ; *ona*, *noa*, *hona*, do., inanimate).

In the interrogative pronouns the difference is not so regular ; here the animate forms end in *-ọe* or *-e* (*ọkọe*, *cele*, who, which), and the inanimate ones in *-a* or *-t'* (*oka*, what, *cet'* what).

In the indefinite pronouns one (a borrowed word) shows different forms, *jãhãe* being used about animates (any one), *jãhã* about inanimates, and *jãhãn* about both.

(*b*) Certain suffixes are used only in connection with words for the animate, and others only with inanimates.

The determinative suffix for the animate is in the singular *-ic'*, in the dual and plural, respectively *-kin* and *-ko*, and for the inanimate *-ak'* (*-aṅ*) with *-akkin* and *-akko* respectively in the dual and the plural. Here the animate *-i* and the inanimate *-a* are again met with. *E. g.*, *bogeyic'*, the good one (animate), *bogeak'*, the good thing ; *gọčič*, the dead one (who was a living being) ; *gọčak'*, the dead thing.

Certain suffixes used to express what corresponds to genitive (the construction is really a kind of adjective formation) are different in animate and inanimate construction.

With inanimate construction we here again meet the above mentioned *-ak'* (or *-aṅ*) ; with animates a suffix ending in -*n* is now generally used (see below para 59 (f)). *

E. g., uniren hopon, his, or her, child; *mare hapṛamko reak katha*, the words of, or about, the Ancestors, i. e., the traditions; *horten hoṛ*, a person who passes along the road, a wanderer; *hoṛ aṛe teak ghãs*, road-side grass.

The determinative suffixes mentioned above are very commonly used in connection with the postpositions and suffixes that do service for the declinations of our languages.

(*c*) The verbal constructions show differences in certain respects.

As to the verbal subject:

Words of the animate class are fully represented, the subject-pronoun being used in the singular, the dual or the plural, as needed, in the Active, the Medium and the Passive.

Words of the inanimate class are not so represented. There is no subject pronoun, with one exception.

In many cases a subject pronoun in the singular (-*e* or -*i*) is used in connection with the active verb to represent the supposed or implied agent.

---

* It should however, be noted that this form is possibly not originally and necessarily animate, as this suffix ending may take the inanimate determinative suffix -*ak* (-*aṅ*). It has, however, now become customary to use the suffixes *ren* and *ten* about animates, and *reak*, *reaṅ*, *teak* or *teaṅ* about the inanimate. To use these suffixes otherwise would be considered a dreadful blunder by the present-day Santals.

It seems, as if *re* has been formerly used to some extent to express our genitive; *renak* is frequently used to express what naturally is supposed to belong to; it is somewhat more indefinite than *reak* (*ato reak*, of the village; *ato renakko*, matters concerning the village or village life).

The use of this personal subject pronoun is the invariable rule in connection with the description of natural phenomena.*

The same subject pronoun is also used, although not as an invariable rule, in connection with other conceptions to represent the active principle, the force acting. In case more than one subject is mentioned this does not cause plural ; this subj. pr. is always singular.

In the Passive there is never any subject pronoun with the inanimate, and in the Medium very seldom, only when a medial verb has an active meaning.

As to the direct and indirect object :

With animate object this is fully represented with infixed personal pronouns of the singular. the dual or the plural, as needed.

With inanimate object there is no infixed object pronoun, except as mentioned below.

In certain verbal forms there is an infixed *-k̓* (the same *-k̓* as the *-k̓* found in the above mentioned *-ak̓*), viz., (*1*) in the Indeterminate and the Future of the active verb when having indirect object, and in the verbal forms based on the Indeterminate (i. e., in the Imperative, in the Present and the Imperfect tenses);

(2) in the same tempora of the so-called Intentional (or Reservative) Form, and (but here optional) in the Imperative of the same ;

(3) in one form of the Anterior Past (*-lak̓*).

It should further be noted that pronominal genitive-infixes (*tiń*, *tam*, *tae*, etc.), so frequently used in verbal constructions, referring to the subject or the object of the verb, only refer to the animate.

---

*Present-day Santals declaring the Creator (or *Cando*) to be the subject or agent.

E. g, (for animate constructions) *mĩhũi at'lena, ńamkedeako*, the calf was lost, they found it; *toyo barea sime ạtkirket'kintalea*, a jackal has run away with two fowls of ours; *dụrup' ocokom*, make them sit down; *dụrup'enako*, they have sat down; *lạiat'koae*, he told them; *pẹ hoṛko calaoena, bareakin ruạṛena, mit' hoṛ dọe okayen cọń*, three men went, two returned, one who knows what has become of him; *sẹn ocoakom*, let them go; *hoṛiń ńẹlkedea*, I saw the man;

(for inanimate constructions) *bẹṅgẹt'ak'me*, look at it; *nahele benaoket'a*, he made a plough; *nahelena*, it became a plough; *janhẹye dalet' tahẽkana*, he was threshing janhe millet; *janhẹ dal sạtena*, the janhe millet was all threshed; *kicric' hoṛọg-me*, take your clothes on; *kicric'e hoṛọk'ana*, he put on his clothes (the *e* is the animate subject pronoun); *buru dọ usula*, the mountain is high; *oṛak' lọyena*, the house was burnt; *hoṛiń ńẹlket'a*, I saw the road;

dak'et'ae, it is raining (but *dak' ńurok' kana*, rain is falling); *hudụret'ae*, it is thundering (but *rimil sadẹk' kana*, the clouds are sounding); *arelket'ae*, it hailed; *arelteye ṭuṭi gọc'kedea nui cẽṛẽ*, this bird was killed by hail, lit he shooting with hail killed this bird;

oṛak' lọyentińa, my house was burnt; *sukriko gọc'kedetaea*, they killed his pig; *poesae ẹm ruạṛadetaea*, he returned him his money;

giḍikak' kanań, I am throwing it away; *dọhọkak'me* or *dọhọkam*, put it down, in the meantime or for good;

poesae ẹmlak'a, he gave the money; *rọṛlak'ae*, he spoke, or, had spoken.

The *k'* in these forms occupies the place of the infixed pronoun in animate constructions (*-kae, -kakin, -kako*, as *ḍaṅgrań idikakin kana*, I am taking the two bullocks away somewhere, for some purpose or other).

Number.

25. Santali distinguishes three numbers, the singular, the dual and the plural.

The singular with or without any suffix or other addition, is the base.

Number is shown by the addition of suffixes to the singular, not by any declensional alteration in the word or word-combination itself.

The only exceptions in the language from this rule are —besides the numerals—the personal pronouns that in Santali, like in other languages, have separate words for the different numbers; see also below para 27.

26. The suffixed forms of the personal pronoun of the third person in the dual and the plural are used to express the dual and the plural (*-kin* and *-ko* respectively).

27. Certain forms can only be used in the singular, viz., when the personal pronoun of the third person singular is part of the word. This is the case with the animate demonstrative pronouns (*nu-i*, *un-i*, *hun-i*, *ni*, *in-i*, *hin-i*, *ạn-i*, *hạn-i*, with the corresponding lateral demonstratives). It is further the case with the animate determinative suffix *-ic'* (*i-c'*, cp. *ac'*), where the *i* is the personal pronoun of the third person singular.† When the dual or the plural are to be used, this singular *i* or *ic'*, as the case may be, has to be substituted by the pronouns of the dual or plural. Thus: *un-i*, he or she, *un-kin*, they two, *on-ko*, they (plural); *ẹrọkic'*, the sower, *ẹrọk'ko*, the sowers.

While the *i* mentioned is singular and animate, the corresponding vowel for the inanimate (*a*) obviously only stands for *genus*. It has consequently to be retained in the dual and the plural, both in the demonstrative pronouns and when found in the inanimate determinative suffix (*-ak'*). Its omission would change the expression from inanimate to animate.

E. g., *on-a*, that; *onako*, those things; *nọṇḍẹnak'*, what is here; *nọṇḍẹnakko* the things here; *onko*, those (animate); *nọṇḍẹnko*, those here (animate).

28. In connection with the dual and the plural the following should be noted :

---

† This *i* is a suffixed form of the third person singular of the personal pronoun, now found in the language as the verbal subject pronoun (when suffixed to an *u* or an *ạ*; see Mat. I., para 40).

Santali has no honorific pronouns; Santals consequently make use of the actual number in addressing others and speaking of themselves, with the following exceptions :

(*a*) Parents-in-law and children-in-law (*hoṅharea* and *hanharea*; concerning these terms see below, para 35 (b)) address one another in the dual (using *aben*, you two), and when talking together and referring to themselves they use the exclusive form of the dual pronoun (*aliṅ*, we two, i. e., he or she and I), when only one person is meant. The reason for this is that the wife or the husband, as the case may be, is mentally included. In their relation to each other the other (present or not-present) partner of the pair is never left out. Any of these relatives making use of the singular in addressing each other would be considered to commit a dreadful insult.

The same form of address, &c., is used by all relatives who by Santals are counted as standing in the same relationship to each other, viz., *bahoṅharea*, a man and his younger brother's wife, or, a man and the wife of his wife's younger brother; *ajhnarea*, a woman and her younger sister's husband, or, a woman and her younger brother's wife. Further all who are counted *hoṅharea* or *hanharea*, such as *mamo hoṅharea*, *kaka hoṅharea*, *hatom hanharea*, &c.

E. g., *cekayenaben, bahu?* what is the matter with you, daughter-in-law? *ruak̔ kanaliṅ*, I am ill, have fever; *bokome laiat'liṅa*, your younger brother (who is my husband) told me; *hatteben senlena?* did you go to the market?

Children of the parties do not influence this way of speaking; it is always the dual.

When speaking to others of the relative mentioned the singular is used, although there may be a certain tendency to speak of the pair.

When speaking to each other about anything concerning them both, the inclusive dual is used, not the plural. *E. g.*, *hatrelaṅ ńapamok̔a*, we two (e. g., father-in-law and son-in-law) shall meet on the market-place.

(*b*) In threatening language (really or jokingly) the speaker will frequently make use of the inclusive dual about himself, especially addressing, but also speaking of an other or others, these, however, always referred to in the singular or plural, as the case may be.

E. g, *hapeṭlaṅ ńeḷmea*, wait, thou and I shall see thee; *dalmealaṅ*, we two shall thrash you; *onkolaṅ—*, quos ego —.

(*c*) People whose children have married (*balaea*, and those who according to Santal social courtesy are counted as standing in the same relationship to each other) address one another and speak to one another of themselves in the plural, when meaning only one person. The explanation is on the same lines as that of the custom of using the dual mentioned above under (*a*). The inclusive plural is used; when absolutely necessary for the meaning the exclusive form may be used, also the plural of the personal pronoun 2nd p. (*ape*).

E. g., *henda ho, sumdhi, cet' leka menakbona? ạḍi din khon babon ńapam akana*, how are you, co-parent in-law? we have not met for a long time; *ạḍi muskilrebon paṛao akana*, we (meaning only himself) are in great difficulties.

29. The dual is frequently used about a pair, but not necessarily so; it is just as often used to show that there is more than one, but not more than two.

E. g., *ạkin haṛam buḍhi*, the husband and wife themselves; *adọ babon ạkinkạkina?* shall we not make these two a pair? (used in the village council about a boy and a girl whose behaviour ought to result in marriage): *barea sukrikin bọl.-yena*, two pigs came in.

30. The plural is often used to express the indefinite, the class, one of a number of possibilities, but not singled out, part of the whole mentioned.

E. g., *goṭa họṛmọ hasoyediń kana, jaṅgako, tiko, deako, bọhọkko*, my whole body aches, legs, arms, back, head; *bọhọkko hasoedea*, his head aches all over; *canḍbọlkoreye tunum baṛakedea*, she felt with her hand (the jackal) over his tail; *noakore*, in these parts; *oṛak'kore*, in the houses, or, somewhere in the house; *alope okakotektabona*, do not go anywhere away for us; *eṅgat apat cet'ko mẹna*, what will the parents say; *nawa peṛako hẹc'ena*, new friends have come (the standard way of announcing the birth of a child).

31. (*a*) The plural is further the rule when enumerating a number of different articles or living beings, even when only one of each kind may be actually meant or referred to. In such enumerations the plural is used even when the words used otherwise never take a plural suffix.

E. g., *hoṛko, dekoko, muslạko, sahebkoko jarwayena*, Santals, Hindus, Mohammedans, Europeans came together (where, e. g., only one European was seen); *gạiko, kaḍako, merọmko menaḱkotaea*, he has cows, buffaloes, goats (when he may have only one or two of each); *biṅko bọtọlko okare cọko giḍikat'*, they have thrown the snake and the bottle away somewhere (heard used about a bottle in which a snake had been put on spirits); *hoṛoko, gundliko, jonḍrako, buluṅko, sunumko*, paddy, millet, maize, salt, oil.

(*b*) In this connection might be mentioned the peculiar way of addressing or referring to the whole of a company, when only one is meant (or two as the case may be).

E. g., *mit' hoṛ hijuḱoen*, come one of you two; *mit' hoṛ calaḱpe*, go one of you; *mit' hoṛ dọkin gọc'ena, mit' hoṛ dọ menaḱkina*, one of them is dead, one is living; *mit' hoṛ dọko gọc'ena, bar hoṛ dọ Asamteko calaoena, ar noṇḍẹ tinạḱ cọko tahẽ akan*, one of them is dead, two of them have gone to Assam and a number has stayed on here; *ọkọeben dalkedea, am sẹ uni?* which one of you two struck him, you or he?

(*c*) The plural suffix is very commonly added to the plural forms of the personal and demonstrative pronouns, this added *ko* conveying the idea of something indefinite superadded to the word used, those mentioned and those belonging to the class mentioned, all possible. *

* One might in this connection refer to the objection the Santals apparently have to making a definite statement, unless they are sure that they can be exact; their sense of concrete reality demands this. *E. g*, *tinạḱem ạguket'a?* how much did you bring? *turui pạị hoyoḱa*, it will be six pai: *nọṇḍẹ khon eae kọs hoyoḱa*, it will be seven kos (14 miles) from here. If they have ascertained the exact quantity they will naturally tell this.

E. g., *apeko*, you and yours, those belonging to your class; *alekoko sap'ket'lea*, they caught us (some mentioned and others included; *akokoko roporena*, they quarrelled among themselves; *gidrako do onkoko kasni bhedrekin dohokakoa*, they saw to it that they children kept a careful watch on these; *bonga do neko goc' horkoge tinak' haram budhiko goc' akan, enkokogebon bakherakoa*, the spirits are these dead people, as many men and women as are dead, to all these we offer our invocation; *onko kul tarup' doko seta kantakoa*; *onkoko uni kora doko tiak' bara ocoyea*, tigers and leopards are the dogs of these people; they made the young man lead these about; *alekoak' racare*, in our court-yard.

32. Collectives, referring to animates, are constructed in accordance with the meaning as plural.

E. g., *phadko jarwayena*, a crowd assembled; *barea phadko larhaiyena*, two hosts fought; *sendra gadko boloyena birte*, the hunting crowd entered the forest.

33. As regards the use of the dual and the plural suffixes the following may be noted :-

If the number is otherwise shown or evident, the suffixes are not ordinarily added. If they are used in such cases, they generally get the meaning of our definite article or even of a demonstrative reference.

Inanimates do not take the dual or plural suffix, unless needed to show number.

E. g., *perako hec'ena*, friends have come (here *ko* is the subject pronoun; it may refer to several or to only one visitor; see above, para 31 (b)); *perakoko hec'ena*, the friends (those expected, all) have come; *dareko makket'a*, they cut trees (one or more); *darekoko makket'a*, they cut the trees (the number to be cut); *bar hor*, two men; *barea nahel*, two ploughs; *nahelkin doe idiket'a*, he has taken the two ploughs away; *horko rora*, people say.

34. (a) A kind of indefinite or distributive plural is formed by the repetition of a word. The same may also signify extension.

E. g., *ato ato menak'a*, there are villages (all over); *lac' lac' hasoyede kana*, he has pains over the stomach: *cot cutteye udauena*, he flew along high up.

(b) Repetition is also often used to show common usage, or so to say, to fix a statement.

E. g., *Paṇḍu Paṇḍuko hohoae kana*, they call him Paṇḍu (that is his name);

35. In connection with certain numerals and certain names of relationship, and a few other words, a suffix *-ea* (after final vowel often *-ya*, the *e* becoming a *y*) * is used to denote collectivity.

(*a*) In Santali this collective-termination is found with four numerals, viz., *bar*, *pe*, *pon* and *isi*, i. e., *barea* (two), *pea* (*peya*, as Santals often write it) (three), *ponea* four) and *isia isiya*), a score.

In other Kol languages the same *-ea* is found with the numerals from two up to ten.

(*b* When suffixed to a word denoting relationship, the termination is used, not to signify a number of persons having the same relative-position in the family, persons called so and so, but always a person and he, or she, or they, who stand in such a relationship to the relative named as to call him or her by the name of relationship to which the termination is added. Suffixed to a word denoting relationship it generally (although not necessarily) conveys the meaning of a pair. The termination is always suffixed to the word denoting the higher position in the relationship-scale, if there is any difference in position.

This *-ea* is used in connection with the following:

dadaya, an elder brother and one or more of his younger brothers;

---

* It has been stated that this *ea* is the Dravidian possessive suffix. Whether there is any such suffix in the Dravidian languages I am unable to say. The Santali suffix has probably no connection with this. The Santali *ea* is likely demonstrative in its origin.

ajiya, an elder sister and one or more of her younger brothers or sisters;

hiliyea, a woman and her husband's younger brother or sister who call her *hili*;

honharea, father-in-law and son-in-law, or daughter-in-law;

hanharea, mother-in law and do. do.

and all called *honhar* or *hanhar*, such as *mamo honharea*, *kaki hanharea*, *etc.*;

bahonharea, a man and his younger brother's wife, or his younger sister's husband, or his wife's younger brother's wife;

ajhnarea, a woman and her younger sister's husband, or her younger brother's wife;

gongoya, a man and his younger brother's son or daughter;

kakaya, a man and his elder brother's son or daughter;

kakiya, a woman and her husband's elder brother's son or daughter, or, a woman and her elder brother's son or daughter;

hatomea, a woman and her brother's son or daughter (*i. e.*, *hatom* and *homon*);

mamoya, a man and his sister's son or daughter;

kumaya, a man and his wife's brother's son or daughter;

guromea, a man or a woman and his or her grandchild, namesakes;

balaya, co-parents-in-law, persons whose children are married;

tenaya (also called *tena era*), a man and his wife's younger brother or sister;

dhuliya, the same as *tenaya*;

natea, the wives of brothers (two or more) (from *nata* -*n*, -*m*, -*t*, or possibly from a now otherwise not used *nat*);

sadgeya, the husbands of two (or more) sisters;

hiromea, the (contemporary) two or more wives of the same man;

tataya, grandfather and grandchild;

jiaya, grandmother and grandchild;

hagaya, relatives, especially *kaka gongo boeha*, cousins (from *haga*, a rarely used word).

(*c*) This same collective termination is found used in connection with a few other words also, apparently only when the word may be used as a mutual appellative, where the persons referred are in some way or other 'joined' together. We have *beneya*, enemies (from *bene*, usually with *bairi* added); *juriya*, the pair (from *juri* a pair; used about husband and wife).

36. Number in verbal constructions :

With inanimates no subject pronoun is used, except as mentioned above in para 24 (c) ; there is consequently ordinarily nothing to represent number.

With animates number is always shown, both in the subject and in the direct and the indirect object, as already described, para 24 (c).

37. The dual and plural suffixes may be added to what we call the noun, or to the adjective (generally not to both). The word representing what we call the noun may, in cases where the number-suffix is added to the adjective, perhaps be better taken as standing in a kind of apposition to the adjective. When a word is preceded by a pronoun, the general rule is to add the suffix to this with animates; with inanimates the suffix may be added to either.

E. g., *unkin hoṛ*, those two persons; *onako dare*, or *ona dareko*, those trees.

Determinative suffixes.

38. The Santal language makes use of certain determinative suffixes, one suffix for animates and another for inanimates.

The one for animates is in the singular *-iḱ*. In the dual and the plural there is no separate determinative suffix for animates; the suffixed forms of the personal pronoun third person (*-kin* for the dual, and *-ko* for the plural), ordinarily employed to show number, also serve as determinative suffixes.

The inanimate determinative suffix is *-aḱ* (or *-aṅ*) added to the base-word in the singular, and kept on both in the dual and in the plural (*-aḱkin* or *-aḱko* respectively, also *-aṅkin* and *-aṅko*). *

* As will be observed, we have a formation quite analogous to what is found in the demonstrative pronouns (*un-i, un-kin, on-ko; on-a, on-a-kin, on a-ko*), only that we have here an *-c'* or an *ḱ* (*ṅ*) added.

39. These suffixes are used to single out concretely and to identify; added to a word the meaning of the construction is that the animates or the inanimates referred to in concrete existence represent the concept mentioned. They often do service for our determined article (see below para 51).

In certain combinations these suffixes may, when the meaning of the word admits such use, serve to show what we call superlatives, in Santali the reality as compared with anything else.

E. g., *bogeyic'*, the good one, the best one; *kharapak'*, what is bad, the bad; *aguakko*, the things brought; *kiriñakko modre bogeak'*, the best among the things bought; *aleyic'*, our one (e. g., husband, master); *joto khon sebelak'*, the most savoury; *mõṛẽ gɔṭec' gidra apatic' kanae*, he is the one who is father of five children (without *-ic'* it would be a simple statement that he has five children; as spoken it shows the man as such a one)

raranic', one who administers medicine; *goc'ic'* the dead one; *goc'kedeyic'*, the one who killed him; *hijuk'ic'*, the one who will come; *hijuk'ak'*, what will come; *hukamade lekaket ic' hoṛ*, the person who did as he was ordered; *hukumadeak' lekaket'ae*, he did in accordance with what he was ordered *rohoṛenak' gidi got'ka me*, throw away what has become dry; *dadalic' do phatna, ar dal oco akanic' do nuige, ar dadalteak' do nõkõe noatet'ge*, the one who struck is so & so, and the one who has been beaten is this one, and here is the very thing with which the beating was done.

40. The here mentioned suffixes may be used to form a possessive 'adjective' (pronoun) doing service for our genitive.

E. g., *amic' koṛa*, your boy (this animate form is not so very common in Santali, but is used; it is frequent in some of the related Kol languages); *amak' katha*, your word.

---

41. In this connection mention may be made of a suffix used to emphasize, especially the identity, viz., *tet'*. This may be added to both animates and inanimates, and is often used to emphasize words already having taken the determinative suffixes examined above, that is to say, in the singular; if added to a word in the dual or plural the *tet'* precedes *kin* or *ko*.

E. g., *noatet'*, this very; *ac'tet*, he himself; *nũkũi bodmastet' do*, here is the real rascal, the rascal himself; *dartet'ko aguime, daretet' ikakakme*, bring the branches, let the tree be; *apattet' do bale ńeiledea, eken hopontet'ge*, we did not see the father, only the son; *sariak'tet'*, the real truth; *kamitet'reń tebakkedea*, I caught him in the very act; *ńũroktet' do alga, rakabok do mus.il*, to fall down is easy, to get up is difficult.

Words functioning as nouns.

42. As repeatedly remarked, the Santal concept-word is not specialized or narrowed down to be only a noun, an adjective, a verb, etc. This peculiarity does not, however, prevent, that words, on account of their special meaning or their general application, function especially as a noun, an adjective or a verb very much as in our languages, only that in genuine Santali the functioning of a word is not limited to one class only.

43. There is no gender, except as previously stated (see chapter on Gender).

44. Number is shown, when needed, by adding the dual and the plural personal pronoun suffixes (see chapter on Number).

45. There is no declension, that is to say, the base-word is not altered. What is in other languages effected through declension is in Santali attained by the employment of a number of postpositions (see chapter on Postpositions).

46. There is nothing in the words themselves to show the difference between the animate and the inanimate, in spite of the strict way in which the language distinguishes between the two classes (see chapter on this subject above in connection with Gender.).

E. g., *kul*, tiger, leopard; *kulkin*, *kulko*, two tigers, (many) tigers; *merom* (*-kin*, *-ko*), goat (-s); *hor* (*-kin*, *-ko*), road (-s); *orak'ren hor*, the man of the house; *hor reak orakko*, the houses of the man; *orak'te idime*, take it to the house.

47. Santali comes near to forming nouns by infixing an *n* or a *t* after the first vowel of a word and repeating the vowel after the infixed consonant (in words with *e* as first vowel and *o* or *o* as second, this second vowel is spoken after the infixed *t*).

This formation is not very frequent in Santali; an infixed *n* appears to be much more extensively used in e. g. Mundari.

It might seem, as if the *t* infixed is used in words where the point of view is from the agent forwards, and the *n* where the object is in view, but there is no fixed rule.

E. g., *etohop'*, beginning (from *ehop'*); *munucat'*, end (from *mucat'*); *anirgo*, descent (from *ãrgo*); *ranakap'*, ascent (from *rakap'*); *anacur*, turning (from *acur*); *anak*, also *anaka*, something to hang on (from *aka*); *anatan*, receptacle (and several other special meanings, from *atan*); *benet'*, a stopper, a lid (from *bet'*); *hanas* (also *hanaso*), pain (from *haso*); *enetet'*, partition (from *etet'*); *banak'*, a hook (from *bak'*); *banar*, both (from *bar*); *pene*, the three, all three (from *pe*); *ponon*, the four, all four (from *pon*); *sunudur*, waterfall (from *sudur*); *otor*, warp in weaving (from *or*); *setelet'*, accompaniment, together with (from *selet'*); *satarec'*, remainder (from *sarec'*); *satahet'*, breath (from *sahet'*); *rotok'*, a seam (from *rok'*); *jeteleń*, length (from *jeleń*, long); *onosar*, breadth (from *osar*); *binida*, departure gift (from *bida*, send away).

48. It should, however, be noted, that this kind of word-formation is not restricted to nouns, and as a matter of fact, any of the examples cited may be used as adjectives or verbs, only that they are mostly used as nouns. Some words formed in the same way are especially used as verbs, e. g., *otor*, to pull down, demolish (from *or*, foundation, beginning), *unum*, submerge (from *um*, to wash).

49. The base with the suffix of Medium added (*ok'*, *-ok'*, or, after single vowel, generally only *-k'*) seems to lend itself to express the general idea, perhaps not quite the abstract, but

something on the road to it. The agent is hidden; the action is what is emphasized, and there is no object, or definite end. With *tẹt'* added this meaning is coming even more strongly out. *

E. g., *ẹmọk'*, to give, the giving; *gujuk'*, to die, death, das sterben.

The Article.

50. The numeral *mit'*, one, is made to serve for an indefinite article, either in this simple form, or with *ṭẹn*, *ṭẹc'* or *ṭaṅ*, or also *gọṭẹn*, *gọṭẹc'* or *gọṭaṅ*, added.

Gọṭẹn, etc., is used to signify a unit and is very commonly combined with any numeral or, e. g., *ạḍi*, very many, *aema*, do., or similar words. *Gọṭẹn*, etc , does not take dual or plural suffixes.

---

* This Medium form is of value when certain terms are to be translated into Santali. A few examples will show this. If one has to translate a word like 'offering' using the word *samaṅ* for 'to offer', it would be fatal to use the active form about the general term; *samaṅak'* or *samaṅic'* could only mean what has been offered (inanimate or animate). These terms have to be used, when special reference is made to an already performed offering; but when one has to refer to the general act, the medial form has to be employed, which implies, that the offering will be performed, and is not performed as yet. A similar use is found in *baḍha*, to adopt, adopted; *baḍhak'* has to be used about the general term, if one is not to use a full verbal construction, with subject and object.

Any number of examples might be adduced; they all show, that the Santal language has not what we could call proper abstract nouns; their expressions in some way or other all refer to concrete reality; but for most practical needs the expression here shown will serve the purpose. There is a concrete base and the concept has the possibility of future development, without reflection as to mode and time.

These particles are used indiscriminately for both animates and inanimates; if there is any difference in use, it is individualistic, one person being accustomed to use the one, another the other. Santals have attempted to reserve the forms ending in *ṭen* or *ṭec'* for animates; but it has no real foundation in the language.

Whether *mit'* is to be taken as the numeral or as doing service for an indefinite article, depends on the stress. With stress it is more the numeral; without stress it is more the indefinite article. *Mit'* alone is probably more the numeral; the same may be said of *mit' goṭen*, etc. With any of the particles added the word itself generally has the stress.

E. g., *mit' ghaṛi tahenme*, remain one moment; *mit' dine hec'lena*, he came one day; *mit'ṭan din seterok'a*, a day will come; *bir reak' dare*, a forest tree; *bir reak' mit'ṭec' dare*, a tree from the forest; *mit' goṭec' hoṛiń ńelledea*, I saw a man.

51. To express our definite article the language makes use of the demonstrative pronouns, and of the determinative suffixes.

The demonstrative element is scarcely ever quite absent from the pronoun, but it may be much attenuated, in this way that the demonstrative acts as a reference to what has already been mentioned.

The determinative suffixes may often be translated by our definite article; in this case the personal reference is attenuated, but not quite lost.

In many cases Santali has the naked word without any prefixed word and without any suffix, while we have to translate it with a word and the definite article. This is all due to the concrete reference natural to the language.

E. g., *uni haṛame menlet' leka*, in accordance with what the old man had said; *ona silpiń dqe aṭkirket'a*, he carried the door away; *onko hoponteṭ' kuṛi*, the daughters; *bahutteṭ'*, the wife, his wife;

dokanteye calaoena, he went to the shop; *dokan menak'a,* there are shops (or, is a s.); *mit' dokan menak'a,* there is one shop; *mit'ṭaṅ dokan menak'a,* there is a shop; *manḍwari dokan menak'a,* there is a Marwari shop, or, the Marwari shop (both meanings possible).

52. From what has been stated it will be gathered, that while Santali in *mit'ṭec'*, *mit'ṭe̱n* and *mit'ṭaṅ* has a word that generally corresponds to our indefinite article (although perhaps not quite, in as much as the numeral meaning is nearer the surface than in our indefinite article), the language has properly speaking no single word to express our definite article, but has, for the purpose, to use the demonstrative pronouns or the determinative suffixes, or to rely on the context in a general way. One everywhere experiences that the language is not a literary language; very much has to be deducted from the spoken word, i. e., especially from the stress and intonation.

With reference to the suffixes mentioned it should be noted, that they do not formally correspond to our definite article, but are a kind of substitute, making a definite article unnecessary. It should also be noted that the language makes much more extensive use of demonstratives than our languages do. This is probably to be accounted for by the constant reference to the concretely existing.

Words used as adjectives.

53. Any word of the class here mentioned may be used as what we call an adjective, that is to say, two or more words may be placed side by side, one acting as the noun, the other or others serving as adjectives, describing, explaining, qualifying, etc., the word functioning as a noun.

As a rule, but not necessarily, the adjective precedes the noun.

Words expressing qualities, which consequently more or less need a concrete substrate, are naturally used more as adjectives; and when rendering such into our languages we find it natural to use our adjectives. There is, however, nothing to show formally, that the words are adjectives, and what has been stated previously with regard to all concept-words in Santali should be borne in mind.

54. Words functioning as adjectives are subject to the same laws as when serving as nouns, so far as gender, number and lack of declension are concerned.

There is no special form to show gender, except in a number of borrowed words where words used about males end in *-a*, and words for females end in *-i* (see chapter on Gender). The same base-form is used for the animate and the inanimate.

Adjectives may take dual and plural suffixes, the same as nouns, when concrete objects are implied, i. e., when it is possible to distinguish countable concrete objects. In such cases the words should perhaps not be counted as 'adjectives', but be classed with base-words used as nouns.

Words with a determinative suffix, with a verbal suffix or a whole sentence (always without the finite *-a*), or with a postposition may function as an adjective.

55. The formation created by adding the determinative suffixes may be thought to be, to some extent, approaching the formation of adjectives in inflexional languages, bearing in mind that Santali does not formally distinguish between the genders, but between the animate and the inanimate.

56. Adjectives formed by a base-word having a verbal suffix added are very frequent; the form corresponds to a participle in our languages; in Santali we have a very large number of such, every verbal suffix with infixes of sorts being used as participles. These constructions very frequently do service for our relative sentences.

One of these suffixes, the one used forming the Medium Reflexive Past (*-an*) is especially common and signifies possession of what the word implies. *

---

* It may be questioned, whether a Santal using this form is conscious of the *-an* being also a verbal suffix. The two suffixes may possibly also be of different origin.

E. g., *boge*, good, goodness; *boge hoṛ*, a good man; *boge ran*, good medicine; *bogeyenae*, he became well, recovered; *bogekedeako*, they made him well; *bogeak*, what is good (opposite to what is not good, or also, the best of the lot); *bogeyić*, the good one; *bogeko*, the good ones (anim.); *bogeakko*, the good ones (inanim.); *hende*, blackness, black; *hende merom*, a black goat; *hende horo*, black paddy; *hendeyić*, the black one (anim.), as distinguished from one of another colour; *hendeak*, do. (inanimate); *calak*, to go; *calak hoṛ*, a man who will go; *hijuk lagidok kan tahẽkan hoedak*, a storm that was just coming up; *bań hiṛińok katha*, a word that will not be forgotten; *baliń hiṛiń daṛeae gidra*, the child we two are unable to forget: *ḍakuko jeret'kede hoṛ*, the man whose house the dacoits set fire to; *mucat' cando*, ending month (i. e. the last days or the end of the month); *bir dare*, forest tree; *mutul ṭhenak dare*, the tree at the gable of the house;

kaḍawan hoṛ, a man who has buffaloes; *dakanak kũi*, a well with water; *senlen hoṛ*, the man who went (and is back again); *calaoen hapta*, last week, the week that is gone; *heć akan koṛako*, the boys who have come (and are here); *janamoktae gidra*, a child that will be born to her.

The termination *-n*.

57. The termination *-n* has to be discussed somewhere, and it is taken here, because a word with this *n* suffixed often is a near approach to what is called an adjective. As will be seen it may be added to many classes of words. Here below its use will be shown in its several occurrences. This *n* is possibly a demonstrative element.

58. Every word in Santali having final single vowel may take a suffixed *-n*. The addition of this *-n* makes the word to which it is suffixed, function, according to the meaning of the base, as an adjective, a verbal noun, or a neutral verb.

It denotes the concrete application of a concept, what belongs to, comes within the sphere of, is fit for, what the base-word denotes. When used in connection with the verb (it cannot be properly called a verbal suffix), it functions somewhat like the Medium or the Passive suffix *-ok̇* (*-k̇*), with which it may in certain respects be compared.

The termination is extensively used, and in connection with a few words, so much so that the language appears to have lost the feeling of an *n* having been suffixed. *

59. The following examples will show, how this *n*- termination is used in the language.

(a) Added to the personal pronouns that have final vowel.

(a)bo, we (inclusive pl.), *(a)bon*, do., we and all who may be counted as such, or included.

(a)lẹ, we (exclusive pl.), *(a)lẹn*, do., with the same qualification.

(a)pẹ, you, *(a)pẹn*, do., as stated.

(a)ko, they, *(a)kon*, do., as stated.

While *alẹn*, *apẹn* and *akon* are very rarely heard in the present-day language, *abon* is very common and generally used without any apparent difference from *abo*. The two words may be heard in the same sentence about the same persons.

Abo abo dọ babon rọpọra, we shall not quarrel among ourselves; *nitok̇ dọbon aboyena, baha sọhraere gidrạ dọ babon jọm ẹnḍẹlkoa*, now we are found to be of the same sept, we shall not let our children go without giving them of the food at the baha and sohrae festivals; *alẹnić dọe calaoena*, our one went; *alẹn alẹnkogelẹ hẹć laha akana*, we who belong to the same family (or tribe) are come in advance; *alẹn kanalẹ*, we belong to the same sept; *alẹnok̇geale*, we shall be found to belong to the same tribe; *apẹn họṛ kanapẹ nokotẹpẹ dọ*, you and these belong to the same sept; *apẹn apẹnrẹn mọtọ lại-akope*, inform only those who belong to your sept; *apẹnok̇-apẹ?* will you be (are you) of the same sept? *akongeako*,

---

* This *n* is in connection with certain classes of words apparently more frequently used by Santals living in Southwest Bengal and in Orissa than by those living in the North and East.

they belong to the same sept; *akon akon hoṛko ṅgota akat'koa*, they have invited their own people.

The same *n* may be heard added to the infixed forms of the personal pronouns of the singular having final vowel (*me* and *e*). With *me* it is fairly common, with *e* very rare. The added *n* may possibly serve to emphasize the concrete actor, and may in such cases seem to belong to the whole expression.

Idiket'menič, the one who took you away; *lạ̃i akawat'menič*, he who has told you; *idiyenič*, the one who will take him away (not commonly used, as it is liable to be mixed up with the verbal suffix *-en*).

In connection with the infixed and suffixed possessive and object pers. pronouns this *n* is scarcely ever used, except with *-bo* (*-bon*, *tabo* and *tabon*).

(b) Added to the demonstrative pronouns and adverbs that have final single vowel.

Practically all demonstrative pronouns may take this *n*, both animate and inanimate ones. The meaning conveyed is some quality concretely demonstrated.

Nuin, this one, showing himself as exhibited; *unin*, that one; *hunin*, that one over there; *noan*, this; *onan*, that. *honan*; that over there; *nin*, this one (i. e. *ni*+*n*, pronounced with a long *i*, sounding nearly like *ni-in*, which seems to show that *ni* really is *nii* or *nei*, cp. *neko*); *onkon*, *nokon*, those ones, these ones, etc.; *ṅgk'ẽn*, such as this here; *oṭẹn*, listen to such as that (one) there; *ghẹn*, so (much, etc.); *ịạn*, such & such; *nhuin*, this one on the side; and so on.

The demonstrative pronouns, as stated, very rarely take this added *n*; it is possibly going out of use; at present these forms seem to be more or less individualistic.

The demonstrative adverbs, both of place and quality, with final single vowel all take this *n*, the word thus formed denoting anybody or anything belonging to the place or direction pointed out, or having such and such a quality.

Oṇḍẹn (*-ic'*, *-kin*, *-ko*, *-ak'*, *-ak'kin*, *-ak'ko*), that one there, that there; *noṇḍẹn*, *neṇḍẹn*, *hanḍẹn*, *nhoṇḍẹn*, etc.

Onkan (*-ic'*, *-kin*, *-ko*, *-ak'*, *-ak'kin*, *-ak'ko*), such a one (anim. or inanim.).

Nonka lekan (*-ic'*, etc., like the preceding).

Nonkan lekan (*-ic'*, etc.)

Any word with *leka* added.

The *ka* of *onka* and *leka* is probably the same as the *ka* of the Intentional (or Reservative) form of the verb, and of the verb substantive (*kan*; see below).

(c) The Interrogative pronouns of the same form also take this *n*, viz., *celen* and *okan*, what kind, which.

Celen kanae, what kind, who is he? *okanko dǫ aleak'*? which are ours? *noa ḍhǫknić dǫ okana*? where does this cover belong?

(d) Among the indefinite pronouns an added *n* is common in connection with one word (*jãhã*, *jãhãn*, *jãhãn tãhãn*, *jãhãn kũhãn*). The *n* here discussed may be the same, and, in any case, influences the form, but it may also be due to an oblique form of the borrowed Bengali word.

(e) Words functioning as nouns, adjectives, and verbs, with final single vowel.

All such may take this *n*, also monosyllabic words, although less frequently.

With the *n* added these words are used especially as adjectives and as neutral verbs (i. e., in the Indeterminate and Future and from this formed tenses, in the Imperative), as a participle and a verbal noun. The form denotes belonging to, also fit for, concretely of the nature of, what the word expresses. The employment of this *n* naturally to a great extent depends on whether the meaning of the word will lend itself to the construction.

Some words with this added *n* are constantly used by all: others especially women will employ.

Aton kanako, they are founding a village (they are village-ing); *aton hǫr*, a man who is settling in a new village; *ẹkẹn ayonko kanako*, they are only women-folk; *babanko*, males, men; *bonġan hǫr*, a spirit-worshipper; *ạḍiye edrena*, he is very short-tempered; *alom ẹrẹna*, don't be a fool (made a fool of); *ạḍiye hasona*, he takes easily offence, is soon hurt; *goṅgon*, one who is father's elder brother, or younger brother's child (very rarely used); *bogen hǫr kanae*, he is a good natured man; *sẽṛãn kanre hǫ̃ budge bańtam*, although you are getting grown up you have no understanding; *marenko kanako*, they are old (inhabitants, etc.); *ạuṛin katha kana, asǫl dǫ bań kana*, it is a false statement, it is not the truth; *bąń bągina*, I am not one who gives up, am not going to let it be; *hǫpǫhǫnko kanako*, they are calling each other; *tapańgin kanako*, they are waiting for each other; *eton ḍańgra*, a bullock fit to be broken in; *gutin lągit'*, who is) to become a servant; *lagan hǫṛ kanae*, he is a man who will be chased (driven away); *okare mandena*, where is there to be a manure heap: *okare dǫhǫn kana*, where is the place where it is to be put; *haren pharenok'me*, be quick; *teńgon kanae*, he is standing, able to stand; *tahẹn hǫṛ*, a man who stays (does not run away); *tahẹnok'ak'*, dwelling place; *tahẹnme*, remain.

(f) This *n* is suffixed to the postpositions *rẹ* and *tẹ*, making the base-word with the thus enlarged postposition function like an adjective, with the meaning of something or somebody being in, belonging to the sphere of, or moving along or towards what the base-word expresses.

As elsewhere stated, custom has in the present language resulted in this *n* (when not followed by any determinative suffix) being constantly and exclusively used about animates only. In itself the *n* is not animate, but simply concrete, as is shown by the possible addition of the inanimate determinative suffix *ak'* (*ań*). *

Oṛak'renko, those belonging to the house; *birren janwar*, an animal of the forest; but *atorenak'ko*, matters concerning the village; *birtenko, hǫrtenko*, people moving in the forest, along the road.

It is possibly the same *n* that is found as an integral part (i. e. not removable in the present language), alternating with *c'* in three postpositions, *ṭhẹn* (*ṭhẹc'*), *khǫn* (*khǫc'*), and *sẹn* (*sẹc'*).

---

* *Renak'* might also be ex- plained as *re+nak'*; this is not, however, likely. Cp. sec. (b) above.

(g) **In verbal suffixes and the verb substantive.**

It is possibly the same *n* that is found in a number of verbal suffixes of the Medium and the Passive, alternating with *t'* of the Active voice (*en*, *et'*, *len*, *let'*, *kan*, *kat'*, *akan*, *akat'*, *ken*, *ket'*). But in these suffixes it is an integral part of the suffix.

The verb substantive or copula of the language, *kan*, very probably is this *n* added to the suffix of the Indeterminate tense of the Intentional form of the verb (*ka*).

Ka appears to convey the meaning of acting the concept of the word with a purpose, or consciously. With *n* added this would consequently mean 'actively being', 'that acts as', 'is' what the word denotes; it is a concrete, not a qualitative statement.

Aṇḍią kanae, it is a male; opp. *aṇḍiągeae*, he is a male (not emasculated); *ini kanae cecet'ic'*, that one is the teacher (not anybody else); but *inigeae cecet'ic'*, that same one is the teacher (there is no one else).

Degrees of comparison.

60. Santali has no suffixes by which to express degrees of comparison; comparison has to be shown in other ways.

Comparative is expressed

(*a*) by putting the postposition *khon* (or *khoc'*) after the word or words with which comparison is to be made, and leave the other as it is. The *khon* may take the determinative suffix.

E. g., *nuiren kaḍa do iñren khone marańa*, this one's buffalo is bigger than my one; *hana dare do noako khon usula*, that tree over there is higher than these ones; *ona khonak' noa do bogege*, this is better than that.

(*b*) by putting *bąṛti* (more), *ar*, *arhǫ̃*, *artet'* (more, still more, additional), also *ar bąṛti*, *arhǫ̃ bąṛti* and *artet' bąṛti*, before the compared word, with or without a *khon* after the other.

E. g., bọṛti sebel, more savoury, *artẹt' kisạ̃ṛ*, still more rich; *nui dọ pahilko khọn artẹt' bọṛti kẹṭẹc'e ńẹlọk' kana*, this one looks even stronger than the first ones.

61. The superlative degree is expressed:

(*a*) in a way similar to that of the comparative, by putting *khọn* after *jọtọ*, *sanam* (all), and compare with this.

E. g., jọtọ khọn nui dọe husiạrena, this one is more cautious than all, i. e., he is most cautious; *sanam jọ khọn ul dọ bọṛti sebela*, mango is the most delicious of all fruits;

(*b*) by adding *utạr* (the highest, the top, the very, the thing itself, etc.) to the adjective, the whole being an absolute statement.

E. g., boge utạr, the very best; *cọṭ utạr*, the highest.

(*c*) Our superlative is sometimes rendered by using a word denoting the limit. *E. g.*, *rạskạ reak' sẹs*, the end, the limit of joy, the greatest possible joy; *phạsiạraren sẹs*, the greatest hypocrite, the limit.

(*d*) Positive, with a determinative suffix, or without any addition and without the preceding postposition, may be used to express our superlative, as an absolute statement. *E. g.*, *ọkọeye maraṅa? nuiye maraṅic'*, who is the bigger one (lit. is big)? this one is the biggest one.

The Numerals.

The Cardinal Numerals.

62. The Santals have the following numbers:

1. *mit'* (*mit'ṭẹn, mit'ṭẹc', mit'ṭaṅ, mit' gọṭẹn, mit' gọṭẹc', mit' gọṭaṅ*).
2. *bar* (or *barea*).
3. *pẹ* (or *pea, pẹya*).
4. *pon* (or *ponea*).
5. *mõṛẽ*.
6. *turui*.
7. *eae* (*eyae*).
8. *irạl*.
9. *arẹ* (or *are*.
10. *gẹl*.
11. *gẹl mit'* (or *gẹl khọn mit'*).

H

12. *gel bar* (or *gel khon barea*).
13. *gel pe*, (*gel pea*, or *gel khon pea*).
14. *gel pon* (*gel ponea*, or *gel khon ponea*).
15. *gel mõṛẽ* (or *gel khon mõṛẽ*).
16. *gel turui* (or *gel khon turui*).
17. *gel eae* (or *gel khon eae*).
18. *gel iral* or *gel khon iral*).
19. *gel are* (or *gel khon are*).
20. *mit' isi* or *isia*, or *bar gel*.*
21. *mit' isi mit'* (or *bar gel mit'*, or *mit' isi khon mit'*).
22. *mit' isi bar* (or *bar gel bar*, etc.).
30. *mit' isi gel*, or *pe gel*.
40. *bar isi*, or *pon gel*
50. *bar isi gel*, or *mõṛẽ gel*.
60. *pe isi*, or *turui gel*.
70. *pe isi gel*, or *eae gel*.
80. *pon isi*, or *iral gel*.
90. *pon isi gel*, or *are gel*.
91. *pon isi gel mit'*, or *are gel mit'*, or *pon isi khon gel mit'*, or *pon isi ar gel khon mit'*.
100. *mõṛẽ isi*, or *mit' sae*.
146. *eae isi ar turui*, or *mit' sae pon gel turui*.
1000. *hajar*, or *mit' hajar*.
10,000. *ojut*, or *mit' ojut*.
100,000. *lak*, or *mit lak*.

63. The numerals from 100 and upwards, i. e., multiples by 10, are all borrowed from Hindi or Bengali. The ordinary Santal will know the names *sae*, *hajar*, *lak* and perhaps *kuṭi* (100 lakhs, or ten millions).

64. Now-a-days the Bengali or Hindi numerals are very commonly used, pronounced according to Santal phonetics.

All who attend school learn either the Hindi or the Bengali numbers, and one may perhaps expect that, except for

* Counting is often done on the fingers and toes, commencing with the little finger or little toe. They also count the finger joints (on the inside) commencing from the inner joint of the little finger; counting the tips also they in this way reach nineteen, the whole hand being twenty. Some also count three joints on the thumb and in this way reach twenty.

the first numerals up to ten, and for twenty and multiples of this, the Aryan numerals will gradually oust the Santali ones.

Although the numerals for 1000 and 100,000 are known to everybody, * it does not seem, as if many has any idea as to the real meaning of these, provided they have not been in school and been drilled, and perhaps not many of these either.

65. (*a*) From the numerals given it will be understood, that the Santals generally count up to ten and then add the units to this up to twenty; higher numbers are multiples of twenties, or of tens, adding the necessary units. This is sufficient for the ordinary wants of village life. If they must tackle higher numbers, they will mostly use the Hindi or Bengali numerals.

(*b*) As to the way of counting from eleven to twenty, it might be remarked, that *gel* + the unit is the most common way; *gel khon mit*, *bar*, etc, is more deliberate and heard with people more or less unaccustomed to count. In stead of the postposition *khon* (from) some people will use the conjunction *ar*, and. If a person has to mention a number one or two short of twenty or multiples of twenty (sometimes also of ten), he may express himself *mit'tec'* (*barea*, or *pea*) *kom mit' isi* (or *mit' gel*), one (two, or three) less one score (or, one ten). In counting this expression is naturally not used.

66. As regards the forms *barea*, *pea*, *ponea* and *isiya*, see para 35. With *ea* (*ya*) suffixed the numeral is a collective (a pair, a triplet, a quadruplet, or a score): this special meaning does not, however, seem to be very conspicuous, both forms being now used indiscriminately.

67. *Ganda* or *gonda*, a quadruplet, is very commonly used as a unit in counting; five *ganda* make one *kuri* or one *isi* or *bis*; four *isi* make one *pon*, i. e., eighty. Certain things connected with their agriculture and household-work are counted in *pon*, such as *gachi*, paddy seedlings, and *ar*, bundles of straw.

68. The language has names for halves and fourths; *adha* is a half (used as a noun, or prefixed, not after a word); *atra* and *tala* or *tara*. half, and *powa* or *poa*, a quart.

---

* A Santal folktale tells of a dog said to eat '*lak pońcas raban*,' that is, fifty laks cold. I remember once hearing an otherwise quite intelligent Santal explain, that there existed 'thousand' kinds of something. On being asked to name these, he managed to mention four. It is very much the same as what is found among other peoples; these numbers really represent uncountable possibilities.

E. g., *adha disom*, half the country, *adha sẹr*, half a seer; *adhatẹt'*, the half part; *tala sẹr*, half a seer, *tala moka*, half a cubit; *bar poesa tala*, two and a half pice; *atra họr*, half-way; *mit' din tala*, one and a half day.

These words for fractions always have reference to concrete things, and no thought of arithmetics should be attached to them.

When needed, the following expressions may be made use of to render fractions: pẹ hạṭiṅre mit' hạṭiṅ, in three parts one part, one third, gẹl hạṭiṅre pẹ hạṭiṅ, three tenths, and so on, also gẹlak' hạṭiṅ, one tenth.

In all schools Hindi or Bengali arithmetics are taught, and the Hindi or Bengali nomenclature naturally comes in.

69. When counting persons *họṛ* is used (e. g. *gẹl họṛ*, ten persons); for families *oṛak'* (house) or *gharọṅj* (family) is used, both constructed as animate collectives in the plural. If *oṛak'* is to mean the building, it is naturally constructed inanimate. *Sạṛim* (lit. roof) is also used about the number of households in a village (always inanimate). About cattle *bohọk'* (head) is used (constructed animate). *Mit' oṛak' menak'koa họṛ*, there is one house Santals.

Distributive numerals.

70. Santali forms distributive numerals of the first ten by reduplicating the first consonant and vowel, if the numeral commences with a consonant, or by inserting an *-k'* after the first vowel, if the numeral commences with a vowel. It is the same formation as is found in the Performative form of the verb; the literal meaning may be said to be "making it one, two, etc."

mimit', one each.
babar, two ,,
pẹpẹ, three ,,
popon, four ,,
mọ̃mọ̃ṛ, five ,, (or, perhaps commonly, *mọmọṛ*)
tutur, six ,,
ek'ae, seven ,,
ik'ral, eight ,,
ak're, nine ,,
gẹgẹl, ten ,,

babar gel, twenty each, or *mimit' isi*,
pepe gel, thirty „ *mimit' isi gel*, *babar isi*, etc.,
and so on up to ninety.

71. (*a*) The distributiva from 1 to 10 require something added; this may be a word showing what is referred to, or it may be *gotec'*, *goten* or *gotan* (piece, see above para 50). Very frequently *kate* is added, either to the distributive numeral direct or after the words just mentioned (see below para 71).

(*b*) The forms *babar gel*, etc., are very seldom used and likely a fairly late development. The construction is in this case the same as with 1 to 10 and a noun.

(*c*) Distributives may otherwise be formed by simple reduplication of the whole numeral, generally with *kate* suffixed.

(*d*) Distributiva are also frequently formed by simply putting *kate* after the cardinal numeral.

E. g., *mimit' phuruk' emakope*, give each one leaf-cup (is also expressed *mimit' phuruk' kate*, or *mimit' gotec' phuruk'*, or *mimit' gotec' kate phuruk'*); *dinre mimit' takako arjaoa*, they earn each one rupee per day; *pepe hor* [or *pepe hor kate* or *pepe kate hor*, or *pepe gotec' (kate)*] *ko hecena*, they came in parties of three; *momor gel kateko uthauena*, they broke up and left in parties of fifty; *mit' mit'*, one by one, some, one each; *bar bar kate hataope*, take two each; *pepe kate jo ko ńamket'a*, they got three fruits each (*note*, the distributiva of 2, 3, and 4 are frequently *bar barea*, *pe pea*, *pon ponea*, in two distinct words, with *kate* added); *turui turui kate bolokpe*, enter in parties of six; *gel turui gel turui kateko hajirena*, they presented themselves in batches of sixteen; *sae sae cetanren sordarko*, the overseers over hundreds; *hajar hajar cetanren subedarko*, the captains of a thousand (each); *isi isi hor kate* (or *isi isi kate hor*), in batches of twenty;

ponea kate poesa emakom, give them four pice each; *bighare gel bar ana kate khajna lagaoale kana*, we have a rent of twelve annas per bigha; *pepe pepe kate emakom*, give each one three;

mimit mimit' hor, some people, one here one there; but *mimit' mimit'te*, one by one, each one, the one after the other.

72. The above mentioned repetition (here of numerals) to express distribution is a common feature of the language Repetition may mean plurality, a mass spread over a space of room or time (see above under Number), but may also mean

distribution over what is named (*oṛak' oṛak'*, house by house, every house, *ghonṭa ghonṭa*, hour by hour, every hour, *hoṛ hoṛte*, along the road).

In the same way not only the numeral, but also the word to which the numeral refers may be repeated, with or without *kate*, to show distribution.

E. g., *pe hoṛ pe hoṛ kate agukope*, bring them three and three persons at each time. *

Ordinal numerals.

73. Santali has properly speaking only three ordinal numerals, namely *pahil*, *dosar* or *dosra*, and *tesar* or *tesra*, first, second and third (all borrowed from Hindi). Sometimes *cauṭha*, fourth, also borrowed from Hindi, may be heard; this last word does not, however, seem to be fully adopted as yet, i. e., for common use, although understood by all.

The ordinals mentioned are used about both animates and inanimates; standing alone they generally take the determinative suffix (*-ic'* or *-ak'*, as the case may be).

It should be noted, that the first two ordinals also have other meanings that may be deducted from their original signification; this is especially the case with *dosra*, which may mean the second, but generally means another, just like *anden* in Norwegian or Danish.

74. (a) The need of ordinal numerals is very limited in the daily life of the Santals. Where ordinals might be used they manage in one way or another.

When, e. g., inside the family the need for knowing the sequence or order arises, they use maraṅ (big) and huḍiṅ (small) for the two extremes and tala (middle) for the middle one. If there are more they use saṅjhla (m.) or saṅjhli (f.) for the third and maṅjhla or maṅjhli for the fourth; maraṅ tala (big middle) and huḍiṅ tala (small middle) are also used for the second and fourth. As is seen, they manage very much like many others. These expressions naturally only refer to a place within a known whole.

(b) Very frequently they will refer not to the whole, but to the relative position of two; in such cases sotok' (following, next

---

* As is seen, distributiva are formed by constructions commonly met with in connection with the verb.

in order) is used. Iń sotok' dọ nui, this one is next to myself; Pạṇḍu sotokić dọ Leḍha, Ledha is in age next to Pandu. Sotok' is used mostly about children of the same parents.

(c) Tayọm or taenọm (after, behind) is used like sotok', but has a wider or more common application, about anything following after. (Cp the expressions ọtọń tayọm, following one after another, in single file, and tayọm maṛań, lit. behind in front, one after the other.)

75. A few examples will show, how the language finds means of rendering what we express by ordinals.

E. g., turui bad kate (or *bạgikate*) *ona tayọmak'* (or, *panteak'*) *ạguime*, leaving six bring the one behind, or next (or, beside it): *ato kulhite calak'me, pon oṛak' parọm kate pạhil oṛak'te bọlọk'me*, walk along the village street, when you have passed four houses enter the first one; *ona hana sawak'* (*noa sawak'*), the one on the further side (on this side), and so on.

76. The most commonly used postposition is tayọm (after), but, as will be understood, this does not give the number, only the next in relation to something named.

Many Santals have tried to render the ordinals by putting *tayọm* with a determinative suffix after the cardinal number; thus *turui tayọmić'* (or *-ak'*), the one after six, i. e., the seventh; also *gẹl tayọmren* (or *reak'*), the one in the place after ten, the eleventh. The late Mr Skrefsrud in his Grammar has given this last form for the ordinals. It should, however, be noted that, while the expression is quite understood by the people, it is only occasionally used and cannot be said to form a system. But it is used and is not something purely made up.

77. Ordinals are or will become necessary, and it has been found that the common cardinal with the determinative suffix, *-ic'* for the animate and *-ak'* for the inanimate, added is quite understood as an ordinal. As a matter of fact the form may be heard used quite unconsciously even by illiterate people. E. g., hanko gạị ńẹlkom; leṅga sa khọn lekha kate eaeyić dọ ińrenićge, look at the cattle over there; commencing to count from the left the seventh one is the one belonging to me. *

* It seems, as if this form is natural, and we have adopted it in our schools and elsewhere when there is need for ordinal numbers. It is a misunderstanding, when it has been said that this form cannot be used as an 'adjective'. There does not seem to be anything repugnant in the expression; it is actually heard, and a word with a determinative suffix may be and is constantly used also as an adjective.

78. (*a*) In arithmetics the Hindi or Bengali ordinals are used, and these may possibly in time also be adopted by the language; but as yet they are quite outside the vocabulary of the villagers. except the first three (or four) ordinals. With the present cultural development, or rather lack of such, there is little need of ordinals.

(*b*) It might be remarked, that nọmbọr (i. e., Engl. number) has in recent years been freely adopted in the language; in connection with this the cardinals are used, just as in English. Nọmbọr mit̕ sae pẹ gẹl turui, No. 136. *

79. In stead of pạhil one may in certain combinations hear pọrthọm (borrowed from Bengali), also combined with pạhil (e. g., pọrthọm cas, the first crop; pạhil pọrthọmre, at the first beginning). Instead of dosar one sometimes hears laha tayọm, next the first.

Laha, generally with the determinative suffix, is also used about the first, the one in front.

80. The language has three *inclusive* or *collective* numerals, formed by infixing an *n* after the vowel which is repeated, viz., *banar*, both, *pẹnẹ*, all three, *ponon*, all four.

E. g., *banar kaḍa*. both the buffaloes; *banar sarege*, on both sides; *dẹnẹ banar sẹc'renko*, the persons of both sides (e. g., in a law-suit); in stead of *banar* only *bana* is heard in the combination *bana họr; pẹnẹń ạgu akat'koa*, I have brought all three; *pẹnẹ-mit'*, all three one, triune §; *ponon kombṛoko sap'ket'koa*, they have caught all four thieves.

81. (*a*) An *approximate number* is expressed by naming two consecutive numbers, the lower numeral first, the higher one last, without any conjunction.

Mit̕ bar, a couple, bar pẹ, or barea pea, two to three; pẹ pon, or pea ponea, three to four; mọ̃ṛẽ turui, five to six (a very frequently used expression); ursiń bạrsiń, or mursiń bạrsiń, a couple of days, lit, one day two days, ur (also pronounced ạr) or mur not being otherwise heard in the present language.

(b) If one wishes to be a little more deliberate, one may put sẹ, or, between the numerals; this is always done when the numbers quoted are not consecutive, and generally also with higher numbers.

---

* People may be heard to say, e. g., bar gẹl pạhilak̕, meaning to say the twenty-first; the expression really means the nineteenth, the one before twenty.

§ Pẹrẹ-mit̕ may mean 'one in three', i. e., among three.

E. g., ponea se mõṛẽ hoṛko senlena, four or five persons went; *gel se gel bar ko jaorayena,* ten or twelve persons came together.

(*c*) If one wants to be still more approximate (as is very common) a *leka,* with or without a *gan,* may be added, after the numeral, or after the noun, or an *amdaj,* about, be prefixed.

Bar pe sae leka gan, something like two to three hundreds: amdaj mit' isi gan hoṛ, about one score of people.

Santali 'arithmetics', counting in play, etc.

83. (*a*) The Santals have, properly speaking, no arithmetics. When they have to perform an addition, etc., they speak of juṭuč or juṭič, add to, lekha guṭ, add up, lekha jarwa, do., bad, deduct, miṇạ, subtract, gunạn, multiply (probably only learnt in schools); dhao, time, eae dhao, seven times; gun, fold; hạṭiń, divide, bhag, divide, hĩs, or hisạ, share, portion, division; joṛo, portion.

(*b*) The principal names for accounts of sorts and matters connected therewith are the following, and it should be remembered that practically all accounts are with people of other races, traders of sorts.

Hisạb, account; lekha, count; lekha jokha, account, render an account; jokha, measure (length); soń, measure (capacity or area); ọjọn, weigh; tulạ, weigh; rin, debt (carrying interest); sud, interest; ḍiḍhi sud, fifty percent interest (charged on paddy); siki sud, 25 percent interest; mas koraṛi sud, (monthly) one anna in the rupee interest; bar ana sud (ṭakarc), two annas interest (in the rupee); raudạṛi sud, an interest of two annas per month in one rupee (charged during the months from Magh to Jheṭ on money borrowed during this slack season; as soon as the rains commence (i. e. from Āsaṛ) the interest is changed to siki sud); khorali sud, the same as raudạṛi; bạki, balance due; jer bạki, do., especially on old accounts having run for some time, brought forward from previous accounts; usul, pay up, to one's credit; hala, refund; hala ruạṛ, repay; sod, repay in full with interest, settle up; haolat, loan for a few days not carrying interest; pańca, loan without interest (in money or in kind);

(*c*) In olden times before money came into use, utiń, barter, was the custom; utiń ạkriń, sell by barter; utiń sunum, barter oil, the common name for a kind of mustard oil, used for culinary purposes; kiriń, buy; ạkriń, sell; dhar, credit; dhar pańca, do.

(*d*) When a present-day Santal, e. g., measures out paddy to pay what he has borrowed, he will always make use of the

Hindi or Bengali numerals, generally commencing in Hindu fashion with Ram, repeating the numeral, as he is measuring out the next pạị (half a seer) thus: ram, ram, ram, du, du, du, tin, tin, tin, etc.), until he has reached solo or bis (it depends upon what kind of measure is used): the suli (20 half seers) is then measured, and he puts a small handful of paddy down as a sola, tally, counting-mark, and commences to count from one again.

Four suli is one kaṭ, or, muṛi, one maund; five muṛi is one bis (20 suli, used in certain parts).

Where accurate measure is not needed, as when they take stock for themselves of what they have, they use the haṭak̔, winnowing fan, as a rough measure; similarly they have baskets of various sizes, one suli, two suli, three suli, four suli, or muṛi, baskets, and also larger ones.

Tulạ is the common name for scales, tạrju tulạ or tạrjuạ tulạ, for a weighing beam.

Ḍheo, or baṭ kara, weights; the common Indian weights are being introduced, tola, coṭak (five tola) and sẹr being commonly known; posori, a stone weighing five seers, especially used in weighing matkọm; coṭak, five tolas, pawa or poa, one quarter seer, pạị, half a seer, pạilạ or sẹr, one seer *

---

* In connection with numbers the following may be noted:

(a) When testing the 'luck' of a bedstead, they count the cords along the long piece of the frame wood from the foot to the head saying: ind, cand, jọm, raja, or sometimes only jiọn, mọrọn. If the last interval counted is cand, raja or jiọn, it means luck, otherwise the opposite.

(b) Children playing will count in the following way:

1. ekam, 2. dukạm, 3. tinik, 4. likiṛ, (or lạkuṛ, or lạbuṛ), 5. ḍẹnḍ, 6. kọnḍ, 7. salae, 8. sapae, 9. kiṭic̕, 10. kọṛọk̔ (or kọṭọk̔). 11. ṭhakṛọk̔.

There are some variants; some count salae, sapae, ḍẹnḍ, kọnḍ (also pronounced kọ̃ṛ), and some count up to fourteen, the words from four on being: lạbuṛ, sạbuṛ, bokoṭ, buyạk̔, ḍẹnḍ (here 8), kọnḍ (9), sạlại, sạpại, kiṭik̔, kọṭọk̔ (13), ṭhakṛọk̔ (14).

The first three are easily recognized.

(c) In ṭir ẹnẹc̕ they count: 1. mona, 2. dona, 3. ṭena, 4. cara, 5. maca (or sometimes paca), 6. choi, 7. goi.

The first four are easily recognized, so also the fifth in its seldom used form, and also six; goi in Santali means a water-pool; it is the end.

(d) In a play called raja paṭa the following ways of counting are used:

1. lạuṛạ, 2. phauṛa, 3. dater loi, 4. kạṭhi upor, 5. bhela dada, 6. ṭhae, 7. ṭhui, 8. ṭhikạn.

Postpositions.

84. As several times remarked the Santal language has no declension corresponding to what is found in the inflexional languages. In stead of declension and also to do service for prepositions (which are not found) the language makes use of a number of postpositions. *

85. The different uses and meanings of the postpositions will be examined in connection with each of these. It may at once be stated that the postpositions may be added to both primary and secondary words, to words with or without a determinative suffix, and to tense and mood suffixes, but not to the finite verb, nor to the Imperative, and not to enclitic particles, nor to Interjections.

86. Some of the postpositions are used to form constructions corresponding to our adverbs.

Most of the postpositions may, when functioning, take the determinative suffixes and the suffixed personal pronouns

---

Or : 1. iciṅ, 2. biciṅ, 3. jãwãe biciṅ, 4. jamae bolẹ, 5. jogọnat, 6. haṇḍi, 7. kuṇḍi, 8. tel kuṇḍi, 9. hoelo ram, 10. khạilom, 11. dạilom, 12. del pat, 13. baṛe, 14. choi, 15. sat.

In the same play when counting the fingers they count :

1. nim juri juri, 2. koire, 3. pal libona, 4. kodal libi, 5. sokti korọ, 6. bọl nại khọ, 7. busur bọtọr, 8. dhọr.

(e) If no one will confess or admit having done something or other, they count as follows :

1. ạmki, 2. jạmki, 3. pat goṇḍa, 4. pitol goṇḍa, 5. dolwari, 6. boswari, 7. gại cara, 8. habar habar, 9. mutiạ ki, 10. damboli, 11. sea bele suriuṭ.

Or : 1. adle, 2. padle, 3. kẹ padle, 4. nimnạ, 5. kọrkoṭa, 6 padle tũi.

In both cases the fingers are counted ; when 11 or 6 is reached, the finger is bent ; the one on whom the last sea bele suriuṭ or tũi falls, is the culprit.

* Where possible the etymology of these postpositions will be looked into. Many of them seem to be of Aryan origin, but furnished with a Santali final consonant, generally one of the three consonants *n*, *c'* and *ṭ*.

(when showing number), the whole combined expression in this way serving for nouns, adjectives, relative sentences, &c.*

87. Postpositions used to express *rest*, stay or being *in*, inside, within, within the sphere of, belonging to :

rẹ (or *re*), *rẹn* (*ren*), *reak*, *reañ*, *renak*, *ṭhẹn*, *ṭhẹc'*, *talare*, *mọṭre*, *modre*, *mudre*.

(*a*) *Rẹ* † is used to denote being in, inside, within, within the sphere of, within the boundaries of the concept to which this *rẹ* is added.

It refers to space, time, action or relation. It may be translated *in*, *on*, *at*, *during*, *while*, *in - case*, or with similar words.

E. g., *oṛakre*, in the house, *birre*, in the forest, *sạṛimre*, on the roof, *Bhagalpurre*, at Bhagalpur, *ọtre*, on the ground, *cọṭre*, in the height, i. e. high up, *latarre*, down below, *dakre*, in the water, *họere*, in the air, *setoñre*, in the sun, *ñũtre*, in the dark, *dukre*, in grief, *rạskạre*, in joy ;

jọkhẹc're, at the time, *caluoen sermare*, last year, *pon sermare*, in four years, i. e., within four years, at the end of, or after (not, however, in the course of four years ; then *te* is used) ; *inạ takreko hẹc'ena*, at that moment they came ; *tisre*, when, which time or day ? *tinre*, which time of the day ? *cando hạsurokre*, at sunset (as a general statement) ; *khẹtre hoṛoko irok kan tahẽkanre*, when they were cutting paddy in the rice-field, *jọjọmre ñũñũre dọ nokokotam peṛa*, *gujukre gurokre okorkotam oaris*, when eating and drinking, these are

---

* The verbal suffixes are a peculiar class of postpositions, essentially different from the postpositions that are to be examined here below, more especially in this respect that a word with an added postposition may form a new concept taking verbal suffixes, which naturally a word with a verbal suffix cannot do.

† This is the original pronunciation and used where the law of harmonic sequence does not demand *re* ; see Materials I. paras 36 & 37. As in all ordinary writing only *re* is written, the learner should have this in mind. As to the possible origin of *rẹ* there does not seem to be anything to explain it in Santali. Uṛia has a locative *re*.

your friends, when dying and falling where are your helpers (heirs)? (quoted from a Santal song); *nitre ge, bañkhan tisre hõ bañ*, now, otherwise never; *ruhedere hõ bae mongaka*, even when they scold him he does not mind; *hijuk̕reye agukedea*, he brought him when coming;

enrė hõ, even then; *endere ma bogege*, in that case, if such be the case, it is well; *hẽgre hõe bañre hõ katha dọ sạri kangea*, whether he admits it or not, it is true;

nui haṛamre dọ bạñ jãwãeok'a, I am not going to be married to this old man (lit. in this old man I will not be husband-ed); *kisũṛre bhorsatiñ*, my hope is in my master; *iñ dọñ dak̕ sẹc'anrege*, I must before anything else go towards water; *bicạrreye jitạuena*, he succeeded in the judging, gained his suit; *dak̕reye ñurhạyena*, he fell into the water; *kul sẹ bana hoṛko ñẹl ñamlekoreko lạpại sadek'a*, when people catch sight of a tiger or a bear, they inform one another; *sanamreko gọpọṛọa jạruṛ jọkhẹc'*, they help each other when needed in all matters;

jãhã ato namdakena mẹnkhan, ona atoren hoṛ, jãhãnak'reko jarwa ñupamlenre disom hoṛko tuluc', buru leka usulko ạikạua, ato manteko bạḍạijoña, ondoko tahẹn tuluc're hõ, if a village becomes famous, then the inhabitants of this village when they in connection with something or other meet with the people of the country, feel tall like the hills; they are proud on account of the honour of the village, even when they are dunces.

(*b*) *Rẹn* (*ren*) is formed form *rẹ*, *n* being added. This *n* is discussed above para 59 (f), q. v.

Ren added to a word produces what virtually corresponds to an adjective, conveying the meaning of somebody being inside of, belonging to the sphere of the concept of the word. In practical use it generally does service corresponding to our *genitive*.

Standing alone, without determinative suffix, *ren* in present-day language always refers to an animate word.

Ren may, however, take the inanimate determinative suffix *ak̕*, and with this the number suffixes, especially the plural one; *renak̕* seems to be getting out of use now-a-days;

younger Santals do not seem to regard it as proper language.

Ren very frequently takes the animate determinative suffix *-ic'*, with *-kin* and *-ko* to form the dual and the plural, that is to say, a word with *ren* added is treated as an adjective or a noun, a concept with a possesive determination.

Renic' (or generally now *rinic'*) has got a special meaning attached to itself and is used as a separate word in the meaning of wife, frequently with *tẹt'* (*rinic'tẹt'*) added.

A word with *ren* added may take a verbal suffix.

E. g., *atoren hoṛ*, a man of the village, belonging to do.; *iṅren hopon*, my child (who is a child in my sphere, belonging to me); *dhuṛiren manwa*, man belonging to dust, of dust; *sermaren siṅ boṅga*, the day-god in the heavens; *hasarene benaokedea*, he made him of earth; *ac'renkoe ạkriṅket'koa*, he sold his own ones; *ac'renket'koae*, he made them his own (e. g. adopted); *uni rinic'* his wife; *atorenak'ko*, things relating to the village.

(*c*) *Reak'* (or *reaṅ*, both are used indiscriminately, some people having got into the habit of preferring the one and others the other) corresponds to and is used like *ren*, and with the same meanings, but only about inanimates. It is *re* with the inanimate determinative suffix added.

A word with *reak'* added is often treated as a new concept or base-word. *

E. g, *bir reak' dare*, a tree of the forest (note the slight difference that may attach to *bir dare*, a forest tree); *nahel reak' pal dọ kumare benaoa mẽṛhẽt' reak'*, the plough-share a blacksmith makes of iron; *hapṛamko reak' katha*, the word of the ancestors, the traditions; *uni reaṅko rọṛa*, they speak of him; *uni reak'ak'koko lạiket'a*, they told his story, what concerned him; *oṛak' reak'ak'ko*, the things belonging to the house;

* The origin of *reak'* and *reaṅ* (*re*+*ak'* or *aṅ*) is often forgotten; they do not think of *ak'* or *aṅ* being the determinative suffix. Hence the determ. suffix *ak'* (I do not remember having heard *aṅ* used) may be added anew (*reak'ak'*, *reaṅak'*, *reak'ak'ko*, etc.).

kạmi reaṅko cepet'ena, they took council together concerning the work.

Ren, reaḱ and *reaṅ* may consequently be rendered by : *of, consisting of, belonging to, concerning, about,* or our genitive. It should be borne in mind that it is not a genitive as we understand it, but a formation, doing service for an adjective or an apposition to the word thus qualified.

The use of the determinative suffixes to serve for our genitive has been mentioned previously. See paras 38-41.

(*d*) *Re* is frequently added to another postposition (see previous examples, as e. g., *sẹc're, tuluc're, ṭhẹnre*), or also suffixed to a word combined with which it forms a separate, compound postposition. Such are *talare, modre, mudre* and *mọtọre.*

(*e*) *Talare* is *tala,* the middle, with *re* suffixed, and is used to express : in the middle, between.

E. g., talare menaea, he is in the middle ; *oṛaḱ talare,* in the middle of the house ; *oṛaḱkin talareye teṅgo akana,* he is standing between the two houses ; *hoṛ talare aṅjọmọḱ kana,* it is being heard among people ; *tala malatẹt're,* in the very centre ; *abo talare noa dọ tahẹna,* this matter shall remain between us ; *unkin talare laṛhạ̃i calaḱ kana,* a fight is going on between those two ; *niạkin barea talare bachaojoṅme,* choose between these two.

(*f*) *Modre* (or as spoken by some, *mudre*) is *mod* (a word adopted from Bengali, used only as part of a postposition in Santali) and *re,* in the middle, midst, between, among, in, within. *Talare* and *modre* are often synonyms ; when there is a difference, it is this, that *talare* may also mean between, without belonging to the concept stated, while *modre* presupposes belonging to.

E. g, abo modre mit' hoṛ, a person among us ; *noako modre hataojoṅme,* take among these things ; *noko modre kombṛo menaea,* the thief is among these ; *ṅindạ modre* (- *mọtọre*), during the night (inside-) ; *eae mãhã modreye sẹtẹroka,* he will arrive inside a week ;

(*g*) *Mọtọre* ('*re* added to *mọtọ*, a word that is in Santali used in the meaning of alone, limited to, possibly the same word as *mod*) is used exactly as *modre*, but may also be heard with the meaning of 'exclusively in'.

In some parts *mọtọre* is more frequently used than *modre*; in other parts it is apparently not used in this meaning.

E. g., *uniren gạiko mọtọre iñren menaea*, my one is among his cows; *nia ato mọtọre menak̕a*, it is within the limits of this village, or, only in this village.

(*h*) *Mọdhẹ* and *mọdhẹre* are, in some parts, or perhaps only by certain people, used in stead of *modre*; *mọdhẹ* is pure Bengali.

(*i*) All compound postpositions having final *re* may take the -*n* and the determinative suffixes, in full analogy with *re*.

88. To express *rest with*, staying with (as distinguished from 'in', 'within the sphere of') the postposition *ṭhẹn* (with its equivalent *ṭhẹc̕*) is used.

(*a*) The original meaning of the word is likely 'of the place of' whatever it is added to.* It may be used of both animates and inanimates, and may also be added to both classes. It denotes co-existence in the same place, but may also be used about non-material relation. In certain cases the person with whom somebody or something is may represent superiority, authority or possession, but far from always; it depends on the context. Naturally the distance between the 'parties' must be observable and small; the word presupposes immediate proximity.

Ṭhẹn is often used to express the logical subject in Passive.

---

* *Ṭhẹn* (*ṭhẹc̕*) is most probably to be explained as derived from the Skr. root *stha* from which we in Santali have *ṭhãi*, place, and *than*. With the adjective termination *n* this may easily become *ṭhẹn*. A Bengali dialect has the form *ṭhe*.

E. g., apat ṭhẹn menaea, he stays with his father; *guru ṭhẹne cet' akat'a,* he has learnt it from (with) his teacher; *mutul ṭhẹn mit'ṭẹc' loa dare menaka,* a fig tree stands at the gable end of the house; *ọkọe ṭhẹnin ńama,* with whom shall I get it? *culhạ ṭhẹn dọhọeme,* put it at (not on) the fire-place; *dhiri ṭhẹne teṅgoyena,* he stopped at the stone; *ojha ṭhẹne ran ocoyena,* he was treated with (i. e., by) the ojha; *ḍaktọr ṭhẹne gẹt' ocoyena,* he was operated on with (i. e., by) the surgeon; *mit' jan ṭhẹnko ńumena mẹnkhan ḍạnko dọ, hajar jan ṭhẹnko sẹnlenre hõ inạgeko rọṛa,* if the witches have been named with (or, by) one witch-finder, even if they went to a thousand witch-finders they will say they same thing;

uni ṭhẹn daṛe menaka, there is power with him (i. e. conferred on); *phalna ṭhẹn kulijońme,* ask so and so (for information, advice, etc.); *mạńjhi ṭhẹn gọṛọm ńama,* you will get assistance with the headman;

mit' ṭhẹn, at one place; *mạńjhi ṭhẹne lại sọdọrket'a,* he told it to the headman.

(*b*) *Ṭhẹn* takes the determinative suffixes like *rẹn* and *rẹ*.

E. g., paranik ṭhenic', he who is with (or at the side of) the deputy headman; *oṛak' ṭhenic' dọ bań, kaḍa ṭhenic'ge bẹṅgẹt'aeme,* look at the one standing close to the buffalo, not at the one at the house; *band ṭhenak'ko,* the things at the embankment.

89. To denote *movement towards* the following postpositions are used: *ṭhẹn* (*ṭhẹc'*), *tẹ* (*te*), *sẹn* (*sen*), *sẹc'* (*sec'*), *dhạbic', hạbic', dhạric', hạric'*.

(*a*) *Ṭhẹn* is the same word as the *ṭhẹn* denoting rest with; it is used about moving towards when the object to which anything is moved is an animate being, further with inanimates, when it is desired to express movement to the immediate proximity, up to, but not inside.

E. g., jan ṭhẹnle calaka, adwa caole aema ṭhẹne curuc' idia, caole curuc' ṭhẹne sindur idiaka, we go to the witch-finder, he puts small heaps of sun-dried rice down at many places; at the heaps of rice he makes marks of sindur; *hạkim ṭhẹn kathako aderket'a,* they brought the matter in before the court; *mit' ṭhẹnbon ạgu jarwakaka,* we shall bring it all together at one place; *kukańteko them pera horokle calaka*, we shall go to my uncle's on a visit.

(*b*). *Te* (*te*, see remarks on pronunciation of *re*) is used to denote movement to, or direction towards, or along, but only suffixed to inanimates. It may also convey the idea of into, inside, although this meaning does not need to be stressed.

It is possibly this *te* (which is to be distinguished from the *te* conveying the idea of instrumentality) that is found as a component part of certain demonstrative adverbs denoting direction (see para 162). *

In analogy with *re* also *te* takes a suffixed *n* (with or without a determinative suffix), and the determinative suffix *ak* (*añ*), the result being an adjective. It also takes verbal suffixes.

E. g., *orakteko calaoena*, they went home; *sendra gad birteko bologena*, the hunt crowd entered the forest; *okatem calak kana? atotege*, where are you going? to the village; *Rañgate*, to Ranga (a village); *dakteye bologena*, he went into the water, was immersed; *hor horteko hecena*, they came along the road; *alope okakotek tabona*, do not go anywhere (presence is wanted); *horten hor*, a wanderer; *hortenko daharteñko*, wayfarers, people going along the roads; *ottęko hecena*, they came walking; *ottenko*, walking people; *gada are areteak dareko*, the trees along the river bank.

(*c*) *Te* is often combined with other postpositions, denoting direction.

E. g., *bir sente*, in the direction of the forest; *sec'te*, towards (see below *songete*, *sãote*).

In recent years *lagit'te* is often heard with some people in the same meaning as *lagit'*.

(*d*) *Sen* (*sen*) with the parallel form *sec'* (*sec*) is a postposition formed in analogy with *then* and *khon*; its literal

---

* *Te* has apparently nothing to explain it in Santali, but may in spite of this be a pure Santali word. As regards the *te* here mentioned the Bengali locative suffix might be compared, and as regards the instrumental or causative *te* the Hindi ablative suffix may be compared. The reader is referred to the works of Aryan scholars discussing these suffixes.

meaning is likely 'of the side'* ; it denotes direction towards ; it is used in connection with words denoting movement or rest. It may be translated : towards, in—direction, on the side of, in favour of.

E. g., *oka sẹc'e calaoena ?* in what direction did he go ? *ato sẹc'ko rakap'ena,* they went up towards the village ; *dak' sẹc'e sẹn akana,* he is gone towards water ; *họk'lọpic' sẹc'ge jọsọk' kana,* it hits the one who administers the oath ; *cecet'ic' sẹc' bẹñgẹdme,* look towards the teacher ; *iń sẹc'ko gujrạua,* they will testify in my favour ; *onko sẹc' ạcurok'me,* turn towards them, in their direction (lit. and figuratively).

Like the other postpositions with final *-n* also *sẹn* (*sẹc'*) may take the determinative suffixes and be furnished with verbal suffixes.

E. g., *ac' senic'*, the one on his side ; *ape senak'ko lạipe,* tell how matters stand in your parts ; *abo sẹc'enako,* they have turned over to our side ; *nọtẹ sẹc' hijuk'me,* come here in this direction ; *dẹnẹ banar sẹc',* towards both sides ; *dẹnẹ banar sẹc'renko,* those of both sides, both parties.

(*e*) To denote the concept of 'up to', 'unto', 'until', *dhạbic'* or *dhạric'*, with the parallel forms *hạbic'* and *hạric',* are used. They are used about space and time and also figuratively, with words denoting motion or rest ; they signify the *limit* or border up to which anything or anybody is or moves.

All four forms are used indiscriminately, some persons showing possibly a predilection for the one or the other ; in certain combinations it may be felt to be phonetically easier to use the forms that have thrown the initial dental away and only kept the aspirate (so done in accordance with a frequently observed phonetic development in Aryan words). †

E. g., *ato dhạbic'*, up to the village (not further) ; *buru*

---

*Cp. *sa*, side, region.

† All four words are likely an Aryan root with the Santali *-c'* added ; as regards *dhạric'* and *hạric'* there does not seem to be any difficulty (cp. Skr. *dhara*). As regards *dhạbic'* and *hạbic'* one may compare Skr. root *dhav*, and *dhavita*, runing towards.

muthni dhạbic'le sẹnlena, we went right up to the top of the hill (i. e. even so far); *sakọ hanasa dhạbic' iń ńẹl gọt'kat'koa,* I followed them to the other side of the bridge to see them off; *oka hạbic'pe khudạukedea? bir dhạbic'ge; ọnḍẹle at'kedea,* how far did you chase him? up to the forest; there we lost him; *mucạt' dhạbic'e tahẽyena,* he stayed up to the end; *teheń hạric',* until to-day; *nịạ cando reak̕ gẹl eaeak̕ tạrik dhạbic' ọrak̕reye tahẽna,* he will remain at home up to the seventeenth of this month; *Kolkata dhạbic'ko sẹnlena,* they went so far as Calcutta (not further); *gujuk̕ dhạbic',* until death; *tis dhạbic'?* until when? *gẹl ṭaka dhạbic',* up to ten rupees; *hatlak̕ dhạbic' dak̕ menak̕a,* there is water up to the armpit (so deep); *un dhạbic',* up to so much, up to that (time, event); *jivi dhạbic' bọlọyena,* it intered unto the soul; *bik̕ dhạbic' jọmme,* eat until satisfaction.

A very common use of this postposition is found in connection with a verb (in the Future) preceded by *ạuri,* denoting 'until such and such happens'.

E. g., ạuriko hijuk̕ dhạbic' alom okakotek̕a, do not go away anywhere, until they come; *ạuriko mọkọńọk̕ hạbic'ko ẹnẹc'a,* they dance until they are satisfied; *ạurim lại cabawako dhạbic' alom hẹc' ruạṛok̕a,* do not return, until you have informed all.

90. To denote departure from the postposition *khọn* (always so pronounced, but generally written *khon*), with its parallel form *khọc',* is used.*

The essential is not the moving, but the starting, departure, origin (in the meaning of separation from; cp. use of *reu* and *reak̕*) from, the separation from, distinguishing from; it is used as regards space and time, and about source. Its use to form comparative has been mentioned above para 60.

Khọn and *dhạbic'* are frequently used to denote the limit from to the limit up to.

E. g., Sikhạr khọn Ṭuṇḍitele hẹc'ena, we came from Sikhar to Ṭuṇḍi; *bhugạk̕ khọne tot'ena,* he came out from the hole; *khẹt khọne rakap' hẹc'ena,* he came up from the paddy-

* With *khọn* (*khọc'*) might be compared Sindhi Ablative suffix *khõ,* derived from Skr. *kakhsa,* armpit, side (Sant. *kokha*).

field; *Rampur khonko odokena*, they have left Rampur (or, came out from R.): *rehet' khon kahle janamok'a*, shoots will grow out from the root; *sedae khon*, from old times; *un khon*, from then; *dher din khone rua kahil akana*, he has been seriously ill for a long time; *gapa khonbon ehobok'a*, we shall commence from tomorrow; *Dumka khon nonde do eae kos hoyok'a*, it is seven kos (fourteen miles) from Dumka here; *uni khon joto noa gulmal do or akana*, all this trouble has its origin from him; *ona khon hataome*, take from that; *gel khon baream odoka*, you shall take two from ten; *abo tala khone odokena*, he has gone out from among us; *am khone marańa*, he is bigger (older) than you; *gai toa do bitkil toa khon sebela*, cow's milk tastes better than buffalo cow's milk; *dare khone ńũren khon do kahilge menaea*, he is seriously ill from the time when he fell down from the tree; (*hasa khone benaokedea*, would, if used, mean 'he made him from the earth' there being, while *hasarene benaokedea*, means 'he made him of earth); *am then khonko calaoena*, they went away from being with you.

Khon is frequently attached to other postpositions, such as *then* and *ren*.

Khon, but commonly not *khoc'*, frequently takes the determinative suffixes, more especially the inanimate *-ak'*, (*an*), giving the meaning of 'what is, exists, etc., from' that which is mentioned, distance, time, etc.

Un khonak', from then on, from that time up to the time referred to; *onde khonak'*, the distance from there to the place alluded to.

91. To denote *association with*, accompaniment, being with, engagement with, the following postpositions are used: *tuluc'*, *selet'*, *salak'*, *songe* (*-re*, *-te*), *são* (*-re* *-te*), *lagae* (*-te*).

Motion or rest are not reflected on, except in connection with the compound postpositions, where *-re* signifies rest and *-te* motion, as a general, but not absolute rule.

(*a*) *Tuluc'* denotes being with, association with, meeting with (also in opposition), from the most casual to the most intimate relations. It is suffixed to both animates and inanimates.

The idea of activity of some sort or other seems generally to be implied. *

Takes verbal suffixes.

E. g., nui tuluc' tahẹnme, alom jãhã sẹjoḱa, stay together with this one, don't go anywhere; *kakańteko tuluc' haṭreń ńapamoḱa,* I am to meet with my uncle and his people at the market-place; *phalna tuluc' menaea,* he is with so & so (used about two persons of different sex this expression practically always signifies being on intimate sexual terms, here, he or she lives with so & so); *onko tuluc' alom midoḱa,* do not become one with them, i. e., one of their party, their partisan; *iń tuluc'e hẹćlena,* he came with me (wherever he may now be); *mohajọn tuluc'e gate baṛaḱ kana,* he is making friends with the money-lender; *lạtkuṭạ hoṛ tuluc'e sọtasọń akana,* he has become intimate with shameless people; *atoren hoṛ dọ raj tuluc'ko lạṛhaiḱ kana,* the village people are fighting with their landlord; *hoṛo tuluc' gundli dọ bań somanoḱa,* gundli millet is not to be compared with paddy; *puthi tuluc' sẹlẹṭ hõ aguime,* with the book bring also the slate.

(*b*) *Sẹlẹt'* is used to denote addition to, association with, company with, and is used in connection with both animates and inanimates. †

Sẹlẹt' is really an independent word, used as a postposition. It is frequently used corresponding to what might be called a postpositional adjective, the whole being a fresh compound concept; in such cases it may be translated 'in

---

* Cp. Muṇḍari and Ho postposition *lo*, used very much like Santali *tuluc'*. Cp. also Santali *lọe*, found as the second part of a composite verb in the meaning of 'assist', 'be with in any operation'.

† It is difficult to do more than guess at the origin of *sẹlẹt'* and the following *salaḱ'*. The final letters of both words (*-t'* and *ḱ'*) are undoubtedly Santali. The final letters may be either *ẹt'* (*-aḱ'*) or *let'* (*laḱ'*), Santal suffixes. In the last case one might take it to be a compound of *sa*, side, and the suffixes mentioned; but such a formation is scarcely ever met with in Santali. In the first case one might compare *sal mesal*, mixed.

connection with', 'concerning', 'regarding', &c. Used in this way it is often, furnished with the inanimate determinative suffix. *Sẹlẹt'* is also used as a verb taking the verbal suffixes.

E. g., *apat sẹlẹt'ko hẹc'ena*, they came together with their father; *hopọn sẹlẹt' bana eṅgako gọc'kedea*, they killed the she-bear with her cub;

am sẹlẹt' cet' hõ bako rọrlak'a, they did not say anything in connection with you; *boṅga buruko sẹlẹt' lelha katha*, the superstition connected with the spirits; *hisạb sẹlẹt'ak'ko dọ auriye ceda*, he has not as yet learnt accounts (things in connection with arithmetics); *kombro tuluc' alom sẹlẹdok'a*, don't mix with thieves; *uni hõ sẹlẹt'e tahẽkana*, he was also mixed up in the matter; *dakare up'e jọm sẹlẹt'ket'a*, he swallowed a hair together with the rice; *sagaṛ sẹlẹt'e calaoena*, he went taking a cart along (*note*: not, with the cart).

(*c*) *Salak'* is used very much like *sẹlẹt'* with which it might be said to be interchangeable. When used as a verb *salak'* may possibly convey a meaning a little less materialistic than the other.

E. g., *gidrạ salak'ko ńirena*, they have run away taking their children along; *baklak' salak' dọ alope aguia*, don't bring (the timber) with the bark on; *noa kathare iń dọ alope salagińa*, don't mix me up into this case;

(*d*) *São* really means companionship, also equality, attachment; it is an independent word used as a postposition to denote accompaniment, generally with *-re* or *-te* suffixed.*

E. g., *onko são calak'me*, go with them (i. e, in their company); *alẹ são hoṛ dọko bạruḍańok'a*, people together with us become bull-frogs; *apat sãore menaea*, he is together with his father; *sagaṛ sãoteye calaoena*, he went along with the cart;

sãosãore tahẽnme, remain in constant attendance;

mit' sãa, level, smooth; *mit' sãoko hara akana*, they have grown to the same size; *sãorenko, sãotenko*, companions, those who come along with; *sãoteak'*, what is (sent) along with; *sãobak'ḍaeak'*, conscience.

(*e*) *Sọṅge*, a word directly borrowed from Bengali, is of

* *São* is a borrowed word of Skr. descent. Cp. Dr Chatterji, The Origin and Development of the Bengali Language, p. 774.

the same class as *sāo* and similarly used and constructed, except that the meaning of equality (cf. *mit' sāo*) is not found. *-re* or *-te* is very commonly suffixed.

E. g., *sǫṅgẹ hǫṛ*, a companion ; *am sǫṅgẹñ calak'a*, I shall go with you; *sǫṅgẹrenko*, those who are with ; *sǫṅgẹtenko*, those who come or go with ; *sadǫm sǫṅgẹte hijukme*, come along with the pony ; *sǫṅgẹte poesa ạguime*, bring money along with you ; *phạd sǫṅgẹ sǫṅgẹte*, along with the crowd.

(*f*) *Lagae* (*-te*) is used to denote presence, inclusion with, in conjunction with, along with. It is used in connection with both animates and inanimates. The person or thing that *lagae* (*te*) refers to is always an integral part of the 'company', often the most important and absolutely necessary part. *

E. g., *mạñjhi ar mõṛẽ hǫṛ lagaete apat dǫ ọt baṛge ar jutọe hạṭiñakoa*, in conjunction with the headman and the village men the father gives the land and all in shares to them ; *ọṇḍẹn peṛako lagaete kulikope, cet'ko mẹna*, in conjunction with the local friends ask them what they have to say ;

nẹsak' lagaete turui serma reakge hoyoka, when that of this year is included it will be for six years ; *hǫṛ lagaete galmaraok' dǫ lajao bañ ạikạuk'a*, to have talk with people present (i. e. to settle some matter) is not felt to be a shame ;

niạ lagae pon dhaoe hẹc'ena, including this time he has come four times.

(*g*) *Sudhạ*, a word borrowed from Hindi, is frequently postpositionally used to denote inclusion ; what is referred to (animate or inanimate) is not left out ; the whole, all of it is there.

E. g., *ato sudhạko jarwayena*, the whole village came together ; *rẹhẹt' sudhạ maraome*, destroy it, the roots included ; *iñ sudhạko tǫlǫpket' lea*, they summoned us all, myself included.

92. To express instrumentality, cause and means the following postpositions are used : *ṭhẹn* (*ṭhẹc'*), *tẹ* (*te*), *tẹrọñ* and a number of compound postpositions consisting of a

* The word is of Skr. origin.

word to which *tẹ* (*te*) is suffixed, such as *iạte, hoṭẹte, hũyạte, kạhĩste, kạhite, karonte, karnete, khạtirte, kate, dhọroste, taraste, niạte, niyete, lasãṛhẽte, uthumte, satate.*

(*a*) *Ṭhẹn* (*ṭhẹc*) (see para 88) is often used to express the means through or by which something happens, also the agent of the Passive. The literal meaning of 'with' is not, however, lost sight of. *Ṭhẹn* is in this sense used only about animates, or inanimates acting as animates (so often in folktales), and is naturally mostly coupled with the passive voice; when used to convey the same meaning with the Active voice the causative *oco* has to be added. With the Passive this is generally, but not necessarily added.

E. g., guti koṛa ṭhene lajao ocoyena, he was put to shame by the servant boy; *ojha ṭhene ran ocoyena,* he was treated (or let himself be treated) by an ojha; *kaḍa ṭhene rọk'ena,* he was gored by a buffalo; *kamar ṭhen palko hulsiń ocoea,* they let their plough-shares be sharpened by the blacksmith; *mõṛẽ họṛ ṭhenko ḍanḍom ocokedea,* they caused him to be mulcted by the village council; *matkọm dare ṭhen bon bicạr ocoea,* we shall let the mohua tree judge.

(*b*) *Tẹrọń* is used to express the cause, reason or motive, generally with inanimates, also added to a full sentence.*

When used with animates the reference is not so much to the individual, as to what he represents, his state or act.

E. g., tobẹ tẹrọń, therefore; *ona tẹrọńe hẹc'ena,* on account of that he came; *ona unạnko añjọmket tẹrọńko dạrket'a,* they ran away because they heard that rumour; *rugi tẹrọńko agukedea,* they brought him because he was ill.

(*c*) *Tẹ* or *te* † (as to pronunciation see remarks on *rẹ* or *re*, para 87 (a)) is used to denote the instrument or the means, by, or with which anything is done or accomplished or becomes what is stated, also the cause of any action, and the price

* *Tẹrọń* may, if it is not an original Santal word, be compared with *te.* See para 89 (b), footnote.

† See para 89 (b), footnote.

for which anything is sold, bought, etc. Cp. also (d) here below.

It is used in connection with all classes of words and constructions. *Tẹ* takes the *n* suffix (see para 59 (f.)).

E. g., *ṭẹṅgọc'teye mak'kedea*, he cut him with an axe ; *pạhil sarteye jọskedea*, he hit it (the animal) with his first arrow ; *titeye dalkidiṅa*, *jaṅgateye kolsakidiṅa*, he struck me with his fist, he kicked me with his foot ; *hoete bindạṛena*, it was brouht down by the wind ; *ceṭẹrteye gọc'ena*, he was killed by lightning ; *ac'teye hẹc'ena*, he came of his own accord ; *jãhãe ọkoeko gọṛọat'mete noa dọm benaoket'a, sẹ am eskartem tearket'a*, has somebody helped you to make this or have you prepared it yourself alone ; *iṅtegeṅ tear akat'a*, I have made it myself ; *jãhã lekate*, in some way or other ; *cet' lekate*, how, in which way ; *onkatege*, in such a way ; *sadọmteye dẹc' calaoena*, he went away riding ; *ac' acte*, of itself (an. & inan.) ;
bọtọrteye dạṛket'a, he ran away from fear ; *ạimạiak' katha sẹnal'te ac'ren jọtọ hopọn sạrigeye jọm cabaket'koa*, having listened to the woman's word he (the sun) really ate all his children . *tarwaṛe sap'kate buḍhi khudạu tiok'kedeteye mak'kedea*, catching a sword he (the sun) chased the old woman (the moon), reached her and cut her ; *hijuk'te hõ hijuk'me*, lit. by coming also come, i. e., come necessarily, under all circumstances, absolutely ;
pon analeṅ kiriṅket'a, I bought it for four annas ; *eae ṭakate gạiye hataokedea*, he bought the cow for seven rupees (lit. took the cow by the means of) ; *utiṅte*, by barter ; *ṭakate ṅamok'a*, it is to be had for money.

(*d*) The following special use of *te* should be noted :

te is very frequently added to the word that is the (animate) subject of a verb, signifying that the action is performed by or through the person or persons mentioned. It must in this connection be remembered that the animate subject is always represented in the verb by a suffixed personal pronoun.

E. g., *pẹ hoṛteko hẹc'ena*, they were three who came ; *jọtọ hoṛtebon calaka*, we shall all of us go ; *jọtọ hoṛteko jọmket'a*, all of them ate it ; *ac'teye lạiket'a*, he told it of his own accord ; *amte kạmime*, do it yourself. See also above (c).

(e) *Te*, when suffixed to a word, may take a determinative suffix.

When this is for the inanimate (generally added to a word functioning as a participle), the construction denotes the means by which the action is done, or also the concrete result of an action.

E. g. calak'teak'ko, means for going, travelling expenses; *hak'lateak' banuk'taea*, he has nothing to pay with; *casteak'*, agricultural produce.

(*f*) When animate, the determinative suffix will in the constructions referred to always be in the dual or the plural.

When added to a word in the singular, this construction is used to denote, as it may be, a pair or a company or a collection, the principal or best known, or (as is very frequently the case) the most easily mentioned one of a company, etc., being the word or name taking the suffix. This construction is more especially used in connection with personal names and relationship names, signifying 'such & such and party.' The determinative suffix shows the number, whether two or more, all included.

When added to a word in the dual (or what represents this number), or to a word in the plural, the construction denotes the composition of a party, i. e. the means by which it is made up.

E. g., Haritikin, Hari and another, e. g. Hari and his wife; *apatteko*, the father and those with him; *makuteko thenko sen akana pera horok'*, they have gone on a visit to (our) young girl's people (said e. g. by the mother of a girl about the family into which the girl has been married); *Duliteko orak're*, in the house of Duli and her people (Duli being as likely as not the name of the last addition to the family);
bahu jāwāetikin (*tikin* for *tekin*), the bridal pair, the bride and bridegroom together; *haram budhitikin*, husband and wife, both of them.

93. *Tẹ* or *te* is very frequently suffixed to another word, together with this forming a compound postposition, the first part of the compound denoting the particular means, cause or way through, by or in which anything is effected or brought about. Above mentioned *sãote, sọṅgẹte* and *lagaete* (see para 91, d, e, f) are examples of the same kind.

The postpositions following here and para 94 are those most commonly used of this construction.

(*a*) *Iạte*, composed of *te* and *iạ* (a kind of reference or indefinite pronominal); *iạ* may here be said to summarize and point to what has been stated. *Iạte* really means, 'by so & so', 'by what is just stated', and may be rendered by 'because of', 'on account of', 'owing to', or by similar expressions. *Iạte* may be suffixed to any base-word or to a sentence or participial construction.

E. g, *ona iạte*, therefore ; *am iạteṅ hẹc'akana*, I have come because of you ; *ruạ iạte bae hẹc'lena*, he did not come on account of fever ; *ạḍi hoṛ iạte bae sorlena*, she did not come near on account of the multitude of people ; *mẹrọm ạḍiko jọm iạtele ẹṭẹt' akat'a*, we have fenced it in, because goats are constantly eating it.

(*b*) *Hoṭẹtẹ* is used to show instrumentality, mostly added to words denoting living beings or persons, although it is sometimes heard used also in connection with inanimates.*

Hoṭẹtẹ is constantly used to express the logical subject in the Passive. Cp. the similar use of *ṭhen*.

Hoṭẹtẹ takes *n* and the determinative suffixes like *tẹ*.

E. g., *nui hoṭẹteye bogeyena*, he was cured through him ; *nui hoṭẹtenic' dọ nige*, the one got through him is this one ; *dak' hoṭẹte baṅ sẹnlena*, I did not go on account of the rain (then falling) ; *ḍhelak hoṭẹteye bańcaoena, dhirite khan dọe gọc'-kok'a*, he was saved, by its being a clot of earth ; if it had

* The use is easily understood, when it is considered that *hoṭẹtẹ* is composed of the Hindi adverbial participle *hote*, on being, and *tẹ*, thus lit. by being (present).

been with a stone, he might have been killed; *am hotẹteaḱ arjaoaḱ*, what has been gained by you.

(*c*) *Hũyạtẹ* is used somewhat like *hotẹtẹ*, but not so extensively, and only in connection with animates *; it conveys the meaning of by being, because of being (viz. what the word to which *hũyạte* is added implies). Not used about the Agent in the Passive.

E. g, *amren hopon hũyạte bae dalledea*, he did not beat him because he is your son; *apat hũyạte bako botorae kana*, they do not fear him, because he is their father.

94. (*a*) *Karonte* (the Bengali *karon+te*, lit. by cause) is used somewhat like *iạte*, naturally without any veiled reference. It may be rendered: for - reason, because of, etc.

E. g., *cet' karonte?* for what reason? *niạko karonte bań sẹlẹdoḱ kana*, for these reasons I am not joining; *ruạḱ kan karonte*, on account of illness.

(*b*) *Karnete* is a parallel form to *karonte*, but not so commonly used as this.

(*c*) *Satate* (Hindi *sata+te*) is used to express: on account of, in lieu of, through, by being present, on the pretext of.

E. g., *am satate jel daka khubiń joana*, on account of you (because I was with you) I got a splendid meal with flesh curry; *sahan satate sẹnẹrko ạguket'a*, pretending to bring fire-wood they brought rafters.

(*d*) *Khạtirte*, on account of, owing to, for - reason.

Khạtir (an Arabic word borrowed from Hindi) is sometimes used without the *te*; more commonly the *te* is added.

E. g., *thoṛa khạtir bań joslena*, on account of a little I was not hit (I just missed being hit); *cet' khạtirteye pạsiyena?* for what reason did he hang himself? *am khạtirteye ḍanḍomena*, he was fined because of you.

(*e*) *Kạhĩste* (*kạhĩs*, annoyance, + *te*), on account of, roused by.

* Like the preceding *hote*, *hũyạ* is also to be derived from Skr. rt. *bhu*.

E. g., noa kahĩsteń piṭaukedea, I thrashed him on account of this.

(*f*) *Kahite* (Hindi *kahi*+*te*), for - reason, owing to.

E. g., cet' kahitem edreyena, for what reason did you become angry? *bin kahite,* without cause.

(*g*) *Taraste* (Hindi *tras*+*te*), on account of;

dhoroste (*dhoros*, fear, +*te*), equal to *taraste.*

E. g., ghao tarasteye ruak kana, he has fever on account of the sore.

(*h*) *Niate, niyete,* on account of, owing to.*

E. g., mańjhi niyetele calak'a, owing to the headman (because he comes along) we shall go; *am niate noań ńamket'a,* on account of you I have got this.

(*i*) *Lasãrhẽte* (*lasãrhẽ*, pretext, +*te*, by), on pretext of, owing to.

E. g., jãhãn lasãrhẽte am hõ seledok'me, on some pretext or other you also go along; *lac' haso lasãrhẽte bae kami kana,* owing to (pretended) stomach-ache he is not working.

(*j*) *Uthumte,* on account of, owing to, in consequence of. Especially used in connection with bodily ailments.

E. g., manda uthumte bohok' hasoyedin kana, I have a headache on account of a cold; *langa uthumte adi ãtiń japit'ket'a,* I fell into a very heavy sleep in consequence of being tired.

(*k*) *Gunak'te* (composed of *gunak'*, a rarely used word, meaning quality, character, and *te*) is commonly used as a postposition, signifying on account of, because of, as a result of, for the sake of. *Gunak'te* may be added to words functioning as nouns and adjectives and to verbal constructions.

E. g., hasa gunak'te bań hoyok' kana, it does not come to anything on account of the soil; *uni gunak'teko bańcaoena,* on account of him they were saved.

---

* Borrowed from Hindi; this *nia* should not be confounded with the Santali demonstrative pronoun *nia.*

95. *Kate*, by doing, or having done, is a very extensively used postposition that will be further mentioned in connection with the verb, where it properly belongs. It is the *ka* of the Intentional form of the verb with the instrumental *te* added.

Kate is in narratives often used alone as a kind of conjunction, with the contents of the previous sentence or statement tacitly implied, in such cases generally translatable by 'thereupon', 'after this'.

Kate is also used in connection with distributives; it is not, however, *kate* that gives the distributive sense; the meaning given above is always discernible. See para 71.

E. g., duṛup'kate onkoko ęm maṛańakoa; *kate Jǫg Mąńjhi tetre kuṛiye hǫhǫukoa*; *hǫhǫ ągukateye metakoa, Dę sunum sasań ǫjǫk'kotabonpe. Ojǫk'ket'koako, pąhil dǫ naeke tekin haṛam buḍhi, onakate kuḍąm naeketekin,—inąkate atoren jǫtǫ buḍi era,* when they have sat down they give them first; thereupon (this done) the village *custos morum* calls the anointing girls; having called and brought these he says to them: Please anoint them for us with oil and turmeric. They anoint them, first the village priest and his wife, thereupon the backside village priest and his wife, this done all the elderly ladies (married women) of the village;

sęnkate ńęl ąguime, having gone seeing bring, i. e., go, see and come and tell.

Babar ṭakakate, making it two rupees for each; *bar ṭakakate emakom*, give them two rupees each.

96. To express the purpose, intention, designation, benefit and similar concepts the following postpositions are used: *lągit'*, *lagat'*, *ńutumte, męntę, mante, marte.*

(*a*) *Lągit* * probably literally means, being applied, joined up to; it has in Santali the meaning of: 1. being on the point of (doing, becoming); 2. for the purpose of. The first meaning is especially observed in

* *lągit'* is probably formed by adding Santali *t'* to Hindi *lagi*.

connection with verbal constructions, when *lạgit'* is added to the Indeterminate of the verb, giving an inchoative meaning, and takes the suffixes of certain tenses.

E. g., *calak' lạgit'*, about to go, for the purpose of going; *dale lạgidok' kan tahẽkanae*, he was on the point of striking him; *katha lạiako lạgit'*, in order to tell them; *ṭaka lạgit'-iñ hẹč akana*, I have come for money; *ran lạgit' rẹhẹt'ko la ạguket'a*, they have dug and brought roots for the purpose of medicine; *noa ciṭhi dọ okoe lạgit'?* for whom is this letter? (It might be remarked that a Santal addressing a letter invariably puts *lạgit'* after the name; thus: *Suna Hãsdak' lạgit'*, to S. H.)

(*b*) *Lagat'* * is parallel to *lạgit'* with the same meanings and used in the same ways.

E. g., *koṛa lagat' kicric'iñ kiriñket'a*, I have bought clothes for the boy; *utu lagat'*, for curry; *ñẹl lagat'*, in order to see.

(*c*) *Ñutumte* is composed of *ñutum*, name, and *te*, the postposition being the instrumental *te*. It is used partly as 'in the name of', partly as 'by the name of', partly as 'for the purpose of', 'for the sake of'.

E. g, *ruạk'ic' ñutumte ran koekom*, ask them for medicine for the patient; *am ñutumteñ calaka*, I shall go in your name, for you; *phalna ñutumte emañme*, give for so & so's sake (lit. by his name).

(*d*) *Mẹnte*, composed of *mẹn*, say, and *te* (lit. by saying): for the purpose of, for.

Mẹnte is also used as a postposition to substantive clauses and to show *oratio recta*, where we use 'that', 'saying', or nothing. †

It should be noted that when *mẹnte* is used as a postposition to a full sentence, it is invariably and immediately

* Formed like *lạgit'* from Hindi *laga*.

† Under the influence of Bengali or Hindi many Santals have lately commenced to use the conjunction *jẹ* prefixed, instead of this *mẹnte*.

preceded by the finite verb (the subj. pronoun may come between the finite *a* and *mẹnte*), or by the Imperative.

E. g., *cet' mẹnteye calaoena?* for what purpose did he go? *ṭaka ńama mẹntege*, in order to get money; *ṭheṅga mẹnteye mak̇ ạguket'a*, he cut and brought it to make a stick; *aloko lạiakoa mẹnteko manaket'koa*, they admonished them that they should not tell them; *kulikom, cet'ko ceka akat'a mẹnte*, ask them what they have done.

The literal meaning is with this *mẹnte* nearly always more or less perceptible, especially is this the case when *mẹnte* is used in connection with the finite verb. †

(*e*) *Mẹnte*, *mante* and *marte* are used to form adverbs, to show the manner or mode in which an action is performed or anything happens. *

E. g., *saṭ mẹnte*, suddenly; *ṭhus mante rạput'ena*, it broke with a crack; *lapak̇ marte ńūr gọt'ena*, it fell down with a flop.

97. To denote possession and accompaniment *ante* and *ate* are used.

(*a*) *Ante* is formed by adding *te* (the instrumental postposition) to *an*, a suffix used to show possession. (*-an* is used to form adjectives (see para 56), taking the determinative suffixes, *mocawan*, who has a mouth; *poesawanic'*, who has money; *dak̇ anak̇*, which has water; it is also used to form a verbal tense (see the verb)).

Ante may be translated 'having', 'with'.

---

† It might be noted that the pronunciation of the postposition *mẹnte* is a little different from the pronunciation of the same word when functioning regularly as a participle; in this last case the verb and the postposition are distinctly pronounced, so it is heard that it is a compound (verb + postposition), the vowel of *mẹn* having the principal stress. In the first case *mẹnte* is heard as one word, the vowel being l. f. w. and somewhat shortened with the nasal correspondingly lengthened.

* *Mante* is probably old Beng. *man* (cp. mọn in ẹmọn, etc.), and *mẹnte* when used as here is possibly the same word; *marte* is possibly to be connected with the Aryan *mar*.

E. g., *hoṛanteye hędena*, he came having people with him; *aḱ sarante*, having bow and arrows.

(*b*) *Ate* (a demostrative element *a* + *te*) denotes the accompanying circumstances, what is taken along with, or done at the time.*

E. g., *sereńate*, singing, with song; *ruate*, drumming; *hatiate*, with an elephant; *daḱateko duṛup' akana dǫs jǫna, sęngęlate dǫ bań*, the village council is sitting with water, not with fire (i. e., to quench, finish the matter, not to stir it up); *ạḍi marań tamasawateko baplayena*, they celebrated the marriage with great show and splendour.

98. To denote time after, or condition, the postposition *khan* (with its parallel form *khač*) is used. It is especially used corresponding to a conjunction, added to a sentence, and will be further mentioned under the verb.

Khan may be translated 'when', or 'if', or by words expressing the same idea.

Khan or (with the emphatic *ge*) *khange* is also used alone adverbially at the commencement of a sentence; in this case the preceding statement has to be implied or tacitly understood, the meaning being, 'what has just been stated - having happened, come to pass, been done', etc. It is then translated 'then', 'thereupon', or similarly.

E. g., *amem hędenkhan*, when you had come; *bam rǫṛle khan cet'le cekaea*, if you will not speak, what can we do; *hoṛ khan*, if a Santal; *bań khač dǫ*, if not, otherwise, of course, naturally; *męnkhan*, lit. when (or, if) saying (or, said), used to express our 'but', when at the commencement of a sentence; at the end it has a conditional meaning (lit. if said); *rǫreḱako, męnkhan iń dǫ bań pạtiạu akana*, they are saying (this), but I do not believe it; *am kanam męnkhan dela*, if it is you, come.

* This *ate* has nothing to do with the *ate* or *ete* used in Muṇḍari and Ho and other Kol languages, where this postposition is borrowed from Hindi.

Words used as Adverbs.

99. (*a*) Bare base-words may be used also as adverbs, in this case frequently reduplicated.*

Whether a base-word may be so used or not, depends on the meaning of the word, whether this lends itself to, or is suitable for such a use or not. Words denoting quality, manner, form, mode, etc., are naturally those mostly serving as adverbs.

(*b*) Santali has a fairly large number of words which are mostly, or nearly exclusively used as adverbs; they are either originally regular concept-words the use of which has been restricted, or demonstratives of sorts.

Even if these words are not any longer regularly used as nouns or adjectives, they may take suffixes of sorts, showing their true nature.

(*c*) A few examples to show how ordinary base-words may be used as adverbs are given here.

Sanamak̕ bogeko bicạreťa, baḍae bhor dọ, they judge well in all matters, as far as they know; *hẹrẹl họpọn reak̕ katha ar bań calak̕ kana*, the word of the man does not go any longer (he has no longer any authority); *sim rak̕ jọkhẹc̕ oṛak̕teko ruạṛ hijuk̕a*, they return home at the time of cock-crow; *bẹbạric̕ko ruheťkedea*, they scolded him awfully; *nahuke calaoena*, he went in vain; *usạrae hẹċena*, he came quickly; *ạḍi sermae tahẽyena*, he remained for many years.

Purṭhạń bẹńgẹťeťa, I am seeing clearly, distinctly; *koṛa koṛae ńẹlok̕ kana*, he is looking like a young man; *thopa thopage jọ akana*, it has fruited in clusters.

---

* The working of the Santal language being as elsewhere described, it may be questionable, whether, apart from the adverbs formed by adding postpositions, many of the adverbially used base-words should not be taken as the object of the verb, or as an apposition to the object or the subject. This is possibly how the Santal mind understands this way of expressing itself.

100. Except for bare base-words used adverbially most adverbs are base-words to which a postposition has been suffixed.

The term adverb has consequently to be understood a little differently from what we ordinarily take it to denote.

Besides the adverbially used words, mentioned here below, Santali has a large number of adverbs formed from demonstrative, interrogative and indefinite pronouns and pronominal elements. These will be conveniently dealt with in separate sections under the pronouns.

The words given in the paras following are intended to show those most commonly in use; the lists might be multiplied.

101. Words used adverbially denoting *place* :—

Goṭa ṭaṇḍi, everywhere (also *goṭa ṭaṇḍire*).
Sanam ṭaṇḍi, do.
Ṭaṇḍi ṭikur (or, - *ṭukur*), all over, anywhere.
Ṅoa sa(re), this side or part; *hana sa*, that side.
Nọ (*nẹ-*) *parọm*, on this side (of anything to be crossed, e. g. a river); *ọn* (*ẹn-*) *parọm*, on that side; *họn* (*hẹn-*, *han-*) *parọm*, on that far off side.

Towards (direction or movement).	In (rest).
Laha, *lahate*, in front.	*Lahare*, *laha sẹc're*, in front.
Laha sẹc'(te), towards the front.	
Tayọm, *tayọmte*, behind, back.	*Tayọmre*, behind, somewhere
Tayọm sẹc'(te), do.	*Tayọm sẹc're*, behind.
Taenọm = *tayọm*, do.	
Samaṅ sẹc'(tẹ), towards the front.	*Samaṅre*, in front.
	Samaṅ sẹc'(re), do.
Latarte, downward.	*Latarre*, below, under.
Latar sẹc'(tẹ), downwards.	*Latar sẹc'(re)*, do.
Cetante, above, up, on top.	*Cetanre*, above.
Cetan sẹc'(tẹ), upwards.	*Cetan sẹc'(re)*, on top of.
Cọṭ, high up.	*Cọṭre*, *cọṭ sẹc'(re)*, on top, high up.

Coṭte, upwards.
Coṭ sẹc'(tẹ), do.
Beṛhaete, round about.
Beṛhae sẹc'(te), do.
Bahrete, outside.
Bahre sẹc' (te), do.
Bhitrite, in, inside.
Aṛe aṛete, alongside.
Dak' sẹc'(te), towards water (generally to ease oneself).
Racate, to the court-yard (generally to pass water).

Beṛhae, beṛhaere, beṛhae sẹc'(re), round about.
Bahre, bahrere, bahre sẹc'(re), outside.
Bhitri, bhitrire, inside.
Aṛere, along side.
Mucạt're, at the end.

Otọṅ tayọm (-taenọm), in file, one after the other (place, time, manner).

102. Words used adverbially denoting *time* :—

(a)

Tehẹṅ, to day.	*Gapa*, to-morrow.	*Hola*, yesterday.
Tehẹṅok', * to-day.	*Gapanok'*, do.	*Holanok'*, yesterday.
Tehẹṅ gapa, at the present time.	*Meaṅ*, day after to-morrow.	*Mahnder*, the day before yesterday.
Nit, now.	*Endrae*, three days hence.	*On mahnder*, three days ago.
Nitok', do.		
Nitoṅ, do.		
Nãhãk', *Nahak'*, } now, at present, presently.	*Pher endrae*, four days hence.	*Taṛik(h)*, date.
Nẹs, this year.		
Nẹtar, now-a-days.	*Kalọm*, next year,	*Din kalọm*, last year.
Nẹbẹtar, now-a-days, at the present time.	*Satọm*, two years hence.	*Hol kalọm*, two years ago.
Siṅ, day, during daytime.	*Pher satọm*, *Mah satọm*, } three years hence.	*Pher kalọm*, *Mah kalọm*, } three years ago.
Ber, sun, daytime.	*Ṅindạ*, night, at night.	*Sedae*, formerly, long ago.
Bela, sun, time of day (hour).	*Sim rak'*, cockcrow, at cockcrow.	*Aṅga*, dawn, at dawn.
Setak', morning, in the morning.	*Ạyup'*, evening, in the evening.	*Tikin*, noon, at noon.

---

* This form, a word with the suffix of the Indeterminate Medium or Passive (*ok'*), will be found mentioned in its place under the verb.

And a large number of words.

Practically all the words mentioned may take postpositions of sorts. *E. g.*, *nitre*, now, at present, during the present time; *gapate dọ sạtoka*, it will be finished by to-morrow; *teheń khon gapa dhạbic'*, from to-day until to-morrow

(*b*)

Jaoge, constantly, repeatedly.
Jao hilok setak, every morning.
Setak piche, every morning.
Jaejug, always.
Mit' din, one day.
Mit' dinok, one day, some day.
Ursiń bạrsiń, a few days.
Mursiń bạrsiń, do.
Bar cando, two months.
Mit' dhao, once, one time.
Mit' dhaote, at one time, all at once.
Pạhil, first, before.
Pạhilre, before.
Laha, before, first.
Maṛańre, first (in time).
Ạuri, later on, not yet.*
Enan (re), } a while ago, some-
Enań (re), } time ago.
Jao hilok, daily, every day.
Jao hilok ạyup', every evening.
Ạyup' piche, do.
Siń sạtup', all day long.
Din hilok, daily, every day.
Bạrsiń, two days.
Pẹ mãhã, three days.
Gẹl din, or, *gẹl mãhã*, ten days.
Mit' cando, one month.
Mit' serma, one year.
Bọchọr din, a year.
Bar dhao, twice.
Pạhilte, at first, before, previously.
Lahate, first, before, in front.
Lahare, before (in time).
Dinạm hilok, every day.
Dinạm(ge), daily.

(c) When words are used repeated adverbially, the meaning may be, either, habitual reoccurrence, or, (the possible conative idea involved in repetition prevailing) the concept of the single word not quite realized.

Setak setak, morning after morning, every morning, or, as it becomes morning, towards morning.
Ạyup' ạyup', every evening, towards evening.
Serma serma, every year. *Cando cando*, every month.

---

* We generally translate this word 'not yet'; but learners of the language should note that there is no negation in it. A Santal will translate a sentence like 'he has not come as yet,' saying *ạuriye hijuk'a*, he will come later; it is rather frequent for beginners to translate *ạuriye hẹc' akana*, which is a howler. *Ạuri* is always constructed with the Future.

Din din, day after day, every day.
Din kẹ din, day after day. *Cando kẹ cando*, month after month.
Serma kẹ serma, every year.
Juge jug, for ever and ever.

(*d*) As it may be of some interest to know how the Santals who have no watches manage to show time the following list of most of their names for the different times of day and night is given, commencing from the time after midnight. All the words may be used adverbially.

Ghaṭao ńindạ, (lit. diminished night) about 1 a. m.
Maraṅ sim rak', first (lit. big) cock crow; about 3. 30 to 4 a. m.
Huḍiń sim rak', second (lit. little) cock crow, about one hour or a little less later.
Aṅga, dawn (general name).
Paha poho, first dawn.
Piạṅ payaṅ, grey morning, break of day, (also called *pirtọṅ pọrtọṅ*).
Gại aṛak' dela dili (or - *ọktẹ*), time for taking cattle out (just before sunrise).
Setak' sim rak', morning cock crow (at sunrise).
Setak', morning (in general).
Ber rakap', sunrise.
Jẹḍẹr, (lit. sunshine) shortly after sunrise (mostly used during the cold season).
Jẹḍẹr kẹṭẹc', (lit. sunshine strong) when the sun is getting hot (a time noticed more especially during the cold season).
Baskeak' (*ber*), lit. (time for) stale food (what is cold and left from last evening's meal), about 9 a. m.
Bạsiạm ber, about 9 a. m. (the same as *baskeak'*).
Khara bạsiạm, about 11 a. m. (also called *khara baskeak'*).
Tikin dela dili, shortly before noon.
Tikin, noon.
Tikin ńọ̃ṛak' (or - *lọ̃ṛak'*), about 1 p. m.
Maraṅ tarasiń, (lit. big half-day) about 2 p. m.
Huḍiń tarasiń, (lit. little do.) about 3 p. m.
Maraṅ dak' lo ber, (lit. big water drawing time) about 4 p. m.
Huḍiń dak' lo ber, (lit. little do.) about 5 p. m.
Ber jhik jhikạuk', (lit. sun dazzling) time just before the sun touches the horizon.
Ber hạsur, sunset.
Ayup', evening (in general, cp. *setak'*).

Gąi ader jǫkhẹc', (lit. cow bringing-in time) time shortly after sunset.

Ńuhum, twilight, before it is dark.

Gąi ader harǫp', time just after housing the cattle.

Mąci andhar, (lit. stool dark) nightfall, when it is dark.

Kedoḱ jǫm, (lit. supper eating) supper time (especially *rẹṅgẹc' hǫṛ* - -, poor people's evening meal).

Kedoḱ jǫm harǫp', time just after supper.

Kaḍa ader jǫkhẹc', time for housing the buffaloes (a couple of hours after housing the other cattle).

Kisạṛ hǫṛ kedoḱ jǫm ǫktẹ, about the same time as *kaḍa ader*.

Gitic' jǫkhẹc', bed time.

{ *Gitic' heṛep'*, time just after bed time.
{ *Gitic' saṛa sạtiń*, the time when people have fallen fast asleep.

Ṭala ńindạ, midnight.

Mit' gitic' ẹbhẹn, first time awake (about midnight).

As is seen the hours are named after light and darkness, after the cock's crowing, after the work or the time for taking the meals, and so on. The actual hours will vary a little according to the time of the year. The hours after nightfall are somewhat variable; from midnight to sunset they are fairly constant. A grown up Santal will generally be able to tell the hour fairly accurately, even at night looking at the stars; but they have no hours named after the stars.

(*e*) In connection with the adverbs the Santal names for the phases of the moon might be mentioned. The moon is more easily observable in India than in our northern latitudes; the moon and the phases of the moon mark the time for them, and certain superstitious beliefs are attached to some of the moon's phases. The words mentioned here below are used as adverbs, mostly with a postposition added.

The Santals have one name for both the sun and the moon, viz., *cando*; when necessary to distinguish the two *siń cando* (lit. day luminary) is used for the sun and *ńindạ cando* (lit. night luminary) for the moon. *Cańdo* is also used in the meaning of a month, lit. a moon.

The phases are named as follows:

Ambas, or *ambabạsiạ*, the time of the change of the moon, when it is not visible.

Molok' cando, new moon (greeted by the Santals, *nawa cando, johar*! be greeted, new moon!)
Bale molok' (cando), (lit. tender new moon) the moon a couple of days old.
Molok' tikin, the moon at first quarter.
Kunạmi, full moon (a general expression).
Buru kunạmi, the full moon as seen just before actual full moon, just above horizon at sunset (lit. hill full moon).
Ol kunạmi, (lit. ground full moon) the time just after actual full moon, when sun and moon 'see each other' in the morning (as the Santals express themselves).
Kunạmi kecak', (lit. full moon broken off) third quarter.
Ńirjạu dela dili, about middle of the fourth quarter.
Ńirjạu, the moon a couple of days before *ńir* (lit. running away).
The time when no moon is seen in the evening is called *ńulạt*, the dark time, differently understood, as from after *kunạmi* to *ambas*, or, as practically only the time of the fourth quarter, and never after *ambas*.

103. Words used adverbially denoting *quantity*:

(*a*) *Ạḍi* (or, *uḍi*), very, very much (frequently used to intensify or emphasize the meaning of the word to which it is prefixed). *Ạḍi boge, ạḍi bạric'*, very good, very bad; *ạḍi* (*uḍi*) *marań*, very big; *ạḍitet'*(*ge*), very (much) indeed.
Dher(*tet'*), much, mostly.
Ekẹn, only; *ẹkẹn hẹndẹ*, only black.
Bạric' (lit. bad), very; *hẹbạric'*, awfully.
Thora(*thuṛi*), a little.
Bejae, very, extraordinarily.
Nase nase, a little.

(*b*) *Ńǫk'*, a little (about quantity, quality and time), always used added to another word to be qualified.

Hẹc' ńǫgok'me, come for a short while; *ẹm ńǫk'adeae*, he gave him a little (something substantial); *rǫr ńǫk'kedeae*, he scolded him somewhat; *esel ńǫk'*, fairly fair, lightcoloured; *sebel ńǫk'*, fairly savoury; *nẹ ńǫk'*, a while ago, just now.

Macha, approximately, somewhat like. *Ponḍ macha*, whitish; *hẹndẹ macha*, blackish; *enka macha*, somewhat like this; *oktẹ macha*, at the aproximately proper time. *Macha* is only used added to an other word.

104. Words used adverbially denoting *quality* and *manner* :

Besides bare base-words used adverbially the language has such adverbs formed by suffixing postpositions and particles. The postpositions, etc., most commonly used are the following :

leka or *lekate* (added to any word); *kate* (mostly added to demonstratives and words commonly used as verbs); *tẹ* (*te*) (the instrumental or causative *tẹ*, added to any word, especially adjectives, and to reiterated words); *ge* (the emphatic particle, added to words used as adjectives).

Hako pako, hako phare, hare phare, quickly ; *eskar,* alone ; *ẹkẹn ti,* empty-handed ; *hoṛ leka,* like a Santal ; *bes lekate,* according to what is good, thoroughly ; *sanam lekate,* in every way ; *ạdi lekate,* in many ways ;

bareakate, in twos ; *ẹṛẹkate,* falsely ; *sạrikate,* truly ; *duṛup'kate,* sitting, in a sitting position ; *rañgaokate,* angrily ; *ạuṛikate,* wantonly, without cause ; *bẹạbrukkatẹle laga ńiret'ko tahẽkana,* we were driving them (the witches) away in a disgracing way ;

joṛmoṭte, by force, forcibly ; *mit'te(ge),* in one, together ; *sulukte,* peaceably ; *mạgnite,* gratis ;

bại bạite, slowly ; *jute jutete,* in a nice way (opp. forcibly) ; *gitic' gitic'te,* lying down ; *hoṛ hoṛte,* along the road : *taṛam taṛamte,* walking ; *hạri hạrite pańjako ạḍao idia,* calling out they follow the tracks along ;

bogege * *menak'lea,* we are well ; *rạput'ge* * *sẹṭẹrena,* it arrived in a broken state (note, not *rạput'ak',* which would mean 'what was broken', and would be the subject).

105. In many cases where Santali has double-worded verbs we have to translate the second word with an adverb.

Sẹn goḍok'me, go quickly ; *hẹc' ńọk'lenae,* he came for a short while ; *dạṛ tap'ket'ae,* he ran away (through).

---

* In Santali the word functions as an apposition to the subject or object.

The Pronouns.

106. With certain restrictions Santali may be said to have the ordinary six kinds of pronouns, viz., the personal, demonstrative, interrogative, indefinite, possessive and relative pronouns.

The restrictions concern the possessive and relative pronouns, for which the language has no separate or special pronouns, but makes use of the personal, demonstrative and interrogative pronouns, with or without suffixes, prefixes or postpositions.

With few exceptions, all due to the nature of the words in question, the pronouns are all treated like ordinary base-words, i. e.. they may function as nouns, adjectives and verbs, taking suffixes of sorts.

Certain (demonstrative, interrogative and indefinite) pronouns are different for animates and inanimates. The demonstrative *elements* may be said to be neutral, as they may be used with reference to both animates and inanimates.

The Personal Pronouns.

107. Santali has the ordinary personal pronouns for the three persons. These pronouns are found in the singular, the dual and the plural, with separate forms for the 1st pers. in the dual and the plural, according to whether the speaker includes or excludes those addressed.

As regards the 3rd pers. the independent form is wanting, if one is not to take *ac'*, *ạkin*, *ako*, self, selves, as representing it. A demonstrative pronoun is generally used to serve for the independent 3rd p. pers. pronoun, this having separate forms for the animate and the inanimate.

The pers. pr. 3rd pers. is there for the suffixed and infixed forms in all numbers for animates.

Sex is not distinguished.

There are separate forms for the independent, suffixed and infixed personal pronouns.

		The Independent Forms.	The Suffixed Forms.
Singular	1st pers.	*iń*, I.	*-iń* (or (after single vowel) *-ń*. I.
"	2nd "	*am*, thou.	*-ẹm* (or *-em*) or (after single vowel) *-m* thou.
"	3rd "	*ac'*, himself, herself. *uni*, he, she. *ona*, it, that (inanimate).	*-ẹ* (or *-e*, or *-i*), he, she. Only about animates, except in certain cases for the subject when inanimate (see para 24 c)).
Dual	1st pers	*alaṅ* (inclusive), thou and I, we two.	*-laṅ*, thou and I.
"	" "	*ạliń* (*aliń*) (exclusive), he and I, we two.	*-liń*, he and I.
"	2nd "	*abẹn* (*aben*), you two.	*-bẹn* (*-ben*), you two.
"	3rd "	*ạkin* (*akin*), they two themselves. *unkin*, they two (animate). *onakin*, those two (inanimate).	*-kin*, they two (only about animates).
Plural	1st pers.	*abo*, *abon* (inclusive), we, you and I.	*-bo*, *-bon*, we (inclusive).
"	" "	*alẹ*, *ale* (*alen*) (exclusive) we, I and they.	*-lẹ*, *-le*, we (exclusive).
"	2nd "	*apẹ*, *ape*, you.	*-pẹ*, *-pe*, you.
"	3rd "	*ako*, they themselves (animates. *onko*, they (animates). *onako*, those (inanimates)	*-ko*, they.

109. The infixed forms, used in verbal constructions, for the direct and indirect object, are the following :—

Singular	1st	pers.	*-iń-*, *-eń-*, or (after single vowel) *-ń*.
„	2nd	„	*-mẹ-*, *-me-*, or (after *ka* and as indirect object) *-m-*.
„	3rd	„	*-ẹ-*, *-e-* (only used about animates).
Dual	1st	„	*-laṅ-* (inclusive).
„	„	„	*-liń-* (exclusive).
„	2nd	„	*-bẹn-*, *-ben-*.
„	3rd	„	*-kin-* (only animates).
Plural	1st	pers.	*-bo-*, *-bon-* (inclusive).
„	„	„	*-lẹ-*, *-le-* (exclusive).
„	2nd	„	*-pẹ-*, *-pe-*.
„	3rd	„	*-ko-* (only animates).

It will be seen that the infixed forms are the same as the suffixed ones, with the following exceptions : As direct object with monosyllabic verbs the infixed pronoun of the 1st p. sing. is generally *-eń-* (always having the stress). See Mat. I, para 29. In the 2nd pers. sing. the infixed form is *mẹ*, (*me*), whilst the suffixed one is *ẹm* (*em*), and only *ẹ* (*e*) is used infixed for the 3rd pers. sing., never *i*. *

The forms used for the indirect object are the same as those for direct object. It is a mistake to say that the infixed pronouns for the indirect object is *a* + the pronoun. This *a* is a suffix, a part of the verbal construction. See under the verb and below para 122.

It does not come under the personal pronouns, but it may be remarked also here, that in the Indeterminate (Future) and from this derived tenses an *-k* is infixed to show the inanimate direct object in the Intentional (Reservative), and the same *-k* for the indirect inanimate object in the same tenses of the simple verb. It may be omitted, and it may be substituted by an infixed genitive of the personal pronoun.

* In Muṇḍari the infixed pronoun 3. p. sing. is *i*.

110. The infixed, or suffixed forms of the personal pronouns, denoting possession, are the following :—

Singular	1st pers.	*-tiń*, my, mine.
„	2nd „	*-tam*, thy, thine.
„	3rd „	*-tae*, his, her (only for animates).
Dual	1st pers.	*-talaṅ* (inclusive), mine and thine.
„	„ „	*-tạliń* exclusive), mine and his, or her.
„	2nd „	*-taben*, you two's.
„	3rd „	*-tạkin*, they two's (only animate).
Plural	1st pers.	*-tabo*, *-tabon*, our (inclusive), your and mine.
„	„ „	*-tale* (*-talẹ*), our (exclusive), their and mine.
„	2nd „	*-tape* (*-tapẹ*), your.
„	3rd „	*-tako*, their (only animate).

111. Besides the forms of the personal pronouns mentioned Santali has three suffixed ones, always doing service as possessive pronouns; but as there is formally nothing to show that they are possessives, and as they, except for the 3rd pers., are identical with the suffixed forms mentioned above, they are recorded here.

Singular, dual & plural	1st pers.	*-iń*, *-ń* (or in one single appellative *-ṅ*), my, our.
„ „ „	2nd „	*-m* (or, in certain cases, *-me*), thy, your.
„ „ „	3rd „	*-t* (frequently intensified to *-t* (*tẹt'*) his, her, their.

The same forms are used for the dual and the plural as for the singular. Their use will be shown below.

112. The independent forms are really compounds, consisting of the bare pronoun and a prefixed *a*. This *a* is not

preserved in the 1st. pers. sing. in Santali; for some reason or other it has here been lost; it is found in some other Kolarian languages (such as Muṇḍari and Hö), but is also wanting in several. *

It is probably unnecessary to demonstrate that this *a* is not an inherent part of the personal pronoun. We see, that this *a* is wanting in the pers. pr. of one person, so it cannot be a component part of this; we see, that this *a* is found in all the personal pronouns, except in that of the 1st pers. sing., which shows that it is something that does not concern the different persons as such; and we see, that all the personal pronouns are used as subject pronouns without this *a*, while the forms with *a* cannot be so used. All this taken together seems to prove, that we have to do with a compound word consisting of this *a* + the real pronoun. †

The language has several other *a*' s; but it seems, that we cannot be far out, if we take the here discussed *a* to be a demonstrative element or part of a demonstrative, intended

---

* We find the same peculiarity in the Mon-Khmer languages. In Khmer I is *añ*, in Bahnar it is *iñ*.

† E. g., if you ask a Santal who he is, or a number of Santals who they are, you will invariably get for an answer in the first case *iñ*, and in the second case *ale*, and not *le*.

If we investigate what this *a* is, we are at once reminded of the same vowel, pronounced in the same way, and heard in a number of words and classes of words, In the finite verb we have always an *a*, without which a statement does not belong to demonstrable reality; in the inanimate determinative suffix we are met with the same *a* (*a* + *k̇* or *n̈*, as distinguished from the animate *i* + *c̓*); in the demonstrative pronouns we hear an *a* for inanimates, as opposed to the *i* for animates, viz. one demonstrative element emphasizing the demonstration and another (*a* or *i*) showing what or which is referred to.

One might compare the pronoun to expressions like 'it is I', 'it is they', etc., although the verb of our phrases has to be eliminated. Taking the demonstrative *ona*, this may be said to consist of the demonstrative, pointing-out part *on*, and what is pointed out, or at, *a*, that, it, the concrete reality referred to.

to show the concrete reality of the person or persons alluded to.

113. (a) It will be seen that the independent personal pronoun of the third person has in all numbers got a particular meaning, apart from what we should expect, viz. the pronoun and self (or selves). In the singular the pronoun consists of *c'* to which *a* is prefixed. *

(b) The special meaning attached to the independent form of the personal pronoun of the 3rd pers. has resulted in a demonstrative pronoun being used in stead of the personal pronoun. When the demonstratives have been shown among the independent personal pronouns, it should be kept in mind, that this is done to avoid a vacuum, and that the words are demonstrative pronouns.

One result of this is that we in the third person get a distinction between the animate and the inanimate, a distinction that only occurs in connection with the third person.

Otherwise, as is natural, there is no difference as regards the animate and the inanimate, and no difference between the sexes. We find practically the same state as in our personal pronouns.

(c The personal pronouns refer only to animates and to what is at the moment treated as being animate, that is

---

* This is the same *c̓* as that found in the determinative suffix *ic̓*. For some reason not now ascertainable the *i* or (more likely here) *e* (cp. Muṇḍari *ae*, corresponding in meaning to Santali *uni*) has been dispensed with (if an *i* had been there and eliminated, it would have been pronounced *ạc̓*, in analogy with *ạń*; but *ạc̓* is a pronunciation never heard), and *c̓* is what represents the animate third pers. sing.

It is understandable, how the animate concrete identification in the one case has developed into the determinative suffix, and in the other case to the special meaning of self; it is the demonstrative restriction, this, and no one else. This *c̓* (or possibly *ec̓*) takes the place of the *e* or *i* found in the bare (suffixed) forms of the pronoun.

to say, considered or addressed as so acting. Any inanimate object may be addressed in the second person.

(*d*) As already mentioned (see para 24 (c)), the suffixed pronoun in the singular is often used about inanimates as subject pronoun, always in connection with the Active voice or the Medium of a deponent verb, about the acting force or the agent, e. g., in connection with natural phenomena, when the ordinary Santal explains that the real subject is the Supreme Being.

114. As to the forms of the personal pronouns the following may be further remarked :

The second pers. sing. in its compound form is *am*, *a* + *m*. The suffixed form shows *m* alone, or, after a consonant *em* (*ẹm*) ; the infixed form is *me* (*mẹ*), except in the Intentional (Reservative) form after *ka*, where it is only *m*. In the Imperative *me* is always heard after a consonant or dipthong, after a vowel it is *m* or *me*. In the forms used for indirect object we also find *m* after a vowel and *me* after a consonant to represent the second pers. sing. To express genitive or possession *m* is used after words with final single vowel and *me* after a consonant; in a very few cases *me* is heard used after final vowel. *

* The question arises, what is the real bare form? As to the *e* of the suffixed pronoun, there does not seem to be any necessity of taking this to be an inherent part of the pronoun ; it seems more likely to be a kind of assistant vowel needed to get the *m* pronounced after a consonant, possibly the neutral vowel sound inherent in the labial *m*.

What can be said against this is, that *em* may be heard used also after a vowel, in this case with an inserted euphonic *y*, when any one (perhaps especially a woman) wants to be emphatic ; forms like *aloyem rọṛa*, or *alogeyem*, or *aloteť geyem rọṛa*, do not speak so, *kanayem*, thou art, are fairly common. In such cases the *em* probably is the form accustomed to be used after consonants, to which habit has given a certain right of independent existence, and nothing more.

The final *e* of the infixed *me* is in a different position. We have here, as remarked, a form with *m* alone ; but *me* is persistently also used, where there should be no necessity for it. *Me* is further used as the subject pronoun in the sing. Imperative, here changing with *m*, when immediately preceded by a single vowel.

115. The pronoun of the third pers. singular shows some peculiarities.

(*a*) The independent compound form with *a* does not exist in the present language; what is wanted when reference is to be made to a third person or party is something functioning as a demonstrative, and such a one is constantly used. This does away with the practical necessity of the compound form. We get in stead a special form denoting reference to self, consisting of the *a* + the animate determinative particle *c'*. It may be said to be the pers. pr. of the third pers. sing., but in a restricted or limited and determined meaning.

(*b*) With reference to *ac'* the following special uses should be noted: In answering *ac'* may be used synonymous with *am*, yourself; e. g., *okoe noa doe ror akat'a*? who has said this? *ac'ge*, he himself, i. e., you yourself. When so used *ac'* is generally constructed with the 3. p. sing.

(*c*) Further, *ac'* is used about the inanimate, significantly enough, mostly with the instrumental or causative *te* added, denoting 'by itself', 'of itself'; e. g., *ac'tege noa do janamentiña*, this (e. g., ringworm) has come by itself; *ac' ac'te nonka harayena*, it has grown to be such of its own accord.

All this seems to point towards *me* being either the original bare form of the personal pronoun of the second pers. sing., or at least a parallel form. The first supposition seems the probable one. In support of this may be quoted the use of the same pronoun when suffixed to a noun to show possessive, when this word ends in a consonant. It is *hopon-me*, thy son, not *hopon-em*. Cp. also forms like *eñgam* and *eñgame*, *moca-me*.

That the form *me* should be an object-form, as one might be tempted to think from the fact that it is specially used for the second pers. when this is the object (cp. also the use of *me* in the impersonal verbs, as *rabañ-me-a*, you will feel cold, *banuk'mea*, you are not present), does not seem to recommend itself. This would point towards inflection, not otherwise observed.

It might be noted, that the same forms of this pronoun may be observed in other Mundari languages.

One may compare this use of *ac'* with the use of the animate *e* (*i*) to represent the agent in certain inanimate verbal constructions. See para 24 (c).

(*d*) For the suffixed and infixed pronoun we have the bare *e*, *ẹ* or *i*, the same pronoun, changing in sound in accordance with the laws of harmonic sequence; *i* is possibly the original form, but it seems more reasonable to assume two parallel forms, *i* and *e*.

In practical use *e* (*ẹ*) is the general and common pronoun. It is always used when infixed, also in the forms used for the indirect object and the possessive (*ae* and *tae*); *i* is used only in the suffixed form, as verbal subject, when the word to which it is suffixed has as final vowel an *u* or a resultant vowel with which the *i* forms a diphthong, and only in such cases, and even then the *e* is often used, suffixed with the help of a euphonic *y* (e. g., *burui tiok'ket'a*, he reached the mountain, or *buruyẹ tiok'ket'a*). *

(*e*) The bare pronouns for the third pers. dual and plural require only a few remarks; they show no peculiarities as to form. In the suffixed and infixed forms their meaning corresponds to the *e* or *i* of the singular. The compound forms *ạkin* and *ako* correspond in meaning to *ac'*; the idea conveyed by our 'self' is, however, often much attenuated or even nearly absent.

116. With reference to the form of the personal pronouns in the plural it will be observed that the inclusive plural of the 1st pers. shows two parallel forms, one with a final *n* and another without this.

This *n* is the same *n* as that found so frequently suffixed to words ending in a single vowel; this *n* is specially examined elsewhere to which the reader is referred. (See para 59 (a)). The present day Santals use both forms ap-

* Compare the *i* that we find in *un-i* (he, she, the animate demonstrative pronoun), *nu-i*, *hạn-i*, etc., also in the determ. suffix *i-ć*.

parently indiscriminately; the difference between the two forms is not, as has been stated, that *abo* is the more familiar one, and *abon* more ceremonial or formal. *Abo* means we who are actually known or present; it refers to known reality; *abon* on the other hand refers to all that will come in under the category of 'we, I and you', all known and unknown. As a matter of fact the choice seems with this pronoun now-a-days largely to be decided by phonetic and individual convenience and habit or predilection.

It should, however, be noted, that although this *n* is not generally, or one might say, is scarcely ever heard with other personal pronouns in the plural than *abon*, it may be suffixed to them all. The forms *alen*, *apen* and *akon* are found, but very seldom used. *

117. In connection with the personal pronouns mention has to be made of a couple of words used as a kind of personal pronouns, viz., *apnar*, *apṛẽ* and *nẹ*.

Apnar is really a Bengali genitive of B. *apọn*, meaning belonging to oneself. The word is used in Santali in this meaning, but is also constantly used to denote 'self', in connection with all personal pronouns, the ordinary pers. pronoun being prefixed or not, as the case may be.

E. g., *apnarte bae jọma*, he will not eat of his own accord; *am apnargem mẹn akat'a*, you have said it yourself; *abo apnargebon jarwaka*, only we belonging to the same family shall come together.

The word has also other uses in Santali. The word is a fairly recent introduction. There is nothing honorific in it.

Apṛẽ is probably related to the same root as *apnar*; it is used about oneself, mostly as 1st p. sing. It is more a women's word and rarely used by men. It has a deprecatory meaning, something like 'poor me'.

---

* I had been in the country for about twelve years when my attention was first called to these forms. Investigation revealed, that the forms with *n* are known, perhaps not to all, but generally to old people in certain parts of the country. Santals living in or near Orissa seem to use this *n* much more frequently than the more northern branch of the people.

E. g., phalna bąhu kuṛiń ńęlledea, apṛę̄ lekangeae, I saw such and such's daughter in-law, she is like myself (no better); *apṛę̄ leka cet' hõ bąnuk'takoa noko dǫ*, these have nothing just like myself (or ourselves).

A third word *nę*, acc. to form a demonstrative element, is heard used somewhat like *apṛę̄*, referring especially to 1st p. sing. or pl., also conveying a deprecatory meaning.

E. g., Mahle leka nę hoṛ dǫ ǫhǫm gǫk' daṛelea, people like us are unable to carry (on the shoulder) like the Mahles (note, 2nd pers. used in the sense of an indefinite pronoun, like Engl. you); *nę hoṛ dǫ ǫhǫe puchąulema*, he will certainly not take any notice of people like yourself (i. e. me).

118. For inanimates there are no suffixes or infixes, with the exception of the previously mentioned use of the animate suffixed pronoun 3. p. sing. for an inanimate subject.

There is, however, an -*k'* used as an infix for the direct and indirect object in certain verbal constructions.

This -*k'* belongs to the third pers. and represents all numbers. Used for the direct object it is met with in one of the verbal suffixes for the Anterior Past (*lak'*), and in some tenses of the Intentional form, viz. in the Indeterminate (Future) (*kak'*) and from this formed tenses, naturally all of the Active voice.

With indirect object this same infixed -*k'* is always used (*ak'*) for the inanimate third pers. in the Indeterminate (Future) and from this derived tenses of the Active verb, when it is not substituted by the genitive infix. It is consequently also used in the Imperative with indirect object in the same way.*

This *k'* is the same as that found in the determinative suffix for inanimates, corresponding to the animate *c'* in *ic'*.

119. As to certain uses of the personal pronouns the reader is referred to what has been stated in the paras dealing with number (the special use of the dual and the plural by certain relatives, and also the use of the plural for the indefinite).

* A form of this Imperative with indirect object and without this *k'* or a genitive infix is, however, also met with.

The second pers. sing. may be used about the indefinite, corresponding to the similar use of 'you' in English.

They have no honorific pronouns; they do not say you, but thou to a single person (except, as mentioned in para 28 that certain relations address each other and refer to each other in the dual or the plural).

When using threatening language, it is very common, (as mentioned para 28 (b)) that a Santal uses the inclusive dual (*alaṅ*, *-laṅ*) about himself, in stead of singular (*iń*).

Otherwise there are no remarks called for; with the exceptions noted the Santals use the pronouns in their literal and natural meaning.

120. With reference to the suffixed forms recorded para 111, the following may be remarked:

(*a*) The same forms are used for the singular, the dual and the plural.

(*b*) For the first pers. there is a parallel form (*ṅ*) used only in the vocative, and, I think, only found suffixed to *ạpu*-(*ạpuṅ*), mostly, if not exclusively, about the father of many.*

(*c*) The suffix for the 2nd pers. is the same as that for the infix of the direct object of the same pers. sing, *m* and *mẹ* (not *m* and *ẹm*). Cp. the remarks made above about this *me*.

---

* How this *ṅ* is to be explained it is difficult to say. The only other *ṅ* found in the personal pronouns is in Santali seen in the inclusive dual second pers. (*alaṅ*); in Muṇḍari a similar *ṅ* is found in the third pers. dual *kiṅ* (here in Santali *kin*), and in the same language *iṅ* is used for the Santali *iń*. In Kurku this *ṅ* is found in several more, *iṅ*, *aliṅ*, *alaṅ*, *abuṅ*, *apiṅ* (=*aben*), *dikiṅ* (they two). The most likely explanation would appear to be, that *ṅ* is a parallel form for *ń* for the consonant of the 1st pers. sing., but now not used any more in Santali except in this single word (*ạpuṅ*).

This *ṅ* should not be confounded with the *ṅ*, alternating with *k̔*, found in certain suffixes (*-ok̔* and *-oṅ*, as *nitok̔* and *nitoṅ*, *reak̔* and *reaṅ*, and the final, but frequently eliminated *ṅ* of certain words (*ba* and *baṅ*, *cẹ* and *cẹṅ*).

(*d*) For the third pers. we find *t* suffixed.*

121. The following examples will show, how the different forms of the personal pronouns may be used.

(*a*) The compound forms are treated like base-words. i. e., they may do service as nouns, adjectives and verbs. When directly connected with the verb the pers. pronouns are in all cases shown in their suffixed or infixed form in the verb, whether they are otherwise mentioned in the sentence or not, whether they are the subject (in this case the suffixed form is immediately joined to the verb), or the direct or indirect object, or stand in any other direct relation to the verb (in this case repeated by one or the other of the infixes).

Alele calak'a, we shall go (the personal pronoun when standing alone and then repeated in the verb, generally to some extent emphasizes the statement, and may often be properly translated by 'as for' (us, etc.); here it may be translated as above, or 'as for us we shall go', or, 'we (and not others) shall go');

abo orak', our house; *ape haram*, your old man, head of family; *abokedeako*, they made him one of us; *babon ạkinkạkina*? shall we not make those two a pair?

ape dọ bako emapea, they will not give you; *ale dọ lako lại-at'lea*, they did not tell us; *iṅtegeṅ rọra*, I shall speak myself; *amiṅ metam kana*, I am telling you (this); *hudurket'ae*, it (lit. he) thundered; *amrenko idikedelama*, they took your one away.

(*b*) Above will show the use of the independent, the infixed and the suffixed personal pronouns. With reference to the suffixed pronouns, used only as verbal subject-pronouns, it

* As regards *t* one might compare it to the initial of the possessive infix *t* (*ta*), also remembering that this suffixed *t* always has a possessive significance. This *t* is, however, very often followed by the genitive infix (*tae, tạkin, tako*), so we, if this is correct, should have a double genitive. Such redundance is not uncommon in the language.

One might also compare it to certain demonstrative particles; cp. *tẹt'*, often found suffixed to a word with this *t*.

should be noted, that the pronoun subject is generally enclitically suffixed to the word immediately preceding the verb, if there is any such preceding word. Nothing not belonging to the verb must come between this and the suffixed pronoun.

The negations always have the subject pronoun attached to them (*bań calak'ae* is not said, but *bae calaka* ; *alom calak'a*, do not go ; not *alo calakam* ; *ọhọń mẹnlea*, I am unable to say ; not *ọhọ mẹnleań*) ; with the verb substantive (*kan*) the subject pronoun is very frequently suffixed to this in stead of to the word preceding what with *kan* forms the verb.

122. The infixed pronouns are, as will be seen, the same for both the direct and the indirect object.

When they have been shown as different, this is due to a misunderstanding. The *a* prefixed to the personal pronoun when used for the indirect object, does not belong to the pronoun, but is a verbal suffix used in the Indeterminate (the Future) and from this derived tenses. If it belonged to the pronoun, we should have to establish two different forms for this infixed pronoun, one for the tenses just mentioned, and another without an *a*, for all other tenses. It is *lại-a-koa-e*(not *lại-ako-a-e*), *lại-at'-ko-a-e*, *lại-uka-w-at-ko-a-e* (not *lại- at'-ako-a-e*), he will tell, told, has told them. It is also *ọhọ-ń lại-le-m-a* (not *lại-le- am-a*), I am certainly not telling you.

Tulket'koae, he lifted them up ; *tulakoae*, he will lift for them ; *tulat'koae*, he lifted for them ; *dalmeae*, he will beat thee ; *dalamae*, he will help thee beating ; *lạikadeae*, he informed against him ; *lạiadeae*, he told him.

123. (*a*) The infixed or suffixed personal pronouns denoting possession are the compound pronouns with a prefixed *t*, i. e., *t* + *a* + the bare pronoun (except in the 1st pers. sing. where the *a* is wanting).

Like all other suffixes and infixes these also will do service only as suffixes or infixes, not as nouns, adjectives or verbs.

(*b*) These personal pronouns are used in two ways : (1) they are suffixed to base-words, doing service for possessive pronouns. In case the base-word has a number-suffix the possessive pronominal suffix follows the number-suffix The poss. suffix may also be suffixed to a word preceding the word to which it has reference.

E. g., *oṛaktako*, their house; *gaikotae*, his cows; *hantḙre tako oṛak*, their house over there; *okorkotam oaris*, where are your helpers; *kisāṛtabon*, our master.

(2) They are used as infixes in verbal constructions. When so used with the active verb they always follow (although not necessarily immediately) the direct or indirect object infix, if there is any such; they may also take the place of the inanimate object-infix -*k*. When there is no object-infix (with inanimate object), the possessive pron. infix may be used in a way representing this, following the verbal suffix. The same infixes are also constantly used in the Medium and the Passive, following the verbal suffix.

The infixed possessive pronoun may refer either to the subject or the object (so mostly), in the Medium or the Passive always to the subject. See further under the verb.

E. g., *peṛa bạnuk'kotaea*, he has no friends (relatives); *dakte khete baṛic'ket'tiñ*, water spoilt my paddy field; *gaiko idikedetiña*, they took my cow away; *añjomtakom*, listen to what they have to say; *beṅget'aktakome*, look at what they have; *beṅget'atakom*, look at what they have (here the possessive infix takes the place of -*k*); *ạuriataea*, he is not as yet ready with (it); *calaoentabonae*, he is gone our one (e. g. dead); *johartabon*, our greeting, be greeted (all).

(*c*) What is referred to as possessed may naturally be either animate or inanimate, but the 'owner' is always animate.

The Possessive Pronouns.

124. Santali has, as already remarked, no special possessive pronouns. To render our possessive pronouns the language uses the personal pronouns, with or without a prefix or a postposition, also the interrogative and (for the 3rd pers.) the demonstrative pronouns.

125. (*a*) The independent form of the personal pronouns, prefixed to a noun, conveys the meaning of a possessive pronoun, provided the pronoun functions as an adjective, and not as a noun to which the second word stands in the position of an apposition.

A personal pronoun preceding an inanimate noun always stands for our possessive pronoun.

As will be seen the independent personal pronouns may function like any other base-word to express the genitive relation.

E. g., *iñ hopon*, my child; *ale koṛa*, our boy; *ape haṛam*, your old man; *ako oṛak'*, their house, home; *ale hoṛ*, we Santals; *ale maejiu*, we women (so generally, but may also mean, our man, a man of ours, a woman of ours).

(*b*) When functioning as possessive pronouns the personal pronouns are frequently given a determinative suffix, *-iċ*, *-kin* and *-ko* for animates, and *-ak'*, *ak'kin* and *-ak'ko* for inanimates. *

With reference to the animate determinative suffixes, *-iċ* is common; but the dual and plural animate determ. suffixes are in the present-day language not generally used to form possessive pronouns prefixed to an animate base-word.

E. g., *iñiċ koṛa*, my boy; *aboiċ gai*, our cow (as distinguished from somebody else's); *amak' ṭheṅga*, thy stick; *apeak' khetko*, your ricefields (also, and just as commonly *apeak'ko khet*, lit. your ones (inanim.), ricefield).

126. To make the personal pronouns function as possessives the postposition *re* (*re*) may be suffixed, with *n* added for animates, and *-ak'* or *-aṅ* for inanimates, i. e., *ren* (for animates), *reak'* or *reaṅ* (for inanimates). See para 87, (b) (c).

* With regard to these forms it may be questioned whether we have a possessive pronoun used as an adjective, or a concrete noun-formation with the second word standing in a kind of apposition to the pronoun. This last seems more in accordance with the working of the language.

Ren is an adjective formation (see para 59). This is in the present language used about animates only, that is to say, when no determinative suffix is added. The forms *renak'* or *renań* are, however, heard used for inanimates.

Ren takes the determinative suffixes for animates (and, as remarked, in certain cases also for inanimates).

What was said above concerning the personal pronouns with the determinative suffixes added holds good for these forms also, with this addition, that the animate determinative suffixes are quite common also in the dual and the plural. The forms are: *renič, renkin* and *renko* (for animates), and *reak'* (*ak'*), *reak'* (*ak'*)*kin* and *reak'* (*ak'*)*ko* (for inanimates), added to the personal pronoun.

E. g., *aboren gai*, our cow; *ac'rinic'* (for *ačrenič*), his one, especially his wife; *aperenko*, those belonging to you; *iń reak' katha*, my word, or, what is told about me; *ape reak' boge juda*, (lit. your well otherwise) your circumstances (how you are); *am reak'ak'ko*, your matters; *atorenak'ko*, village matters.

127. Besides the hitherto mentioned personal pronouns used prepositively as possessives the language makes use of the same pronouns suffixed or infixed for the same purpose.

There are two forms; these have already been given under the personal pronouns (see paras 110 and 111).

128. As regards the so-called genitive suffix or - infix, (which is the independent form of the personal pronoun with *t* prefixed), see para 123, where this pronominal form has been dealt with.

129. (*a*) As stated in para 111 certain forms of the personal pronouns are used suffixed serving as possessive pronouns. These suffixed pronouns are only used in their singular form, this doing service for all numbers.

(*b*) The 1st person is *-ń* or *-iń*, according to whether the word to which the pronoun is suffixed ends in a single vowel or in a consonant or diphthong. For the second person *m* is used after a single vowel, otherwise *me*, although *me* is also heard after a vowel in certain words, in such cases the meaning conveyed generally having a disparaging taint.

(*c*) For the third pers. *-t* is suffixed to words with final single vowel, very frequently amplified or intensified by the addition ot *tet'* (see para 41). In words ending in a consonant or a diphthong no *t* is added, but this *tet'* is very frequently used instead.

The suffixed pronouns here mentioned are used especially in connection with words denoting relationship, many of these not being used without one of these suffixes.

The use is not, however, restricted to such words alone.

(*d*) The examples given here below mention most of the relationship-words that take these suffixes.

apu (*-ń*, *-m*), *apa-t*, my, our, etc., father; *eṅga* (*-ń*, *-m*, *-t* (*tet'*)) my, etc., mother (the form *iṅgań*, with resultant vowel and *i* for *e* is frequently heard; in a low kind of abuse *eṅgame* is used, see Materials I, para 132, (e)); *goṅgo* (*-ń*, *-m*, *-t* (*tet'*)), my, etc., uncle (father's elder brother); *kaka* (*-ń*, *-m*, *-t* (*tet'*)),* my, etc., uncle (father's younger brother); *era* (*-ń*, *-m*, *-t* (*tet'*)), my, etc., wife; *misera* (*-ń*, *-m*, *-t* (*tet'*)), my, etc., sister (word can only be used by a man, a woman not having a *miserat*); *hoponera* (*-ń*, *-m*, *-t* (*tet'*)), my, etc., daughter; *dada* (*-ń*, *-m*, *-t* (*tet'*)), my, etc., elder brother; *boko* (*-ń*, *-m*, *-t* (*tet'*)), my, etc., younger brother or sister (*kora*, boy, or *kuri*, girl, is added, if necessary to make meaning clear; this word is used also by and of women); *aji* (*-ń*, *-m*, *-t* (*tet'*)), my, etc., elder sister; *hopon* (*-iń*, *-me*, *-tet'*), my, etc., child (son or daughter); *gorom* (*-iń*, *-me*, *-tet'*), my, etc., namesake; *goromiń haram*, my grandfather (paternal or maternal); *goromtet' budhi*, his, her, grandmother; *jae dada* (*-ń*, *-m*, *-t* (*tet'*)), my, etc., great grandfather; *jae tata* (*-ń*, *-m*, *-t* (*tet'*)), do.; *tata* (*-ń*, *-m*, *-t* (*tet'*)), my, etc., grandfather; *aja* (*ń*, *-m*, *-t* (*tet'*)), my, etc, grandfather; *jia* (*-ń*, *-m*, *-t*

---

* Note, these suffixes are not used with the single forms, *ka*, *da*, *etc.*

(*tẹt'*)), my, etc., grandmother (often with *buḍhi* added); *koraṛ* (*-iń, -me, -tẹt'*), my, etc., grandchild; *jae koraṛ* (*-iń, etc.*) my, etc., great grandchild, *mamọ* (*-ń, -m, -t* (*tẹt'*)), my, etc., maternal uncle; *kạki* (*-ń, -m, -t* (*tẹt'*)), my, etc., aunt, paternal uncle's wife; *goṅgoń etc., era*, my etc., father's elder brother's wife; *hatọm* (*-iń, -me, -tẹt'*), my, etc., father's sister; *jãwãe* (*-iń, -me, -tẹt'*), my, etc., husband (but *ale* (*ren*) *jãwãe*, or *jãwãetale*, our son-in-law); *bạhu* (*-ń, -m, -t* (*tẹt'*)), my, etc., wife (the suffix for the 1st and 2nd persons are only rarely used, for the 3rd pers. generally the *tẹt'* is added, and also *tae*; (*bạhutako* (etc.) means their daughter-in-law); *hońhar* (*-iń, -me, -tẹt'*), my, etc., father-in-law; *hanhar* (*-iń, -me, -tẹt'*), my, etc., mother-in-law (the two last words frequently with *haṛam*, *buḍhi* or other suitable word added); *bala* (*-ń, -m, -t* (*tẹt'*)), my, etc., co-parent-in-law; *balań era*, my do. female (*bala* is, except in a couple of expressions, not used without the suffix; it is used about parents whose children have been married, one's son to the other's daughter: as a rule a word showing who is meant is added, *balań hoṛ, balań hẹrẹl*; *balattẹt' buḍhi*, etc.); *oaris* (*-iń, -me, -tẹt'*), my, etc., heir, helper (forms like *oarismekotam*, even with a prefixed *amren*, are heard, thy helpers).

The number suffixes are, in case they are required, added after the pronominal suffix.

(*e*) The second pers (*me*) may be added to inanimates; *joharme*, greet (Imper.), or (so commonly) thy greeting, thy honour or salute; in the last case it is the here mentioned suffix; *mocame lań koṭẹjlama*, I shall punch your mouth for you; *ḍaṭamelań ńũr ocoetama*, I shall make your teeth fall out for you; *time*, your hand; *mẹt'me*, your eye; *jaṅgame*, your leg; *khẹtme*, your paddy-field.

This use of a suffixed *me* is probably archaic, now not often heard. I am told, that men do not use this *me* as a rule (except in *johar-me* and *eṅga-me*, which last is possibly to be explained as inanimate), but that women, and following them, herding boys and girls make use of it. It is generally used in threatening or disparaging language, coupled with *lań*. See above examples.

Used with a word denoting something inanimate the *me* always refers to the singular.

Cp. the use of *me* in Muṇḍari, also in Kurku.

The Demonstrative Pronouns.

130. The Santal language has a very large number of demonstrative pronouns, differing in form for the animate and the inanimate, and distinguishing distances, having different demonstratives for what is close by and further off, also for what is general and what is singled out (the identity), besides a whole separate series for what is on the side, as distinguished from what is in front.*

131. The demonstrative pronouns proper are compounds, consisting of a demonstrative element, and, as the case may be, an animate or an inanimate pronominal determinative, the demonstrated concrete reality towards which is pointed or attention is drawn.

In order to properly understand the Santali demonstrative pronouns we shall first examine the demonstrative elements. These cannot be properly called pronouns; they are demonstratives pure and simple; they form part of the demonstrative pronouns. The demonstrative elements that have initial vowel or aspirate are also found alone, as prefixes to other demonstratives, the prefixed element being identical with the first part of the following demonstrative. See below para 149. One may be tempted to compare these demonstratives to one of the Performative forms of the verb. It seems in both cases to be a similar working of the mind. There is, however, this great difference that the demonstrative element is a separate word, not a syllable. Some of the demonstrative elements with initial *n* may function as a demonstrative pronoun.

The Demonstrative Elements.

132. These, as will be seen, consist of a vowel, with an *n* prefixed or added, and when something at a distance is

---

* What is behind has naturally no separate demonstratives; one does not point that way demonstratingly without turning; hence the language for such demonstration makes use of the ordinary demonstratives with an added statement giving the particular direction.

alluded to, or rather pointed at, with the aspirate prefixed to the forms with an initial vowel. The vowel varies in accordance with the meaning wanted, and within certain limits, in accordance with the laws of harmonic sequence.*

133. The demonstrative elements are the following:

(*a*)

Nu, with parallel form *no*, when demanded by the law of harmonic sequence, pointing towards what is near (not found outside the compounds †).

Nǫ, with the same meaning as *nu* (not found outside the compounds, except in a few expressions, where it functions as a pronoun, *nǫ parǫm*, this side, *nǫ kuṭ*, this part, and a few others) (joined to inanimates).

Ni, with parallel form *ne*, when demanded by the law of harmonic sequence, pointing to what is near by, at the same time singling out or identifying (not found outside the compounds, except when standing for *nei* or *nii*).

Nẹ, pointing to what is near and singling out (not found outside the compounds, except in some combinations where it is used as a demonstrative pronoun, *nẹ parǫm*, this side, *nẹṭar*, *nẹbẹṭar*, at this time or season, *nẹ ńǫ̆k'*, a while ago, *nẹ nḍi*, this little, just this, or as an adverb in the meaning of just now, a moment ago, in a moment; this *nẹ* is found only in connection with inanimates; *nẹ* is also used as an interjection).

Na, with parallel *nạ*, as demanded by the law of harmonic sequence (not found outside the compounds, except in a certain expression where *na* functions as a pronoun).

---

* Whether this *n* is the same as that met with in so many formations of the language, we shall not take up for discussion. It shall here only be just pointed out, that we instead of the *n* in certain forms of the demonstrative pronouns find a *t*, when the demonstrative refers to direction or to sound; in this case the *t* is, however, always followed by *ẹ*, and an element consisting of a vowel + *t* alone is not found. The question therefore arises with regard to these forms, whether we have not to do with a demonstrative element (sometimes consisting of a vowel alone) and the postpositional suffix *tẹ*; could this *te* originally be a kind of demonstrative element denoting direction?

† Compound is here and in the following to be understood as referring to the ordinary demonstrative pronouns, such as *nu-i*, *nu-kin*, *no-ko*.

(*b*)

Un, with parallel form *an*, pointing to what is near, but not close by, corresponding to *nu* and *no*. Used in the compounds and alone as a demonstrative and also as an adverb (in the last case always *un*).

Qn, with the same meaning as *un*, corresponding to *nq*; used in compounds and alone, but always joined to inanimates.

In, with parallel form *en*, corresponding to *ni* or *ne*, used in the componnds and alone, also as a demonstrative adverb, pointing to what is near, singling out or identifying (animate and inanimate).

En, corresponding to *nẹ*, pointing to what is near and singling out or identifying; used in compounds and alone (inanimate), also used as a demonstrative pronoun (*en betar*, *en hilok'*, etc).

An, with parallel form *ạn*, pointing to what is at a distance and significantly enough, also denoting astonishment, found only in the compounds (animate and inanimate).

(*c*)

Hun, with parallel form *hon*, pointing to what is at a distance, otherwise corresponding to *un* and *nu*, found in the compounds and alone (animate).

Hqn, corresponding to *qn* and *nq*, pointing to what is at a distance, used alone and in compounds (inanimate).

Hin, with parallel form *hen*, corresponding to *in* and *ni*, pointing out what is at a distance, singling out and identifying, in the compounds and alone (animate and inanimate).

Hẹn, corresponding to *ẹn* and *nẹ*, pointing to and singling out, identifying what is at a distance, in the compounds and alone (inanimates).

Han, with parallel form *hạn*, corresponding to *an* and *na*, pointing to what is far off, in the compounds and alone (animate and inanimate).

Besides those mentioned the forms with initial *n* have a side-form with aspirated *nh* having the same meaning as the forms with *n*, but with this peculiarity that they only point to something on the side.

(*d*) The above demonstrative elements will be found in the different kinds of demonstratives, in the pronouns and in the adverbs, and none of these (except those referring to sound) is without one or the other of these demonstrative elements.

134. We shall later on refer to these demonstrative elements; we shall here only draw attention to a few peculiarities, observable in the elements and in the compound demonstratives.

(*a*) As will be seen, we have three different sets, one with an initial *n*, referring to what is close by; another with an initial vowel, and followed by this same *n*, referring to what is near, and a third set, which is the same as the second one, only with a prefixed aspirate, referring to what is at a distance, or far off.

(*b*) Inside each set we further meet with a series of vowels, running from *a* to *u*, with modifications due to the influence of the laws of harmonic sequence, and possibly to the concept of animate and inanimate; the latter is, however, doubtful; but it is a fact, that the open *e̱* and *o̱* sounds in the dem. elements only occur in connection with reference to inanimates. On the other hand a demonstrative pronoun with the vowel *u* refers only to animates. As to the difference in meaning of these several vowels, it does not seem, as if they should refer only to distance; this has already been shown in another way, as mentioned above.

(*c*) There seems to be no reasonable doubt that the *i* (or *e* or *e̱*) has the special meaning of identifying, singling out, pointing out, asserting, a reference to an easily and exactly observable fact or conclusion. A demonstrative having this vowel may be translated by a demonstrative to which a 'just' or an 'exactly', or some such word is added, or, in many cases, 'there you see', 'it is so', or a similar expression,

(d) As regards the *u* (*o* or *ǫ*) this seems to be generally demonstrative with reference to anything within reach or easy, detailed observation, whilst the *a* (*ạ*) seems simply to signify observed reality.

(e) It should be noted that these demonstrative elements may refer not only to what is actually observed, but also to what is stated, so to say, to mental observation, and when referring to time or sequence, the forms with initial *n* may have reference to what follows, while the forms with initial vowel preferably refer to what is 'behind'. *

* With reference to the vowels met with there may be some doubt as to whether they have originally been three or five.

Have the vowels been originally *u* or *o*? *i* or *e*? or all these?

Something may be said for both suppositions. Following the pronunciation of old Santals one is tempted to think, that *o* (*no*, *on*, *hon*) is the original vowel; I have often here heard the resultant *ǫ* (*nǫkin*, *ǫnkin*, etc.). In support of *u* the words *un*, *unạk*, *nun*, *nunạk* may be quoted; on the other hand why should it be *ona*, *noa*, *hona*, and not *unạ*, etc.? It does not seem possible, however, to assume an *u* for the animate and an *o* for the inanimate (cp. *un*, *uni*, *ona*).

In connection with *i* we find something analogous, forms with *i* and others with *e* (*ni*, *nikin*, *neko*, *niạ*, *in*, *inạk*, etc.) without being able to say, whether it is originally an *e* or an *i*.

While the law of harmonic sequence might be sufficient to explain *uni* for *oni*, *onko* for *unko*, *ni* for *nei*, *nikin* for *nekin*, *neko* for *niko*, it will not explain the forms *ona*, *noa*, *un*, *nun*, *niạ*, *inạ*, etc.

The most likely explanation seems to be, that we have to do with originally two parallel forms, one with *u* and *i*, another with *o* and *e*.

In support of this one may refer to the suffixed and infixed pers. pronoun 3rd pers. sing., where we have to do with a similar double form.

Another possibility might be to assume an original close sound that has developed into two different sounds; this does not, however, seem to have much to recommend it.

With reference to the demonstrative elements showing *ǫ* or *ę* as their vowel, it seems most likely to assume that these forms are original, there being no visible reason why *o* and *e* (or *u* and *i*) should be turned into *ǫ* or *ę*. As remarked the dem. elements having one of these two vowels are used only with reference to inanimates.

Might *ǫ* possibly have been originally *a*? Cp. the sound of the originally short *a* in Bengali and Bihari.

The Ordinary Demonstrative Pronouns.

135. The ordinary demonstrative pronouns are the following :

Animate.	*Inanimate.*
Nui (dual ***nukin***, plural ***noko***), this one here close by.	***Noa*** (dual ***noakin***, plural ***noako***), this thing here close by.
Uni (dual ***unkin***, pl. ***onko***), that one there near.	***Ona*** (dual ***onakin***, pl. ***onako***), that thing there near.
Huni (dual ***hunkin***, pl. ***honko***), that one there further off.	***Hona*** (dual ***honakin***, pl. ***honako***), that thing there further off.
Ni (for ***nii***, dual ***nikin***, pl. ***neko***), this very one, just this one here, close by.	***Niạ*** (dual ***niạkin***, pl. ***niạko***), this very thing, just this here, close by.
Ini (dual ***inkin***, pl. ***enko***), just that one, that very one there, near.	***Inạ*** (dual ***inạkin***, pl. ***inạko***), that very thing, just that thing there, near.
Hini (dual ***hinkin***, pl. ***henko***), that very onẹ, just that one at a distance.	***Hinạ*** (dual ***hinạkin***, pl. ***hinạko***), that very thing, just that, at a distance.
Ạni (dual ***ạnkin***, pl. ***ạnko***), that one far off (scarcely ever heard, but frequently used by the Mahles).	***Hana*** (dual ***hanakin***, pl. ***hanako***), that thing far off.
Hạni (dual ***hạnkin***, pl. ***hanko***), that one far off.	***Nẹ*** (dual ***nẹkin***, pl. ***nẹko***), this very (mostly used adverbially, but also as a demonstrative pronoun).
Hạ̃i, the same as ***hạni***, found only in the singular.	***Nọ*** (only in the singular), this.
	Na (***nah***) (only in the singular), this.

136. (*a*) The demonstrative pronouns proper are all compounds, consisting as already remarked, of a demonstra-

tive element, one or another of those already mentioned, and an animate or an inanimate pronominal suffix, the demonstrated concrete reality.

With the regularity of the language we should have expected also *ana, nạị* and *naa*; but these are not found in the present language. The lateral demonstratives presuppose both *nạị* and *naa* (*nawa*). The intensified pronouns also presuppose *nạị*.

(*b*) The demonstrated concrete reality is for animates expressed by suffixing in the singular *i*, in the dual *kin* and in the plural *ko*, suffixed to the demonstrative element.

For the inanimate the corresponding suffixes are in the singular *a*, in the dual *akin* (note, no resultant vowel, if this is not found also in the singular; it is *noakin*, but *niạkin*), and in the plural *ako*.

(*c*) The *i* denotes the single animate being to which the demonstrative element draws attention; in the dual and the plural it has consequently to be substituted, as in the corresponding determinative suffixes by *kin* and *ko* (i. e. the personal pronouns), respectively. *Kin* and *ko* may possibly have originally been denoting animates, since nothing besides these is used to show the animate, in opposition to what is needed for the inanimate.

The inanimate is represented by *a*, apparently the demonstrable inanimate, and has as such to be retained also in the dual and the plural.

(*d*) It will be observed that the formation corresponds to the determinative suffixes both for the animate and the inanimate, only with the omission of the *c'* in the animate singular, and of the *k'* throughout the inanimate numbers.

(*e*) *Nah* is heard used as the second part of a double demonstrative: *hana nah*.

The Intensified Demonstratives.

137. Besides the already mentioned demonstrative pronouns Santali has a set of intensified demonstratives, formed from certain of those mentioned above by inserting an *k̓* after the first vowel, * which is repeated after this *k̓*. Strangely enough the vowels of these intensified demonstratives are generally nasalized, perhaps always, although it may be more or less pronounced; there is no apparent cause for this.

It is only the demonstratives having initial *n*, that are intensified in this way.

The intensified demonstratives are the following:

Animates.

Nũk̓ũi, this one you see here (only singular, from *nui*).

Nĩk̓ĩ, just this one you see here (only singular; from *ni*).

Nụ̃k̓ụ̃i, that very person over there (only singular; from a *nụi*, not found in the present-day language; cp. the lateral demonstratives).

Inanimates.

Nọ̃k̓ọ̃e (dual *nọ̃k̓ọ̃ekin*, pl. *nọ̃k̓ọ̃eko*), this thing you see here (from a non-existing *nọe*, cp. *ọnẹ* and *nọ*).

Nẽ̱k̓ẽ̱ (dual *nẽ̱k̓ẽ̱kin*, pl. *nẽ̱k̓ẽ̱ko*), just this thing you see here (from *nẹ*, cp. *ẹnẹ*).

138. One might be tempted to include among the intensified demonstratives *nẹk̓*, which is the dem. element *nẹ* + *k̓*; but apparently it is not the same formation; the *k̓* is not an infix, but a suffix, with which may be compared the suffix of the Medium or the determinative suffix. This *nẹk̓* is used like the demonstrative elements intensifying; it is rare. *Nẹk̓ nẹndẹ*, just here as may be seen. As to form one might be tempted to compare a word like *hẽ̱k̓*, from *hẽ̱*, yes.

* The *k̓* is apparently the same as the *k̓* found in the Performative form of the verb and in the distributive numerals. Whether it is the same *k̓* that is found in the inanimate determinative suffix and in the inanimate object infix (in -*k̓*, -*ak̓* and *kak̓*) may be doubtful, but is possible.

139. As already remarked Santali has, in addition to the ordinary demonstratives, also a number of

Laterally Demonstrative Pronouns.

The laterally demonstrative elements have been previously just referred to; the laterally demonstrative adverbs will be shown further on.

The lateral demonstratives are formed from the ordinary ones that have an initial *n*; this *n* is in these demonstratives aspirated; consequently all laterally demonstrative pronouns, etc., have an initial *nh*.*

The lateral demonstratives are interesting also in this way, that we have among them preserved certain forms that are not any longer met with among the ordinary demonstratives.

Animates.

Nhui (dual *nhukin*, pl. *nhoko*), this one here, on the side (corresp. to *nui*).

Nhi (dual *nhikin*, pl. *nheko*), just this one, this very one here, on the side (corresp. to *ni*).

Nhạ̃i (dual *nhạkin*, pl. *nhạko*), that one at a distance, on the side (corresp. to a not found *nạ̃i*; cf. the intensive *nạ̃kạ̃i*).

Inanimates.

Nhoa (dual *nhoakin*, pl. *nhoako*), this thing here, on the side (corresp. to *noa*).

Nhią (dual *nhiąkin*, pl. *nhiąko*), just this thing, this very thing, here on the side (corresp. to *nią*).

Nha (dual *nhakin*, pl. *nhako*), that thing there at a distance, on the side (corresp. to a very rarely used *na*).

Nhawa (i. e. *nha-a*)=*nha*.

---

* As regards the form it may be noted that an initial aspirated dental nasal is in Santali found only in these demonstratives (elements, pronouns and adverbs). See Materials I, para 87. Why an aspirate should convey the idea of 'on the side', is not self-evident; the aspirate never does so elsewhere in the language. An aspirate sometimes seems introduced to denote some kind of energy (cp. *ḍhismis* for Engl. *dismiss*, and similar words). Demonstrative elements with an initial *h* refer to what is at a distance, while those with an initial *n* refer to what is close by. In any case we here have the fact that demonstratives with an initial aspirated *nh* denote what is on the side, or off the straight line in front of the speaker.

140. The intensified forms of the laterally demonstrative pronouns.

Animates.	*Inanimates.*
Nhũkũi, this one you see here on the side (only singular, corresp. to *nũkũi*).	*Nhǫkǫe* (dual *nhǫkǫekin*, pl. *nhǫkǫeko*), this thing you see here on the side, (corresp. to *nǫkǫe*).
Nhĩkĩ, just this, this very one you see here on the side (only singular, corresp. to *nĩkĩ*).	*Nhẹ̄kẹ̄* (dual *nhẹ̄kẹ̄kin*, pl. *nhẹ̄kẹ̄ko*), this very thing, just this thing you see here on the side (corresp. to *nẹ̄kẹ̄*).
Nhụ̃kụ̃i, that person over there on the side (only singular, corresp. to *nụ̃kụ̃i*).	*Nhãkãe* (dual *nhãkãekin*, pl. *nhãkãeko*), that thing over there on the side (no corresponding form, but cp. *nha*).

141. With reference to the demonstrative pronouns hitherto mentioned the following should be noted :

(*a*) As regards number all ordinary demonstrative pronouns take the same dual and plural suffixes as the nouns, with the modifications and exceptions mentioned para 136 (b), all of which concern the animate forms.

(*b*) The animate intensified demonstrative pronouns are used only in the singular.

The inanimate forms of the same all take number suffixes, added to the singular.

(c) All forms in all numbers take the same postpositions as words used as nouns or adjectives. They may also in certain circumstances take verbal suffixes, very much in the same way as the personal pronouns.

(*d*) When a number suffix is added to a demonstrative pronoun immediately followed by a word used as a noun, the noun generally takes no number suffix. Such suffixes may, however, be added, when it is wanted to identify or, it might be said, to restrict the demonstrated animates or inanimates to a certain demonstrated number.

With the pronoun having the number suffix it would seem natural to take the demonstrative as a noun and the noun as an explaining apposition.

142. The demonstrative pronouns may take a suffix *ṭak'* (seldom *ṭaṅ*), specifying the unit, corresponding to the suffixes added to *mit'* (*-ṭaṅ*, *-ṭen*, *-ṭẹc'*) and to *gọ* (*-ṭaṅ*, *-ṭẹn*, *-ṭẹc'*). Cp. para 50.

Some other peculiarities, as the possible addition of *n* to any pronoun with final single vowel, will be dealt with further on.

143. The following examples will show the way in which the demonstratives hitherto mentioned are used :

nui koṛa, this boy ; *nukin kuṛi*, these two girls ; *noko gại*, these cows ; *noko gạiko*, these the cows ; *nhui ṭhenge menak'a*, it is with this one here on the side ; *nhoa oṛak'*, this house here on the side ; *onageye rọṛket'a*, he said that ; *onako katha*, those words ; *onako reaṅ lạiaṅme*, tell me about those matters ; *hana ṭạṇḍire hạnkin barea mẹrọmem ṅẹlet'kina* ; *unkin ạgukinme*, you see those two goats on that field over there, bring those two ; *nũk'ũitae maraṅic' họpọn dọ*, see this one here, his eldest son ; *nọ̃k'ẽetam ṭheṅga*, here is your stick ; *bicạr dọko onaket'a*, they settled the matter in that way ; *katha dọ onayena*, the matter became that, was settled that way.

Demonstratives referring especially to sight and sound.

144. Besides the demonstrative pronouns already mentioned the language has two sets of demonstratives of a nature somewhat different from those hitherto dealt with. They are in use restricted, in as much as they refer to, *draw attention* to what is seen and heard. In some cases they may also refer to what is felt or tasted, and may also draw attention to what is obvious or apparent, to facts as shown by evidence and logic. See below para 147.

They are the following :

Referring to sight.	*Referring to sound.*
Ọnẹ (dual *ọnẹkin*, pl. *ọnẹko*), that you see there (corresp. to *ona*).	*Otẹ* (dual *ọtẹkin*, pl. *ọtẹko*), that, or this one, you hear there.
Họnẹ (dual *họnẹkin*, pl. *họnẹko*), that you see over there (corresp. to *hona*).	*Họtẹ* (dual *họtẹkin*, pl. *họtẹko*), that, or that one, you hear over there.
Ẹnẹ (dual *ẹnẹkin*, pl. *ẹnẹko*), just that you see there (corresp. to *inạ*).	*Ẹtẹ* (dual *ẹtẹkin*, pl. *ẹtẹko*), just that, or this one, you hear there.
Hẹnẹ (dual *hẹnẹkin*, pl. *hẹnẹko*), just that you see over there (corresp. to *hinạ*).	*Hẹtẹ* (dual *hẹtẹkin*, pl. *hẹtẹko*), just that, or that one, you hear over there.
Anẹ (dual *anẹkin*, pl. *anẹko*), that you see over there (corresp. to *ạni*).	*Atẹ* (dual *atẹkin*, pl. *atẹko*), that, or that one, you hear over there.
Hanẹ (dual *hanẹkin*, pl *hanẹko*), that you see there far off (corresp. to *hana*).	*Hatẹ* (dual *hatẹkin*, pl. *hatẹko*), that, or that one, you hear there far off.
Hăe (dual *hăekin*, pl. *hăeko*), the same as *hane* (cp. *hāi*).	

145. (*a*) With reference to the forms of these demonstratives we note, that whilst we have three sets, the form with initial *n* is wanting in all, the reason for this probably being that reference of this kind naturally is not made to anything very near. In such cases one of the intensive forms may be used.

The forms referring to sound show a medial *t* instead of medial *n*. *

(*b*) All these demonstratives have final *ẹ*, compared with the animate *i* and the inanimate *a* occurring in the regular demonstratives. This *ẹ* very likely is a demonstrative root

* This *t* should not, perhaps, be compared with the *tẹ* found in some of the demonstrative adverbs, where we possibly have to do with the postposition *tẹ*. We have probably here to assume a demonstrative root with a *t*. Both the *n* and the *t* might be compared with the same consonants found infixed in base-words ; there may perhaps be some idea of direction combind with the *t*.

that may stand for the pure demonstrative without reflecting on its reference being animate or inanimate.

146. These demonstratives for drawing attention may all take the dual and the plural suffixes, added to the singular form; they may take the determinative and the possessive pronominal suffixes, but no postpositions. Verbal suffixes may also be heard added. By adding a final *n* they may be turned into constructed demonstrative pronouns. See para 59 (b).

The meanings have been given above.

The following examples will show, how these demonstratives are used:

anẹ, alo sẹn laṛaoka, look at that there, don't move; *anẹ, arhõm ẹhọp'et'ge*, there you see, you are at it again; *anẹkoaṅ ọṇḍẹ khọnak itạ dọ*, that over there is the seed brought from that place; *atẹ rimil okare cọṅ saḍek kan*, listen there, it is thundering somewhere; *atẹko torako calak kan*, hear them, they are walking off; *hanẹ disạime*, remember that of that far off place (seen); *ãṛgọm dọko hanẹket'a*, they put the clod-crusher over there (as seen); *ọnẹ dọ cet' kana?* what is that there (seen); *ọnẹlaṅ ńapamlen ṭhẹc'*, at the place where we two met; *ọnẹko dare dọ*, those seen there are the trees; *ọnẹ thọye ọnẹwat'pe*, there you see what he did for you; *ẹnẹkidińam*, that much you did me (you were not able to trouble me a bit); *baṅ dọ ọnẹyaṅokklako onkoak cas dọ*, is it perhaps their cultivation seen there; *ọnẹ sạri jọ akan barea utạr*, really that there has set fruit, even two; *ẹtẹko anẹc' katha dọ*, there, that is just the matter, *ẹtẹko kanako rọṛọṛko*, hear just those, they are the speakers; *ẹtẹyic'e hijuk kana*, listen, that is just him coming; *ẹtẹak rak dọ*, listen just to that, that is the call; *ẹtẹko bọlẹ alerenko dọ*, listen there, they are our ones; *ẹtẹ tale bọlẹ ale buḍhiạ họr reaṅ aṛaṅtae dọ*, there you hear the voice of our old lady (grandmother); *ẹnẹ ẹṇḍẹ menaka*, it is just there (as shown); *ẹnẹ enkate calakme*, go in that direction (as shown and told); *ẹnẹko inạkgea*, it is so much as shown and no more; *ẹnẹko tale katha*, that is what we have to say, our case; *ẹnẹ nãhãkem bạṛic'et'a*, look there now, you are spoiling it; *ẹnẹ cọm sẹn sorlen*, there you see (according to your telling) you went near; *ęnęye emac kana, ńęltaepe,* there he is giving him, see what it is; *nun din khonem mokordomayet'a, ęnę tom ęnęyedea,* so long a time you have brought law-suits, that is the only thing you are able to do him; *ęnęyenae,* he was done for (i. e., not at all); *ęnęgeye ęhop'et'a,* now first he is commencing; *hanęnko hanko,* those there shown); *onęnic' doe apenic' kana?* he there (whom we see) is he one of yours? *bań do otęańokitako,* I wonder, whether it will be (proved to be) theirs that is heard.

147. (*a*) While all the demonstratives mentioned in para 144 refer to what is seen and heard respectively, *onę* and *otę*, to some extent also *ęnę* and *ętę*, have a wider application.

(*b*) As stated *onę* refers to what is seen, not only to what is seen with one's eyes, but especially also to what is evident (we also may use 'see' in the same way), and to known or demonstrated facts.

Onę very frequently refers to a statement of fact, often followed by a sentence that functions like a kind of apposition to the demonstrative, showing what is pointed out.

Onę is further used in combination with a personal, demonstrative or interrogative pronoun to express what corresponds to our relative pronouns. See below para 188.

E. g., onęm metadiń, onań agu akat'a, I have brought what you spoke to me about; *onę anań katha do,* there that is the case; *onę ńęlme,* there look; *onękoa dare do,* those there they are the trees; *onękidińam,* that you did me (i. e. you did not trouble me a bit); *onę onę arhõkin jhograk' kana,* there you see, they are again at loggerheads.

(*c*) *Otę* besides drawing attention to what is heard, is also used referring to taste, feeling and smell, and to what is told, a story, a rumour, the meaning of what is heard.

E. g., otę rearge coń, there you can feel it, it is cold; *otę labit'gea,* don't you feel it, it is soft; *otę harhat'gea,* feel it, it is bitter; *sedae do otę noa birre adi marak'ko tahękana,* formerly, we hear, there were many peafowls in this forest; *sari otę noa ato doko dakuket'a,* is it true what is told that they have committed a dacoity in this village? *ote bole katha*, hearsay, rumour.

148. The demonstrative pronouns are very frequently found in doublets, two of the same class, sometimes the same demonstrative repeated, sometimes different ones. In the first case the repetition signifies simply repeated drawing attention to. When the demonstratives are different, they are sometimes to be taken quite literally, sometimes they convey a more general, comprehensive idea. Cp. remarks para 17.

There is no rule which pronoun is to come first; it seems, however, to be the most common method to take the one signifying what is at a distance first and then the word for what is nearer.

When intended to convey a comprehensive or general meaning the second demonstrative or (sometimes the first one) may be one of the laterally demonstrative pronouns.

Both demonstratives take the same number suffix. Postpositions may be added to both (in such a case the same), or only to the last one.

E. g., uni nui, onko nhoko, hanko neko, hana nah, hana nhawa.

149. (*a*) The intensified demonstrative pronouns have been dealt with para 137, viz. pronouns with intensification effected through the infixing of an *k'* after the first vowel.

The language also has another way of effecting intensified demonstration, viz., by prefixing a demonstrative element (see para 133), identical with the first syllable of a demonstrative pronoun or dem. adverb, to this. It is not done with demonstratives having an initial *n* (possibly because the word itself is felt to be sufficiently strong) or a medial *t*, only with the demonstratives having initial vowel or aspirate and medial *n*.

E. g., un uni, un unkin, on ona, on onko, ǫn ǫnẹ, ǫn ǫntẹ, ǫn ǫndẹ, in ini, in inkin, en enko, an anẹ, ẹn ẹnẹ, hẹn hẹnẹ, in inạ, hạn hạni, hạn hạnkin, han hanko, han hanẹ, ẹn enka, ẹn ẹndẹ.

(*b*) This 'intensification', like the formation dealt with para 137, to a certain extent is also in analogy with the Performative form of the verb, however, with this difference that while in the verb words with initial vowel always take an infixed *k'* and repetition of the first syllable does not take place, here in the pronouns we are met with repetition of the initial vowel and following consonant, and, in the case of a pronoun with initial aspirate, of the first three sounds. It is similar to what is referred to in the Passive of the Performative, only that it is here initial and there final. See para 208. The analogy is not complete, and it is alluded to here only to show how the Santal mind uses similar methods to find expression for similar needs. In the corresponding verbal forms an expression is wanted for the active performance of a concept; in the pronouns an intensified demonstration is aimed at.

Naturally the forms here mentioned are not the result of a repetition of the first syllable. It is the corresponding demonstrative element prefixed to the demonstrative pronoun proper. It may possibly also be that this process is inverted, in as much as the demonstrative element may be the primary one taking the following demonstrative for completion and specification, in analogy with the formation of the demonstrative pronouns.

(*c*) Somewhat in analogy with the prefixing of a demonstrative element to a demonstrative pronoun the language makes use of a kind of double demonstration by prefixing the demonstratives that draw attention to sight (see para 144) to another demonstrative or to a demonstrative adverb. In the demonstratives referred to we have no forms with *u* or *i* as initial vowel; the forms with an initial vowel nearest in sound to that of the following demonstrative is made to serve (*ǫnẹ* with following demonstrative having *u* or *o*, and *ẹnẹ* with following demonstrative having *i* or *e*), except that *ǫnẹ* may apparently serve with all.

(*d*) The prefixed *ọnẹ*, etc., may take the dual and plural suffixes; *ọnẹ*, etc., may be prefixed to both animate and inanimate demonstratives, and also to demonstrative adverbs.

E. g., *ọnẹko onko, ẹnẹ ina̩, ẹnẹ ẹnḍẹ, ọnẹ ọnẹ, ọnẹ uni, ọnẹ unkin, ọnẹ ona, ọnẹ onka, ọnẹ ọntẹ, ọnẹ ọnḍẹ, ọnẹ ini, ọnẹ ina̩, ọnẹ hina̩,*

ẹnẹ ini, ẹnẹ ina̩, ẹnẹ enka, ẹnẹ ẹnḍẹ, ẹnẹ ẹntẹ,

hẹnẹ hina̩, hẹne hini, hanẹ hana, hanẹ ha̩ni, hanẹ hanḍẹ, hanẹ hantẹ.

(*e*) The intensive form with infixed *k'* may be followed by the corresponding demonstrative pronoun, animate or inanimate. *E. g.*, *nũk'ũi nui, nĩk'ĩ ni, nọ̃k'ọ̃e noa.*

(*f*) The intensive form of the lateral demonstratives is in the analogous construction followed by the corresponding ordinary demonstrative, and not by the lateral do., possibly in analogy with the law that two aspirated consonants are not to be found inside the same stress-unit. We have two stress-units here, but it would be heavy to pronounce the two aspirated words together. Or the use of two lateral demonstratives may be considered unnecessary.

It is, e. g., *nhũk'ũi nui* and not *nhũk'ũi nhui.*

---

150. In connection with the demonstratives a few particles ought to be mentioned, because they are of a demonstrative nature. They have no separate existence, but are always suffixed to or added to a word, a verbal construction or a demonstrative element.

Principal among these demonstrative particles is:

a, generally called the finite or the categorical *a*, added to the finite verbal construction.

Remembering the peculiar formation of the inanimate demonstrative pronouns, together with the apparent necessity of the Santal mind of having to do with concrete reality, it seems not only possible, but natural to connect this finite *a* with the *a* of the demonstrative pronoun. It refers to concrete matter or fact, and is the means by which the language makes a verbal statement enter the world of reality. It is significant that when the verb takes the optative particle *ma* or the particle *cọṅ*, or any other word denoting mental uncertainty, the finite *a* is not used. Thus *calak'ae*, he will go; but *calak'mae*, may he (let him) go; *calak' coe baṅ cọṅ*, it is uncertain whether he will go or not; *baṅ dọe calak'*, (I wonder) whether he will go.

151. This *a* may be enlarged by suffixing an *n* (see para 59), and we get *an*. This *an*, as an expanded finite verbal *a*, is not ordinarily used in the present language, but occurs in occasional forms of the verbs *menak'* and *bạnuk'* (*bạnugic'an*, *bạnuk̃an*, etc.).

We find *an* used as a possessive suffix, added to a word denoting what is possessed (see para 56). It may possibly be the same *an* that is used as the verbal suffix to form the Medium Reflexive Past; this last *an* and the *an* here dealt with are, however, of different application, whatever their origin may be.

The *an* is again expanded by the addition of certain suffixes, *-ic'* (corresponding to the animate determinative suffix), *-ak'* or *-aṅ* (corresponding to the inanimate determinative suffix), and *-ẹc'*; thus: *ạnic'*, *anak'*, *anaṅ* and *anẹc'*. *

Of these *ạnic'*, *anak'* and *anaṅ* are commonly used as possessive suffixes also taking number suffixes (*ạnkin*, *anko*, *anak'ko*, etc.); *anẹc'*, *anak'* and *anaṅ* are frequently used in stead of the finite *a* in the same two verbs mentioned above, *bạnuk'* and *menak'*, mostly with inanimate logical subject.

151. Apart from the meanings mentioned these four particles (*ạnic'*, *anak'*, *anaṅ* and *anẹc'*) are used with a demonstrative denotation; used with another demonstrative the demonstration becomes more pointed. Often, perhaps

---

* We may possibly here have to do with two different particles, *an* + *ẹc'* (etc.) and *a* + *n* + *ẹc'* (etc.). Where the finite *a* is dealt with under the verb, a very curious individualistic use of *a* + *nẹc'*, instead of *a*, will be found mentioned. The constituent parts of the particles may be the same, but the formations may belong to different stages of development.

generally, we cannot give a literal translation. In many cases the addition of *anẹc'*, *anak'* or *anaṅ* conveys a meaning of 'at last', 'then only', or something similar. The three particles mentioned are especially used with the Anterior of the verb (see verbs).

E. g., *ọnẹ anẹc' katha*, that is the matter (as stated); *ẹnẹ anẹc' inreń sẹnlena*, just at that time I went (and not at any other time); *ẹnẹ anẹc' iń ńẹl akat'a, baṅkhan tisre hõ baṅ*, that is the only and first time I have seen it, otherwise never; *ọtẹ ạnic' darae kana*, listen there, now he is coming; *ọtẹ anko anẹc'*, listen there, now only they are coming; *ọtẹ anko tae*, listen there his ones are heard; *ọtẹaṅ tako anaṅ onkoak' sagaṛ*, listen, now there is their cart to be heard coming; *ọtẹ anaṅ uni cẽṛẽ*, listen, there is that bird heard.

153. The language has a number of demonstrative particles, formed like those dealt with in the last two paras, but with an initial *e* in stead of *a*; it is the demonstrative element *en* or *ẹn* with certain suffixes, viz., *-a*, *-ak'*, *-aṅ* and *ẹc'*.

These particles are the following:

ena, used in the meaning of 'then only', 'not until';
ẹnẹc', do.;
enak', do.;
enaṅ, do.

Enak' and *enaṅ* are rarely used; *enaṅ* should not be confounded with another very common word, *enaṅ* or *enan*, used as a noun, meaning a while ago (same day, or, in some parts of the country, same year).

These particles are mostly heard in connection with verbal constructions and adverbs, but may also be heard after the demonstrative pronouns. The original meaning may possibly be 'that happened', or something similar.

E. g., *uniye calaoen ena noko dọko hẹc'ena*, only when he had left these came; *nit ẹnẹc'* now first; *hola ẹnẹc'*, only yesterday (not before); *kalọm ẹnẹc'*, only next year; *nọṇḍẹ ẹnẹc' jut ạikạuk'a*, here only it is pleasant to feel; *nui ẹnẹc'e chinḍạuket'a*, this one only managed to unravel the case.

Demonstrative adverbs.

154. The language has a large number of demonstrative adverbs, all derived from the demonstrative elements. They are dealt with here, in connection with the demonstratives, for the sake of convenience.

These adverbs may be single or compound.

The demonstrative adverbs show the same classes as the ordinary adverbs, there being different ones to denote place (rest in or direction towards), quality, manner and quantity.

155. Demonstrative adverbs denoting *place* (rest in).

Noṇḍẹ, here, at this place.
Oṇḍẹ, there, at that place.
Hoṇḍẹ, there, at a distance.
Haṇḍẹ, over there, far off.
Nẹṇḍẹ, just here.
Ẹṇḍẹ, just there, just at that place.
Hẹṇḍẹ, just there, at a distance.

These demonstrative adverbs seem to be a compound of a demonstrative element and the word *ḍi* (place, site), the nasal being changed from dental to cacuminal on account of the *ḍ*.

As will be observed, we have, corresponding to what is found in the demonstrative pronouns, sets of adverbs with certain variations in accordance with distance and identification. The adverbs with initial *n* point to what is close by, *nẹṇḍẹ* denoting a more accurate, better definable place, nearer or more exact, than *noṇḍẹ*, which leaves a little more latitude.

Those with initial vowel show the same qualities, but denote what is at a little distance.

Those with initial aspirate (*h*) only point to what is further or far off.

156. Parallel with those enumerated the language has also some *laterally demonstrative adverbs*, the same as those with initial *n*, but aspirated (*nh*). They are: *nhoṇḍẹ*, here

on the side; *nhẹnḍẹ*, just here on the side; and *nhaṇḍẹ*, there at a distance on the side.

157. The demonstrative adverbs are very commonly heard used in doublets. The meaning is literal, distributive or generalizing.

Of the adverbs mentioned above the most common doublets are the following:

oṇḍẹ noṇḍẹ, here and there; *oṇḍẹ nhoṇḍẹ* here and there; *eṇḍẹ neṇḍẹ*, just here and there, just in these places; *eṇḍẹ nheṇḍẹ*, do.; *hoṇḍẹ nhoṇḍẹ*, here and there; *haṇḍẹ nhaṇḍẹ*, do.

In these doublets the lateral meaning is not specially dwelt on; but the laterally demonstrative adverb seems to imply an ampler scope and is very commonly used in these doublets.

158. The language further has a series of four demonstrative adverbs, viz., *neman*, *eman*, *noman* and *oman*, conveying the meaning of hereabouts, thereabouts. These are, however, very rarely used.*

E. g., *nomanre*, hereabouts; *oman darakote dẹñ dāṛī akat'a*, I have walked about to those parts, *iñ khonak' eman darateko sẹnena*, they went from me to some such place.

159. All the above mentioned demonstrative adverbs may take postpositions, provided these go with the meaning.

This taking of postpositions shows the real nature of these adverbs: compound base-words used adverbially.

E. g., *noṇḍẹrẹ*, within here, here in this place; *hoṇḍẹrẹ*, there in those places further off; *eṇḍẹrẹ*, just there in that place (this last expression is very frequently used figuratively, denoting 'in that case,' 'if that is the fact,' 'then'; the other demonstrative adverbs with *rẹ* may also be so used, but not so frequently); *eṇḍẹrẹ ma bogege*, in that case all is well; *noṇḍẹ khoṇ*, from here; *noṇḍẹ habic'*, up to here;

* Cp. footnote to para 168 and para 194.

hande lagat', for that place; *endete enec'*, then only (*te* is here the instrumental postposition). The laterally demonstrative adverbs take postpositions like the others; there is no difference.

160. Demonstrative adverbs denoting *direction*.

Corresponding to the demonstrative adverbs denoting rest in a place the language has the same number of ordinary and laterally demonstrative adverbs denoting direction. They are formed in a similar way, here (in stead of *di*) *te* being added to the demonstrative element, the two parts being so melted together as to have formed a new word. *

It should be noted that direction does not necessarily imply movement. The forms with initial *n* imply movement or direction towards the speaker, if movement is at all reflected on.

Note, hither, to this place, part.
Onte, there, to that place.
Honte, over in that direction.
Hante, over in that far off direction.
Nhote, hither on the side.
Nhate, over in that direction off on the side.

Nete, just to this place.
Ente, just to that place.
Hente, just over in that direction.
Nhete, just hither on the side.

161. Also these demonstrative adverbs take postpositions, *te* and *sec'* (*sen*) denoting direction towards, *khun* direction from, and *re* rest in some direction or other. Any postposition not incompatible with the meaning of the adverb may be used. The following examples will show, how the postpositions are used.

* One is tempted to identify this *te* with the postposition *te* denoting direction or movement towards. On account of the postpositions taken by these adverbs one will in this case have to presuppose that the speakers are no longer conscious of this *te* being a postposition.

Notete, in this direction.
Ontete, in that direction.
Hontete, over in that direction.
Hantete, over in that direction far off.
Nhotete, nhetete, in this direction on the side.
Note sec', towards here, in this direction.
Notere, here in this direction.
Note sec're, in these parts, towards here.
Note khon, from these parts.
Netete, just in this direction.
Entete, just in that direction.
Hentete, just over in that direction.
Nhatete, over in that direction far off on the side.
Nhate sec', towards that direction away on the side.
Hantere, over there in that direction.
Nete khon, just from hereabouts, etc., etc.

162. The demonstrative adverbs denoting direction are also very frequently used in doublets, the meaning being on the one hand distributive, on the other giving a more comprehensive and general idea than that of the single word. Cp. para 157.

{ *Onte note*, / *Onte nhote*, } hither and thither, everywhere, round about, to both sides.
{ *Ente nete*, / *Ente nhete*, } to this and that side, in both directions.
{ *Honte note*, / *Honte nhote*, } to this and that side, in both directions (further off).
{ *Hante nate*, / *Hante nhate*, } to this and that side far off.

163. Demonstrative adverbs denoting *quality* and *manner*.

These adverbs are formed in analogy with the two classes of demonstrative adverbs already mentioned, in this case by suffixing *ka* to the demonstrative elements *non, on, nen, en, hon, hen, han*, with their lateral variations, all having the same meaning, differing only as to proximity and exactitude of comparison.

Nonka, thus, in this way.
Onka, thus, in that way.
Honka, thus, in that way (further off).
Nenka, just in this way.
Enka, just in that way (often with a disparaging side-meaning).

Hanka, thus, in that way, like that far off.
Nhonka, thus, like this on the side.
Nhanka, thus, like that far off on the side.
Henka, just in that way (further off).
Nhenka, thus, just like that on the side.

164. (*a*) All the adverbs mentioned para 163 may have *leka* added. With *leka* added there is not much difference in meaning, the adverb with *leka* apparently having its demonstrative sense especially turned towards the performance more than to the state of what is referred to; *leka* conveys a meaning corresponding to 'like', 'in accordance with'. Cp. paras 104 and 308, footnote.

Nonka leka, in this way.
Onka leka, in that way.
Honka leka, in that way.
Hanka leka, in that way, like in that manner far off.
Nenka leka, just in this way, like in this manner.
Enka leka, just in that way, like in that manner.
Henka leka, just in that way, like thus further off.

Nhonka leka, *nhenka leka*, *nhanka leka*, same meanings as above, only with the lateral qualification.

(*b*) This *leka* may be added to any pronoun or other word the meaning of which will suit *leka*, the result being an adverb denoting a way, manner or functioning like that which is expressed by the word to which *leka* is added. Thus: *noa leka*, like this, *am leka*, like you, *dak̇ leka ạikạuk̇ kana*, it feels like water, or, like rain coming; *kạhni leka*, like a tale.

165. These demonstrative adverbs of quality and manner also take postpositions, most frequently *te* and *re*, but also others, as may be required.

Onkate, in that way, so, thus.
Enkate, so, thus, just in that manner; in the condition in which it is found.
Enkare, just so, just in that condition, in such case.
Enka lekate, just in that way, manner.

166. Of these adverbs also doublets are in constant use, conveying meanings analogous to what has been mentioned in connection with the others. Cp. paras 157 and 162.

Onka nonka, onka nhonka, in such and such ways.
Enka nenka, enka nhenka, in just such and such ways.
Honka nonka, honka nhonka, do.
Enka enka, in such and such a way (generally : not quite well).

For the use and several meanings of these demonstrative adverbs the reader must be referred to the dictionary.

Demonstratives used as adverbs denoting *quantity.*

167. The language has some demonstrative elements adverbially used referring to quantity. Also in these we find the same series of changing initials and vowels as in the demonstrative pronouns, although not to such a large extent. As is natural with this class the elements referring to what is at a distance are not occurring. Forms with an initial aspirate are not heard single.

They are the following :

Nun, so, so much, this much.
Un, that much, so many.
Nin, so, this much, just this much.
In, just so much, that very.

With the corresponding laterally demonstrative adverbs : *nhun, nhin,* and *nhạn.*

These demonstrative adverbs are also used about time, then, at that time.

E. g., nun marañ, so big ; *nun serma,* so many years ; *un din,* so long a time ; *nun jeleñ,* so long ; *nin tirit',* so much (as shown) ; *nin hoṛgeako,* they are just so many people ; *in kaṭic',* so small ; *in dhao,* so many times ; *in gan,* about as much ; *in aṅgc', in ena, in anañ,* then only, not till then.

168. The following demonstrative adverbs are seldom heard in the presentday language :

Numin, so much, so long. *

Nimin, so much, just so much, so big.

E. g., *numin marań* (*kal*), so long (a time); *nimin tirit'*, so much.

169. The following, all heard also as interjections, are used adverbially about quantity :
Nẹ, this much.
Ẹhẹ, so (much, — big).
Iọ, so (big, — much).

Nẹ has been mentioned previously (see para 133 (a)). *Ẹhẹ* and *iọ* are generally accompanied by a gesture showing the size or the quantity.

E. g., *nẹ uḍi jọmme*, eat the little I put before you ;
ẹhẹ tirit'e jọmet'a, he eats this much; *ẹhẹ marań biń*, a snake so big as this (shown); *ẹhẹ tiń*, - *talań* (etc.), so much (as shown); *ẹhẹ ẹhẹ talań*, just so much; *ẹhẹnak'* (this is women's language);
iọ talań, so big; *iọ marańiń ńẹlledea tạrup'*, I saw a leopard so big as this (shown).

---

* It may be questioned whether we here have an infix (*mi*), or a compound of *nu* + *min*, or *ni* + *min*.

I cannot call to mind any other *m* infix in Santali; following the rules for infixes we should expect the same vowel in the first and the second syllable; this is without exception the case in all words formed by an infix from monosyllable words. Here we should have to accept a *mi* infix, not only *m*.

In Muṇḍari and Ho a similar *min* is found added to the interrogative *ci* (Santali *cet'*), also in a couple of other words, and declared to be demonstratives of quantity (*nimin*, *imin*, *niminuń*, *nimińań*, *iminań*).

In Santali we find the same *min* in *timin* (that might come from *tin*) and in *cimin* (*leka*, very rare and used only by women, equal to *cet' leka*; in this case there cannot well be any possibility of an infix). We meet with a similar addition in certain other words, only with another vowel (*a* for *i*), in *noman*, *neman*, *oman* and *eman* (see para 158). This seems to point towards a demonstrative element with an added *min* or *man*, in the case of *man* most probably the same word as that found in *ẹmọn*. Cp. para 96 (e), footnote.

The *man* in *jande man tande*, *jãhã man kãhã*, etc., is likely also to be explained in the same way (borrowed from old Bengali).

170. **When adverbially used these demonstratives are followed by an adjective; when taking a postposition they function combined with this as an adverb. The demonstratives** mentioned **para 167** all **take postpositions**; **especially** *re* **and** *te* are **of constant occurrence.**

E. g., ***unre***, **then, at that time**; ***inre***, **at that very time**; ***ninte***, **by this time** (now gone); ***inte***, **by that time**; ***inkote***, **by about that time** (note the plural suffix ***ko***, about the indefinite time); ***intekote***, **by about that time**; *unkote*, **by about that time.**

171. The **demonstratives mentioned para 167** have **taken the** inanimate **determinative** suffix (***aḱ***, in one case *aṅ*), so **melted together with the demonstrative as to have become one word with it; when the demonstrative** has *u* or *i* **as its vowel this causes the** *a* **of the suffix to become a resultant** *ạ*. This is constant in the demonstratives here dealt with; it seems to be forgotten, that we have the determinative suffix. *

The forms are the following:

Nunạḱ, this much. *Ninạḱ*, just this much.

Unạḱ, that much. *Inạḱ*, just that much.

Hạnạḱ, that much (as that at a distance).

Hạnạṅ, do.

With the corresponding laterally demonstrative forms: *nhunạḱ*, *nhinạḱ*, *nhạnạḱ*. †

These demonstratives function like adverbs, prefixed to an adjective; further as nouns or as verbs, and as adjectives.

E. g., *inạḱ gan soroḱme*, come near about that much; *unạḱ marạṅ*, so big; *inạḱ usul*, just so high;

---

* Another explanation is possible, viz., that there is a demonstrative *ninạ*, etc., with *ḱ* added; but this is scarcely likely. The form *hạnạḱ* might be brought forward in support, as there is nothing to explain the resultant vowel; but then again we have *hạnạṅ* which could not well be explained on the same lines.

† *Nhạnạḱ* presupposes a demonstrative *nạn* or *nạnạḱ*, but such a one is not heard in the present language. A *nanaḱ* is heard, but very rarely.

unạk' phạd, such a multitude ; *unạk' hoṛ*, so many people ; *ninạk'e emadiña*, he gave me just this much ; *nunạk'ena*, it became this much.

172. Also these forms take postpositions, *te* and *re* being common.

E. g., *inạk'te*, by that much, by that time ; *nunạk're*, in so much.

173. These forms with final *-ạk'* are frequently found in doublets, the meanings being of the same nature as those of similar doublets of other demonstratives. These doublets function as nouns, adjectives and verbs.*

E. g., *unạk' nunạk'*, so and so much ; *inạk' ninạk'*, just so and so much (or little).

174. All demonstrative adverbs may, like the dem. pronouns, be intensified by prefixing one of the demonstrative elements, viz., *un*, *on*, *ọn*, *in*, *en*, *ẹn*, *hun*, *hon*, *hẹn*, *han*, *hạn*, or the demonstratives *ọnẹ*, *ẹnẹ*, *anẹ*, *honẹ*, *hẹnẹ*, *hanẹ*. The prefixed demonstrative element is always the same as the initial syllable of the adverb ; the same holds good also for the corresponding forms with final *ẹ*, with the addition that *ọnẹ* and *ẹnẹ* are also used with following dem. adverbs having as first vowel respectively *u* or *o* and *i* or *e*. Cp. para 149. The forms *un*, *on*, *ọn*, *in*, *en*, *ẹn*, *han*, *hẹn*, *hon*, *hun*, *hạn*, are pointing to, showing, while the forms with suffixed *ẹ* more draw attention to the fact that what is pointed to is there.

Thus : *ọn ọndẹ*, there (pointing, showing), *ọnẹ ọndẹ*, there (as you may see) ; *ẹn ẹndẹ*, *ẹnẹ ẹndẹ*, *hẹn hẹndẹ*, *hẹnẹ hẹndẹ*,

---

* In the present-day language it is not uncommon to hear the Bengali demonstratives *ẹmọn*, *ẹmọn tẹmọn*, *ẹmọn sẹmọn*, *jẹmọn tẹmọn* used as demonstrative adjectives and adverbs, denoting : so and so, such, such like, only so and so, indifferently. The words have very frequently a derogatory side-meaning. *Ẹmọn hoṛ*, such a person ; *ẹmọne ruheṭ'kidiña*, he scolded me something awful ; *ẹmọm tẹmọn hoṛ dọ alom bujhạuea*, do not take him to be an ordinary person ; *jẹmọn tẹmọne kạmikeṭ'a*, he worked only so and so, unsatisfactorily.

han haṇḍe, hane haṇḍe, hon hoṇḍe, hone hoṇḍe; un unte, han hante, one onka, han hanka, un unak', in inak', one unak', ene inak', han hanak', han hanan.

The whole expression is a demonstrative element or pronoun with a localizing demonstrative adverb. When these forms are used they are very frequently supported by a pointing gesture.

175. The forms with initial *n* (cp. para 149) do not take these prefixed demonstrative elements; as a kind of substitute the intensified demonstratives *nũk'ũi, nĩk'ĩ, nõk'õe* and *nẽk'ẽ* (or *nẽk'*) are used, according to what is pointed to or shown being animate or inanimate.

E. g, *nũk'ũi noṇḍe, nõk'õe nonka.*

176. All demonstrative pronouns, adverbs and adverbially used demonstrative pronouns of any class with final single vowel may take a suffixed *n*, the words thus formed becoming demonstrative adjectives of sorts.

This *n* has been dealt with paras 58 and 59.

With the Santals living in the Santal Parganas and the northern districts of Bengal and in Assam it is seldom to hear this *n* suffixed to the demonstrative pronouns proper. I understand this *n* is much more frequently added to these pronouns by the Santals living in Southwest Bengal and Orissa. The *n* added to a demonstrative pronoun seems to convey a reference to quality or class, being such as demonstrated, belonging to what is referred to.

The addition of this *n* to the demonstrative adverbs is regular.

The following examples will show the use.

Nuin, such as this one; *onan*, that; *onanko kangea aleak' do*, those (things) are ours; *onan dharae ạikạuk' kana*, he seems to be of that sort; *sedaere mit' atorebon beṛel ńapamlen, unin kanae*, it is him with whom we in olden times settled in the same village (it must be him); *noko hǒko onkongea*, these are also some belonging to those; *iṇạn hoṛako*, they are so many people; *onko tinạk̔ menak̔ko, noko hǒko iṇạnena*, they are also as many as those are; *ọnẹn*, he, she, that there (both animate and inanimate); *ọnẹn dọ cet' kana*, what is that there; *ọnẹnic' dọe apenic' kana?* the one there, is he one of yours? *ọtẹn dọ cele kanae?* who is the one heard there? *ọtẹnic' dọe aleic' kana*, he who is heard there is our one; *ọtẹnak̔ dọ cet' añjọmok̔ kana?* listen to that there, what is being heard? *ọtẹnko*, those heard there;

ọṇḍẹn, ọṇḍẹnak̔, ọṇḍẹnic', ọntẹn (-ic', -kin, -ko, -ak̔, -ak̔kin, -ak'ko);

onkan (-ic', -kin, -ko; -ak̔, -ak̔kin, -ak̔ko);

uni lekan (-ic', -kin, -ko);

onka lekan (-ic', -kin, -ko; -ak̔, -ak̔kin, -ak̔ko);

onkan lekan (-ic', -kin, -ko; -ak', -ak'kin, -ak'ko);

nẹṇḍẹren (-ic', -kin, -ko);

nọtẹren (-ic', -kin, -ko);

hantẹren (-ic', -kin, -ko);

hantẹten (-ic', -kin, -ko), etc., etc.

The Interrogative Pronouns.

177. (*a*) The language has two classes of interrogative pronouns, one for the animates, and one for the inanimates. Inside each class there is one pronoun that simply singles out, and another that refers to quality and reality.

For animates.	*For inanimates.*
Ọkọe (dual, *ọkọekin*, pl. *ọkọeko*), who, which one.	*Oka* (dual *okakin*, pl. *okako*), what, which one.
Cele (dual *celekin*, pl. *celeko*), which, what kind.	*Cet'* (dual *cet'kin*, pl. *cet'ko*), what.

(*b*) *Ọkọe* and *oka* in the singular often take the suffix *ṭa, ṭak'* or *ṭaṅ* (cp. para 142.) Of these *ṭak̔* is probably the most commonly used; it signifies the unit, in a way makes the question more pointed. It is a mistake to say that *ṭak̔* makes the pronoun into a noun; with *ṭak̔* it is used also as an adjective.

When asking for one's name *cele* is used.

They may all be used as adjectives, and also as verbs. All take suitable postpositions.

(*c*) The interrogative pronouns are often repeated, such repetition denoting plurality or distribution.

E. g., *okoe kanae*, who is it? *okoekoko calaoena*, who went away? *okoe okoeko heċ' akana*? who, which different ones, have come? *okoekin noa dokin hoeket'a*? who are the two persons who did this? *okoe hor kanae*, which person is it? *cele hor kanae*, what kind of a man is he (or, what named person is it)? *oka hortem heċ'ena*? by which way did you come? *cet'tem heċena*? how did you come? *cet' katha kana*? what matter is it? *oka kathako sap' akat'a*? which matter is it that they have taken up? *cet'iń aguia*? what shall I bring? *puthi aguańme*, bring me a book? *oka puthi*? which book? *cet' puthi*? what book? *cet' cet'kom cet'ket'a*, what (different things) have you learnt? *cet' cet'kope jomket'a*, what different things did you eat?

okoe badae? who knows? (a very common expression: it may be noted that in this question *oko* and *hoko* may be heard used instead of *okoe*, *hoko* being used by impatient or angry persons.)

okoe kan tamae? what relative of yours is he? *okoe horme kanam*? what sept do you belong to? *nui dope okoekedea*? whom did you make this one to be? *okoeok'ae nui do*? what sept does this one belong to? *nui haram doe okoeyentapea*? what kind of relation of yours is this old man? *okoeko heċ'-at'bona, abo se onko*? (expression used by women when asking the sex of a newborn babe) who came to us, we or they? *okoeantem senlena*? with whom did you go? *okoe theċ' theċ'ko ńamket'a*? (equal to *okoe okoe then*) with whom (several) did they find it? *okortak'em akrińkedea*? which one did you sell? *okoren*? whose? *okaren*, from where?

celeama ńutum? what is your name? *onko do celeak'ako*? what is their relationship to one another? *celeak'kom kami barayet'a*? what are you occupied with?

okam dakana, where did you go? *okayenae*? what is become of him? *gai dom okakedea*? where have you left the cow? *okakoauko aleak' do?* what has become of ours? *oka okape senlen, onde onde idiboupe,* take us to the places where you went; *katha dom okatakket'a?* what did you agree upon? *okateyic' hor kanae?* what place is this person going to?

cet' lagit'? for what purpose? *cet' iate?* why?

cet' bań se, what not, wonderful (exclamation of wonder); *cet' bań se, holanok' hatteń senlena, ar deko bebaric'ko tapamena,* you have never seen the like of it, I went yesterday to the market, and the dekos had an awful fight.

178. *Cet' - - cet',* preceded by *ge* put after words corresponds to 'whether - or', 'both-and'; *takage cet', poesage cet',* whether rupees or pice (all of it;) *nãhãk' do jotọ hor reak' pagra menak'takoa, aimaige cet', herelge cet', korage cet', kurige cet',* at the present time all Santals have ear-rings, whether women or men, whether boys or girls.

179. *Cele* is frequently used to introduce a question, where we might translate it with an interrogative 'well', 'how is it'? It is also used inside sentences adverbially to express 'presumably', 'likely', 'perhaps'.

E. g., cele, jarwayenabon sebon baṅa? well, how is it, are we all here or not; *cele tearena se bań,* how is it, is it ready or not?

nui gai do cele mĩhũi busagea hapen, this cow will probably soon have a calf; *pon hor celeko tahẽkana,* they were, I presume, four people.

180. (*a*) *Celec'* and *celet'* are sideforms to *cele* used adverbially, more especially when the speaker refers to hearsay.

E. g., henda ho, phalua doe hec'ena se? hẽ celet', onkageń ańjom akat'a, look here, has so and so come, or how? yes, very likely, so I have heard; *phalua do hatteye calaoena se bań? hẽ celet', onkage holae menet' tahẽkana,* did so and so go to the market? yes, I presume so, he was saying so yesterday; *hijukgeae celet, gate onkako ror barayet'a,* he will come, I presume, for so they are saying.

(*b*) A form *celet* is heard, but is very rare.

Celettet'ko coṅ din hilokko hijuka, some ones or others, who knows who they are, are coming daily.

(c) *Cetat* (or *cetat'*), possibly connected with *cet'*, is used as an interrogative inanimate pronoun, in a meaning somewhat like *cet*, but with a derogatory side-meaning. As an interrogative pronoun it is rare, but used with *hõ* or *ge* added as an indefinite pronoun it is common. See para 191 (e). *Noa baṅ cetat* (or, *cetatak'*), what is this? (it is of no account).

181. *Okor* is an interrogative pronoun to some extent corresponding to the demonstrative *ọnẹ*; it is used objectingly, remonstratingly, when a person does not see or find what or whom he is expected to see or find. *Okor* takes the animate determinative suffixes, also *an*, *anaṅ*, *anẹc'* (see para 151. A), but not the inanimate do., although it is used about both animates and inanimates. Its adverbial use will be dealt with below. It may be translated: Why, where (is it, is he? etc.).

E. g., *okoric'*, *nit hõ bae hẹc' akana*, why, where is he? he is not come even now; *ukuric' tako apat họṛ dọ*, why, where is their father? I do not see him anywhere (note *ukuric'*, on acc. of the law of harmonic sequence); *ukuric'tako an bahu họṛ dọ*, why, where is their daughter-in-law? *okorko okare*, why, where are they? (I do not see them); *okoran tako katha dọ*, why, where is what they have to say? *okoran tako anaṅ onkoak' khẹt dọ*, why, where is their ricefield (I cannot find it); *okoric' anẹc'* (or *-ạnic'*) *oka ṭhẹc' menaea*, where is he? near what? (I cannot see him); *okor anaṅ oka ṭhẹc'em ńẹl ńamket'a*, why, where is it, where did you catch sight of it? *okoric'an uni dọ*, why, where is he?

Interrogative adverbs.

182. In analogy with the adverbially used demonstratives and demonstrative adverbs the language has also a number of interrogative adverbs of a similar nature, not always and not necessarily, but generally compounds of an interrogative pronoun and a postposition or a postpositionally used word.

Interrogative pronouns used adverbially referring to *place*.

183. (*a*) The interrogative pronoun *oka* is sometimes used adverbially without any addition, mostly, however, with a postposition (*tẹ, rẹ, ṭhen, sẹc', khon, dhạbic'*).

E. g., okam dukạna, where did you go ?

okate, whereto ? *okare*, where ? *oka sẹc'*, in which direction ? *oka ṭhen*, at which place, near what ? *oka khon*, wherefrom ? *oka dhạbic'*, up to where ? *okare hõ baṅ*, no where; *okate hõ baṅ*, to nowhere.

(*b*) *Okor* (see para 181) is used adverbially in the meaning of where ? why not ? It is also used as an impers. verb with indirect inanimate object.

E. g., okore hẹc'ena, where did he come ? (he is not come); *okorem sẹnlena*, why, you did not go ; *calak' dọ okoratae kana*, he is unwilling to go ; *okorat'takoa ẹmok' dọ*, why, they did not give at all.

184. Interrogative adverbs referring to *time*.

Tis, when ? referring to time in general, but not the same day.

Tisok', when ?
Tin, when ? referring to the time of the day.
Timin, when ? (time of the day).
Timinạk're, do.
Tis (*tisok'*) is used only about time.

Tis, tin and *timin* may all be used adjectively referring to time when the word to which they are added denotes time. Standing alone *tin* and *timin* when referring to time always take a postposition. *Tin* and *timin* otherwise refer to quantity.

E. g., tis, when, which day ; *tisre*, at what time ; *tis khọn*, from what time, since when ? *tis dhạbic'*, up to what time ? *tisre hõ baṅ*, never (in stead of *baṅ* any other negation may be used) ; *tisok'* (*tis* with the Medium suffix added), when, when will it be ? *tis jọkhẹc'*, at what time ?

tinre, at what time of the day, at what hour ? *tin khọc'*, from what hour ? *tin hạbic'*, up to what hour ? *tinte*, by what hour ? *timinre*, at what time of the day ; *timinạkre*, do. (*timin* is only rarely used).

185. Interrogative adverbs referring to *quantity*.

(*a*) *Tin*, how much, how many, how big.
Timin, do. (rare in the present-day language),
Tinạk', how much, how many.
Timinạk' (or *timinạn*), how much (seldom used).

As to the forms *tinạk'* and *timinạk'* see para 171, and as to *timin* see para 168, footnote. It will be seen that the forms here dealt with correspond to the demonstratives *nin*, *ninạk'* and *nimin*. *

Tin and *timin* are used prefixed to a word; when this refers to time *tin* and *timin* naturally also refers to time (time of day; see para 184), otherwise when prefixed to any other word it is always quantity.

When having a postposition *tin* and *timin* always refer to time (several European languages also refer to the time of the day as a matter of quantity).

E. g, *tin maraṅ*, how big? *tin sạngiṅ*, how far away? how distant? *tin tirit'*, how much? *tin ụdi*, how much, i. e., a little; *tin ụdic'*, do., a few;
timin maraṅ, how big? *timin sạngiṅ*, how distant?

(*b*) The remarks made regarding *ninạk'* and *inạk'* (see paras 171 & 172) hold good for *tinạk'*, when it is borne in mind that we have here an interrogative meaning.

E. g., *tinạk' maraṅ*, how big? *tinạk' gan*, about how much? *tinạkte*, at how much, at what price?

(*c*) Note the correlatives: *tin - nun*, *tinạk' - nunạk'*.

186. Interrogative adverbs denoting *manner*.

These are all compounds, consisting of an interrogative pronoun with *leka* added. To *leka* a postposition may be added, mostly *tẹ* or *re*, but also any other that may suit or be needed.

Cet' leka, lit. like what, in what way, manner; *cet' lekate*, in what way; *cet' lekare*, in what manner, in what

---

* In connection with the initial *t* one is reminded that the interrogative pronouns ordinarily having an initial vowel in Santal poetry mentioned get a prefixed *t*. See Mat. I., para 122. It should have been there, that in poetry also *oho* takes a prefixed *t* (*toho*).

circumstances; *cimin leka* = *cet' leka* (used by women, see para 168, footnote), *oka leka*, in which way, manner; *oka lekate*, in which manner; *oka lekate hǫ̃ bań*, in no way at all (note: *hǫ̃* with a negation goes with *oka leka*, but not with *cet' leka*); *tinạk leka*, in how many ways, like how many.

Note the correlatives:

cet' leka—onka leka (*enka leka*, *hanka leka*, etc.)

187. (*a*) All interrogative pronouns and adverbs with single final vowel may be made into adjectives by getting *n* suffixed, some, however, very rarely in the present day language.

(*b*) An interrogative pronoun with a postposition may also take the determinative suffixes of the singular, the dual and the plural. The adjectives and nouns thus formed may be both animate and inanimate, according to the suffixes employed.

Okan, which, belonging to what, where; *noa ḍhạknic' dǫ okana*, where does this cover belong? *okanko dǫ aleak'*, which ones are ours? *okaren* (*-ic'*, etc.), from where? *okaten* (*-ic'*, etc.), whereto? *oka senakko*, things belonging to what direction; *celen*, what kind; *cet' lekan* (*-ic'*, *-kin*, *-ko*; *-ak'*, *-ak'kin*, *-ak'ko*), of what kind; *oka lekan* (*-ic'*, *etc.*), like what; *ǫkǫe lekan* (*-ic'*, *-kin*, *-ko*), like who; *cele lekan* (*-ic'*, *-kin*, *-ko*), like which one.

(*c*) The word *ceka* (what do, -doing, -done) * is used as an interrogative adverb and with *n* suffixed as an interrogative pronoun.

Ceka, how, why; *cekam hẹc'ena*, how did you come? *cekan*, what sort; *cekanic'* (=*ceka* + *n* + *ic'*), what kind of (found only in the singular); *ceka lekan* (*-ic'*, *-kin*, *-ko*), of what kind; *cekan lekan* (*-ic'*, *-kin*, *-ko*), of what sort; *cekate*, how, why, in what way.

The Relative Pronouns (and Relative Sentences).

188. As already mentioned, the language has, properly speaking, no relative pronouns, and has to make use of

* We may possibly have an interrogative *ce*, not found outside compounds; we might then take the composition to be *ce*+*t'*, *ce*+*le*, *ce*+*leć*, *ce*+*let*, *ce*+*tat*, *ce*+*ka*, *ci*+*min*.

other classes of pronouns when such are needed; or it manages to render our relative sentences without any pronoun at all.

(*a*) The easiest and, to a Santal, probably the most natural way of rendering our relative sentences is to take the whole relative sentence as an attribute to the governing word, omitting all pronouns. In such cases the 'relative sentence' always precedes the word to which it is attached.

We may in such cases have either a full sentence with constructed verb (without the finite *a*, the word to which the clause refers, so to say, taking the place of this *a*).

Or we may have only a participial construction, in as much as the verbal subject may be left out. While we may have to translate the last named construction with a relative sentence, it is in Santali nothing more than what is shown. The construction is participial, but it must be borne in mind that a Santali participle, or what we for the sake of convenience call so, is different from the participles of an inflexional language. We have in Santali the base-word with any tense-suffix, according to need with or without a direct or indirect object infix and a possessive infix; only the subject and the finite *a* are wanting. When this construction is mentioned here, it is due to the fact that we ordinarily and most easily may translate it with a relative sentence or render our relative sentences in the way described.

E. g., *sẹnen hoṛ*, the man who went; *kombṛoket' hoṛ*, the man who stole; *kombṛokede hoṛ*, the man from whom something was stolen (so ordinarily, but might also mean, the man who stole it, e. g., a goat); *teṅgo akade janware tuń tap'kedea*, he shot an arrow through the animal that had been put standing (there);

ḍaṅgrae kiriṅkede haṛam, the old man who bought the bullock; *ghạṛdi jãwãeko ạguade kuṛi*, the girl for whom a house-husband has been brought (whose husband lives in his father-in-law's house).

(*b*) The same construction as mentioned above, with *onę* prefixed. *Onę* is the demonstrative pronoun referring to sight (see para 144). It is constantly used in connection with relative sentence constructions, but its real meaning is never lost sight of.

E. g., *onęm hęćen hilok'*, the day you came; *onęm metadiń onageń ągu akat'a*, I have brought what you told me.

Onę in this construction more or less refers to the whole sentence and precedes what it refers to.

(*c*) The interrogative pronouns *okoe* (for animates) and *oka* (for inanimates), with or without a prefixed *onę*, are used corresponding to our relatives 'who' and 'which', or 'that'.

This kind of relative sentence may stand before or after the word to which it belongs.

E. g., *mit'ten hor, okoe noae kami dareak'*, a man who will be able to do this (may also be expressed thus: *okoe noae kami dareak' mit'ten hor*, or, *noae kami dareak' mit'ten hor*, or, *mit'ten hor, onę okoe*, etc., or, *onę uni*, etc.); *ona dare okam mak' akat'*, the tree that you have cut (or, *okam mak' akat' dare*, or, *ona dare, onę ona*, etc., or, *onę okam mak' akat' dare*); *haharawakko, onę okako bam ńel akat'*, wonderful things that you have not seen.

(*d*) *Cet'* and *cele* may also serve as relative pronouns. In such cases the relative sentence always precedes the word to which it refers.

E. g., *cet'e khoj kan ona emaeme*, give him what he wants; *cele coko metae hore hęćena*, the man whose name I don't know came (the what-do-they-call-him man).

The interrogative sense is easily felt.

(*e*) The demonstrative pronouns (generally those with initial vowel) and the personal pronouns may serve as relative pronouns, always having *onę* prefixed.

E. g., *uni sadom, onę unim kirińkede*, the horse that you bought; *ona khęt, onę ona teheńko rohoe akat'*, the ricefield that they have planted to-day; *abon, one abon nonde menak-bon,* we who are here (cp. the German way: wir, die wir hier sind); *iń, one iń noań gok akawat'pe,* I who have promised you this (ich, der ich).

(*f*) Some of the indefinite pronouns may be used to introduce relative sentences, thus *jãhãe* and *jãhãe okoe* for animates, and *jãhã* and *jãhã oka* for inanimates*. These function like the relative sentences introduced by an interrogative pronoun, but as a rule without *one*.

E. g., *jãhãe* (or *jãhãe okoe*) *pe ńamko agukope,* bring any you may find; *jãhãtak' bogepe metak' onage,* whichever you think good, that.

(*g*) A relative sentence proper has no finite *a* in its verb.

A good many Santals may, however, be heard to use this *a*, especially when the sentence has an interrogative pronoun at its head. When the finite *a* is used the sentence can scarcely be called a relative one, but is a disjointed full sentence.

The Indefinite Pronouns.

189. Santali has two indefinite pronouns proper; further, these two with an interrogative pronoun or another word added, and besides these a number of words that may be used as indefinite pronominals.

The interrogative pronouns when repeated, or, when getting *cẹ̃ń*, or *hõ* or *ge* with a negation, attached, also function as indefinite pronouns (see below para 191).

Some of the indefinite pronouns are used about animates, others about inanimates only. Others may be used about the one or the other, when needed taking a determinative suffix to show the animate or the inanimate.

---

* Any of the pronouns that ordinarily may have *tak'* added, may have the same added also when functioning as a relative pronoun.

For animates.	*For inanimates.*
Jãhãe, any one, some one, whosoever.	*Jãhã*, anything, whatever.
Jãhãe ọkọe, any one, whosoever,	*Jãhã oka*, anything which, whatsoever.
Jãhãe kahae, any one, some one or other.	*Jãhã kaha*, some or other.
Jãhãe tãhãe, any one, some one or other.	
Jãhãe man tãhãe, some one or other. *	

190. With reference to the above mentioned the following may be noted : they take the number suffixes. In the singular *ṭak'* is frequently added, in the same way as with demonstrative or interrogative pronouns. They also take postpositions.

The inanimate *jãhã* (with final single vowel) very frequently has *n* added, making it into an adjective that is used both about animates and inanimates.

E. g., *jãhãeṭak'*, any one ; *jãhãṭak'*, whatever, anything ; *jãhãn janwar*, *jãhãn kaṭ*, any kind of animal, any kind of timber ;
jãhãnic' (*jãhãnkin*, *jãhãnko*), any one ; *jãhãnak'* (*-kin*, *-ko*), anything ;
jãhã tinạk', howsoever much (or many) ; *dal jãhãnkemako*, they may beat you or do something to you ; *ńẹl jãhãn akat'am*, have you chanced to see it (at any time)?

191. Some of the interrogative pronouns are, as remarked above, in certain circumstances used as indefinite pronouns. The circumstances are the following :

* As to the pronunciation of *jãhãe*, *jãhã* and their jingles it might be remarked that while generally both vowels are nasalized some Santals in writing nasalize only the last vowel. The nasalization is often not very pronounced, scarcely heard.

(*a*) *Cọ(ṅ)* * may be added to the interrogative pronoun (single, or having a number suffix, or any postposition); *cọṅ* conveys the meaning of uncertainty and indefiniteness to the interrogative pronoun.

Ọkọe cọṅ, somebody, unknown who, whoever it may be.
Cele cọṅ, do., unknown which.
Cet' cọṅ, something or other, unknown what.
Oka cọṅ, something or other, unknown which.

Cọṅ must not necessarily immediately follow the interrogative. If it has especial reference to the verb, it is not compatible with the finite *a* (see para 326 (d)); this *a* is often left unspoken, even when *cọṅ* has no connection with the verb. *Ọkọe pẹṛa cọko hẹc' akan*, some visitors have come, whoever they may be; *calaoenako, oka họṛte cọṅ*, they went by some way or other; *ọkọeren kan cọko*, they belong to somebody or other, whoever it may be; *cet'ko cọe rọṛet'*, he is talking something or other, whatever it may be (also = nonsense).

(*b*) *Hõ* or *ge* with following negation added to an interrogative pronoun makes this serve as an indefinite pronoun. The negations *ba(ṅ)*, † *ọhọ* and *alo* are all used, *ọhọ* and *alo* always immediately connected with the verb. The negative verb *bạnuk'* serves the same purpose.

Ọkọe hõ baṅ, no one (lit. who also not).
Cele hõ baṅ, no one, not a soul.
Oka hõ baṅ, nothing at all.
Cet' hõ baṅ, nothing.

E. g., *ọkọe hõ bako cet' akat'a*, no one has learnt (or knows of) it; *cet' hõ bạnuk'a*, there is nothing; *oka hõ ọhọe ẹmlena*, he is absolutely unwilling to give any; *cele hõ alom lạiakoa*, do not tell any one; *ọkọege bako hẹc'lena*, not a single one came; *cet'ge alom rọṛa*, do not say a word.

* With a pronoun suffixed, it is generally, but not necessarily, only *cọ*; without anything suffixed it is *cọṅ*. The velar nasal is, however, often only slightly audible.

† What was stated regarding the pronunciation of *cọ(ṅ)* holds good for *ba(ṅ)*, with this addition that the full *baṅ* with the pronoun added generally conveys some emphasis (*e. g.*, *bako hijuk'a*, they will not come: *baṅko hijuk'a*, they will certainly not come).

(*c*) *Cetat* (or *cetat'*) followed by *hõ* or *ge* and a negation is used to serve as an indefinite pronoun, conveying the meaning of nothing at all. It is commonly used with a contemptuous side-meaning. See para 180 (c).

E. g., *cetat hõ bañ luraea*, he has no sense (or ability) at all ; *cetat'ge bae dhẹj daṛeak'a*, he is unable to accomplish anything ; *cetatak' hõ bañ kana*, it is nothing, of no account, valueless.

(*d*) The interrogative pronouns *ọkọe* and *oka* may reduplicated have the meaning of an indefinite pronoun, the first animate, the second inanimate. The reiteration conveys the idea of plurality ; when animate, the verbal construction has to be in the plural. Cp. para 31 (*c*).

E. g., *ọkọe ọkọe dọko mẹna*, some people say ; *oka oka jaegare ñamok'a*, it is found in sundry places, here and there.

(*e*) *Ọkọe* and *oka* are used like indefinite pronouns standing singly, but repeated in coordinated sentences or expressions. When functioning in this way the pronouns are always taken as referring to an indefinite plural.

E. g., *ọkọeko dọko baḍaea, ọkọeko dọ bañ*, some people know, others do not ; *oka ran dọ gune ẹma, oka dọ bañ*, some medicines give effect, others not (also : some times—some times).

(*f*) The interrogative meaning is perhaps never quite absent from these pronouns in the Santal mind.

(*g*) *Ja* and *je*, both recently borrowed, are now in frequent use, when used as an indefinite pronoun, with *ge* or another word added.

Ja uḍi, a little ; *ja ge*, whatever, wherever ; *je ge*, what ever ; *je kichu*, whatever ; *jẹ jẹmọn*, in accordance with ; *je ọtreko tahẽkanko*, as many as were on the ground.

192. Indefinite *pronominals*.

The language has a number of indefinite pronominalia, the most common ones being the following :

Adǫm, some (animate and inanimate, taking plural animate determinative suffix, and inanimate do. in singular and plural); *adǫm adǫm*, some; *adǫmko*, *adǫm adǫmko*, *adǫmak'*, *adǫmak'ko*, *adǫm adǫmak'ko*; *adǫm hoṛ*, some people; *adǫm dare*, some trees; *adǫm dǫ - - adǫm dǫ*, some - - others.

Adha, half; *adhan*, lit. the half, some, some - - others; *adhan menak'koa, adhanko calaoena*, some are here, some have gone.

Buje, some, some - - others (not used by all in this meaning).

Eṭak' (*-ic'*, *-kin*, *-ko*, with parallel form *eṭagic'*), an other, others; *eṭak'ak'* (*eṭagak'*) (*-kin*, *-ko*), another, others (inanimate). *Eṭak'* is used about both animates and inanimates. With reference to *eṭag* see Materials I., p. 82.

Kichu, some, a little; *kichu kichui phạria ńǫk' akana*, he has improved a little; *je kichu*, whatever (little).

Ar (commonly used as a conjunction to signify 'and') is also used as a pronominal signifying 'more', 'others'; also doubled, *ar arko*, others. Used about both the animate and the inanimate. *E. g.*, *ar ẹmǫk'me*, give more; *ar hoṛko*, other people (additional to already mentioned ones). Especially common combined with *hõ* (*arhõ*), also, again, more.

Ạḍi (with parallel forms *uḍi* and *ạṛi* or *uṛi*) mostly used as an adverb, but also as a pronominal meaning much or many.

E. g., *ạḍi hoṛ*, many people; *tin uḍi*, a few; *jāhātin uḍi*, some few, a little; note, *ạḍi* does not take final *n*; a word *ạḍin* is heard used, especially by women, in the meaning of shameless; it may possibly be *ạḍi*+*n*; if so, the connection is forgotten.

193. The language has a couple of words that function as indefinite pronominals and are of very extensive use, viz. *ia* and *eman*.

(*a*) *Iạ* functions as a kind of reference or indefinite pronominal, used when the speaker from some cause or other, also from excitement, does not for the moment remember the proper word or name that should be used. In this case the proper word is as a rule spoken practically at once, coming as a kind of explanatory statement; or the proper word may be supplied interjected by somebody present. *Iạ* is also used when the speaker from delicacy or some other reason wants to avoid using a direct expression, in this case leaving it to the hearers to supply a word or to understand what is meant.

Iạ is constructed as the proper word referred to would be constructed, as a noun, an adjective, a verb, or an adverb. It may refer to both animates and inanimates.

Iạ is ordinarily used corresponding to 'so and so', 'such and such', 'what-do-you-call-it', or similar expressions. Cf. its use in the postposition *iạte*; see para 93 (*a*).

Iạ is also frequently used as an interjection, in this case always at the commencement of an address, corresponding to 'I say', 'listen', or some similar expression.

E. g., *iạń ńẹlledea, hankateye calaoena, Pạṇḍuge*, I saw what's-his-name, going over there, Pandu (I mean); *iạ aguańme, mit̕ tẹć buler*, bring me so and so, I mean a rope; *iạkedeako, ḍanḍọmkedeako*, they did so and so to him, they mulcted him; *iạk̕ kanae, ńũrok̕ kanae*, he is what-you-call-it, he is falling down; *iạ buḍhi*, this unspeakable old woman; *iạ, do sẹ calak̕me*, I say, please go.

(*b*) *Eman* functions as a kind of indefinite pronominal referring to somebody or something similar to what is mentioned or tacitly implied. It may function as a noun (always in the pl.), or as the second part of a compound, in this last case corresponding to 'such like', 'that kind'. *

* While *iạ* in all probability is a pure Santal word, *eman* has likely at some time been borrowed from an Aryan source; cf. the Bengali *ẹmọn* and the remarks para 176, footnote, and para 158.

Especially with *teak'* or *ten* added *eman* functions as a noun or adjective, translatable 'such like', 'and so on', 'etcetera'.

E. g., tite dọ alom hạtrạua, emankoko takẹna, don't grope with your hand; various ones (e. g., snakes) may stay there; *noa birre emanko menak'koa,* in this forest various ones (dangerous animals) live;

emantenko noa dọ alope emakoa, do not give this to all kinds of people; *ñindạ motọre dọ babon calak'a, emantenkoko daṛana,* let us not go during the night; all sorts of beings (dangerous animals and especially witches) are roaming about; *bạṭi eman dọ bahrere alope bạgiak'a, kọe emantenkoko idikea,* don't leave cups and that sort outside, begging people and such ones might take them away;

edre eman bạnuk'taea, there is no anger or anything of that kind in him; *kul eman menak'koa,* tigers and such ones are there; *binti eman dọ bạnuk'a, mabon jọma,* there is no rigmarole or anything of that kind, let us eat;

hoṛko ñẹl emankema, people might see you or become aware of you; *añjọm eman akat'ape noa katha,* have you heard or become aware of this matter? *emanteak'ko ẹm emankema,* they might give you various (bad) things or do you something or other;

noa bajarre emanteak' ạkriñok' kana, in this bazar all kinds of things are sold; *dak' emanteak'tele harkhetok' kana,* we suffer from the lack of water and other things; *emanteak' jinis,* different kinds of things; *kaṭko, mat'ko, emanteak',* timber, bamboo, etc..

Eman is used in a very few expressions, prefixed to *dara*: *hạṇḍi eman darate,* with rice beer or stuff of that kind; *katha eman darate dọ ọhọñ pạtiạulena* I shall certainly not believe it by simply hearing about it.

194. The language makes use of an indefinite postpositional particle or pronominal, *tan.*

Tan has always a determinative suffix added (*tạnic', tankin, tanko* for the animates, and *tanak', tanak'ko* for the inanimate); it is always preceded by a base-word in the singular or a demonstrative referring to sound (*ọtẹ,* etc.); it may be translated 'such like', 'that kind', 'something like', etc. *Tanak'* may be used also with animates.

Tanak' is added also to verbs, often with a *pasęt'*, perhaps, in the sentence.

E. g., *toyo tanak'*, a jackal or the like; *toyo tạnic'*, do.; *otę tạnic' kanę bań dọ*, listen, perhaps it is he who is heard; *otę tanko pasęt' onko gạige*, listen there, it is perhaps those cows; *pasę uni dọm landa tanak'ade*, perhaps you laughed to him or did something of a similar kind; *pasęt'em ruhet' tanak'-lede*, perhaps you scolded him or did something of that kind.

The difference in meaning between *eman* and *tanak'* (*tạnic'*, etc.) may be said to be that the first expresses 'and that kind', 'and various', while the second more stands for 'or something similar'.

Indefinite pronominal adverbs.

195. Some of the indefinite pronouns, without or with postpositions, singly or as special compounds, may be adverbially used. It is especially the (from Bengali borrowed) *jãhã* (with compounds) that is so used. The following are examples only, not a complete list.

Jãhã gem calak', wherever you go; *jãhãre*, wherever; *jãhãte*, wheresoever; *jãhã sęc'*, in whatsoever direction; *jãhã khọn*, from whereso ever; *jãhã tinạk'*, whatsoever, however much; *jãhãtinre*, at any time during the day; *jãhãtisre*, at any time, whensoever; *jãhãtis jãhãtis*, now and then; *jãhãtin jãhãtinre*, now and then in the course of the day; *jãhã leka(te)*, in some way or other; *jãhã kãhã*, here and there; *jãhã tãhã*, here and there, somewhere; *jãhãn tãhãn*=*jãhã tãhã*; *jãhã man tãhã*, any where, here or there; *jãhãn man tãhãn*, *jande mande*, *jande lande*, *jande man tande*, *jande munde*, *jane tane*, *jane man tane*, anywhere, at random, here and there; *jatna*, *jetna*, howsoever much.

Bajek khanek, sometimes.

Some of the above mentioned adverbs, ending in a single vowel, take an *n* added and are turned into adjectives.

Compound adverbs, consisting of an indefinite pronoun with a postposition, are treated in analogy with others of the same class.

The Verb.

General remarks.

196. As previously (para 5) stated every Santal word may be used or function as a verb. The Santal word-concept differs from ours, in as much as it seems not yet to be fixed for functioning as only a noun, a verb, etc.

197. To show what is meant and intended, the functioning of a concept in its relation to reality, in casu, to make a word function as a verb, the word has to be treated in a special way, given a place in a sentence and, according to need, be supplied with the required working accessories. These are mentioned here below.

198 (*a*). A subject is needed.

Provided the subject is animate, it is always shown in the form of a suffixed personal pronoun (see para 108), added to the verb or to the word immediately preceding the verb. When the subject is a personal pronoun, it has to be repeated in its suffixed form in the verb, even when the independent form of the same is mentioned in the sentence, perhaps immediately preceding the verb.

When the subject is inanimate there is no subject pronoun to represent it.

With this exception that in case an actor or a force is supposed to be behind and to be the real cause of the action then the 3rd pers. sing. of the suffixed pers. pronoun may be and generally is used to indicate this subject, but only in the singular, however many subjects there may be according to our estimation. See para 24 (c). This subject is shown with the Active verb, and with the Medium when this has active meaning. In the Passive an inanimate subject is not shown.

Consequently a word may, without any accessory, function as a verb, not, however, as a finite verb.

E. g., hoṛoko casa, they cultivate rice; *calak'am? hẽ, iñiñ calak'a,* will you go? yes, I shall go (*calak'añ* may be said, but not *iñ calak'a*; it would have to be *iñiñ calak'a,* or *hẽñ calaka*); *holae dak'ket'a,* it rained yesterday; *hola dak' ñũrena,* rain fell yesterday; *amak' ghaṭkogeye baṛic'ket'mea,* your misdeeds have ruined you.

If the verb stands alone, i. e., is the whole sentence, or is the initial part of a sentence, the subject pronoun naturally comes at the end of the verb (in the finite verb after the *a*); when preceded by a word, the verbal subject is generally affixed to the preceding word. With the prohibitive *alo* this is invariably the case. When the verb has the copula *kan,* the subject is quite frequently added to this.

When two or more complete verbs follow each other without conjunction, the subject may be heard alone before the second and subsequent verbs without being affixed to any preceding word. In such cases it never has stress. *E. g., unreñ raskak'a, iñ hulasok'a,* then I shall be glad, I shall rejoice.

(*b*) What has been stated regarding the subject holds, mutatis mutandis, good for the object.

When animate, the object is always shown in the Active verb by an infixed personal pronoun (see para 109), whether it is a direct or an indirect object.

When the object is inanimate it is not represented, provided the inan. object is not supposed to represent some animate being (as sometimes in folktales). There is no inanimate pers. pronoun; an *k'* is, however, found representing the inanimate object in certain verbal forms and tenses.

The object infix, whether direct or indirect, always immediately follows the base functioning as a verb, if there is no suffix (i. e. in the Indeterminate or Future of the Active verb with direct object, and tenses formed from this by adding *kan* and *kan tahẽkan*, and in the Imperative). When a suffix of the Active verb is used, the object infix pronoun always immediately follows this. For examples see below under (*c*).

(*c*) In apposition to either the object (so generally in the Active) or to the subject (so always in the Medium and the Passive, but also in the Active) the Santal verb may take a pronominal genitive infix (see para 110), always following, but not necessarily immediately after, the object infix (see below under (*d*)) ; or, if there is no object infix, then immediately after the tense suffix, as, e. g., in the Medium and the Passive. With inanimate object this genitive infix may take, so to say, the place of an object infix.*

E g., *idiyeako*, they will take him away; *gạiye ạkriñkedetaea*, he sold his cow; *lạiaeme*, tell him; *lạiadeañ*, I have told him; *iñko dusạuiña*, they will blame me; *irket'taeako*, they have cut his (paddy); *cas khub hoeyentakoa*, they have got excellent crops; *khẹte aṛeyet' kan tahẽkantakoa*, he was occupied making ridges for their ricefields.

(*d*) Then we have a number of verbal suffixes, conveying meanings corresponding to our tenses, moods and voices.

The verbal suffixes always follow immediately after the conjugational base, pronominal infixes, if any, coming after the suffix, as mentioned above.

---

* Two genitive suffixes may be heard; in such cases the first infix refers to the object, the second to the subject. The late Mr. Skrefsrud in his grammer gives many instances of two possessive infixes in verbal constructions. Whatever may have been the frequency of such constructions when he wrote his grammar, they are now very seldom heard. I have heard the construction used with the meaning stated, not as given by Mr. Skrefsrud. I may add that I do not remember to have heard the double genitive infix used by men, but have heard them acknowledged as correct language by men. I remember an old woman saying with some pride, *họpọniñ dọ khubegeye kạmiket'laetiña*, this son of mine worked very much and well for him.

When a verbal form has *kan*, *tahẽkan* or *kan tahẽkan* added, the object infix always precedes these; a genitive infix may precede these, but may also follow the *kan* or the *tahẽkan*.

(*e*) With the accessories mentioned we have a word functioning as a verb. It does not, however, as yet refer to actual reality. To make a Santal verb do this, to make it function as a finite verb, the addition of a determinate *a* is required. This *a* has been called the finite *a* and also the categorical *a*. Its function is to convey the idea that what is stated in the verb will be, is or has been referring to actual reality. This *a* is probably a demonstrative element. See paras 150 and 330.

---

199. The Santal base-word concept being what it is, there may occur a need of showing certain verbal functionings in the base-word itself; how this is done in words with final single vowel and with final checked consonant in the Indeterminate or Future and the Imperative of the Active voice, will be found dealt with paras 240 ss.

Besides the alterations referred to, that may be classified as occasional, because they are restricted to certain forms and tenses, the language shows certain alterations of the verbal base of a different character. A fresh base may be formed by certain infixes or by the reduplication of an initial consonant with its following vowel. In this way the base-word concept is given a special significance, narrowed down in one direction.

These alterations of the base belong to the class of word-formation, only that they are formations effected at the present day with consciousness of what is done.

By making these alterations the language gets two conjugational bases that are dealt with here below, viz. the Performative and the Reciprocal conjugational bases.

The Performative Base.

200. When in the absence of verbal suffixes it is required to show that the concept of a word is to be understood as an active performance, or in other words, is to be seen from the viewpoint of the subject or the actor, the language has two methods of effecting this.

(*a*) One is to prefix to the base word its initial consonant with its folowing vowel. This method is, or may be, resorted to only with words having initial consonant or initial aspirate.

(*b*) Another way is to infix an *k̔*' after the initial or first vowel. See Mat. I., p. 76. This may be done with all base-words.

(*c*) A combination of both methods is sometimes heard, naturally only in words having initial consonant.

201. The rules followed are in the main these:

(*a*) As stated above, in words with initial consonant any of the two methods described may be employed, habit giving the one or the other method the preference in certain words.

Monosyllables with initial consonant have reduplication as the general, but not the absolute rule.

Polysyllabic words have a preference for the *k̔*'.

With reduplication of the initial consonant and following vowel of dissylabic words the first vowel of the fresh base has stress, sometimess to such a degree as nearly or wholly to eliminate the first vowel of the original word.

When monosyllabic words are reduplicated as here mentioned the second vowel of the fresh base has the stress.

E. g. bebenao and *bek̔'nao*, from *benao*, make; *dadal* (never *dak̔'al*) from *dal*, strike; *ńik̔'ir* (and *ńińir*) from *ńir*, run, hurry; *hẹk̔'nọsta* from *hẹnọsta*, despise; *kuk̔'li*, besides *kukli*, from *kuli*, ask; *sasna*, besides *sak̔'na*, from *sana*, desire.

(*b*) Words with aspirated initial consonant, when reduplicating the initial sounds, keep the aspirated consonant as the initial of the new base, while the second consonant of this is unaspirated. This rule naturally does not apply to words with initial *h*.

E. g., *jhajaṛ*, from *jhaṛ*, exorcise; *ṭheṭep'*, from *ṭhep'*, tap with the finger; *haha̤r*, from *ha̤r*, pick up.

(*c*) In words with initial consonant and following diphthong, when the reduplication method is employed, only the first vowel of the diphthong is heard after the initial consonant, the full diphthong following in the second syllable of the fresh word, having the stress.

If in the same class of words the form with inserted *k'* is used, this *k'* is inserted after the first vowel of the diphthong, followed by a slight repetition of the same vowel.

E. g., *la̤la̤i*, from *la̤i*, tell; *jajaora* or *jak'ora*, from *jaora*, collect; *ka̤uma̤ma̤u*, from *ka̤uma̤u*, make a noise, an uproar.

(*d*) Words with initial vowel always follow the method with inserted *k'* after the vowel, this being slightly, if at all, repeated, or in certain cases fully repeated after the *k'*.

In monosyllabic words with initial vowel this is always fully repeated, both vowels of the fresh base having a fairly equal stress, the last vowel, however, preponderating.

In dissylabic and polysyllabic words the first vowel is generally very slightly repeated, often not heard at all, and never written in ordinary writing.

Words with initial diphthong insert the *k'* after the first vowel, the full diphthong following the *k'*.

E. g., *ęk'ęr*, from *ęr*, sow; *ik'ir*, from *ir*, reap; *a̤k'a̤ula̤u*, from *a̤ula̤u*, disorder; *ak'aosan*, from *aosan*, relieve; *ak'ae*, from *ae*, estimate; *a̤k'gu*, from *a̤gu*, bring; *ik'di*, from *idi*, take away; *uk'num*, from *unum*, submerge.

(*e*) The Reciprocal form, when used in the Performative, only takes an inserted *k'*.

E. g., *ńęk'pęl*, make to see one another, from *ńępęl*, see one another, from *ńęl*, see.

(*f*). In compound words (i. e. words that are the result of observable or supposed combination) the reduplication or the insertion of the *k'* may be heard in the principal part of the compound, or, when in polysyllabic words such is not obvious, where found convenient.

In compounds consisting of two or more otherwise separate words, functioning as a base, the reduplication or the insertion of the *k'* may be heard in both words or only in one. In such cases it all depends on the relation between the words making up the compound.

E. g., *nijọjọr*, from *ni-jọr*, without strength; *kurumuk'ṭu*, from *kurumuṭu*, exert oneself; *puruchucun*, besides *puk'ruchun*, from *puruchun*, propitiate; *dadal gọgọc'*, from *dal gọc'*, kill by beating; *ńęńęl gọgọt'*, from *ńęl gọt'*, see off; *dadal babṛa*, from *dal baṛa*, strike now and then; *ńęl ạk'gu*, from *ńęl ạgu*, see and bring result back.

(*g*) With further reference to pronunciation see Mat. I., para 161.

(*h*) As mentioned para 200 (c) a combination of the two methods may be heard, mostly in bases formed from monosyllabics with initial consonant. The explanation of this redundancy probably is that the fresh base with reduplicated initial consonant is not felt to be strong enough. This double Performative frequently conveys the idea of some ineffectual attempt.

E. g., *dak'dal*, from *dadal*, from *dal*, strike; *lạk'lại*, through *lạlại* from *lại*, tell.

(*i*) To obviate misunderstanding it may be expressly mentioned that the alteration of a final checked consonant to its corresponding full, and the adding of an *e* or an *i* to a final single vowel, (both occurring in the Indeterminate of the Active verb) — never occur in the Performative. The final syllable of the Performative form is always the unaltered final part of the original base. It is *gogoc'*, not *gogoj*, (from *goc'*), *babṛa*, not *babṛae*, (from *baṛa*), *ak'gu*, not *ak'gui* (from *agu*), and so on.

---

202. This augmented base has been called the Intensive form of the verb. If, however, intensity is understood as implying the use of special activity or exertion, this name may convey a wrong impression. The name of Performative is therefore here adopted.

The form denotes the active execution, doing, performance of a concept, seen from the viewpoint of the doer. If we had not to use the term Active in its accepted significance, Active might have been a fitting name.

203. As active doing may be resultless, this form may get, and often gets, a side-meaning of ineffectual doing, used about people who are unable to do a thing properly. The performance may be ineffectual, in spite of exertion. In the spoken language the intonation will always show, whether such ironical and often contemptible application is intended. This use is mostly confined to the form with *kan* added.

E. g., *sisi kanae,* he is ploughing (may mean, occupied ploughing, but is very commonly used about one who does not know how to do it properly); *dakka kanae,* she is preparing food (often, just so and so).

204. (*a*) This form is used to denote habitual performance or activity: it is consequently also employed to denote qualities that make themselves felt, further the senses actively operating. The special use of this form to describe implements will be noted further on.

E. g., *dadalae,* he is in the habit of using the stick (from *dal*); *leknjet'a,* lit., it is slipping, causing to slip, i. e.

slippery (from *lẹñjẹt'*, slip); *ñẹñẹl*, see, do seeing (it is, e. g., the common expression used about going to see a festival, or the like), see, about the faculty of seeing, as opp. to being blind, from *ñẹl*, see; *ak'ñjọm*, hear, have the faculty of hearing, from *añjọm*, hear.

(*b*) The bare form is frequently used to express purpose or intention; the postposition *lạgit'* (*lagat'*) may be added.

E. g., *ñẹñẹlko sẹn akana*, they have gone to see (a festival or show); *sim kik'riñko kol akadea*, they have sent him to by fowls; *jọjọm lạgit'ko duṛup'ena*, they have sat down to eat.

205. As to construction the following may be noted:

(*a*) As remarked it is a purely Active form. It does not take tense suffixes. It is found only in the Indeterminate or Future tense and tenses formed from this by adding the verb substantive (*kan* and *kan tahẽkan*). The form may consequently function somewhat in analogy with the Present participle and the Infinitive of our Active verb.

(*b*) As this augmented base signifies only the performance of an action, it may be used referring to any time, past, present or future, according to the context.

(*c*) The form may be heard in the Imperative, but is very rarely so used and only (so far as the writer has observed) with certain words.* A foreigner using the language is advised not to use this Imperative. The Prohibitive (*alo* followed by the Future) is regularly used.

(*d*) The Performative never takes any object-infix to show the direct or indirect, the animate or inanimate object. With a transitive verb there naturally will be an object; but this is not shown or repeated in the verb itself by a personal pronoun being infixed, as is the case with the ordinary verb. The word representing the object of the

---

* Most Santals will not acknowledge a Performative Imperative as proper language, but consider it a slip of the tongue.

action is placed generally in front of the verb, or it may be only mentally implied, but not specifically mentioned.

(*e*) A pronominal genitive-infix (see para 110) may be used, always following *kan* or *tahẽkan*, when these are spoken.

E. g., *hola sahanko sak'gaṛ kantako tahẽkana*, yesterday they were carting fire-wood; *kakatteko hik'riye sẹn akana*, he is gone on a visit to his uncle's; *nui dọ ạḍiye hẹk'nụstawa*, this man is usually showing contempt, speaks contemptuously; *onkoko lạk'lại kanrege ac'geye hẹc'ena*, whilst they were telling he came himself; *alope lạlại babṛawa*, do not tell anywhere; *maṇḍa lak'gape*, keep the threshing cattle moving; *kathae khạk'ṭi kana*, he is making investigations to ascertain the truth of something; *tok'darote calaoena*, he went to investigate.

(*f*) When the finite *a* follows the augmented base having final vowel, the euphonic vowel is always *w* and not *y* (*e*), as might have been expected. An *e* would here be a redundancy or felt as a suffix of the Active verb (see below where the Indeterminate tense is dealt with, para 242 (a)), and the Performative does not take verbal suffixes. It is *ek'towa*, *babṛawa*, *lak'guwa*, etc., and not *ek'toea*, *babṛaea*, *lak'gaea*.

206. The Performative base may take the determinative suffixes. The suffixing of one of these to the bare form is the means by which the language shows, in the case of animate subjects, the doer, the actor, the person whose profession is denoted by the word, and, in the case of inanimates, that which performs or makes an action, or the implement with which an action is performed.

It should, however, be noted, that the form never loses its original sense. It may be used referring to an action in general, or to a special performance. This last will always be the case when the verb substantive is added with the determinative suffix following this.

E. g., *ńẹńẹlic'*, the one who sees (or saw), a witness, or a seer; *ńẹńẹlak'*, that which sees, the eye, or, a mirror; *raranic'*, one who applies or administers medicines (professionally or otherwise), a doctor; *bebenaoko*, the builders (of a house), the makers (of anything); *Bebenaoič* or *Beknaoic'*, the Creator, or the maker (the last form is not generally used about the Creator, but naturally may be so used); *sesreńko* or *sekreń-ko*, the singers; *potam akarsalko*, lit. those who at night throw light for an instant on doves, a common veiled name for witches; *kukṭamak*, anything to hammer with; *papaṛ-haoak*, that which makes reading, a reading portion or lesson; *mamarsalak*, that which gives light.

207. The Performative takes postpositions; these are dealt with paras 84 ss. Here two postpositions may be especially mentioned, viz., *ręe*, used to denote the sphere within which anything is or happens, and *tę*, used to show the instrument or implement with which an action is performed, or by which anything is completed; *tę* with the inanimate determ. suffix (*ak*) is a very common way of naming an implement.

E. g., *jǫjǫmre ńüńüre dǫ nokokotam peṛa, gujukre gurokre dǫ okorkotam oaris?* when eating and drinking, these are your friends, when dying and falling, where are your helpers? (a Santal saying); *bikcarreko gǫṛǫaea*, they will help him when judging; *kuṛi dǫkhǫtege hoyoktaea*, he will have to keep (marry) the girl;

mamakteak, anything to cut with, as an ax; *lalateak*, anything to dig with, as an hoe; *jǫjǫmteak*, the means by which one eats, i. e. food; *haklateak*, that by which refund is made.

Performative Passive.

208. The Performative form is, as already mentioned, Active and not Passive. But just as a form is needed to show plainly that active performance is meant, so a need may also arise to show that real passive is meant. This is effected by a reduplication of the Indeterminate Medium suffix, added as is proper, one might say, at the end of the baseword, i. e., *-ok'* + *ok'* or *-ǫk'* + *ǫk'*, or *-k'* + *ok'* or *-k'* + *ǫk'*, always in the form of *-ogok'*, *-ǫgǫk'*, *-gok'* or *-gǫk'* (these last forms when the Medium suffix after final vowel or diphthong is only *-k'*).

This form is a Passive Performative.

Like the Active it is used in the Indeterminate or Future and tenses formed from this by adding the verb substantive (*kan* and *kan tahẽkan*); in the Imperative, as a Passive Indeterminative participle and Infinitive. It takes the determinative suffixes and also postpositions, in analogy with the Active Performative.

As regards meaning we find this the same as that of the Active, only seen from the point of the object; the act of being performed is emphasized. It is often used in a general way to express what is customary or possible of being done, consequently what may be, or has to be, done; used participially as an adjective it often denotes quality.

E. g., *ẹmọgọk̔a*, will be given, is possible of being given; *rọṛọgọk̔ kana*, is being spoken; *nonka dọ baṅ rọṛọgọk̔a*, such is not spoken, or said (either one does not express oneself in such a way, such is faulty language, or, such matters are not mentioned); *baṅ lạiok̔a*, it will not be told; *baṅ lạiogok̔a*, it may not be told, it cannot be told;

ṅẹlọk'ak̔, what will be seen; *ṅẹlọgọk'ak̔*, what is visible; *baṅ-ṅẹlọgọk̔ak̔*, what is invisible; *siok̔ak̔*, what ploughs, the plough; *siogok̔ak̔*, what is ploughed, the field; *hoyok'ak̔*, what will happen; *hoyogok̔ak*, what has the quality of being able to happen; *jọmọgok'ak̔*, what may be eaten, food, eatable; *baṅ ucrạuk̔a*, it will not be pronounced; *baṅ ucrạugok̔a*, it cannot be pronounced.

The Reciprocal Base.

209. (*a*) A reciprocal base is formed by infixing a *p* after the first vowel of the word. As a rule this vowel is fully repeated after the *p*. This is always the case when the *p* is inserted in monosyllabic and more than dissyllabic bases.

As to stress: the reciprocal base follows the rules of ordinary dissyllabic and polysyllabic words.

(*b*) In reciprocal bases formed from dissyllabic bases the vowel may be omitted after the *p*. This is the case with a few common words where the reciprocity, although being presupposed, is often not the idea that has the stress; we often seem have a fresh concept, the original one being put into the background. *E. g.*, *oprom* (besides *oporom*), from *orom*, recognize, in forms like *ńepel oprom hoṛ*, an acquaintance, lit. people seeing and recognizing each other; *dapram*, meet, from *daram*; *bapla* from *bala*, lit. mutually strengthen, marry.

(*c*) In a few words with *e* or *i* in the first and *o̤*, *o* or *u* (having stress) in the second syllable, the vowel of the second syllable is spoken after the *p* (cp. para 47). Thus *epoto*, from *eto*, break in, train; *iputut'*, from *itut'*, apply sindur to the forehead of a girl; *eporo*, from *eṛo*, tantalize with food: *lipupuk'*, from *lipuk'*, deceive; *e̤po̤ho̤p'*, from *e̤ho̤p'*, begin; *sipukup'*, from *sikup'*, shut up; *tipurup'*, from *tirup'*, lean forward.

The rule is not absolute; they say *mepelot'*, from *melot'*, dart out the tongue, *sipiboṛ*, from *siboṛ*, stripe and rob, *sipiṛog*, from *siṛog*, mock. The composition of such words might perhaps supply an explanation.

(*d*) Words with a diphthong as their first vowel infix the *p* after the first vowel of the diphthong and have the full diphthong after the *p*; thus *upuihar*, from *uihar*, long for, remember with longing; *a̤pa̤ula̤u*, from *a̤ula̤u*, bring into disorder; *la̤pa̤i*, from *la̤i*, tell.

(*e*) When the first vowel of a word is resultant, both the vowel preceding and the one following the *p* become the corresponding ordinary vowel, except in monosyllabic words, in words with initial diphthong, and in dissyllabic words ending in *a̤i*. Thus, *apasul*, from *a̤sul*, support; *tapańgi*, from *ta̤ṅgi*, wait for; but *pa̤pa̤c*, mutually recede, from *paṭ*; *apaulau*, from *aulau*, disorder; *laparhai*, from *larhai*, fight. See Mat. I., para 26 and p. 30.

200. This form denotes reciprocality, doing the same to one another, meeting in performing similar action.

This meaning will always be more or less evident, when the word functions as a verb.

211. It should not, however, be forgotten, that the Reciprocal is not principally a verbal formation, but really a regular word-formation. The formation is also met with, where it is not principally a word functioning as a verb. In such words, functioning as nouns or adjectives, the meaning, conveyed by the infixing of a *p*, is that of a collection, a company, or even a class of such people as are designated by the simple word. The idea of reciprocality, i. e., meeting or coming together, is apparent, the word giving the result of a collective action of the single base-word. The grammatical construction is in the plural. The form is also used to denote the place where a collective action occurs.

E. g., *hapṛamko*, the ancestors; *rapaj*, the collection of kings, or (so generally) the class of kings; *Kisku rapajko*, the Kisku kings (a Santal tribe); *Marndi kipisār*, the Marndi rich ones (another Santal tribe so called); *mapañjiko*, the headmen, those of this class; *maraṅ hopon maraṅ kimin kapṭic'ko reak' ghaṭ guna jokhec̓ teṅgo hoyok'takoa*, the eldest son and eldest daughter-in-law have to stand up any time the small ones (*kapṭic'ko* from *kaṭic'*, small, little) commit any fault or trespass; *gipitic̓*, hunt's night camp.

212. (*a*) The Reciprocal form takes verbal suffixes, and also postpositions.

(*b*) The suffixes of the Intransitive and the Passive verb may all be taken, the suffixes of the Transitive verb only when the meaning of the Reciprocal permits it, viz., when a new concept has been formed, permitting transitive application. In this case the Performative of the Reciprocal may also be used, in the meaning of performing or bringing about the fresh concept. In this case the subject may be any number, also singular. Otherwise the subject of this form, in accordance with the meaning of reciprocality, has to be either dual or plural.

(c) Generally the Reciprocal is formed from the simple, unaltered base; in a few cases, when the original base is monosyllabic, the Reciprocal may be heard formed from the Performative. This is very rare.

(d) The Reciprocal form may be repeated (Repetitive form, see para 213).

E. g., *ńapam*, (from *ńam*, seek, find), meet one another; *ńak'pam*, make to meet; *ńẹpẹl* (from *ńẹl*, see), see one another; *ńẹpẹlket'kinako,* they made (let) them (especially used about prospective bride and bridegroom) see each other; *ọpọl* (from *ọl*), write to one another, correspond; *ọk'pọl kanakin*, they are engaged writing to each other (or attempting to do so); *ak'pasul kanakin*, they are engaged working to support each other; *ak'pasulić*, the one who makes some support one another; *tak'pańgi*, cause to wait for one another; *ḷạk'-pạṛhạị*, cause two parties to fight; *mapak' baṛayenakin*, they cut each other several times (from *mak'*, cut); *ḍapaṇḍọm baṛayenako*, they mulcted each other, got each other fined; *dapramlenakin*, they met each other (*daram*, meet); *gọpọ-ṛọk' kanako*, they are assisting one another (from *gọṛọ*, assist); *sapabok'pe*, catch hold of one another (from *sap'*, catch); *apasulokkin gọk akat'a*, the two have promised to support each other; *ńapam ńapamkat'akin*, they made unsuccessful attempts at meeing each other;

gipitic'reko bicạra, they sit in judgement at the place where the hunt spend the night; *gipitic' ṭhenko calak'a*, they go to do. place; *kulhi dupuṛup' khone hẹc'ena*, he came from the village council gathering;

gẹk'pẹr kanakin, they are biting each other (from *gẹr*, bite, and *gẹpẹr*); *gẹpẹgẹr* (through *gẹgẹr* from *gẹr*), actively biting each other (like fighting dogs); *ḷạpạḷạị*, tell against one another (through *ḷạḷạị* from *ḷạị*, tell; *ḷạpạị* means tell one another).

The Repetitive Base.

213. The repetition of the full base-word is a way of forming a new conjugational base. All words, functioning as a verb, also the Performative and the Reciprocal may be repeated.

This base takes all verbal suffixes, not incompatible with the meaning, and also postpositions, in all cases added to the second word of the new base.

214. The meaning is not different from that of other repeated words, except in so far as we have here to do with words functioning as a verb.

The primary idea is naturally that of repetition or continued performance of an act.

The form may further denote distribution, the repetition of the same act towards different objects or in different places.

Repetition of an act may further be an attempt to do a thing. The form may consequently convey a conative meaning. More especially when having an Intentional verbal suffix of the Simple Past of the Active Voice this form is used to denote an unsuccessful attempt.

E g., *taṛam taṛampe*, walk steadily on, hurry up; *ẹm ẹmọk'me*, give out, continue to give; *dọhọ dọhọket'añ*, I put it down (viz. consecutively, in different places); *ẹm emat'koae*, he gave them (distributed); *hạṭiñ hạṭiñ akawat'koae*, he has given each their share; *bañ dare dare akana*, it has not (as yet) grown much (so much as expected);

tahẹn tahẹnte, by remaining, as time passes; *duṛup' duṛup'teye lañgayena*, he became tired sitting; *bicạr bicạrteko añgaket'a*, they passed the night until dawn sitting in judgment;

ńam ńamkat'koań, I sought for them in vain; *sẹn sẹnkat'-ań* (note the Active suffix), I made an ineffectual attempt at going; *sap' sap'kadeań, bań sap' daṛeadea*, I tried in vain to catch him, but was unable to do so; *duṛup' duṛup'kak'ań, pasẹt' jăhănak'ko emań*, I shall try sitting down, they might perhaps give me something; *duṛup' duṛup'kat'ań*, I sat down in vain (e. g., waiting for something).

215. A special kind of reduplication might be mentioned here. The subject of the verb, when animate, is suffixed to the first baseword, while the second takes the verbal suffix, and a *sẹ* is frequently added after the finite *a*.

In this case the reduplication is somewhat different from the Repetitive described above, in as much as the repeated word alone functions as a verbal base. The meaning conveyed consequently is not so much repetition of an act, as a mode of drawing attention to intense performance. The construction is used to express the idea of something extraordinary, the limit of intensity.

This form is most frequently used taking the suffix of the Simple Past, but also other suffixes.

E. g., dạṛe dạṛket'a sẹ, birạmpaṭe dạṛket'a, he ran at the top of his speed, he ran heels over head; *dalko dalkedea sẹ,* they beat him something awful; *họeye họeket'a sẹ,* it blew tremendously; *ḍaṇḍọmko ḍaṇḍọmmea sẹ,* they will fine you without fail and mercy; *mōṛā mōṛāyena sẹ,* an astonishing number of clumps came out.

Constructed Repetitive.

216. A constructed verb, i. e., a verbal base with a verbal suffix and, in case, a pronominal infix, added, may be repeated, the second word taking what is needed to get the full verbal construction. The subject pronoun does not come in between the two words.

This construction always denotes constant repetition or continuation of an act.

E. g., peṛẹko sẹnako sẹnakoa, friends are constantly visiting them; *bẹṅgẹt' akak' bẹṅgẹt' akako tahẹnme,* keep a constant watch on them; *ona ṭhẹ̃iko sẹnak' sẹnak'a,* they are going to that place again and again; *ḍaṅgrae dalae dalae kana,* he is again and again beating the bullock; *ona jinis hoṛ ḍọko ṅẹlak' ṅẹlak' kana,* people are constantly coming to have a look at that thing; *manawae manawaepe,* warn him again and again (also: *manaye manayepe*); *gidrạị jọmak' jọmak' kana,* the child is eating again and again (running off and returning); *ṭheṅgae saṛak' saṛak' kana,* he is again and again catching hold of the stick; *bẹṅgẹt'ae bẹṅgẹt'aete tahẹnme,* have an eye on him constantly.

---

217. The Conjugational bases formed from the simple baseword by repeating the first two sounds, by infixing a checked or another consonant, or by repeating the whole word, are those described.*

Those hitherto described denote the Performative, the Reciprocal, and the Repetitive functioning of the verbal concept of the base-word.

218. Besides what has been mentioned, conjugational bases may be formed by the combination of two or more base-words, and by the addition of a postposition or other word or particle. More will be found on this subject, when the verbal suffixes have been described. Here we shall describe only two of these compound bases, the Causative (Permissive) and the Inchoative.

Other forms that have been styled conjugations will be found examined under the verbal suffixes where these forms rightly belong (the Continuative *aka* and the Intentional *ka,* both forming part of a series of functional suffixes).

---

* An attempt has been made to tabulate the conjugational bases of the Santal verb in analogy with the socalled conjugations of the Arabic language. The Arabic, or for that sake, every Semitic verb is inflectional and widely different from the agglutinating Santal verb, so a comparison may easily become misleading. The conjugational bases of the Santal verb are not so numerous that it is a relief to use numbers (as in Arabic) instead of a descriptive name.

The Causative and the Permissive.

219. By adding the word *oco* immediately to the conjugational base a Causative, or a Permissive conjugational base is formed.

(*a*) Constructed with direct object the form is causative; with indirect object (the socalled dative-suffixes) the form is permissive, denoting indirect causation, i. e., permission, leave to do, or absence of any attempt to prevent an act from taking place.

(*b*) The base is treated as any other base similarly formed by the combination of two different words. The verbal suffixes and pronominal infixes are added to *oco* (which otherwise functions as a verbal base with final single vowel).

(c) *Oco* may take the Performative infix *k*' and also the Reciprocal infix *p* (*okco* and *opoco*), and may be added to any of the above mentioned conjugational bases.

(*d*) As regards the use of *oco* it may be further noted that it denotes an action as willed and caused or permitted by somebody or something. Consequently the verbal subject is not the direct performer of the action of the baseword.

E. g. hẹc' ocokedeako, they caused him to come; *hẹc' ocoadeako*, they permitted him to come; *ńẹl ocoyem*, make him see it, show it to him; *ńẹl ocoaeme*, let him see it; *gọc'enae*, he died; *gọc' ocoyenae*, he was made to die; *gọc' ocokedeale*, lit. we caused him to die (an expression constantly used where there is no thought of intention to cause death, e. g. when a child in spite of all exertions to save life has died; death has been caused by the ineffective attempts to keep it away); *gọc' ocoadeale*, we let him die, permitted him to die, did not attempt to prevent it; *sẹn sẹn ocoket'leae*, he caused us to go over and over again; *sẹn sẹn ocokat'leae*, he tried over and over again to make us go (but in vain);

nuigeye ńapam ocoket'kina, this one made (caused) the two to meet; *ńapam ok'coic' dọ nuige*, this one is the one who caused (arranged) the meeting; *dal ok'coic'*, the one who caused the striking; *ẹk'gẹr opoco kanako*, they are making them scold each other (*opoco* occurs, but is very rare *ran ocok'me*, be medically treated (by somebody); *hakim thenko bicar ocokedea*, they brought him before the magistrate to be judged; *hakimko bicar ocokedea*, they made the magistrate judge.

(*e*) In a few constructions *oco* with indirect object infix may have a causative (not permissive) meaning. Direct and indirect object infixes cannot both be shown at the same time, so the one who is made (caused) to do something for somebody is referred to in the *oco*. Thus *ran kotec' ocoaepe* does not necessarily mean 'permit him to prepare medicine' (which it may mean), but 'make him (the ojha) prepare medicine for him (the patient)'.

(*f*) When *dare* is used as the last part of a compound verb, *oco* precedes this, and does not follow after, as is the rule. *Dare* is as an Active Verb constructed with the indirect objsect uffixes. This does not mean that *oco* with *dare* always has a Permissive significance; it may be Causative or Permissive. *Sen oco darcaeań*, may I let him go, or shall I make him go?

220. When it has been stated that in the Intensive (here called Performative) form only *oco* is 'intensified', i. e. that the base to which *oco* is added, is not made Performative, this is not correct; as stated above *ok'co* may be added to the simple base-word and also to the Performative. *Parak' oco*, cause to split; *parak' ok'co*, do.; *paprak' ok'coko*, those who cause to split, employers of such.

221. *Oco* is frequently used to show the sufferer, the subject of the Passive, when in any statement there might be some doubt as to who is the actor and who the object of an action. The Performative is in this case employed to show the actor. In formal statements before the village councils this form is constantly used. Thus: *dadalic' do nui, dal ocaic' do huni*, the one who gave the beating is this one, and the one who was beaten is that one there.

The Inchoative.

222. Compound conjugational bases may, as elsewhere remarked, be formed by the joining together of two or more words; such a compound base may also be formed by adding a postposition to a base-word. Among these there is one that is of constant occurrence and conveys a special meaning; it is therefore mentioned here.

By adding the postposition *lạgit'* (or its parallel form *lagat'*) to the Indeterminate tense of any verb a construction called the Inchoative is formed.

The postposition *lạgit'* (or *lagat'*,—there is no difference in meaning or use, some may have a predilection for *lagat'*, but on the whole *lạgit'* seems to be the most commonly used postposition) has several meanings (see para 96, a, b). In the construction here dealt with *lạgit'* is used to show that the verbal subject is on the point of, is just going to, or is bound to do or suffer what the base-word denotes.

223. While *lạgit'* (or *lagat'*) cannot be added, forming a fresh base, to any tense suffix proper, it is, as stated above, added to a constructed Indeterminate (or with this identical Future) tense of the verb, naturally eliminating the finite *a*. The principal word functions as a verb and may in this form take a direct or indirect object infix with or without an added genitive suffix. Further, if the principal word has a single final vowel the *e* or *i* of the transitive verb has to be added acc. to rule (see para 242 (a)); if it has a final checked consonant, this has to be changed in the same way to its corresponding full voiced one (see para 248). If the primary word is Medium or Passive, *lạgit'* (or *lagat'*) is added after the suffix *-ok'*, *-ọk'* or *-k'* (which is not a tense-suffix proper). The examples given below will show the use.

224. The Inchoative takes the suffixes of the Medium, the tenses occurring being the Indeterminate (or the Future)

and the tenses formed from this by adding *kan* or *kan tahẹkan* (i. e. the Definite Present and do. Imperfect), being in this respect analogous with the Performative. Other forms would not be compatible with the meaning of *lạgit'*.

A construction with the bare *lạgit'* (*lagat'*), in all respects following what is stated above, but always without any suffix and the finite *a*, is quite common. It is kind of participial construction.

E. g., *sẹnok' lạgidok' kanae*, he is on the point of starting; *gujuk' lạgidok' kan tahẹkanae*, he was just going to die; *rạṛạṛ lagadok' kanae*, he is just going to speak; *sabe lạgidok' kan tahẹkanako*, they were just on the point of catching him; *ńapamok' lagadok' kanako*, they will meet just now; *ọṇḍẹko atoe lạgidok' kan tahẹkanre ạk'yuric' dọe gọc'entakoa*, as they were going to found a village there their leader died; *seta dọe gẹgẹr lagadok' kana*, the dog is going to bite; *nẹko ńurhạ ocoak' lạgidok' kan tahẹkana*, they were on the point of letting it fall down; *bẹj lạgidok' kanae*, he is on the point of vomiting;

hijuk' lạgit'e, he is due to come (lit. on the point of coming he. Note the subject pronoun; if it had been the determinative suffix, it would have been *hijuk' lạgidokic'*); *nẹko ẹhọbọk' lagat'*, they are just going to commence.

The Verb Substantive.

225. Before describing the verbal suffixes we shall mention the Copula or Verb Substantive, its construction and use. The Copula is in Santali *kan*.

When functioning as a finite verb the determinative *a* is added. The different forms for the different persons and numbers are given here below, as an example, showing how the finite *a* and the subject pronoun (provided it is not attached to the word preceding the verb) are added in all verbal constructions.

Singular	*kan-a-ń*,	I am.
	kan-a-m,	thou art.
	kan-a-e,	he, she is (animate).
	kan-a,	it is, they are (inanimate, identical for all numbers).
Dual	*kan-a-laṅ*,	we two are (i. e., thou and I, inclusive).
	kan-a-liń,	we two are (i. e., he (she) and I, exclusive).
	kan-a-ben,	you two are.
	kan-a-kin,	they two are.
Plural	*kan-a-bo* (*bon*),	we are (i. e., you and I, inclusive).
	kan-a-le,	we are (i. e., they and I, exclusive).
	kan-a-pe,	you are.
	kan-a-ko,	they are.

226. Some variations in the pronounciation of the above may be noted; they all refer to the singular. See para 108.

Kanań is, especially by women, but also by men, frequently pronounced *kạnạń*, with resultant vowels due the omitted *i* of *iń* (see Mat. I., para 23).

The subject pronoun of the second and third person sing. is often, especially by women, added with a euphonic *y* between the finite *a* and the pronoun. Thus: *kana-y-em* and *kana-y e* (or even *kanae-y-em, kanae-y-e*). In such cases the stress is always on the finite *a* (see Mat. I., p. 90). *

227. *Kan* has not the meaning of existing; nor does it signify remaining or staying. For these concepts Santali has other words.

It cannot stand alone, but must always be attached to another word denoting the concept to which it refers. It can never precede the word or words to which it refers, but must always and immediately follow this or these.

The only, and merely apparent, exception to this rule is that it is possible in answering a question or referring

---

**Kan* in all probability is the Intentional *ka* with the formative *n* added (see para 59 (g)). In support of this the corresponding use of *ta* and *tan* in Muṇḍari may be cited.

to an immediately preceding statement, to use *kan* alone; the word to which it refers having being just mentioned is not repeated, but implied (e. g., *hor kanam? Kangeañ*, are you a Santal? I am).

A few examples will show the meaning and use, and incidentally the difference in use between *kan* and *ge*. See also para 59, (g).

E. g., *apum kanae*, he is your father (that is his relation to you); *apumgeae*, he is your father (not anybody else); *mĩhũ kanae*, it is a calf; *mĩhũgeae*, it is a calf (not grown up as yet); *boge kanae*, he is good; *bogegeae*, he is good (of good quality);

roret' kanae, he is speaking, doing speaking just now; *jojom kanako*, they are eating (at the moment of speaking).

---

228. To some extent corresponding to *kan* which always refers to the actual or supposed present time, the language has *tahẽkan* referring to the past. It denotes an incomplete (not finished) or a continuous action or state in the past; it generally corresponds to our Imperfect, was, were; but it should be remembered, that *tahẽkan* is not an Imperfect of *kan*. *

229. While *kan* is a pure auxiliary, *tahẽkan* is more, on account of the *tahẽ*, the idea of being, remaining or of continuation never being absent.

Tahẽkan consequently also functions as the Past of of *menak'*, to exist, to be.

---

* *Tahẽkan* is a combination of *tahẽ* and *kan*, *tahẽ* meaning to remain, stay. This *kan* is, however, not the same word as the just discussed Copula. If we look at the sister language Muṇḍari we have corresponding to *kan* a *tan*, and corresponding with the Santali *tahẽkan* we find *taeken*; In Ho we find the same. The difference is apparent in these languages.

We find further in Santali that the word *tahẽ* when having the Copula added takes the form *tahẽn*, meaning being, staying or remaining.

This *kan* will be found further mentioned para 291.

230. The use of *tahẽkan* in connection with the verbal suffixes will be shown below. When functioning as an independent verb, it is constructed like these, may thus have its subject pronoun attached to the immediately preceding word, which with *kan* cannot be done, because it is an auxiliary.

As a matter of fact *tahẽkan* is often heard as an independent verb added to a participial construction, where it might also be used as part of the tense suffix. Thus: *duṛup' akanko tahẽkana*, besides *duṛup' akan tahẽkanako*, they were sitting.

The Verbal Voices.

231. The Santal verb may be said to have three Voices, the Active, the Medium and the Passive, all formed by the addition of suffixes to the conjugational base.*

232. In connection with the different Voices the following should be noted:

(*a*) The Active Voice naturally functions in analogy with our Active, but is also often used to express the pure Passive. This is in analogy with the working of the language as stated in para 9 and elsewhere. It is naturally not Passive to the Santal mind, but the result or completion of an act, viewed from the standpoint of the actor. We have to translate it with Passive.

(*b*) The suffixes of the Medium and the Passive are identical.

The same suffixes are used to denote:

1. Passivity;

---

* Rev. J. Hoffmann in his Muṇḍari grammar calls the Reciprocal form a Reciprocal Voice. As elsewhere shown the form is of much wider application. The formation concerns the base-word itself.

2. Reflexive action;
3. Transitive or intransitive action, in connection with a number of words, corresponding to the Latin or or Greek deponent verbs.

(c) As regards the Passive: when the simple form is felt to be insufficient, when the Passive sense has to be shown so as to obviate misunderstanding, this may be done (only in the Indeterminate and from this derived tenses) by reduplication of the suffix (*ogok̉* or *o̦go̦k'* for *ok̉* or *o̦k̉*), as described above para 208. Very frequently in connection with the Passive suffixes the causative *oco* is added to show caused passivity. See para 219.

(d) The Medium or Passive suffixes may always have a reflexive meaning. The context only, not the form, will show, whether the meaning is reflexive or not. To make this clear a personal or demonstrative pronoun or some other word with the instrumental postposition *te* is often added. It will be understood, it is a special application of the Passive.

(e) Deponent verbs are in Santali very much like the same class in Latin or Greek, verbs with Passive suffixes, but Active transitive or intransitive meaning. It should, however, be noted that such construction is not confined to special words, exclusively so constructed. Practically all words used as deponent verbs may take the suffixes of the Active, but in many cases the deponent construction is preferred, where a corresponding Active suffix might also be used. The idea of the action is apparently emphasized, the object being put in the background.

As remarked, Santali has not verbs used exclusively as deponentia; this would presuppose a developement not reached and would be against the present genius of the language (see Introduction). There are words that are used practically only with the Passive suffixes when functioning as verbs; but all these may be used as nouns and adjectives and may take certain Active suffixes.*

(*f*) In the Passive the logical subject (the agent) may be shown by adding one of the postpositions *hoṭete*, *ṭhen* or the instrumental *te* to the word representing this. See paras 92 (a) and (c) and 93 (b).

233. The Medium and the Passive Voices may take Possessive infixes, these always having reference to the verbal subject.

Examples will be found under the different headings below.

The Verbal Suffixes.

General remarks.

234. Conjugation is in Santali effected by the addition of suffixes to the conjugational base. Of these verbal suffixes the language has three different sets, with separate suffixes for the Active and corresponding ones for the Medium or the Passive.

235. (*a*) One set of suffixes shows action pure and simple, transitive with a direct object, or intransitive, a statement of performance. All voices.

As an appendix to this set there are certain suffixes denoting a wish, what is preliminary, or a possibility, these suffixes being identical for the direct and the indirect object.

* As a curiosity it may be mentioned that the Passive or Medium suffix of the Indeterminate may apparenty be treated as a part of the baseword. We have thus *peṛa hoṛ*, a relative, a friend or a visitor, *peṛa hoṛok'* means to visit; this form may be heard used as a base taking verbal suffixes both Active (not with direct, but indirect object) and Medium as e. g., *aḍi ghaṛi bañ peṛa hoṛok'ape kana*, I am not paying you a long visit; *peṛa hoṛok'at'koañ*, I paid them a visit; *peṛa hoṛok'enako*, they visited.

(*b*) Then there is one set of suffixes corresponding to the first, but denoting action with indirect object. The corresponding Medium suffixes have a reflexive meaning.

(*c*) There is a third set used to denote action performed with a purpose, viz., as regards the result of the action.

As an appendix to this set we find certain suffixes denoting continuation.

236. The first mentioned set has suffixes for all tenses of the Active voice. The other sets have no suffixes for certain tenses, the Santal mind apparently not acknowledging the actuality and need of such. In the Medium or the Passive (suffixes are, as remarked, identical) no suffixes occur for the Indefinite Present and do. Imperfect.

237. From what has been stated regarding the Santal word-concepts it will be gathered that no suffix is needed to express an action in general, that is to say, when the word functions as an active verb. See para 198 (a). For the Medium and the Passive a suffix is in the same case needed, not a tense suffix, but a suffix showing the view-point from which the concept is to be regarded.

238. Suffixes are found

(1) for the Indeterminate and the Future (in the Medium or Passive, in the Active no suffix, except in certain cases, as detailed below);

(2) for the Present ;

(3) for the Past, *a*) performed, *b*) performed, but finished or superseded, *c*) performed and continuing in its results ;

(4) for the Preliminary and the Conditional ;

(5) for the Optative or Desiderative.

By the addition of the verb substantive (*kan*) and the verb denoting the unfinished continued performance of the Past (*tahẓkan* or *kan tahẓkan*) certain tenses are formed, viz. a Definite Present, an Indefinite and a Definite Imperfect, and two Pluperfects. These will be shown in their proper places.

239. As regards the verbal suffixes the following arrangement is followed here below: The different sets are taken separately. Inside each set the suffixes, etc., used to denote the different tenses will be shown under separate headings, the different suffixes being shown at the top. The Active, Medium and Passive suffixes of the same set are shown under the common tense-heading.

The examples will show, how the full verbal form is made up; the reader is for certain details referred to paras 197 and 198, and to para 225.

The verbal subject and the finite *a* are not mentioned outside the examples, except when for some reason it is necessary to deal with them.

Ordinary Verbal Constructions with Direct Object.

The Indeterminate and the Future.

240. (*a*) The Active Voice.

Suffixes: *Ordinarily no suffix.* For apparent exceptions see below para 242.

(*b*) The Medium and the Passive Voice.

Suffixes (identical): *-ok̔*, *-ọk̔*, *-uk̔*, or (after final single vowel and after certain diphthongs) *-k̔*.

Note: the language has no separate form for the Future tense; the Indeterminate functions, when required, for the Future.

Remarks concerning the Active Voice.

241. (*a*) The quality of the Santal base-word, as previously described, being borne in mind, it will be understood that the language does not for the Active voice need and does not use any suffix to express this tense. Every word may function as a verb; it is consequently unnecessary to add any suffix of a tense-character, when the concept of the base-word is to be taken functioning as a verb in general without reference to time.

(*b*) What is needed for this tense, in addition to the word functioning as a verb, is a subject pronoun (if this is animate), an object, when it is a transitive verb, and if it has to function as a finite verb, the finite *a*. See para 198.

242. (*a*) While in this tense no suffixes are ordinarily used, it should be noted that all words ending in a single vowel, provided they function as a transitive verb and have no pronominal object infix, get an *e* or an *i* suffixed, i. e., *e* when the final vowel of the base-word is *a*, *o* or *o̜*, and *i*, when the final vowel is *a̜* or *u*, this *e* or *i* forming a diphthong with the final vowel of the base. Words ending in *e*, *e̜* or *i* do not show this suffix, but the final vowel of the verb may be heard appreciably lengthened.* *Teṅgo-e-ae*, *laṅga-e-ae*, *a̜gu-i-ae*, but *e̜re̜-ae*, *idi-ae*.

Words with final consonant or diphthong do not take

* What this *e* (*i*) really is, it is difficult to decide. It is possibly a remnant of an object-infix. Muṇḍari has an *e* used as an infix for transitive verbs with inanimate object, even when the word has final consonant (see Hoffmann's Muṇḍari Grammar, p. 135). This may possibly be a demonstrative element. Against this might be objected that Santali in certain verbal forms shows an inanimate object-infix *-k'* (see para 24, c). In Kurku is (acc. to Mr. Drake's Kurku Grammar, para 106) found what is called an 'increase' vowel *e* added to transitives, and a corresponding *u* added to intransitives. To this *u* might be compared the above mentioned euphonic *w* in Santali, possibly also a *w* or *o* heard inserted, especially by women, between

this suffix, nor does any verb when taking an object infix.

The Performative and the Reciprocal do not take this suffix.

When the word functions as an Intransitive or a Neutral verb, no suffix is added to words with final vowel.

(*b*) It should further be noted that when a word ending in a single vowel has the finite *a*, the connecting euphonic semi-vowel for words functioning as a Transitive verb is *y*. *Nanha-e-y-ae*, he will make it narrow. *

With words functioning as an Intransitive verb and in the Performative the connecting euphonic semi-vowel is *w*. See para 205 (f). When the same word functions as a Transitive or an Intransitive verb, the euphonic vowel changes accordingly. *Nanha-w-a*, it is narrow, thin.

243. A word having checked final consonant gets in this tense this consonant altered to its corresponding full voiced consonant in the Active, when the word is functioning as a transitive verb, with an inanimate object, consequently without an object-infix added. With animate object infix the alteration does not take place except before an infix with initial vowel (i. e., *-iñ* and *-e*). *Bered(tabon)me, beredeme,* from *beret'*, but *beret'kom.*

The genitive infix does not affect this rule.

Before the *a* of the suffixes of a verb with indirect object the checked consonant is never altered. *Dak'ak'ae.*

When the verb functions as Intransitive the checked consonant is kept. *Beret'(tabon)me.* So also in the Performative and the Reciprocal.

---

a word and its determinative suffix, also when the word has final consonant (as e. g., *bereloak'* for ordinarily *berelak'*). With the Kurku *u* the *o* or *ǫ* of the Santali Medium and Passive might be compared. An *o* or *w* infix will be found mentioned in connection with the the indirect object suffixes of the Santal verb.

* In such cases the euphonic semivowel is not written. It melts into one sound with the *e* or *i* suffix. We write *nanhaeae*, not *nanhayae*, to show that it is not a euphonic semivowel, but a verbal suffix.

Remarks concerning the Medium and the Passive Voice.

244. *a*) To express the Medium or the Passive of this tense an *-ok̉*, *-o̦k̉*, *-uk̉* or only *-k̉* is added to the base. *

(*b*) *-ok̉* may be taken as the general form added to words with final consonant. After an open vowel in the base-word (i. e., *o̦* or *e̦*) it becomes *o̦k̉*, in accordance with the law of Harmonic Sequence (see Mat. I., para 42). When the base-word is a monosyllabic with *u* for its vowel, this suffix becomes resultant and may become *uk̉*, not, however, as a general rule. *Baḍaeok̉*, *ńamok̉*, *e̦mo̦k̉*, *e̦ho̦bo̦k̉*, *dulok̉*, *ńũruk̉*.

(*c*) A base-word with single final vowel in the Medium and the Passive takes only *-k̉*, the vowel of the suffix being eliminated. † *Teṅgok̉*, *laṅgak̉*, *o̦guk̉*, *idik̉*, *e̦re̦k̉*, *do̦ho̦k̉*.

(*d*) With words ending in a diphthong the use varies. Words ending in *ao* or *a̦u* as a rule take only *k̉*, although the full suffix may be heard, especially with monosyllabics (see Mat. I., p. 91, para 114). Words with diphthongs the second vowel of which is *e* or *i*, generally take the full suffix. *Laṛaok̉*, *bujha̦uk̉*, *la̦iok̉*, *ba̦iok̉*, *baḍaeok̉*.

(*e*) When a word with final checked consonant takes the Medium or Passive suffix, the checked consonant is always before the *ok̉* altered to its corresponding full voiced one. This should be especially remembered in connection with the Passive Performative, where *ok̉* is repeated (*-ogok̉* or *-o̦go̦k̉* or *-gok̉* or *-go̦k̉*, for *okok̉*, etc. ; see para 208). *Bagok̉*, *le̦be̦dok̉*, *ńumogok̉*, *ńe̦lo̦gok̉*.

---

* The essential part of this suffix is obviously *k̉*, which may possibly be compared with the *k̉* of the inanimate determinative suffix. See also para 242, footnote.

† The monosyllabic *si* (to plough) generally takes *ok̉* (*siok̉*, pronounced *siyok̉*) ; but *sik̉* is also heard. This is possibly the only exception to the rule.

245. The Indeterminate is naturally found in connection with all conjugational bases.

246. The Indeterminate tense is used to denote the functioning of a concept as a verb without reference to any special time.

247. It is consequently used to denote inherent qualities, general principles, universally accepted statements or truths, or statements believed by the speaker to belong to this class.

Further, regularly occurring actions or happenings, consequently general customs and habits, and recurring natural phenomena.

248. (*a*) The Indeterminate tense corresponds to our Present for the analogous meanings.

(*b*) As stated, the tense does not refer to any special time, but it will naturally be presupposed that the function mentioned is centered in the present time, i. e., the time of the speaker.

Provided the context directly or indirectly makes it understood that the function refers to some other time than the present, that it is centered in the Past or in the Future, there is nothing to prevent this tense being used. As a matter of fact such use is frequent. The statement must only be 'framed', so as to exclude doubt. It must, however, be understood that in such cases the possible cessation of the habit, etc., is not reflected on. Otherwise a past tense will have to be employed for what belongs to the Past.

(*c*) The Indeterminate may be used to denote the name of anything or anybody or of any concept (generally, however, with indirect object infix.).

249. As regards the Medium and the Passive of this tense there is no other difference in meaning than what is due to the difference in Voice.

As elsewhere remarked the Medium is often used to express the reflexive, viz. when the subject and the object of the act are the same. The Medium is also often, in connection with verbs, used as a deponent.

---

250. The language has no special form or verbal suffixes to denote the *Future* tense. The Indeterminate is functioning also for the Future. The context or the nature of the statement will show whether it is to be understood as being an Indeterminate or a Future statement.

This tense is used in final clauses.

In connection with a negative particle (*alo*) the Future is used as a Prohibitive, and with another do. (*ǫhǫ*) to express negative assurance; another tense, the Anterior, is, however, more common with *ǫhǫ*.

251. The examples given here below will show the forms and give the meanings.

Dakako jǫmu, they eat rice (or they will take food); *dakaeań*, (*n*)*utuiań*, *cundburuń* (*n*)*emaea*; (*n*)*ęnrę hǫe męna*, *nui* (*n*)*era dǫ bąń dǫhǫyea*, I cook rice, I prepare food; I give him heaps; still he says, I will not keep this wife (a Santal song); *bako bađaea*, they do not know; *bako onkaea*, they do not do so, such is not done; *din hilo'ko lạṛhąia*, they fight every day; *jel bako jǫma*, they do not eat flesh;

noa churi dǫ khub lasera, this knife is very sharp; *noa hǫtǫt' dǫ haṛhat'a*, this pumpkin is bitter; *alom haṛhada*, do not make it bitter; *kalawae*, he is deaf; *kuṛhiąwae*, he is lazy; *nui hǫṛ dǫ ạḍiye dadala*, this man is much in the habit of beating (people); *lại baṛaeae*, he is in the habit of telling; *lalại babṛawae*, he is always telling;

oṛak'e benaoa (or *oṛagae*), he will build a house; *gapae idikotaea*, to-morrow he will take his ones away; *ęm gǫgǫć-ako*, they are in the habit of killing by giving (e. g. poison);

oṛakreye tahęna, he will be staying (or, ordinarily stays) at home;

usąraeae, he will act (or, ordinarily acts) quickly; *ąḍiye usąrawa*, he is very quick; *usąrak̕an̕*, I shall be quick;

ąḍikin rupuhet̕a, they are scolding each other constantly; *n̕apamok̕alan̕*, we two shall meet; *sǫntǫrtebon pahrawa*, we shall be keeping careful watch; *sǫntǫrtebon pahrayea*, we shall watch him carefully;

nǫnḍę khǫn n̕ęlok̕a, it is to be seen from here (or will be seen); *gujuk̕ae*, he will die; *jǫtǫ gidrąko gujuk̕ tąkina*, all their children die; *nią khęt dǫ ban̕ dagok̕a*, this rice-field never becomes filled with standing water; *ąuri belek̕tege noa dare reak̕ jǫ dǫ n̕ũruk̕a*, the fruit of this tree generally falls down before it is ripe; *ona dǫ ban̕ udugok̕a*, that is not shown (or will not be shown); *piṭąu ocok̕ae*, he will cause himself to be thrashed; *ban̕ bujhąuk̕taea uniak̕ rǫr*, what he says cannot be understood;

ęmǫk̕ae, he will give; *ęmǫgǫk̕a*, it will be given; *ban̕ jǫmǫgǫk̕a*, it is not to be eaten;

hijuk̕ako, they will come (are in the habit of coming); *noa hǫrte rakas dǫ jaogeye hijuk̕ sęnok̕a*, the ogre is always passing this way going and coming; *noa bandreko ąbukok̕a*, they wash themselves in this tank; *khąrąireko ęnǫk̕a*, they thresh on the threshing floor; *gapa sunumle lęnǫk̕a*, we shall press oil to-morrow; *sǫntǫrǫk̕ae, jęmǫn aloe magok̕*, he will be careful in order not to cut himself;

alope rǫṛa, do not speak; *alom bąḍąiok̕a*, don't become proud; *ǫhǫe n̕ęlǫk̕a*, he will certainly not be seen.

252. Some remarks in connection with theuse of the Medium or Passive suffix of the Indeterminate or Future tense.

(*a*) It has to be borne in mind that *ok̕* in itself has no tense significance; *ok̕* (or, as the case may be, *ǫk̕*, *uk̕* or only *k̕*) simply denotes that the concept is to be viewed from a certain point, the object end of an action or the realisation of a quality, not, however, the concept finished, but the concept in the state of being finished or completed. When this is applied to time, we get futurity; when applied to the concept as such, we get possibility of completion, an indefinite or indeterminate reference to what may be, the undefined in stead of the exact, what belongs to the class or the group or the sphere in stead of the concrete or the exact place.

(*b*) With the determinative suffix added we get something or somebody described as belonging to the group, etc., of the concept mentioned.

(*c*) This use of the verbal suffix with the determinative suffix added is very common, also used where the construction at first sight seems strange to a foreigner. In many cases, if not generally, the use of this form seems to be connected with the Santal's instinctive dislike of committing himself to a definite statement.

Some examples will show how it functions; some examples of corresponding verbal finite construction will help to understand the use.

E. g., ńẹlok'a, it will be seen, or is seen; *ńẹlọk'ak'* what is or will be seen; *ńẹlọgọk'ak'ko,* the visible things; *bań-ńẹlọgọk'ak',* what is invisible; *bujhạuk'a,* it will be understood, is to be understood; *bujhạugok'ak',* what is to be understood; *kirińok'ak',* what is to be bought; *bań-hịrińogok'ak',* what cannot be forgotten;

rajok'ic', a zemindar, a man whose work or behaviour makes him out to be do.; *eńgat apatok'ko,* parents (in general); *mạńjhik'ko,* the village headmen (as a class); *ạpumok'ic',* one who is your father; *hạkimok'ko,* judges (as a class).

We have a somewhat similar expression in our languages; we may say, 'this is the owner' (in Santali *nui dọ mạliktẹt'*), or 'this will be the owner' (in Santali *nui dọ mạlikokic'*). It has nothing to do with the Future, except in connection with our personal perception or certainty.

Pon kọs hoyok'a, it will be four kos (eight miles).

(*d*) The same suffix is constantly used in connection with certain adverbs denoting time, naturally without any determinative suffix. The idea is to widen the sphere of the concept (see para 102).

Nitok̇, from *nit*, now ; *nitok̇e calaoena*, now he is gone ; *nitgeye calaoena*, he went just now ; this moment ; *holanok̇*, yesterday ; *holanok̇ din*, yesterday's day, from *hola*, yesterday ; *gapanok̇*, from *gapa*, to-morrow ; *mit' dinok'*, one day, some time (past or future) ;

tisok̇, when? (about any time in general), but never *tinok'*, from *tin*, what time of the day ?

253. As mentioned para 58 every word in Santali having final single vowel may take an added *-n*. In connection with such words functioning as verbs the following should be noted :

The base augmented by an added *n* follows the same rules as any word with the Medium or Passive suffix *ok̇* added, that is to say, this form takes no infixes, except the genitive infixes, and no tense suffixes, but may take the Verb Substantive *kan* and *kan tahẽkan*. The form is a kind of Neutral voice.

As to meanings see para 59 (e).

In a few cases this augmented base is treated as a fresh baseword ; the addition of the *n* has become fixed, a fresh word has been formed ; in such cases verbal suffixes may be added.

The word *tahẹn* might be specially noted ; the base is *tahẽ* with nasalized second vowel ; this is lost in *tahẹn* ; from this *tahẹnok'* is formed ; we have the word *tahẹnok̇ak̇* in the meaning of dwelling, 'remaining' place ; in the Traditions the following expression is found ; *bhagegebon bicạr akat'a, inạ acar ar bicạr baṛẹ tahẹnok' tabon ma nañ leka jug leka*, we have decided well, let this decison and agreement (custom) remain ours for ever and always.

E. g., *teṅgon*, standing (from *teṅgo*) ; *ọnḍẹ dọ alom teṅgona*, do not be standing there ; *teṅgon kan tahẽkanae*, he was standing ; *bạgin*, leaving off ; *uni ạuriñ hoeye dhạbic' bạñ bạgina*, I am not going to leave (him) until I have done for him.

The Indefinite Present.

254. The Active Voice only. Suffix : *et'* (*ẹt'*).

This tense is formed by suffixing *et'* (*ẹt'*) to the unaltered base-word. If the base has a final vowel the *et'* is added with a euphonic *y*, always spoken, but generally written only when the final vowel of the base is *e* or *i*.

Before an infixed personal pronoun (direct object infix) with initial vowel (i. e., *-iń* and *-e*) the *t'* is changed into *d*. Before the finite *a* it is, now-a days, also frequently changed into *d*, but not necessarily so. See Materials I, para 109, B. (c), (d) and (e). *

255. ***Et'*** may be followed by an infixed personal pronoun, showing the animate direct object, and by the pronominal possessive infix. See para 198 (b) and (c).

256. This tense is found only in the Active Voice and only in this set of verbal suffixes, i. e., in the set showing performance pure and simple, with direct object (if a transitive verb). The meaning conveyed (see below) would likely make it incompatible with any other form than the Active with direct object - also with the Intentional form.

257. With reference to the use of this tense the following may be noted :

The Indefinite Present tense (base + *et'*) is used to denote a present unfinished active function, without special reference to the present moment (see para 258). It might be said

* With reference to the origin of *et'* it is only possible to guess. The *e* may be compared with the same vowel found in demonstrative pronouns, in the Indeterminate and in other verbal suffixes ; *t'* is found as the final sound of a number of verbal suffixes used to form several tenses of the Active verb, with both direct and indirect object (*ket'*, *let'*, *at'*, *kat'*, *akat'*, *akawat'*). It obviously refers to active performance, the doing, just as *n* in corresponding Medium and Passive suffixes refers to performed action.

to be the Indeterminate narrowed down to the present time, it may be to the day, the season, the year or even longer periods.

It presupposes that the subject is occupied with what has been commenced, possibly at the present moment, but not necessarily so. The present moment has no stress and is not urged, but the tense is often used when a rigorously exact expression would seem to demand the Definite Present.

This tense is consequently not used like the Indeterminate or our Present about custom or habit. The action is understood as having commenced, and there is a supposed continuing or repetition of the act.

The following examples will show the use :

Hoṛoko rọhọeyet'a, they are planting rice (at the present time, not necessarily just now) ; *sokṛare khẹtle benaoet'a,* we are making ricefields in the depression ; *bogeko bicạret'a,* they are judging well ; *Maraṅ buru dọ mē̱ṛhē̃t' ṭenṭateye sọbọk' daramet'koa, onate arhọ̃ baṛti dukgeko ńamet'a,* Maraṅ buru stabs them with a fish-spear of iron (when they try to get up) ; thereby they get still more woe ; *Kandna ińren barea gạiye gupiyet'kintińa,* Kandna is herding my two cows (he has undertaken that work) ; *nẹs dọ bae daket'a,* it does not rain this year.

The Definite Present.

258. The Active voice. Suffix : *et' - kan,* added to the base.

The Medium and the Passive. Suffix: *(o)k' kan,* added to the base.

This tense is formed by adding the Verb Substantive *kan,* in the Active to the Indefinite Present, and in the Medium and the Passive to the Indeterminate Medium or Passive.

As regards construction it should be noted that in the Active Voice the direct object infix always comes after *et'.*

A pronominal possessive infix follows the object infix or comes after *kan*, where it seems to be preferred. See para 198 (b) and (c).

In the Medium and the Passive Voice the pronominal possessive infix, if used, comes after *kan*.

259. To understand this and other tenses with *kan* attached the actual meaning of *kan* should be kept in mind (see above paras 225-27). The verbal construction to which *kan* is added must be understood as a kind of participle.

When *kan* is added the subject is shown as at the time actively doing or being what the word, with its suffixes, etc., added, denotes.

Kan may consequently only be added to participles that denote incomplete (not finished) action or a continual state.

260. The Definite Present is used to denote what is being done at the present moment, i. e., the time of the speaker or the time referred to.

It is also used about what is constantly being done, what is always happening.

261. As regards the Medium and the Passive the following should be noted: This voice has in all sets of suffixes one form for both the Indefinite and the Definite present.

The cause of this is probably to be sought in the meaning attached to the Medium and the Passive Indeterminate. The act is seen from the side of the object; the agent is hidden; it is something happening, and with the Verb Substantive added it will depend on the meaning of the base-word, whether it is to be understood as something of an indefinite nature belonging to the present, or as something belonging to the present moment.

262. *E. g., bogeteko rak'et' kana,* they are crying very much (just now); *cedak'pe tiąk'ede kana?* why are you lead-

ing him (by a string or the like)? *gaiko idiyet'ko kantaea*, they are just now taking his cows away; *bale arak'ede kana*, we are not letting him loose (so is not our intention);

Candoe ńglet'bon kana, God is seeing us;

onakoreye okok' kana, he is hiding in those parts; *nia cando horoko irok' kana*, this month they are reaping paddy; *dak' ńũrok' kana*, water is falling (rain); *hijuk' sgnok' kanae*, he is constantly going and coming; *abukok' kanae, hijuk'ae nãhãk'*, he is having a wash, he will come presently; *rane emok' kana*, he is giving medicine; *sarimteye dejok' kana*, he is mounting the roof (just now).

263. Verbs with suffixed *n* are used with *kan* added. A pronominal possessive infix may be heard after *kan*. This form is always intransitive in meaning. *Teṅgon kanae*, he is standing; *teṅgok' kanae*, he is standing up, rising (just now); *teṅgon kan tiṅae*, my one is standing.

Such a form might, however, be said to be a verbal adjective with the Copula added. See para 59, (e).

264. When the direct object is animate and the infixed pers. pronoun is that of the 1st or 3rd pers. sing. *kan* is frequently added to the Indeterminate form. In this case the pronominal infix (*-iń*, *-eń*, or *-e*, *-g*) always has the stress.

Formally this form may be compared with the Definite Present tense of the verb with indirect object, or of the Medium and the Passive.

It is strange that this form is used only in connection with the two infixed pronouns mentioned. Phonetic considerations (the stress) may possibly have something to do with it. The verbal base melts into one stress-unit with the infixed object pronoun. This form is especially frequent with monosyllabic bases, but is not restricted to these.

The meaning is the same as that of the Definite Present; Santals will not acknowledge any difference. *

E. g., *ńeleń kanae*, he is seeing me; *dale kanako*, they are beating him; *aguye kanako*, they are bringing him.

The Indefinite Imperfect.

265. The Active Voice. Suffix : *et' - tahẽkan*, added to the base.

The Medium and the Passive : wanting.

This tense, like the Indefinite Present found only in the Active Voice, is formed by adding *tahẽkan* to the Indefinite Present. As regards infixes the same rule is valid for this tense as for the Indefinite Present. The pronominal direct object infix comes immediately after *et'*; the possessive infix (if any) may precede or come after *tahẽkan*.

266. As the construction shows this is the Indefinite Present transposed to the past. It denotes a commenced, but unfinished function in the past, without stress on the moment; something was happening or being done at some time in the past.

This tense is also used to denote what was customary or a habit in the past, i. e., past repeated action.

---

* When Mr. Skrefsrud in his grammar says that the Definite Present (Special Incomplete Present, as he calls this tense) may have a conative meaning ('something is being tried to be effected, but is failing'), the conative meaning is due, not to the verbal form, but to the particular meaning of the base-word and the object employed. He gives as an example *hakoe sabe kana*, he is catching a fish. To be occupied catching one fish (note the object infix) is naturally caused by the inability to catch it at once, which gives a conative meaning. On the other hand *dale kanae*, he is beating him, has nothing conative in it, it would seem rather the other way.

When something is going on at a particular moment, and then something supervenes, the action described may naturally seem to become conative ; it is interrupted at any particular moment and not finished ; this is what there is to it.

E. g., *din kalom noa godare janheko caset' tahẽkana*, last year they were cultivating millet in this field; *calaoen haptare adiye dak'et' tahẽkana*, last week it was raining very much; *mõrẽ hor samanre ma cet' katha hõ bam roret' tahẽkana; ado endekhan nitok' do cet' mocatem roret'a?* you did not speak a single word before the village council; then what mouth are you speaking with now? *ita do negeye er cabayet'tae tahẽkana, khan jhomor jhomor dak'e ehop' got'ket'a*, he was just on the point of finishing sowing; then it suddenly commenced to rain heavily; *noa bandre uniren hakole sap'et'ko tahẽkantaea*, we were catching his fish in this tank;

sedae jugre bulunko benaoet' tahẽkana, in olden times they were making salt; *Tudu hor do mẽrhẽt' reak' khanda bhandako benaoet' tahẽkana*, the Tudu sept were making iron implements and weapons.

The Definite Imperfect.

267. The Active Voice. Suffix: *et' - kan tahẽkan*, added to the base.

The Medium and the Passive. Suffix: *(o)k' kan tahẽkan*, added to the base.

This tense is formed by adding *tahẽkan* to the Definite Present. As regards infixes the pronominal direct object infix is added to *et'*; the possessive infix may stand just after the object infix; as a rule it will come after *kan* or after *tah kan*.

268. As to the meanings of this tense:

(*a*) It is the Definite Present transferred to the past; consequently the meanings stated as applying to the Definite Present are applicable, only that the whole refers to the past. The tense denotes what was being done or happening at a particular time or moment in the past. The act was unfinished at the time referred to.

(*b*) Just as the Definite Present has been stated to convey a conative meaning, so the same has been said about this; but as there it is here also the meaning of the verbal base and the verbal object that will give the conative meaning, not the form itself. See para 264, footnote.

(c) As regards the Medium and the Passive all holds good that has been said about the Active when the reservations due to the difference in Voice are taken, and the reflexive and deponent possibilities of the Medium are kept in mind.

Further : In the Medium and the Passive this tense, being the only one for the Imperfect, may be used also about what was generally (to the Santal mind possibly always) happening, without reference to any particular time in the past.

E. g. hakoe sap'et'ko kan tahẽkana, he was (at some particular moment) occupied catching fish ; *jelko sendrayede kan tahẽkanre mit'ṭen banako ńamkedea,* as they were chasing a deer they met a bear ;

daka isinok' kan tahẽkantabona, our food was being cooked ; *ińiń calak' kan tahẽkanre uni dọe hẹc'ena,* just as I was going away he came ; *nọndẹ khon onkoak' ọrak' dọ ńẹlok' kan tahẽkana, nitok' dọ darete danańena,* their house was to be seen from here, now it has been hidden by trees ; *Kharwar ńutumtele bikạuk' kan tahẽkana,* we were being called Kharwars : *sedaerele ńapamok' kan tahẽkana,* formerly we were in the habit of meeting ; *gidrạ dọ churiteye gẹdok' kan tahẽkana,* the child was cutting itself on a knife.

269. Besides the forms mentioned we have for this tense a form with *et'* omitted, corresponding to the form mentioned para 264. *Dale kantiń tahẽkanako,* they were occupied beating my one (at a particular time) ; *ńẹleń kan tahẽkanae,* he was seeing me.

Verbs with suffixed *n* are also used in this tense.

E. g. teńgon kan tahẽkantińae, my one was standing (at that particular time) ; *teńgok' kan tahẽkanae,* he was rising, standing up.

The Simple Past.

270. The Active Voice. Suffix : *ket'* (*kẹt'*).

The Medium and the Passive Voice. Suffix : *en* (*ẹn*).

The Simple Past tense (also called Recent Past and Aorist I) is formed by adding in the Active *ket'* (*kẹt'*), and in the Medium and the Passive *en* (*ẹn*), to the conjugational base.

The original vowel seems to be *ẹ*; in accordance with the laws of Harmonic Sequence this is changed to *e* when followed by vowels other than *ẹ*. For the sake of convenience only *ket'* and *en* are written. When followed by the direct object infixed pronoun of the 1st p. sing. (*iń*), *ket'* and *iń* melt into one stress unit with stress on the *i*; the is then generally, but not always, changed into *i* (*kidiń*).

As regards the change of *t'* into *d*, see remarks on *et'* (para 254); there is no difference, the same rule is valid for both *et'* and *ket'*, and for all verbal suffixes with final *t'*.

The infixed pronouns of the direct object follow the *ket'* immediately, and thereafter the possessive infix, if any, will come.

The Medium and the Passive are formed by adding *en* (*ẹn*) to the verbal base. The possessive infix, if any, follows immediately after *en*.

271. This tense is used to denote that the concept of the base-word has been performed. It signifies the Simple Past without complications or connotations: the act is done.

It is consequently the tense used as historic, i. e., to narrate past events or happenings.

The reflexive and deponent meanings of the Medium should be borne in mind.

The Simple Past is not used with negations, when these function as such.

E. g., *mẹnket'ae*, he said; *potame ṭuṭikedea*, he shot the dove (with an arrow); *mit' mit'teko sap' idiket'lea raj atote; ọnḍẹ mit' cando leka dọhọkate Kumbrạbadteko ạguket'lea*, they caught all of us and took us to the zemindar's village; having kept us there something like one month they brought us to Kumrabad; *sukriko gọc'kedetiñа*, they killed my pig;

sim rak'reko hẹc' gọt'ena, they arrived just at cock-crow; *kũi dak' bọḍẹyen takore hõ dak' lolo dọ bako bạgilet'a*, although the water of their well became muddy they did not leave off drawing water (note *bạgilet'*, not *bạgiket'* on account of the negation); *gẹt'enań*, I cut myself; *họpọnerae ẹmena*, he gave his daughter;

jạnumiń rọk'ena, I was pricked by a thorn; *am ṭhen ńamena*, it was found with you; *gọc'en tińae họpọniń dọ*, he died my son;

beret'en ńamen, hụni tora huń marteye oḍok calaoen, he got up without warning, off he went in a hurry.

272. (*a*) In vivid narratives the Simple Past tense may be changed into the Present; and in the same way general statements of what is commonly done may be told in the Indeterminate alternating with the Simple Past.

The natural explanation of this is that the narrator 'sees' the happenings described and uses the tenses pertaining to what he 'sees'.

E. g., *onakate jọlọ maejiuko nim dak' mạṇḍiko emakoa; adọ chut meṭaoena, ar gidrạ dọ peṛa talateye bọlọyena*, thereupon they give all the women rice-water with neem; so the religious pollution is wiped out, and the child has come in among the friends (i. e., is henceforth a recognized member of the family); *khange Jhõrẽ dọe dạṛket'a; adọ Bạjun dọ kạpi ńamkate lagae lagayedea sẹ, bẹbạṛic'e lagayede kana; khange adọ mit'ṭań birreye laga at'kedea*, then Jhore ran away; so Bajun took a battle-axe and chased him; he chased him something awful; he chased him until he lost him in a forest; *hoṛo rọhọe din nonka hoeyena, kạmi sạrdiyena mẹnkhan guti koṛa oṛak'te dọ bae hijuk'a*, during the paddy planting season it so happened, that when the work got into full swing, the servant boy was not in the habit of coming to the house; *adọ dihri dọe gạṛpuc'ena, cet'e mẹna bạpuṛic' dọ*, then the hunt-priest becomes (lit. became) downhearted, what can he say, poor fellow?

In narratives the Simple Past with finite *a* is frequently used in describing consecutive events as they generally happen. The narrator 'sees' the different acts performed and describes them as such, although the whole has no reference to something actually happened, only to what is generally done. The long description of the marriage ceremonies in the *Hapṛamko reak' katha* abounds in examples of this.

(*b*) The Simple Past suffix may also be used, where we would use the Pluperfect.

E. g., *Ạimạị reak' etrañ dọ apạṛite bale dạbire tuṅ tap'ket'me leka*, a woman's snappish word is like just as if you had got an arrow shot through your back below the shoulder blade.

The Anterior Past.

273. The Active Voice. Suffix: *let'* (*lẹt'*).

The Medium and the Passive Voice. Suffix: *len* (*lẹn*).

The Anterior Past tense is formed by suffixing in the Active *let'* (*lẹt'*), and in the Medium and the Passive *len* (*lẹn*), to the conjugational base.

What has been stated as to form and infixes in connection with *ket'* and *en*, holds good for these suffixes; there is in these respects no difference. *

274. This tense is used to denote what was done or happened previous to some other event. It denotes a performed action. This may be something that happened long ago, so long ago that the performance is no longer observable. The tense may consequently be used in describing historic events of some time ago or of a former age.

Or it is used to denote a past action, the effect of which

* The difference in form between the suffixes of the Anterior Past and those of the Simple Past is, as is seen, that we here have an initial *l*, while we there have an initial *k* or no initial consonant (in the Medium). We find an initial *l* in another tense, the Preliminary (*le* and *len*), and it is probably the same that we have here. The idea of the preliminary or anterior is observable in the use of this tense.

has been nullified, neutralized, superseded or revoked, formally or by some subsequent action or event; also an action that took place anterior to some other action in the past.

The possible reflexive and deponent meanings of the Medium and the Passive should be borne in mind.

The tense is fairly frequently used in narratives about what happened or took place sometime or other, where one might expect the Simple Past; the action is looked on as performed and finished, without reflecting on whether its effect has been done away with or not. It is an action performed earlier than the time of the speaker or narrator. The tense may often be translated by our Pluperfect.

E. g., *ńel khusi baṛakate pọrthọm dọko lại̤a Saharjuṛiko ato maṛańlet'a*, being pleased at what they had seen, at first, they tell, they first founded Saharjuri village; *eṭak'ic'e bạhuana, tọbẹ ena gidrạ dọe haralet'koa*, he married another woman, then only he got grown up children; *sedae jugre, kathae, nonka hoelena, mit'ṭań bir ạdi bạṛić bagahilena*; *ona birre mit'ṭen ṭạrup' ạḍi bạṛic'e cankelena*, in a former age, people tell, it so happened that a forest became awfully dangerous through wild animals; in this forest a leopard became very fierce;

idiledeań, arhõe hẹc' ruạṛena, I took him away (there); he is again returned; *nọnḍẹko oṛak'let'a, ńirenako*, they built a house here, they have run away; *tọlledeako*, they tied him (he is free now); *ńẹlledeań*, I saw him (but lost sight of him; *ńẹlkedeań*, I caught sight of him, simply stating the fact); *pẹ pon mãhã bọhọk' haso ńọk'ledea, inạtegeye gọc'ena*, he had a slight headache for three four days, from that he died; *holae sẹnlena, teheń dọ oṛak're menaea*, he went yesterday, to-day he is at home;

ṭańgateń mak'lena, I cut myself with an axe (am well now); *ṭakae ẹmlena*, he gave (paid) the money (long ago).

275. While *ket'* and *en* cannot be used with negations, *let'* and *len* are the suffixes used in verbal construction for the simple negation of the past, to state that something

was not done or did not take place. This shows the logical working of the language.

It should, however, be noted that this refers to real negations. When *baṅ* is used in conditional sentences, or in questions with the meaning of negation obliterated (as an assertion), *ket'* and *en* may be used.

E. g., bako sap'ledea, they did not catch him; *daka bae jọmlet'a teheṅ*, he did not take food to-day;

bam kạmiket'a mẹnkhan dọṅ jobabket'mege, if you do not work, I shall dismiss you; *bae dạrket'a?* did he not run away (why, he did); *adọ kaje bae ọr ṅūrket'mea*, then did he not drag you down? (of course, he did); *hẹc'enae baṅ*, why, he has come.

The Anterior Pluperfect.

276. The Active Voice. Suffix: *let' - tahẽkan.*

The Medium and the Passive. Suffix: *len tahẽkan.*

This tense, also called Indecisive Pluperfect, is formed by adding *tahẽkan* to the Anterior Past.

As regards infixes, these follow in the Active the rules mentioned for the Indefinite Imperfect (*et' - tahẽkan*) and, in the Medium and the Passive, the rules of the Definite Imperfect, only that here *len* comes in the place af *ok' kan*

The tense might with some right be called Anterior Imperfect; Pluperfect has been kept, because we generally have to render the tense by our Pluperfect.

277. This tense is used to denote that something had been done or had happened, but had been neutralized, superseded or revoked in the past. It might be said, that the Anterior Past is transferred to a continuative state in the past, so to say framed in a past state.

The tense is also used to denote that something was attempted, was going to happen in the past, but was not done or finished, because something came to prevent it.

The possible reflexive or deponent meanings of the Medium and the Passive should be borne in mind.

E. g., cet' lạgit'em sẹnlen tahẹ̄kana, ma sẹ lạiań talańme, please tell me for what purpose you had gone; *rẹńgẹc' jalate Asamtele sẹnlen tahẹ̄kana, adọ ọṇḍẹ họ̃ bale dhẹj daṛeat'a*, not being able to maintain ourselves (lit. on acc. of hunger pain) we went for a time to Assam; but we were not able to manage there either; *umok'iń sẹnlen tahẹ̄kana, adọ dak' bọḍẹ iạte bạń umlena*, I had gone to take a bath, but as the water was muddy I did not bathe; *hẹc'len tahẹ̄kanań noa lạiam lạgit'*, I had come to tell you this (said by a man who had come during the bespoken man's absence, and who had remained waiting until arrival);

idilet'ko tahẹ̄kantińako, adọ nuiyẹyẹ ạgu ruạṛket'koa, they had taken my (animals) away, then this one brought them back;

nẹsge marań koṛa dẹe hẹc'len tako tahẹ̄kana, this year their eldest son came (on a visit, but is gone again); *alon oarle khan hutẹc' gidrạ dẹe gọc'len tahẹ̄kantakoa*, if I had not rescued their child (out of water), it would have died.

The Optative.

278. The Active Voice. Suffix: *ke* (*kẹ*).

The Medium and the Passive Voice. Suffix: *kok'* (*kọk'*).

This tense, or as it should perhaps be styled, mood, is formed by adding in the Active *ke* (*kẹ*) and in the Medium and the Passive *kok'* (*kọk'*) to the conjugational base.

The pronunciation of the vowels, whether closed or open (*e* or *ẹ*, *o* or *ọ*), is in accordance with the laws of Harmonic Sequence.

279. The pronominal infixes (there is here no difference whether the object is direct or indirect, there is one verbal form for both) are added to *ke*.

With reference to the infixed pronouns of the singular the following should be noted: the vowel of *ke* is eliminated before *iń* and *e*, and the vowel of *me* is omitted (see Materials I., para 132 (b) and (e)). The forms for the three persons singular consequently are: *kiń*, *kem* and *ke*. (The omission of the *e* in *me* is regular.)

The possessive infix follows the infixed pronoun or, in the absence of this, the *ke*.

In the Medium and the Passive the *e* is eliminated before the *ok'*. In analogy with the omission of the *o* when added to words with final vowel one might have expected *kek'*, but no such form is found. (*Kek'* might possibly be taken as *ke* with inanimate object infix). The omission of the *e* before *ok'* corresponds to what happens before *iń* and *e* in the Active; the *e* is apparently weak.

280. The Optative is used to express a wish or willingness on the part of the subject of the verb. It is frequently used to express a prayer, put forward in the form of a question.

It is commonly used to express what the subject will do or may be willing to do, provided certain conditions or circumstances are fulfilled, whether these are expressly mentioned in a protasis, or only tacitly implied.

E. g., *nukin ḍaṅgram ạkriṅkekina?* would you be willing to sell these two bullocks? *ṭhik damiń ńamle khan dọń ạkriṅkekin ge cọń*, if I got a proper price I might perhaps be willing to sell them; *mit' ṭakam ẹmkińa?* would you be willing to give me one rupee? *oṛak'teń idikekoa*, I should like to take them home;

niạm ẹmkok'a? would you be willing to give this? *ojha ṭheniń ran ocokok'a*, I should like to be treated by the ojha; *haṭre nui tuluc'e ńẹpẹlkok'a*, he would like to meet this one in the market place (or: he might chance to meet); *alom họhọlekhan ghaḍlak'reń ńũrkok'a*, if you had not called I should (or, might) have tumbled into the ditch; *amem sẹnlen khan iń họń sẹnkọk'a*, if you go, I should also like to go (note, if *sẹnok'a* had been said, it would mean, I shall go).

281. This form is used in the sacrificial rituals when invoking the spirits to be pleased to receive the sacrifice. The following sentences from a *bakhẽṛ* (invocation) will show the use : *johar toḅẹ - - - - , -le emam calam kanale, niạge khusite kusạltem atańke telakeam ; niạgem sukkok' rẹbẹnkok'-am, - - - - ale dọ bale baḍaea oroma, sahaoke lahaokeape,* Be greeted, - - we are giving thee, handing thee ; mayest thou with pleasure, with enjoyment receive, accept this ; mayest thou agree to, accede to this, - - - we do not know, do not perceive ; may you suffer it, bear it.

This form of the verb is to the Santal mind the most courteous, ingratiating and well-bred way of asking for something. *

The Anterior.

282. The Active Voice. Suffix : *le* (*lẹ*).

The Medium and the Passive Voice. Suffix : *len* (*lẹn*).

This tense is formed by adding in the Active *le* (*lẹ*) and in the Medium and the Passive *len* (*lẹn*) to the conjugational base.

As regards object infixes and possessive infixes, what was remarked with regard to the suffix *ke* and *kok'* holds good for this form. Especially it should be noted that the form is the same whether the verb takes direct or indirect object.

The *e* is eliminated before *iń* and *e*, so also the final *e* of *me*. The forms with object infix in the singular consequently are *liń*, *lem* and *le*.

It will be seen that the Medium suffix (*len*) is the same as that of the Anterior Past Medium.

---

* The writer remembers an old Santal woman who came to him many years ago and said, *Ẹ bacha Saheb, mit' ṭẹċ kicriċem ẹmliń khan ạḍim̐ bhagekea,* O dear young saheb, if you would give me a piece of cloth you would do a very good act. I seem still to hear the old lady's ingratiating voice.

283. This suffix is used to denote an action or a state that takes place or exists previous to something else; it may denote priority in time, possible action, or a condition that has to be fulfilled, before something else will or can take place.

The possible reflexive and deponent meanings of the Medium should be borne in mind.

284. Except in connection with the negation *ǫhǫ* this form is not used with the finite *a*. It is used in the Anterior Imperative (q. v.), also standing without any addition, or with *ye*, *baṅ* and *nọhĩ*, added, in certain conditional sentences, and with certain postpositions.

Examples of the use with finite *a* : *ǫhǫń mẹnlea*, I am unable to tell; *ǫhǫtẹt'geń ạkriṅlekoa*, I am utterly unwilling to sell them; *ǫhǫe sẹnlena*, he is sure not to go; *ǫhǫe ẹmlena*, he will not give; *ǫhǫko cekalena*, nothing at all will happen to them.

Examples of the use without any additions: *gẹc' guric'le jhuṛu jhak' ńẹloka*, only when smearing and plastering with cow-dung it will look smooth; *sapha kicric' jaoyem pheraole pheraole ac' kathae tin maraṅ dawadar hoṛ leka*, he constantly changes his clothes and takes clean ones on, thus he feels himself like who knows how big a Croesus; *nui gidrạ dǫ noa jinis ńẹlte nunạke mạluṅena, ghaṅgẹye sap'le, ghaṅgẹye dǫhǫle, baṅgeye ạrisoka*, this child became so fascinated seeing this thing, now it takes it up, now it puts it down, it never becomes tired of it; *noa dǫ sap'le tǫhǫp'le, mit' tǫhǫp'ge hoelena*, by (over and over again) taking up and grasping, it became one handful.

285. In conditional clauses *le* and *len* are used in the protasis; what is stated in the protasis is what must be fulfilled for the apodosis to take place. The negation, if used in the protasis, is *baṅ*, when a plain statement of the negative condition is to be made, and *alo*, when the condition is prohibitive, or the apodosis refers to what might have happened, in case such and such had not been done.

The protasis sentence is closed by the postposition *khan* (or *khac'*, there is no difference between the two in meaning). This *khan* may be pure conditional, or may also have a reference to time.

E. g., janwariń ńamlekokhan iń agukoa, bań ńamleko khan doń cekaea? if I find the animals I shall bring them; if I don't find them what can I do? *gidrai pharialenkhan poesań emoka,* if the child gets well, I shall pay; *uniye hec'len-khan iń doń chutika,* if and when he comes I shall be free; *ti aloe saprletińkhan doń ńurhakoka,* if he had not my arm, I might have fallen down; *gidra aloko hec' idilenkhan noa iskul do uthaukok'a honań,* if the children should not continue to come, this school will be shut up; *onko bako senlenkhan ińgeń calak'a,* if they do not go, I shall go (with *alo* the meaning would be: if they should not);

ran jomkate batolak' aloe jomle khan honań ohoe cekalena, bogekok'geae, if after having taken the medicine he had not eaten anything that was forbidden, nothing would have happened to him; he would have recovered.

Examples of the Anterior used with postpositions other than *khan*:

hadarlere doe sudura, when it thunders, it becomes wet; *rorlere dhũndgeye beńgeda,* when he is upbraided he sees indistinctly (i. e. scolding makes him downcast).

The Imperative.

286. In all voices. No Suffix, only the subject pronoun.

The Imperative is formed by adding the infixed* forms of the personal pronoun 2nd pers. Singular, Dual or Plural, as the case may require, to the Indeterminate form of the verb in the Active or the Medium or Passive).

* One might be tempted to compare the subject pronoun of the Imperative with the suffixed pronouns mentioned para 111, and explain the Santali Imperative as something like 'yours (to do)', 'for you (to do)'. One objection to such a theory is that the suffixed pronouns there mentioned are fonnd only in the singular, this doing service for all numbers. On the other hand one might in support bring in the haplology always occurring when the Imperative has *tam, taben,* and *tape,* infixed before a not spoken, *me, ben* or *pe.*

In case the verb has an object infix and (or) a possessive infix these are attached to the verb and come immediately before the subject pronoun.

In the singular the subject pronoun is *me*; but when suffixed to the object infix of the 3rd pers. sing. or plural, or to the possessive infix of the 3rd pers. plural (i. e. to *-e*, *-ko* and *tako*) the *e* of the *me* is mostly, but not necessarily, omitted in common speech.

In the Dual and the Plural the subject pronouns are unalterably *ben* and *pe*.

With reference to the haplological omission of the subject pronoun of the Imperative see Materials I, para 136. The subject pronoun is omitted when it should have followed immediately a pronominal genitive infix of the same person as the subject pronoun.

287. As to meaning and use no explanation is needed. This Imperative of the language is as to meaning not different from that of other languages.

E. g., *idime*, take it away; *idikotaepe*, take his ones away; *iditam*, take yours away; *beredme*, raise (anything) up; *beret'me*, stand up; *beredokpe*, stand up; *teṅgoepe*, make it stand; *teṅgonme*, be standing; *dọhọeme*, put it down; *gidrạ dọhọyem*, put the child down; *hanko ṅẹlkom*, see those over there; *mẹrọm idikotape*, take your goats away; *hijuk'tabonpe*, please come and join us; *ẹmọk'talaṅme*, please give; *noare sabok'me*, take hold of this; *ạbukok'pe*, wash yourselves; *durup'tabonben*, please sit down (you two); *mit' họr hijuk'pe*, come one of you (addressing three or more, intending only one to come).

The Anterior Imperative.

288. The Active Voice. Suffix: *le* + subject pronoun.

The Medium and the Passive Voice. Suffix: *len* + the subject pronoun.

The Anterior (or as it might also be called the Immediate) Imperative is formed in analogy with the Imperative by adding the subject pronoun to the Anterior.

All remarks made with reference to the subject pronouns, object and possessive infixes and haplology are applicable also to this form.

289. While the simple Imperative denotes a general order or command, the Anterior Imperative denotes that what is ordered is to be done before something or anything else is done or happens. It is very commonly used, especially when one wants something done immediately.

E. g., *daka jọmlem, adọ laṅ calak'a,* take your food first; then we shall go; *rọṛlem, tọbẹń bujhạua,* speak first, then I shall understand; *ḍaṅgra ạgulekinme, adọń lạia, tinạk'iń ẹmok',* bring first the two bullocks, then I shall say how much I will give; *hẹc'lenme,* come at once (before doing anything else); *teṅgolenme, adọń ńẹltama,* stand up, and I shall see what is the matter with you; *mit' họṛ hẹc'lenpe,* come one of you at once.

The Prohibitive.

290. To express prohibition the Imperative is not used, but the negation *alo* with the finite Future, in all sets of suffixes. It may be softened down by using *ma* instead of the finite *a*.

E. g., *alom calaka,* don't go; *alo sẹ onka dọm rọṛa,* don't, pray, speak in that way; *alotẹt'gem ẹmọk'a,* do not give under any circumstances; *alo baṛẹm sẹnok' ma,* don't go, I pray.

The same form is used in final clauses and unfulfilled conditional clauses, naturally without the finite *a*.

E. g., *sọktọ tọlme, jẹmọn alo raṛak',* tie it fast, that it may not be loosened; *alоń sẹnlen khan uni tuluć ọhọń ńẹpẹllena,* if I had not gone, I should not have met him; *alom sẹnok', ona bọrọń bogege,* if you do not go, that will be the better course.

The Accidental Past.

291. The Medium Voice. Suffix : *ken*.

(*a*) The language has a verbal suffix, now-a-days not frequently used, and apparently only in connection with certain words denoting going and coming, eating and drinking, sitting and standing up.

The suffix has been taken to belong to the Intentional (or so-called Reservative) form, and to be Past with indirect object of the Medium Voice.

This is scarcely correct. The final *n* seems to show that the form is Medium, although the initial *k* makes it difficult to find a place for it among the Past Medium suffixes of the verb. In the Intentional we should expect *kan*, not *ken*; this difficulty has been met by referring to the Medium *kok* of the Intentional, where the *a* has been eliminated; but this will not help through, *kok* not being a Past tense suffix, and of the two vowels *a* is undoubtedly stronger then *e*.

Further: the Medium with indirect object in the supposed corresponding form of the verb has *a* (*an*), and the language has a suffix of the Intentional in the Past Medium with the *a* (*kan*).

Taking all into consideration it seems natural to suppose that we in *ken* have an old Medium form of the ordinary verb, corresponding to the Active *ket'*. It may possibly be the termination *n* added to the verbal suffix *ke* (like *ka*+*n*).* The name proposed for this the tense is meant to convey an idea of a meaning of the form often occurring in the present-day language, but a better name might be found.

So far as the meaning is concerned, there is no verbal suffix with less 'intentional' meaning.

---

* The same suffix is met with in several other Muṇḍa languages, in Muṇḍari, Ho, and Kurku. Hoffmann says *ken* is a weak form of *kan*: this is, however, scarcely sufficient to explain the two co-existing forms.

Ken seems to be gradually getting obsolete in Santali; many of the younger generation declare not to know the suffix; others say it is a form used by the related Mahles (which is quite true).

(*b*) So far as the writer has been able to find out, *ken* is used only in connection with a few words (that is to say, by present-day Santals, whatever may have been its use formerly), such as *jọm*, to eat, *ńū*, drink, *sẹn*, go, *hẹc'*, come, *ruạṛ*, return, *duṛup'*, sit, *gitic'*, lie down, *beret'*, stand up. It does not seem to be used with the finite *a*, but may take the *ge* (like the hypothetic Future, see para 331). It is frequently used in participial constructions, without subject.

(*c*) As to meaning: it will be observed that the suffix is used only in connection with verbs of a special signification, words describing an act, the performance of which has special reference to the human subject.

The suffix conveys the idea that somebody is in the state of having performed what the base-word signifies, to his personal satisfaction or pleasure. An idea of the unexpected or the accidental seems often to be connected with this form.

E. g., *jọmken ńūken cet'ya noakoregepe ạcur baṛae kana?* having had your fill of food and drink what are you fellows loitering for hereabouts? *bạń baḍae akat' tahẽkana, ọnḍẹko kūi akat'a mẹnte, ackagen sẹnken, nẹge bań ńūruka*, I did not know that they had dug a well there, I went there suddenly in my own thoughts, and just managed not to fall in; *jọmken, ńūken, bọrọḍańe gitic' akana, ac' kathae jãhãn kạmi bań leka*, having eaten and drunk as much as he liked he is lying there sluggish, just as if there were nothing to do; *dāṛã dāṛãte ackageń sẹnken tạrup' dander ṭhen, bogeye jạpit' akat' tahẽkan, bańkhane tạhuṛkińa honań*, wandering about I came unawares to a leopard's den; it was well, he was sleeping, otherwise he might have mauled me;

kuṛhiạ họṛ dọ kạṭic' talań tahẹn tako jọkhẹc' ẹkẹn jọmkọk' ńū kok', gitic'kengeko, ḍiṅgạr bańkhanko cekak'a, when lazy people have just a little, it is only eat and drink and then to lie down and sleep: what should happen to them other than become utterly destitute.

Verbal construction with indirect object.

General Remarks.

292. The series of verbal suffixes hitherto dealt with concerns the verb when having a direct object in the Active and its corresponding forms in the Medium and the Passive.

For the verb with indirect object the language has a separate set of tense suffixes in the Active and the Medium. There is no Passive of the verb with indirect object.

The suffixes of this series are less numerous than those of the first series; the tenses for the Indefinite Present and the Indefinite Imperfect are wanting, probably from logical reasons, a function with indirect object presupposing either a momentary or a continuous action (see para 256). This series has in this respect the same tenses as the Medium Voice of the verb with direct object. Anterior Past is also wanting. The Optative and the Anterior have no separate suffixes; they are, as already elsewhere remarked, identical for construction with both direct and indirect object.

293. As regards form there are some peculiarities to be noted.

(*a*) With indirect object we find in the Indeterminate (Future) and from this derived tenses (the Definite Present and do. Imperfect) and in the Imperative a form showing the inanimate indirect object (an infixed *k*').

The pronominal infixes are the same for the direct and the indirect animate object. *

* When it has been stated that the pronominal infixes are different for the direct and the indirect object, this is a mistake. The *a* preceding the infix in the Indeterminate and from this derived tenses does not belong to the pronoun, but is a verbal suffix. The compound form of the personal pronoun is not and could not be used as an infix on account of its nature. If any proof of what is here said were needed,

(*b*) The suffixes themselves show the vowel *a* where the suffixes for the direct object have *e* or no suffix at all.

(*c*) The *k* and *l* found initial in the suffixes of the Active voice in the Simple and the Anterior Past with direct object do not occur, all suffixes for the indirect object having initial vowel (*a*), except that of the Indeterminate Medium and from this derived tenses which have an initial *j* (*jǫṅ*), and those of the Optative and the Anterior which are identical for both direct and indirect object.

(*d*) The final *t'* and *n* are used in the Past tenses corresponding to their use in the direct object forms. In the Indeterminate (Future) and from this derived Medium tenses we have *ṅ* (*jǫṅ*) corresponding to *k'* (*ok'*).

(*e*) Especially women, but also men, may be heard prefixing a *w* or an *o* to the suffixes that have initial *a*. This is not euphonic, as it may be heard after a consonant. It is possibly a remnant of an old suffix. Women may be heard to pronounce also the inanimate determinative suffix with this *w* or *o* prefixed (as *berel - o - ak'* for *berelak'*).

294. Regarding the use and the meanings of the verb with indirect object the following may be noted.

(*a*) The tenses as to time in all cases correspond to those with direct object.

The difference is in the meaning, the relation of the verbal action to its object. With direct object we have the result of the performance, the object becoming, or being directly affected by, what the verb denotes. With indirect object the action is performed with the intention that it is to have special reference or application to somebody or something mentioned. An action is performed

---

it is found in the fact that there is no such *a* in the infixed pronouns in the past tenses, nor in the Optative and the Anterior; moreover this *a* is found as a separate verbal suffix in certain forms, as will be seen below.

with a result for, to, with, or in connection with somebody or something.

The verbal indirect object form presupposes a direct object of the action, the object not being the result, but the result applied to somebody or something.

(*b*) Direct-object and indirect-object infixes can naturally not be inserted at the same time. When, as frequently happens, both are specially referred to at the same time in the sentence, one of the objects, the direct or the indirect, will have to be shown outside the verb. Cf., however, infra (c).

With direct-object infix in the verb the indirect object will be separately mentioned in the sentence with a suitable postposition.

If on the other hand the indirect object is shown by the infix, the direct object is mentioned in the sentence without any postposition.

(*c*) A possessive infix may be added, referring to the direct or the indirect object.

(*d*) A few examples will show how the use of the direct and the indirect object differs. Some words may be constructed with either of these, others only with the one or the other. The examination of these will be dealt with elsewhere.

Q̱jọk'kedeako, they made him anointed, performed the ceremony of anointing him; *ọjọk'adeako*, they anointed him, applied oil to him (as a matter of daily custom without the act having any special significance besides the performance); *kicric'kedeae*, he made him clothed, provided him with the clothes required; *kicric'adeae*, he gave him some clothes (as a matter of course); *lạikedeae*, he made him told, informed against him, told of him; *lạiadeae*, he told him; *jāwāe-kedeako*, they made her husbanded, gave her away in marriage; *jāwāeadeako*, they procured a husband for her.

The Indetermiuate and the Future with indirect object.

295. The Active Voice. Suffix : *a*.

The Medium Voice. Suffix : *jo̤ṅ* (*joṅ*).

(*a*) This tense is formed by suffixing in the Active *a* * and in the Medium *jo̤ṅ* to the conjugational base.

(*b*) In the Indeterminate and the Future tense this *a* has always something added to show the object. When the object is animate, the infixed form of the personal pronoun is added to the *a*, with an optional possessive infix following.

When the object is inanimate, it is shown (*a*) by adding the inanimate suffix *k'* to the *a* (*ak'*), with an optional possessive infix following, or (*b*) by adding the possessive infix directly to the *a*, this possessive infix in a way taking the place of *k'*. †

(c) Especially women, but often also men, pronounce a *w* or an *o* before this suffix, see para 293 (b).

(*d*) Note : this *a* never becomes resultant on account of the vowels *i*, *u* or *a̤* being found in the base-word. The *i* of the infixed pronouns (i. e. of -*ṅ* and *kin*) may make the *a* resultant.

Except in a few monosyllabic words the verbal suffix is a stress-unit separate from the stress-unit of the base.

(*e*) In the Medium the suffix is *jo̤ṅ* (always so pronounced, although generally written *joṅ*), with a reflexive meaning.

---

* In the Imperative we have a form with this *a* without any addition.

† As regards the formation ot these suffixes, one is tempted to compare the *a* of the Active with the *a* found prefixed in certain words, conveying the idea of administering what is understood by the word itself. We have *a̤ṅū*, i. e., *a* + *ṅū*, in the meaning of giving to drink, or to overlay (something with a metal), from *ṅū*, drink ; *ajo̤*, i. e., *a* + *jo̤*, from *jo̤m* (*jo̤*. or *jo*, occurs in the form *jo-w-an*), eat, in the meaning of feeding. It is possibly the same that is met with in *aṅjo̤m*, to hear,

It should be noted that *joṅ* very frequently is untranslatable in our languages. It always conveys the meaning of acting or doing for one's own profit or pleasure, for oneself; but this is often reduced to mean only private or personal occupation with what the verb denotes; one's personal interest is more or less engaged.

296. The meanings are the same as of the same tense with direct object, only that we have here to do with an indirect object. See paras 246—250, and 294.

E. g., *aṭiṅ jaegaṅ arak'aea*, I shall let him have some pasture land; *gapa kuṛaiko emako takoa*, they will to-morrow give them their wages; *thoṛako ẹm juṭuc'akoa jaoge*, they always give them a little thrown in; *bae taṛam daṛeak'a*, he is unable to walk; *jhic'aeae*, he will open (the door) for him; *lạioaeaṅ*, I shall tell him;

mạciko duṛupak'a, they will sit on the stool; *ḍaṅgrako siakoa*, they use bullocks for ploughing;

bako baṅalaea, they do not refuse his request; *bẹṅgẹt'atiṅae*, he will look at my (work); *nonkate am dọ cele baṅ ạuam*, when

---

jọm, to eat, being sometimes used in the meaning of accepting, listening to (*e. g.*, *katha bae jọmlet'tiṅa*, he did not 'eat' my words, did not heed what I said). The *a* of the personal pronouns, of the inanimate determinative suffix, of the inanimate demonstrative pronouns and the finite *a* might also be compared with this *a*. Could the position of the *a*, if there be any connection, in the agglutinating process, regulate its meaning, or rather the application of its possible fundamental meaning?

As regards the Medium suffix *jọṅ* there is very little to compare with; *ṅ* might be compared with the *k'* of the Medium suffix *ok'*. In the inanim. determinative suffix we find *k'* and *ṅ* interchangeable, in a single case also in the Medium suffix (*nitoṅ* for *nitok'*). But we should have to explain the constant pronunciation *ọ* (not changing like in *ọk'* and *ok'*), and the *j*.

In Muṇḍari we find in three or four tense suffixes a *j* (Present Active *jad*, Indefinite Past Active *jan*, and the same in the Passive or Reflexive Simple Past; I have used the terms and forms of the Rev. Hoffmann in his Muṇḍari grammar): the Kurku suffix *yu* might also be mentioned. Connection is, however, doubtful. It has been suggested that the *j* is the same as the *c̓* of the determinative suffix and the personal pronoun *ac̓*. This is, however, very problematic, the *c̓* being only singular, and here something of a general nature is wanted.

you behave like this who will heed you (women's expression);

ṭakako idijoṅa, they will take money along (for their use); *iṅteṅ ṅamjoṅa*, I shall procure it myself; *ąurikin gidrąjoṅa*, they have not as yet had any children; *cet'joṅaṅ*, I shall learn.

The Present and Imperfect tenses with indirect object.

297. The Definite Present in the Active and the Medium. Suffix: *kan* added to the Indeterminate.

The Definite Imperfect in the Active and the Medium. Suffix: *tahẽkan* added to the Definite Present.

(*a*) The Definite Present is formed by adding *kan* to the constructed Indeterminate with indirect object, and the Definite Imperfect is formed by adding *tahẽkan* to the Definite Present.

The infixes follow the *a* just as in the Indeterminate, only that the possessive suffix, if used, may come after *kan*, and in the Imperfect after *kan* or after *tahẽkan*.

In case there is no object infix the possessive infix, if any, always follows the *a* (*atiṅ*, *atam*, *atae*, etc.).

(*b*) The language does not in constructions with indirect object distinguish between an Indefinite and a Definite Present or do. Imperfect. The one form has to do service for both, just as in the Medium and the Passive in all suffix series (see paras 256, 261 and 268). An action with indirect object seems to demand a definite application. It does not, however, mean that the action has to be performed at the particular moment.

(*c*) As to the meaning the reader is referred to what has been stated regarding the same tenses with direct object, only keeping in mind that we here have indirect object (see paras 260, 261, 268 and 294.)

E. g., noako jinis do hante sakak'me, bogete dak' jorgak' kana, put these things over there, here a good deal of water (rain) is falling down on them; *noa kũi reak' dak' dele ńũak' kana,* we are drinking the water of this well; *onem senak' kan hortem calaolenkhanem tiok' goda nãhãk'*, if you follow the road you are going along, you will presently reach your destination; *pańcateye emako kana,* he is giving it to them as a temporary loan;

uniak' kami mimit' gharińbengetatae kana, jãhã lekae baric' botec'kea, I am keeping an eye on what he is doing, he might otherwise spoil it; *hortet' banugic' khan cedak'pe bolo-atae kana,* when the man himself is not at home, why do you enter his premises? *bańatako kan khan alope jormotkoa* if they are unwilling do not force them;

kicric'e bachaojoń kana, he is choosing cloth for himself; *ic'joń kanae,* he is easing himself;

noa horte sedaere do jaogele hec' senak' kan tahẽkana, formerly we were always going and coming by this road; *mundame horok'ae kan tahẽkanre ona do ńurhayente okayen coń,* as he was just putting the ring on her finger it fell down and was lost;

jom joń kan tahẽkanae, he was eating.

The Simple Past with indirect object.

298. The Active Voice. Suffix: *at'*.

The Medium Voice. Suffix: *an*.

(*a*) This tense is formed by adding in the Active *at'*, and in the Medium *an*, to the conjugational base.

As regards the Active suffix: the *t'* is changed to *d* before a pronominal infix with initial vowel (i. e., *iń* and *e* in full analogy with the change of the Present suffix *et'* (see para 254, also Materials I, para 106, B (d)). Now-a-days people are also heard changing the *t'* to *d* before the finite *a*.

(*b*) The personal pron. infixes are inserted in full analogy with what has been stated in connection with *et'* of the Indefinite Present.

(*c*) There is nothing to show an inanimate indirect object.

(*d*) As to meanings the reader is referred to what is written on the Simple Past with direct object, only keeping in mind that we have indirect object, and that there is no Passive, only Medium with a reflexive meaning.

(*e*) In analogy with the Simple Past this form may also be used with *ge* in stead of the finite *a* to express what is called a hypothetical Future (see para 331).

(*f*) A form for Anterior Past with indirect object is not found.

(*g*) Especially women, but sometimes also men, may be heard to prefix a *w* or *o* to these two suffixes. See para 293 (b).

E. g., sagaṛiń bęńgęt'at'taea, I looked at his cart; *siok'ko dakae idiat'koa,* she took food out to the ploughmen; *kaḍako ṭọṭkọwadea,* they tied a wooden bell to the buffalo;

tis hõ bań ńęllet'koa saheb họpọnko dọ, nęs bapoń ńęloan, I had never before seen a European, this year, o dear, I obtained sight of them; *turui gọṭęnkin gidrọwana,* they have got six children;

itạm aphọra, ọmọnkate thoṛa haralenkhanem phoṛaoa, adọ dak'em dulat'ge, adọ bar pę cando parọmkate thamakurem ńawange, you sow the seed, when it has germinated and grown a little you plant it out, then you water it, and after two or three months you have tobacco (leaves).

The Anterior Pluperfect with indirect object.

299. The Active Voice. Suffix : *at' - tahẽkan.*
The Medium Voice. Suffix : *an tahẽkan.*

(*a*) This tense is formed by adding *tahẽkan* to the constructed Simple Past with indirect object. Pronominal infixes are inserted as in the Simple Past, the possessive infix, if any, finding a place either directly after the object infix or after *tahẽkan.*

(*b*) As is seen the language has no Anterior Past tense for the verb with indirect object. The here mentioned form functions as Anterior Pluperfect in this way: it refers to a Past when an act had been performed. It does not say that the result of the Act lasted (for this there is another form); the act had simply been done; as likely as not it had lost its effect.

E. g., *lqiat'ko tahękanań*, I had told them.

The Optative with indirect object.

300. As already remarked (see para 293 (c)) the Optative is the same for both direct and indirect object; there is no difference in form, either in the Active or the Medium.

As regards the meaning, the reader is referred to what is stated about the Optative with direct object.

E. g., *mit'tęc' kicric'em ęmkińa*, would you be willing to give me a piece of cloth; *rinte ṭakam ęmkelea*, would you give us money as a loan.

The Anterior with indirect object.

301. The Active Voice. Suffix: *le*.

The Medium Voice. Suffix: *an*.

In the Active Voice there is no difference in this form, whether the object is direct or indirect. In the Medium the same form as the Simple Past with indirect object (*an*) may be used, not, however, with the finite *a*, to express the Anterior.

Except that we here have indirect object, all remarks concerning the contruction, use and meanings made in connection with the form with direct object hold good, especially also concerning the use of the finite *a*, and of the particles *ge*, and *bań* and *nįhi*. (see para 331).

E. g., *bin damte noa dǫ ǫhǫń ęmlekoa*, I shall certainly not give them this without being paid for it; *nįąm aṛak'leko khan ąḍiko rąskąkok'a*, if you allow them this they will be very glad;

mohajoniń halalege, I must first pay the moneylender his due; *hapẹ, jowangeń, adọbon calak'a* wait, I must first have my food, then we shall go; *jạpit'anregeń, nit dọ ọhọń daṛelena,* I must first have some sleep, just now I am unable to do anything;

sudem ẹmliń bań dọń tirpitok'a, only when you give interest I shall be satisfied;

gidrạ kicric'em họrọkleko nũtĩ dọko sẹn daṛeak'a, only when you put clothes on the children they will be able to go.

The Imperative with indirect object.

302. The Imperative is formed in analogy with the Imperative of the verb with direct object by adding the infixed forms of the personal pronoun 2nd pers sing., dual or plural, as the case may require, to the constructed Indeterminate form of the verb with indirect object, in the Active and the Medium, the personal pronoun taking the place of the finite *a* and the subject pronoun of the finite tense.

As regards the indirect object infix and the possessive infix there is no difference from the Indeterminate tense, except that we here may meet with an inanimate form without an infixed *-k'*. In the Indeterminate we may also find this *k'* omitted, but there always substituted by a possessive infix, which is not always heard in the Imperative. *

E. g., jọm emakope, give them food; *sẹn ocoaeme,* let him go; *kạmi bẹṅgẹt'ataeme,* keep an eye on what he is doing; *ẹm juṭuc'ak' takope,* give them some more;

jẹrẹt'am, set fire to (with stress on *a*; the Indeterminate (Future) would be *jẹrẹdam,* with stress on the second *ẹ*); *onako dạń hõ jẹrẹt' darawame,* as you come along set fire

---

* When I drew the late Mr. Skrefsrud's attention to this form, he at first flatly refused to recognize it as an Imperative and insisted on its being 'Future'. It is undoubtedly Imperative. The Santals themselves recognize it as Imperative. The intonation is different from that of the Future, and the rule regarding final checked consonants (see para 243), followed in the Indeterminate and Future, is not followed here. The subject pronoun may also be *me*, not only *m*.

also to those heaps; *onurege up'am*, put it down on that there: *perec'am*, fill up on it; *mak'ame*, give it a cut; *kuṭamam*, strike at it;

amte ńeljońme, look out for yourself; *dẹ duṛup'jońme*, please sit down; *apete ńẹl bachaojońtape*, see and choose for yourselves what is yours.

The Anterior Imperative with indirect object.

303. The Active Voice. Suffix: *le.*

The Medium Voice. Suffix: *an.*

This is formed in all respects in analogy with the Imperative, but from the Anterior with indirect object.

As to meaning see para 301.

E. g., *peṛa ẹmlekom*, give the visitors first; *daka jowanpe*, take your food first.

Prohibitive with indirect object.

304. This form is the constructed Future with *alo* as negation. In stead of the finite *a ma* may be used, signifying more a wish, than an interdict.

E g:, *alope laiakoa*, don't tell them; *alo baṛẹye tahẽ ocoako ma*, may he not let them stay; *siń modre alo:n gilic'jońa*, don't lie (sleep) during day-time.

The Intransitive Verb.

305. Verbs having an intransitive meaning show certain characteristics that have to be noted.

(*a*) The Intransitive verb takes the verbal suffixes of the Active transitive verb, naturally without the object infix; it may take the indirect object infix and also a possessive infix, if wanted.

(*b*) In connection with the Indeterminate tense and also the Imperative the following intransitive peculiarities should be noted:

Conjugational bases with final checked consonant keep this and never alter it into its corresponding voiced consonant (as is the case with similar transitive verbs with direct inanimate object).

Conjugational bases with single final vowel do not get an *e* or an *i* suffixed, as is the case with the transitive verb with inanimate direct object. The euphonic vowel in the same class of base-words between the finite *a* and final vowel is *w* and not *y*, except in words ending in *i* or *e*, where a slight *y*-sound may be heard, induced by the preceding *e* or *i*.

Both rules hold good when the *kan* and the *kan tahẽkan* of the Definite Present and do. Imperfect are added.

(*c*) In the Medium there is no difference in suffixes.

E. g., *beret'ae*, he will stand up; *beredae*, he will put (something) on end (transit. verb); *beret'me*, stand up; *lọlọ kan tahẽkana*, it was hot;

dak' dọ lọlọwa, the water is hot (but *dak'e lọlọea*, he will warm the water);

banko ruạṛ kana, they do not return, are not returning.

Infixless transitive verbal construction.

306. (*a*) A base-word may function as a transitive verb, without, however, taking any object-infix.

This construction is heard used in what corresponds to the Indeterminate (Future) and tenses formed from this by the addition of *kan* and *kan tahẽkan*, that is to say, in tenses with the base-word used without any verbal suffix, bare or with the auxiliaries mentioned added.

To explain this construction one has to remember the character of the Santal word-concept. It is the transitive concept of this as such that is in function, the object of the action being left out of specific consideration and not specifically shown in the construction. The base functions, as if it were an Active Present participle, either alone or with the auxiliaries mentioned added.

This infixless verbal construction is used, with the unaltered base-word, very frequently in connection with a few words, but otherwise rarely.

It is an analogous construction that is met with in the Performative form of the verb. The deponent verbs may also be compared.

E. g., *nekom ńeleť'ko gidra, jotoge ińren, ado okoeyem ńam kana*, the children you see before you here are all mine, whom are you seeking then? *neko enkole uduk'at'mere hõ bam khusilena, ado tobe celem ńam kana*, even when we pointed out to you these and those, you were not pleased, what kind (of cattle) do you want then? *turui horiń ńam kan tahẽkana* I was wanting six men; *gaiye gupi kana*, he is herding cows; *gaiko horho kan tahẽkana*, they were tending the cattle (note the bare *horho*).

(*b*) The postposition *kate* seems to belong to the kind of construction referred to above. *Kate* is the Intentional *ka + te*; used as a postposition it never takes any object infix; used as part of the Intentional verb the infixes are regularly heard (*kaňte, kaete, kamte, kakole*, etc.).

The Intentional Form of the Verb.

General Remarks.

307. Besides the two series of verbal suffixes already dealt with the language has a third series of a special character, conveying the idea of intentional performance.

308. As to the form the following may be noted: The suffixes have, with one possible exception (that of *lak'*), as their fundament *ka*, to which *t'* or *n* may be added, also

ok' (*ka*+*ok'* becomes *kok'*), and to which an *a* may be prefixed. *

309. In this series we have no Indefinite tenses (of the Present and the Imperfect) and no Optative (except that a *ma* may be added to the Future).

On the other hand we have two tenses, formed by prefixing an *a* to the *ka* and adding an *t'* or an *n*, viz. a Perfect and, with *tahẽkan* added, a Plúperfect, tenses not found in the two series previously dealt with. As an appendix to this series we further have a Continuative form of the verb.

The Intentional has no suffixes for the indirect object (possibly because the object of the action is so prominent as to exclude reference in the verb). The exceptions found in the Perfect and the Pluperfect are only apparent, the here found suffixes for indirect object really belonging to the Continuative.

310. As regards the special meaning of the suffixes of this series :

(*a*) The base-word is not altered and consequently keeps its meaning. The relation of the act as to time is not altered; the tenses consequently have in this respect the same meanings as those of the ordinary verb.

What distinguishes this series of suffixes from the others is that the object of the performance or action gets special

---

* The formal resemblance between the suffixes of the Intentional series and those of the Active verb with indirect object might be noted. By prefixing a *k* to the initial *a* of the suffixes referred to we have an Intentional suffix. It would be rash to build anything on this resemblance; still it may possibly be more than accidental. With indirect object something is done intended to have effect in connection with something or somebody; here the performance is intended to have certain results.

We find this *ka* as a component part of a number of demonstrative adverbs and some other words (*nonka*, etc., *leka*), probably also of the Copula *kan*. *Ka* is extensively used with the postposition *te* (*kate*), see paras 165, 166 and 306 (b).

attention. An act is shown as being performed with some special intention as to its results, with some ulterior purpose. In the Medium and the Passive the continuance of the result is observable.

The ulterior purpose may be one of two. In the one case it is the performance with an absolute or final result of the act, to do and be done with; in the other case it is a performance, reserving the result for some further action, the result to remain for a time with the intention of acting in connection with it at some later time. In both cases the performance has stress. *

(*b*) The form is naturally optional; there is no word that demands an Intentional suffix, with one significant exception. The language has a word *oṭo*, never used independently, but always added to another word, conveying the idea of 'leaving behind'. With direct object *oṭo* is always (except in the Anterior Past) followed by an intentional suffix; with indirect object it takes the suffixes of the ordinary series.

(c) From the meanings given it will be evident that the Intentional suffixes are used when the subject (or the agent) is a logical being. This does not refer to the Passive where the continuance is the preponderant meaning.

---

* Mr. Skrefsrud called this series of suffixes the Reservative, and it is a fitting name for the last mentioned meaning, but does not suit the first. I have therefore ventured to rename this series of suffixes the Intentional for lack of a better name.

When it has been said that these suffixes convey a meaning more emphatic than those of the other series, this is a mistake. *Thirkok'pe*, keep quite (to quote one of the examples given in support of this assertion), is certainly not more emphatic than *thirok'pe*, be quiet, shut up, as this last may be translated. An angry person who may be supposed to use emphatic expressions will use the ordinary Imperative; the Intentional Imperative is deliberate, an order to be quiet, so that something may be done undisturbed.

(*d*) The Intentional Active suffixes are used with the Repetitive conjugational base, conveying a conative meaning, the meaning of an attempted, but resultless, frustrated action. This use is of great assistance in defining the real meaning of these particular suffixes, viz. intentional performance.*

The Intentional Indeterminate and Future.

311. The Active Voice. Suffix: *ka* (+*k'* or object infix).
The Medium Voice. Suffix: *kok'*.

(*a*) This tense is formed by adding in the Active *ka*, and in the Medium and Passive *kok'* to the conjugational base.

(*b*) With inanimate object an *k'* is added to represent this; this *k'* may, however, be omitted when a possesive infix follows (this *k'* may also be omitted in the Imperative without any substitute; see below, para 318 (b)).

With animate object the pron. infix is added to the *ka*, the possessive infix, if any, following the object infix. Consequently we find exactly the same form as in the Active verb with indirect object, only that we have here a *k* prefixed.

(*c*) The object infix 3rd pers. sing. (*e*) is in this form added to the suffix without any euphonic consonant, forming a diphthong with the *ka* (*kae*). Cp. Materials I, para 133 (a).

(*d*) The *k'* is never under any circumstances changed to its corresponding voiced consonant (*g*) before a vowel, thus never before the finite *a*.

(*e*) As to the meaning see paras 246 and 310.

---

* It does something more, it helps to realize the actual meaning and functioning of the verbal suffixes, showing that they have an intrinsic independent meaning. Take a form like *hẹč hẹčkat'aṅ*, a verb otherwise constructed with a Medium suffix, here with the Active Intentional, lit. I performed coming coming, acted with the intention of coming again and again, but did not succeed; I intended to come, but was unable to.

E. g., kalaṅkak'ako, they pick it up (for some purpose); *giḍikak'ae,* he will throw it away for good; *ac'geye idikataea,* he will himself take his things away; *peṛaṅ ạgukakoa,* I shall bring the friends (for a purpose); *ona dare ṭhen saulọmem tọlkaetama,* you will tie your pony at that tree (while you do something else);

ọṇḍẹye duṛuṕkok'a, he will sit there (waiting);

rọṛ rọṛkak'ae, bae pusṭạu daṛeak'a, he will make vain attempts at speaking, he is unable to speak distinctly.

The Intentional Definite Present.

312. The Active Voice. Suffix: *ka - kan.*

The Medium and the Passive Voice. Suffix: *kok kan.*

This tense is formed by adding *kan* to the constructed Indeterminate tense. The possessive infix may come after *kan,* except when in stead of the *k'* it is added immediately to the *ka,* just as is the case with certain forms of the Active with indirect inanimate object.

The meaning is the same as for the Definite Present (see para 260) with the qualification stated para 310.

E. g., gạiko idikako kantakoa, they are just taking their cows away (for some purpose); *jobrae atar giḍikak' kana,* she is just now burning and cleaning away rubbish; *ikạkatako kanae,* he is always forgiving them; *aṅjọmkak' kanaṅ,* I am listening (intending to have it in mind for use);

hapekok' kanae, he is keeping quiet.

The Intentional Definite Imperfect.

313. The Active Voice. Suffix: *ka - kan tahẽkan.*

The Medium and the Passive Voice. Suffix: *kok' kan tahẽkan.*

This tense is formed by adding *tahẽkan* to the Definite Present. Nothing needs to be added as to construction and meaning; it is in all respects the same as the ordinary Definite Imperfect (see para 268) with the Intentional qualification.

The Intentional Simple Past

314. The Active Voice. Suffix : *kat'.*

The Medium and the Passive Voice. Suffix : *kan.*

(*a*) This tense is formed by adding in the Active *kat'* and in the Medium and the Passive *kan* to the conjugational base.

As to the suffix of the Active no remarks are called for; the construction is in full analogy with the same tense of the ordinary verb.

(*b*) The Medium suffix *kan* is found in the auxiliary *tahẽkan,* where the suffix has melted into one word with *tahẽ.** Apart from this word *kan* does not seem to be used with the finite *a.*

(*c*) On the other hand it is frequently used with *ge* (instead of the finite *a*) about a hypothetic Future (like *ket'ge* and *enge*). It is also used in the same way with *pasẹt',* perhaps.

(*d*) The meaning of this tense is the same as that of the Simple Past (see para 271), but with the qualification that the act was performed for a purpose, with some intention as to the result of the completed act.

E. g., bọchọr dinin̉ gupikat'ko tama, ma adọ n̉ẹlkotam, I herded your cattle for you for one year, now look after them yourself; *ẹkẹnem rọṛ giḍikat'a, tayọm daram dọ bam disạlak'a,* you only talked away, without thinking of the afterwards; *tinạk'in̉ hataolak'a, jọtọn̉ ẹm ruạṛkat'tama,* so much as I received, I have given it all back to you;

enan̉rem sẹn akanre hõ nit anẹc'em ruạṛ kan, although you went a long while ago (to day), now only you have returned; *kọe legayem, pasẹt' cọe ẹm kange,* make a trial asking him, he might perhaps give; *masẹ dela legawaeme, pasẹc'e hẹc' kan,* please ask him, perhaps he might come; *noa dare dọ dak' dul idiak'me baṛẹ, pasẹ kalọmte dọ jọ baha kan ge,* keep

---

* The Medium and Passive *akan* might be compared; it is possibly the same *kan* that we have there.

on watering this tree, perhaps it might give fruit next year; *masẹ noa dare jọ dọ lurgau legaeme, pasẹc' mit' bar dọ ńũr kange*, try to poke at the fruit of this tree, a couple might fall down; *ọṇḍẹm sẹnlenkhan pasẹc' amak' sana dọ purạu kange*, if you went there, perhaps you might effect what you wish; *ranko dọ beste lagao idiaepe, pasẹc'e boge kan ge*, be diligent applying medicine to him, perhaps he might get well again; *masẹ biḍạu ocoaeme, pasẹc' cọc pas kan ge*, let him go up for the examination, he might perhaps pass; *dẹsẹ amak' kạṭhi ẹmlenme, pasẹc' onate dọ jhic' kange*, please let me have your key; perhaps it might be opened with that.

The Intentional Anterior Past.

315. The Active Voice. Suffix: *lak'*.

This tense is formed by adding the suffix *lak'* to the conjugational base. It is a form used only with an inanimate direct object;* it is found only in the Active; there is no corresponding form for the Medium or the Passive.

316. It is doubtful where this form should be taken as belonging, whether to the Intentional series or to the ordinary series. Something may be said for both. A verbal suffix with initial *l* is not otherwise found in the Intentional, and we should have expected a form *lat'*. In the ordinary verb with indirect object—the tenses of which are the same as those of the Intentional— we have nothing to express the Anterior. The *k'* is in the verbal suffixes of the Active Voice found only to represent an inanimate object, and there is no reason to think that it is not the same that we have here. As stated the form is used exclusively about an inanimate object.

To explain the form several possibilities might be suggested. It may be a contraction of *let'* (*led*) + *ak'*, or of a possible *lat'* (*lad*) + *ak'*, or it might be an Intentional *la* + *k'*. The difficulty is that we have no analogous examples for

* When Mr. Skrefsrud in a footnote in his Grammar quotes a form *dallakkoae*, this is a mistake; *lak'* with animate direct object does not occur in the language.

any of the possibilities mentioned; on account of the last mentioned possibility the form is tentatively recorded here.*

The form is used apparently indiscriminately with *let'*; it conveys the meaning of a previously performed purpose, now given up or neutralized.

E. g., rorlak'ae, he said (so); *orak'e raput'laka*, he pulled his house down (purposing to build another).

The Intentional Anterior Pluperfect.

317. The Active Voice. Suffix: *kat' - tahēkan.*

(*a*) This tense is formed by adding *tahēkan* to the constructed Intentional Simple Past. It is found only in the Active Voice.

The object infix is added immediately to *kat'*, the possessive infix, if any, following the object infix or *tahēkan.*

(*b*) The meaning of this tense is somewhat similar to that of the Anterior Pluperfect of the ordinary verb.

It conveys the idea, that an act was performed with some purpose in the Past, but that the act did not answer to the intention; one of two happened, either the result was nullified, or the act itself was not accomplished, it became conative.

The form *kan tahēkan* is not Medium of this tense.

E g., gidra do iskulteń idikade tahēkana, bae tahēlena, I had taken my child to school (to be taught), he did not stay;

dar darkat' tahēkanae, adoe ruarena, he had made an attempt at running away, but came back; *ńum ńumkat' tahēkanae, bae dareat'a*, he had repeatedly tried to name it, but was unable to do so.

---

* The writer has formerly been inclined to take *lak'* as contracted from *let'* + *ak'*, but is becoming more and more doubtful how to explain the form. It is probably wrong to presuppose an *ak'* here; the most likely would seem to be *la* + *k'*, only we have nothing analogous.

The Intentional Imperative.

318. The Active, the Medium and the Passive Voice.
No suffix; the infixed form of the pers. pr. added to the Indeterminate.

(*a*) The Imperative of the Intentional is formed in the same way as that of the ordinary verb. The infixed form of the personal pronoun 2nd pers. is added to the Intentional Indeterminate.

The Intentional has only one Imperative, that formed with the Indeterminate as its base.

(*b*) The inanimate object infix *-k'* is often omitted in the Imperative, and the subject pronoun is attached to *ka* immediately, even when no possessive infix follows the *ka*.

The object infix of the 3rd p sing. (*e*) forms, when added to *ka*, a diphthong with the *a* (*kae*).

As to haplology see para 286 (Mat. I, para 136).

The meaning is the same as that of the ordinary Imperative with the qualifications of the Intentional.

E. g, *giḍikak'me*, or *giḍikam*, throw it away; *idikakotape*, take your (animals) away; *sahta bhaote caole kiriń ḍoho̱kak'me*, buy up rice while the price is low; *ma no̱ṇḍe̱ge ḍoho̱kak'me, cele hõ bako cekaea*, place it here (so long), no one will touch it; *idi oṭokaeme*, take him away (to some place agreed on) and leave him there;

thirkok'pe, keep quite; *duṛup'kok'tabonpe*, please sit down with us.

---

319. As has been observed none of the other series of suffixes shows any suffix for the Perfect tense. In connection with the suffixes of the Intentional we have an expanded suffix which, with certain additions, does service for a Perfect tense. In its naked form this is treated as a

kind of base-word and used to make up a Continuative form of the verb.

The expanded form of the Intentional suffix is *aka*, the initial *a* very likely being a demonstrative element. The different forms are dealt with here below. The literal meaning may possibly be: *aka* 'that (*a*) doing, (*ka*)', and *akat'* 'that (*a*) effected (*kat'*)'.

The Perfect with direct object.

320. The Active Voice. Suffix: *akat'*.
The Medium and the the Passive Voice. Suffix: *akan*.

(*a*) The Perfect tense is formed by adding in the Active *akat'*, and in the Medium and the Passive *akan* to the conjugational base.*

As to object infixes and possessive infixes, the same rules as those of the Intentional Simple Past (*kat'*) are valid.

(*b*) The Perfect tense denotes a completed action, remaining in its results at the present time or at the time referred to by the speaker.

As stated the Perfect must be taken as belonging to the Intentional form of the verb; but as the suffix is expanded, the meaning is also a little different. In the ordinary Intentional tenses the intention or purpose of the agent as to the effect of the act is always apparent; this side of the action is not so apparent in the Perfect. The Perfect tenses presuppose intention, but the predominant or principal meaning to be conveyed is the continued effect of the act.

* When the corresponding form in Muṇḍari has been explained partly as a Continuative Present, partly as Perfect, this is unnecessary and may be due to an oversight as to the real meaning of the base-word concerned. It may be questioned, whether *akan* should not in many cases be taken to be the continuative *aka* with the adjective forming *n* added (see para 59).

This should not be lost sight of by those who learn the language.

(c) The Santali Perfect does not correspond to the so-called Historic Perfect.

(*d*) It should be noted that the Perfect goes well with the direct negation (*bań*).

E. g., *okarem dọhọ akat'a?* where have you put it? *Khajnań calao akat' taea,* I have paid his rent for him; *jọtọ kuṛiko jãwãe akat'ko takoa,* they have married away all their girls; *nọṇḍeń ạgu akat'koa,* I have brought them here; *jọtọkogepe hẹc' akana?* have you all come? *ọkọe hõ bale tayọm akana,* none of us have stayed behind.

(*e*) The Perfect tense is often used where we have the Present; this is due, not to any peculiarity of the Santal Perfect, but to the peculiar meaning of the Santal base-word.

E. g., *baḍae akat'koań,* I know them (lit. I have learnt to know them); *jạpit' akat'ae,* he is sleeping (lit. he has shut his eyes); *teńgo akanae,* he is standing (lit. he has risen and is continuing in that position); *pạtiạu akanae,* he believes (lit. he has put belief in).

The Perfect with indirect object.

321. The Active Voice. Suffix : *aka - w - at'.*

The Medium Voice. Suffix : *aka - w - an.*

This tense is formed by adding *aka* + the suffix of the ordinary verb in the Simple Past with indirect object to the conjugational base, i. e., in the Active *akawat'* and in the Medium (there is no Passive) *akawan* (the *w* is possibly euphonic; however, cf. para 293 (b)).

As to object infix and possessive infix the ordinary rules are followed.

The meaning conveyed is the same as that of the Perfect, only that the object here is indirect.

E. g., *lại akawadeañ*, I have told him; *ranko ẹm akawat'koa*, they have given them medicine; *thamakur daк'iñ dul akawat' tiña*, I have watered my tobacco plants;

nẹs dọe ạgu akawana, he has brought (e. g., a wife) for himself this year.

The Pluperfect with direct or indirect object.

322. The Active Voice with direct object.

Suffix: *akat' - tahẹ̄kan.*

The Active Voice with indirect object.

Suffix: *akawat' - tahẹ̄kan.*

The Medium and the Passive with direct object.

Suffix: *akan tahẹ̄kan.*

The Medium with indirect object.

Suffix: *akawan tahẹ̄kan.*

This tense is formed by adding *tahẹ̄kan* to the constructed Perfect forms, either those with direct or those with indirect object, as may be required.

The forms and meanings do not call for any special remarks. The tenses refer to a state in the past, the effect of the action remaining at the time referred to, or when something else happened.

E. g., *hoṛoko rọhọe akat' tahẹ̄kantakoa*, they had planted their rice; *lại akawade tahẹ̄kanae*, he had told him;

teṅgo akan tahẹ̄kanae, he was standing (had risen and remained standing); *lọsọt'reye jọbẹ akan tahẹ̄kana*, he was wallowing in the mud; *ṭaka poesa akawan tahẹ̄kanae*, he had acquired some money.

The Continuative Form.

323. A Continuative is formed by the addition (to the base) of *aka*, plus an object infix, always followed by *tahẹn*.

The continuative meaning is partly due to *taḥen* (remain) to which the tense suffixes used in this form are added.*

324. This *aka* is an expanded form of the Intentional *ka*, the same as is found in the Intentional Perfect suffixes, more especially when constructed with indirect object.

In the Continuative *aka* does not, however, function as a verbal suffix proper, but as a supplement to the verbal base. We have a kind of double worded base constructed as in the Indeterminate, analogous to other double words when the second word has final single vowel (with one exception that will be presently mentioned), and used without tense suffixes, but taking direct or indirect object infixes.

The exception refers to the animate infix of the direct object in the 3rd pers. sing. With inanimate object the form is regularly *akae* (see para 242 (a)); with animate direct object the form should in the Indeterminate Active be *akaye*, but it is *akae* in the Continuative.† The euphonic semi-vowel *y* is not used in the Continuative base; the infixed object pronoun is joined to the *a* so as to form a diphthong with this, as is the case in the Intentional Indeterminate Active (*kae* for *kaye*) with the same infix. Cp. also the Indeterminate with indirect object, where we find a similar phenomenon.

324. (*a*) *Aka* may in the way here mentioned be added to any of the conjugational bases provided the meaning of

---

* In a few cases (participial constructions) *aka* may be heard without a following *taḥen*, but this is possibly a lapsus linguæ; Santals questioned on this point generally deny such solitary use of *aka*.

† As a curiosum it may be mentioned that the language has a word sounding exactly like this *aka*, but of a different etymology and meaning, viz. to hang up. Here we hear, how a word with single final vowel is functioning as a verb in the Indeterminate Active. With inanimate direct object it is, e. g. *akaeae* he will hang (something) up; with animate direct object the same is *akayeae*, he will hang him up.

the verb will permit it, not however, to the Performative, and not to the Inchoative. Thus, when the causative or permissive *oco* is used this follows the base-word, preceding the *aka*.

The following details will show the use.

(*b*) With the reservations taken above it may be said that the Continuative is used in all voices; *aka* with its preceding word may be Active with direct or indirect object: with *n* added we get a Medium or Passive. But as remarked, *aka* does not take any tense suffix.

(*c*) The Active Voice:

With direct object the forms, omitting the *tahẹn* here, are:

- *akań* (1st p. sing.)
- *akame* (2nd p. sing.)
- *akae* (3rd p. sing.)
- *akae* (direct obj. inanimate, for all numbers.)
- *akalań, - - liń, - - ben*, etc.

With indirect object:

- *akawań* (1st p. sing.)
- *akawam* (2nd p. sing.)
- *akawae* (3rd p. sing.)
- *akawak'* (indirect obj. inanimate, for all numbers.)
- *akawalań, - - liń, - - ben*, etc.

(*d*) The Medium and the Passive:

- *akan tahẹn* (corresponding to Active with direct obj.)
- *akawan tahẹn* (do. to do. with indirect obj.)

325. (*a*) The tenses used are the Indeterminate or the Future, the Definite Present and the Definite Imperfect; the Imperative is also commonly used.* An Inchoative form of the Continuative may also be heard, but is very rare. The following forms are consequently met with:

tahẹn, tahẹn kan, tahẹn kan tahẽkan, tahẹn lạgit' (with the tenses of the Inchoative) preceded by constructed *aka*

* Mr. Skrefsrud in his grammar mentions the Continuative as used in a number of other tenses: present day Santals do not acknowledge the use of the tenses mentioned there for this form. Theoretically they are possible.

and followed by the finite *a* and subject. The Imperative is also used, constructed *aka*+*tahẹnme* (- *ben*, - *pe*).

(*b*) The meaning of the Continuative is to continue performing or being performed what the base-word denotes, the tense being regulated by the tense of *tahẹn*.

E. g., *sap' akae tahẹnme*, remain keeping hold of him (or,it); *bẹṅgẹt' akawae tahẹn kan tahẹ̃kanae*, he was continually looking at him; *dil akae tahẹnme*, be courageous; *họrhọ oco akae tahẹnme*, make him keep continual watch; *họrhọ oco akawae tahẹnme*, let him keep continual watch.

Verbal suffixes other than Tense suffixes.

—*a*.

326. (*a*) As previously stated (see para 198 (e)) an *a* is added to the verb to make the statement a finite verb.

This *a* (cp. para 150) seems to be a demonstrative particle, conveying the meaning of 'that', 'that's it', or something similar. It is in all likelihood the same *a* as that forming a part of the inanimate demonstrative pronouns (as in *no - a*, *on - a*, etc.), of the inanimate determinative suffix (*a-k'*), and of other words or particles.

This finite *a*, as we are accustomed to call it, is always the last part of a finite verb, if the subject pronoun is excepted. As a general rule this is suffixed to the word immediately preceding the the verb in the sentence. The subject may be added to the verb, and if nothing precedes the verb in the sentence, it must be affixed to the *a*.

(*b*) When this *a* is omitted, we have the same idea, the concept as qualified by the verbal tense suffix and other suffixes or infixes, but not specifically referred to demonstrated reality. With this *a* we have a demonstrated fact; without this there seems to be no demonstration, provided the idea or concept is not attached as an appendix to a word that in a sense takes the place of this *a* (cf. para 188 (a)).

(*c*) An example will show, how it may work. The Santals have an expression in constant use, viz., *okoe badae*, lit. who knowing? or, who knows? an indefinite question, expressing uncertainty or lack of knowledge on the part of the speaker in common with all others. Used in this way it is never *okoe badaea.* On the other hand, when it is a question with stress on 'who', we have the regular construction generally with the otherwise eliminated subject pronoun, *okoeye badaea*, who knows, who is it that actually knows (this matter ? or *okoeko badaea*, who know ?

(*d*) When reference is made to a possibility, when there is doubt, and even when a concrete fact is mentioned with reference to some one's knowledge, the finite *a* is or may be omitted. Thus, if *paset'* (or any of its parallel forms), or *co* (*ñ*) (whether expressing doubt or used as an affirmation in which case the finite *a* becomes superfluous), or *ba* (*ñ*) (functioning not as a direct negation, but to express doubt or a question) is used in connection with the verb, the finite *a* is regularly omitted.*

E. g., *paset'e hijuk'*, perhaps he will come; *pasere pasec'-ko calaoen*, perhaps they are gone; *okoe badae, hijuk' coe bañ coñ*, who knows whether he will come or not; *ac' coe men akat'*, why, he has himself said so; *goc'en coe*, why, he is dead (as you know); *bañ doe añjom akat'*, whether he has heard (I wonder); *hec'len bae*, provided he comes.

(*e*) The finite *a* is further often omitted in sentences conveying a wish, also in certain conditional expressions. It is

* Santals will often use the finite *a* in sentences with *paset'* or *coñ*; but in such cases the *paset'* or *coñ* is not attached to the verb itself, but to some other part of the sentence, if it is not that the speaker has had his language too much 'educated' in schools, in which case his native idiom may have been tainted by the grammar of a foreign language.

always omitted in the Imperative, but not in the Prohibitive, provided this does not convey the idea of a wish, when it may be omitted or substituted by *ma*. Conditional sentences introduced by *khajuk* do not take the finite *a* (the negation is *alo*).

It is also rather frequent to hear the finite *a* omitted in vivid narratives, the whole possibly being a kind of appeal to one's imagination; often *dǫ* may be heard as a kind of substitute.

As a common rule it may be said that the finite *a* is omitted when there is no demonstrated reference to fact.* It should, however, be distinctly understood, that an omission of the finite *a* does not imply that what is said is not a fact; it is only not 'demonstrated.'

E. g., *teheń bar̥ẹko hijuk'*, might they come to-day; *uniye calak' iń hǫń calak'*, if he goes, I shall also go; *khajukem ẹm ruar̥tiń*, provided you bring back what belongs to me; *alo bar̥ẹm sorok'*, may you not come near;

adǫe ńẹlkede dǫ, carẹc' menak'tae; *adǫ ḍẹkẹye tunum aikauket', tayǫm sẹc' dǫ bhugak'getae*, then he saw (the fish), it has a straw (through the gills); then he felt his hindquarters with his paw, there is a hole in his back (from a folk tale).

(*f*) For the cases where other particles are used in stead of the finite *a*, see paras 330 ss.

327. When two or more verbs follow each other having the same subject, the subject is repeated with each following verb, while the finite *a* is often added only to the last verb. This naturally is the case, when, as frequently

---

* There may possibly in the present-day language be signs of the real signification of the finite *a* not being quite clear to all speakers. It may be heard used, where one would not expect it, and it may often be left out, where a more formal language would seem to demand it. It is especially the use of it in certain cases that does not seem to fit in.

The Santal verb has been compared to a picture: the base is the picture, the suffix etc. is the framing, the *a* is the hanging of the picture.

happens, the first verb does not consist of more than the subject and the conjugational base. It should be noted that a conjunction in such cases is necessary between the verbs. If such is wanting, there is in ordinary speech either a fully constructed verb or a participial construction.

In the peculiar language of the *bakhẽṛ* (invocation of bongas) two verbs constantly stand together without conjunction and with only one finite *a*, also often with only one subject. The same may also be heard in *binti*.

E. g. toyoko sap'kede arko gọc'kedea, they caught and killed the jackal (or - *ko sap' arko gọc'kedea*); but in *bakhẽṛ*: *alope bọlọ ocoe sọṛọ ocoea* do not let it come in, soak through; *tẹnke hạrup'keape*, may you press down, cover up;

ghạṭem mañgao akat'te alegele hataoket' gọk'ket'tamale, as you have acknowledged your transgression we have taken over and carry it for you.

328. (*a*) In subordinate clauses the finite *a* is not regularly added to the verb. If the *a* is heard in sentences that should be classified as subordinate, as, e. g., in relative clauses, the statement is to be taken as an appositional or disjointed principal clause, to which reference is made.*

(*b*) In what corresponds to our relative clauses one might say that the word to which the relative sentence is attached represents what the finite *a* otherwise stands for. This is especially observable when the relative clause precedes the word to which it is an attribute. See para 188 (a) and above para 326 (b).

(*c*) In final clauses the *a* is never used, when these are introduced by *jẹmọn* (in recent time borrowed from Bengali) or by *jãhã lekate* (lit. by somehow), both giving the idea of 'in order that'. If there is any optative sense conveyed, *ma* is often used where the finite *a* would be in the Indicative.

* The use of the finite *a* in what is really subordinate clauses seems to be rather common with many. Cp. remarks above para 326 (d), footnote.

(*d*) Possibly the original form of a final clause in Santali is a sentence with a postpositional *mẹnte* (lit. by saying). This *mẹnte* is always preceded by the finite *a*; in case *mẹnte* is preceded by a word functioning like an Infinitive (i. e., without a subject pronoun and a verbal suffix other than that of the Indeterminate) an *a* is also used, in which case the demonstrative nature of the *a* is very evident.

It will be seen that the real meaning of this construction is 'by saying' or 'thinking' or 'meaning' what is stated in a preceding principal cause.

E. g., *metakom, jẹmọnko calak'*, tell them that they go; *mit' jomkaogeko tahẹna, jãhã lekate ọkọe hǫ̃ õkokate jan aloko lại dareae (ma)*, they all remain together, in order that no one shall be able to inform the witch-finder secretly (*ma* may or may not be used);

sendrare enkogeye boṅgawakoa, aloren họr sendrare bhạganko hoyok' ar boge bogeteko rụạra mẹnte, at the hunt he performs sacrifices to these (mentioned) bongas, in order that the village people may be succesful hunting and return home safe and sound; *kuli jọṅa mẹnteń hẹc' akana*, I have come to ask.

329. In consecutive and descriptive subordinate clauses introduced by *onate*, *cet' leka*, *cet' lekate*, *oka leka*, and *oka lekate*, no finite *a* is used, so long as they are used as subordinate clauses. It is, however, very frequent to hear these sentences treated as principal propositions with finite *a*. Sentences with *onate* in such cases retain the literal meaning of *onate*, which then does not act as a quasi conjunction, but is to be taken literally as 'by that'.

Similarly the descriptive subordinate sentences (with *cet' leka*, etc.) often become interrogative sentences.

E. g, *dalkedeako, onate bae beret' dareat'*, they beat him so he could not stand up; *khange disom họr ẹtọm kọńẹko badaea, lańma, dob hoyena, onate sor sorrenko ńir jarwak'a*, then the people to the right and to the left know, that an accident has happend, so those near by come together in a hurry;

lạiat'leae. cet' lekale bẹbọhar, he told us how we should act; *họr udukaeme, cet' lekateye calak'*, show him the way, how he is to go;

bạń bujhạu daṛeak' kana, oka lekateko ạsulok' kan, I am unable to understand how they are supporting themselves;

pạhil dọ disome ńumtạkoa, inạkate ato, inạkate kulhi oka lekate menak'a, first he gives the name of their country, then of their village, thereupon he tells how their village street runs.

---

330. In a number of verbal forms we find in stead of the finite *a* some other particle or even word, viz., *ge, ma, bań, nạhi*, further *ẹnẹc'* (with parallel forms *ena* and *enań*), *an, anań* and *anẹc'*.

The late Mr. Skrefsrud has in his Grammar taken some of the forms resulting from the particles and words mentioned being added to some verbal suffixes as constituting separate 'tenses (or rather moods)', as he expresses himself. This may be convenient to show the use or meaning, but a good many more names of moods than those used would be required. The difficulty is to decide which agglutinating forms are entitled to get a specific name.

The particles and words mentioned take the place of the finite *a*, when used as here below described. While the finite *a* places the verb, or rather what the verb describes, inside demonstrated reality, these particles may be said to give expression to the relation of the verbal concept to actuality as represented by the subject.

The way in which these particles are functioning will be shown here below.

ge.

331. (*a*) *Ge* is an emphatic particle used in connection with any word or concept that may be emphasized. It is very

commonly used in the verb, directly preceding the finite *a*. In such cases the *ge* is simply emphatic and nothing more. It may also be only emphatic when the verb has no finite *a*.

(*b*) In certain verbal forms the finite *a* is omitted, and the *ge* takes the place of the finite *a*. This happens in connection with the suffixes of the Simple Past, in all sets of suffixes, in the Active, the Medium and the Passive, further with the suffixes of the Anterior.

(*c*) In connection with the suffixes of the Simple Past the *ge* emphasizes the performance of the act, not, however, with reference to past time, but with reference to a succession of happenings or acts performed as the obvious or customary result following some just described or mentioned act or condition. The form does not describe concrete reality, but something supposed to happen, in accordance with known custom; or what will certainly happen in certain circamstances or under certain conditions.

The narrator 'sees' what happens, obviously and naturally supervening, not as something coming, but as already performed. We have the real meaning of the verbal suffix, viz. an act performed without reference to time, simply the act itself performed.

The form is not used and cannot be used commencing a narrative; we have first a general statement of a supposed fact in the Indeterminate or the Future, or even the Imperative; then this tense form comes, sometimes alternating with the Indeterminate.

Mr. Skrefsrud called this form the Contingent; it has also been called a hypothetical or imaginary Future.

(*d*) Besides as stated this form is also used (in the apodosis) to state the consequence, what will happen under certain conditions. This form is especially used when the whole is only supposed.

E. g., gonoṅ toraoni ńamkate bariatko doko johar barawakoa; ado meromko tiak'kedege, handiko dipilket'ge, caoleko ghẽtket'ge, buluṅ sasaṅko sap'ket'ge, hanko tora derate, when the bridegroom's party have received the gifts usual after the payment of the bride-price they make their obeisance to them (the bride's parents); thereupon they lead the goat away, take the beer-pot on the head, tie the rice up in their clothes, take the salt and the turmeric, and there they are off to their lodgings;

gapa bare hijuk'me setak' tora, ado birtelaṅ calaoenge, come to-morrow morning at once, then we shall go to the forest;

aimai do usat' akanre boge katham metaere hõ etraṅat'megeye, when in the sulks, even when you speak friendly to her, a woman will snap at you; *arhõ seṅgel harsurena menkhan adokin sorenge*, when the fire again burns low they draw near; *orak're baṅ ńamleko khan doṅ hec' ruarenge*, if I do not find them at home I shall come back.

(*e*) As remarked above, *ge* is added to the suffixes of the Anterior (in the Active *le* with or without object infix, in the Medium or Passive *len*, or Medium with indirect object *an*). This form is used to express what is purposed to happen before something else is done, or what is willed or must or should be done previously to something else. It will be seen, we have not a concrete reality, only what is purposed and emphasized as such.

This form frequently has the postposition *re* added to the suffix, the *ge* following the *re*, showing what the *ge* means to the Santal mind, viz. its use to emphasize a statement.

E g., aṅjomle takogeṅ, I must first hear what they have to say; *birteṅ senlenge*, I must first go to the forest; *hape, jowangeṅ, adobon calak'a*, wait I must first have my food, then we shall go;

sap'lekore gem cekakoa, even if you catch them what will you do with them?

(*f*) This *ge* is also heard added to the Accidental Past, see para 291.

ma

332. *Ma* is a particle conveying an optative, benedictive, precative, cohortative, permissive or admissive sense.

(*a*) *Ma* is used in many ways, and, what concerns us here, also in connection with the verb. It is very commonly used in connection with the Imperative, toning the command down to practically a wish. On the other hand the verbal form with *ma* in stead of the finite *a* often is a polite Imperative, and a way of giving an order in a person other than the second.

(*b*) We find this *ma* used in stead of the finite *a* in all verbal forms from which an Imperative may be formed, i. e., in the Indeterminate or the Future and tenses formed by having *tahẹn* added (the Continuative form), and in the Anterior, Active, the Medium and the Passive, with direct and in the in direct object, of the general and of the Intentional forms.*

(*c*) As regards construction there is nothing special to remark; we have the full verbal construction of the tenses alluded to, only that *ma* is used in stead of *a*.

The form is used to denote a permission, a wish or an encouragement.

The negation used in connection with this form is always *alo*.

(*d*) *Ma* is also often used in a looser connection with the verb without the finite *a*, but without *ma* taking the place of the finite *a*. This construction is used as a reference to a known fact as an admission or a remonstrance.

E. g., *iń hǫń ńẹlko ma*, let me also have a look at them; *jae korarkom ńẹl tiok'leko ma, ạurim gujuk're*, may you see great-grand-children, before you die; *cako ńũan ma*, let them first have their tea; *gọrọam mako*, may they help you; *dọhọ akako tahẹn mae*, let him continue to keep them; *alo barẹko lạiako ma*, may they not tell them;

* Mr. Skrefsrud treated the forms with *ma* as separate moods, calling them Benedictive or Precative and Preliminary do.

hijuk̓ mako, let them come; *iñ uni lahare baṛẹñ gọc'len ma,* might I die before him; *disom họṛ reak̓ ic' ado jọmteye harakok̓ ma,* may he grow up eating the excrements of the people (a common form of 'blessing' a child); *duṛup' akan tahẹn mako,* let them remain sitting; *Isore bhọrako tam ma,* may God bless your ones.

Ona mañ rọṛ akat', why, I have said so; *ona dọ hẽ ma hẽge,* that is quite so, but-; *iñ ma bañ sẹnlen,* I did not go (as you know).

bañ and nạhĩ.

333. Both these words are really the same, the first being the Santali negation and the second the Hindi *nạhĩ,* by the Santals pronounced as written.

(*a*) *Bañ* is the full form of the ordinary Santal negation, used when functioning as a negation without having a pronoun or *cọ* (*ñ*) attached to it. Before these it is commonly only *ba.* When added to the verb as here below shown it is, however, also often heard as only *ba.*

(*b*) While *bañ* is the common negation, *nạhĩ* is not used outside the construction here below mentioned, except, so far as the writer has observed, in two expressions.

One of these exceptions is akin to the construction here discussed, viz., *nạhĩ* added to a word functioning as an infinitive and followed by *chạị* (as e. g., *sẹn nạhĩye chạilena, ẹkẹne ajare baṛa joñ kana,* go—he did nothing of the kind, he is only going round gossiping); the other exception is *nạhĩ nindhạn,* used in the meaning of 'somehow or other', 'by no manner of means', or, 'approximately' (e. g., *nạhĩ nindhạn judi bae daṛeak' khan jãhãebon ạcukoa,* if he is absolutely unable, we must hire someone or other).

334. (*a*) *Bañ* and *nạhĩ* are used in stead of the finite *a* added to the suffixes of the Anterior in the Active, Medium and Passive with direct or indirect object. Mr. Skrefsrud treated these constructions as separate 'moods', calling the Anterior with *bañ* Preliminary Persuasive, and the Anterior with *nạhĩ* Preliminary Expostulative.

The same two negations may, however, also be in the same way added to other tenses than those mentioned. We find them added to the Indeterminate, both in the General and the Intentional form, and to the Perfect, in all voices, also to the Present and the Simple Past.

(*b*) The postposition *rẹ* is often added to the constructed verb preceding the *baṅ* or the *nḁhĩ*.

(*c*) The construction denotes that the contents of the verb to which the one or the other of the two negations is added are a *conditio sine qua non* for the possibility of the implied apodosis.

(*d*) The meaning may be expostulative, admonitory, persuasive or retorting. There is little difference in the use of the two negations. *Baṅ* seems to be a little more decisive and objective, while *nḁhĩ* possibly has a more subjective turn. Mr. Skrefsrud describes what he calls Preliminary Expostulative (*le nḁhĩ, len nḁhĩ*) as exposing the fallacy of an argument or the unreasonableness of a demand; what he calls Preliminary Persuasive (*le baṅ, len baṅ*) he describes as being used to remind or persuade the person addressed that what he imagines to be easy of accomplishment really requires the adoption of some preliminary measure which may prove unattainable or impracticable. The definitions are quite good; but really what is said about the one form may just as well be said about the other.

E. g., dak'le baṅ dọle si dạreak'a, only when it has rained we shall be able to plough; *kombṛole sap'leko nḁhĩ dọle ạgukoa*, when we have caught the thieves, then only we shall (be able to) bring them; *muṭhiạule bam ṭarhaoea, bae dạṛket'a?* only when you catch firmly hold of him you will be able to keep him; did he not run away? (note the Simple Past after *baṅ*, here not functioning as a regular negation); *peṛako lagaolen baṅ bapla dọ hoyok'a*, only when you get a proposal (lit. friends are applied), there will be a marriage;

khetem sile nāhī dǫm arjaoa, only when you plough your rice-field you will get any crops; *ran dǫń emamgea, adǫm jǫmle nāhī,* I shall give medicine, but you must take it to get any benefit; *cedak' unąk'em diriyena? Ńam hǫt'le nāhīm ągu gǫda,* why are you so late? You must get it quickly to be able to bring it quickly; *jǫlen nāhīm gǫda,* there must be fruit to enable you to pluck;

emamre bań thǫm ąguia, only when they give it you you can bring it;

isinket' nāhīko loama, only when they have prepared (cooked) they will serve you (also *isin akat' nāhī*); *dąṛ dąṛeak' nāhīye dąṛa,* only when able to run he will run; *ańjǫmet' nāhīye gǫńmea,* only when hearing he will answer you.

an, anań, anęč.

335. *An, anań, anęc'* are used in connection with a couple of verbs in stead of the finite *a* (which, however, may also be used; it is entirely optional).

The use of these particles in stead of the finite *a* is restricted to the verbs *menak'* (with its parallel *henak'*) and *bǫnuk'*. They are further used in connection with the interrogative adverb *okor* and certain demonstratives.

The demonstrative character of these particles is evident; their use in connection with demonstratives and the interrogative *okor* clearly shows the fundamental meaning.*

An is mostly used added to *bǫnuk'*; *anań* and *anęc'* are mostly used in connection with inanimates; with animates

---

* *An* seems here to be the finite *a* with the *n* mentioned para 59 added; *anań* and *anęč* may be this *an* further developed.

Curiously enough a number of individuals constantly use *anęč* in stead of the finite *a* in connection with the finite verb. It is a habit they have acquired. This use of *anęč* apparently becomes the custom of the members of a family or even of a whole village. A couple of miles away from the writer's present home there is a fairly large village where about half the Santal population uses this peculiarity, all these being relatives and descendants of a former pargana. The Santals themselves may be heard making jesting remarks on this kind of speech. Such people will say, *holae calaoenanęč,* he went yesterday; or *gapako hijuk̇anęč,* they will come to-morrow.

they are mostly used by people who have acquired the habit mentioned in the footnote of using *anec'* for *a*.

Another use of *anan* and *anec'* will be found mentioned para 336.

E. g., *menak'anan*, it is, exists, is to be found (besides *menak'a* and *menak'anec'*); *banuk'an*, it is not (found) (besides *banuk'a*, *banuk'anec'* and *banuk'anan*); *banugic'an*, he is not (here) (not, however, *banugic'anec'*).

Okor anan, why, where is it? (it is not to be seen here); *okorkoan okare*, why, where are they? (I do not see them); *one anec' katha*, that is the matter (as just stated).

ena, enec', enan, anan, anec'.

336. These particles are added to verbal constructions and to single words, conveying the meaning of 'then first', 'then only', i. e., what is stated must be previous to something else.* When used with a verb there is no finite *a*.

The particles are, added to a verb, mostly used with the Anterior.

Used in connection with the Anterior of the verb these particles serve to emphasize the necessary precedence or previousness of the verbal concept.

The particles are used indiscriminately, some preferring one, others another; *enan* is, however, seldom heard, probably because this word is generally used as an adverb in the meaning of 'some time ago'.

Mr. Skrefsrud in his grammar calls the Anterior with *ena* Preliminary Admissive.

E. g., *ran do jomle jirqule enae guna*, only when you have taken and retained the medicine, it will have effect; *oktere jomle enec' hormore dare bujhauka*, only when one takes one's food at the proper time, bodily strength is felt; *daple anan*

* These particles are all demonstrative elements with certain suffixes added, possibly the same that is found in the verbal suffixes *en* and *an*. The idea is likely something like 'that done'. See paras 151—153.

(or *ṇẹc'*) *ṭhikoka*, when it is thatched then only it will be right; *sẹnlen ṇẹc'*, only when (you) go;

ạyup' enae hijuk'a, he will only come when it has become evening (we would naturally translate 'not until' or 'not before', but it should be noted that there is no negation); *sẹnkate ange'*, only when (you) have gone.

---

337. A construction with a full verb, except the final *a* or any of its substitutes, remains to be mentioned. We have the full verb with the subject affixed at the end where the finite *a* would otherwise be. There is nothing irregular in it; it is only the position of the subject that has seemed strange to some (cf. below para 339 (d)). It is not a participial construction, because we have the verbal subject; we have a parallel participial construction, where the subject is replaced by the determinative suffix, identical with the sentence here dealt with in the Dual and the Plural, but different in the Singular (- *ic'* for - *e*).

With the determinative suffix we have a singling out or identification of the actor; with the verbal subject the act itself has the stress, what the subject has done, or what has been done to the subject. The construction might be compared with a relative clause, but we have not here any word to which there is direct reference; the subject implies this. We have a kind of sentence substantive, if such an expression could be used.

This construction has been used in the translation of the creed (*küṛi kuṛi Mạriạ khon janamlene, - gọc'lene*, etc.). *E. g.*, *dalkedeye*, who committed the act of beating him, but *dalkedeyić* the one who beat him.

---

338. (*a*) We have hitherto considered the verb when having the finite *a*, and when taking certain particles or words in the place of this *a*. With this *a* the verb is in the Indicative;

the statement concerns (actual or supposed) demonstrable reality. Without this *a*, but with something in its place, the contents of the verb becomes applied in accordance with the substitute.

We have further seen the verb without any finite *a* or other particle, as is the case in relative sentences (see paras 188 and 326), in the special construction mentioned para 337, and in final and consecutive clauses (see paras 328 and 329), and nothing further needs to be said here.

(*b*) We shall now deal with subordinate clauses, sentences that are in Santali closed up with a postposition, one or the other of those previously dealt with as added to a single or compound word, but here when added to a constructed verb.

(*c*) When a verb occurs, as is very frequently the case, with a postposition, but without a subject, it should be noted that we have to do, not with a clause proper (naturally except when we have a verb with an inanimate subject), but with a participial construction.

Subsidiary clauses formed by postpositions.

339. (*a*) Except for the above mentioned relative, final and consecutive clauses, all subsidiary clauses are in Santali formed with the help of postpositions; these always come in the place where the finite *a* should have been in a sentence with a fully equipped verb, just following the tense suffix (with or without infixes) and auxiliaries.

(*b*) These postpositions are the same as, although not all, those enumerated paras 87 ss. The most commonly occurring are: ***khan***, ***rẹ***, ***tẹ***, ***ṭhẹn***, ***khọn***, ***dhạbic'***, ***tuluc'***, ***sẹlẹt'*** and ***ịạte***. The meaning conveyed by the postposition and the tense suffix must naturally not be incompatible.

(*c*) These postpositions do service for our prepositions and conjunctions. In the verb the principal reference is to an action, the performance of the concept. If we remember, what has been several times remarked, that the Santal apparently has mental pictures of what he states, the use of the postpositions is more easily understood. The postposition states the relation in which one concept stands to another.

(*d*) It should be noted, that when the subsidiary clause consists of only the verb and the postposition, i. e., when in the clause there is no word preceding the verb to which the verbal subject might be affixed, the subject pronouns is always affixed to the postposition.

(*e*) Examples of the use of these postpositions in connection with the verb have been given previously, and the reader is referred to these (see paras 87 ss.).

(*f*) We shall here examine the use of a few postpositions that are used more especially in connection with verbal constructions, viz. *khan* (*khac'*), *re* and *te*.

—*khan*.

340. (*a*) *Khan* (with its parallel form *khac'*)* is used to mark the time when, or the condition when. It refers to the time, when anything will or may happen, happens or has happened; in analogy with our 'when' it may get the meaning of a conditional postposition. The temporal meaning is, however, the original one, and likely always present. In connection with the Anterior of the verb, we have to translate it with a conditional conjunction.

* As regards the origin of this *khan* or *khač*, it might be tempting to connect it with Sanskrit *kshana* or *kshaṇa*, a twinkling of an eye, instant, moment. Probably the same word is found in the Santal name for time, *jokhan*, *jokha*, *jokhak̃*, more commonly *jọkhẹn* or *jọkhẹč*. The

(*b*) ***Khan*** **is very frequently used as a postposition to single words, then mostly in a conditional meaning. It is also, as mentioned para 98, used at the commencement of a sentence, in the meaning of 'then', 'thereupon'. In this case what has already been told is implied and understood; but the word has in this use probably become something like an adverb. Used as stated it has commonly a *ge* suffixed.**

The same *khan* is added to *men* (*menkhan*, lit. when said, or, when saying) and the word is used, (1) as a conjunction meaning 'but', (2) as a postposition, always preceded by the finite *a*, in the meaning of 'when' or 'if' (conditional).

E. g., *angayenkhan Liţai hec' got'ena*, when it became dawn, Lita came at once; *ser puraulentabon khane idibona hanapurite*, when the seer (what God gives for food at birth) is finished He takes us away to the other world;

jãhãtis jãhãtis banako ńamlekore adi hor iate bako tuń dareako khan, ţhengateko dal gitic'koa, sometimes when they get a bear they will knock him down with sticks, when they are unable to shoot him on account of the number of people present; *amem senlenkhan iń hõń calak'a*, if you go I shall also go;

adoń onkaket' khac', since I have done so (what is to be said?);

adokin mena, kora gidra khan babalań ńumea, then (the parents) say, if it is a boy, we shall name him after father;

ado khange, or *khange ado*, thereupon, thereafter; *khac'ge tho cet' hõ bae ror dareat'a*, then he could not say anything; *khanko menket'a*, then they said;

endekhan, then, in that case; *tobekhan*, then;

nit khanińcalak'a, I shall go if needed now at once;

apeak' khan hataope, in case it is yours, take it;

baben jutok' kan khac' ale mõrẽ hor dole cekaea, if you two cannot hit it off with one another, what can we the village community do?

---

change of *n* to *c* or vice versa makes some difficulty, as this change would seem to presuppose a *kha* with addition of the adjective-forming *n* or *c*. *Khan* and *khin* are found in Hindi in the meaning of moment.

So far as meaning is concerned the derivation would fit very well ('the moment' - something happens).

gidrą auriko baplak're onkoren eṅgate gǫc'lenkhan, onkoren apate chuṭkianre hõ hǫpǫnko begarok' bako khǫj daṛeak'a; menkhan koṛa hǫpǫnko bapla akana mẹnkhan ona jǫkhẹc', sanaleko khan ko begar daṛeak'a, when the mother dies before her children are married the sons cannot demand separation, even if their father has married again; but if the sons have been married at that time they may, if they wish, separate (i. e. divide the land and set up separate households);

hoṛ dǫṅ ṅẹllet'koa, mẹnkhan bạṅ oromlet'koa, I saw people, but I did not recognize them;

bae aṅgǫcket'a mẹnkhan iṅ ṭhen ạguyepe, if he does not confess bring him to me (note the tense suffix, *ket'* after *baṅ*); *nuiye tahẽyena mẹnkhan am tahẹn reak' jạruṛ dǫ bạnuk'a,* if this one remains there is no need for you to stay; *baṅkhac' dǫ,* to be sure, of course, naturally; otherwise; *hẹc' baṅkhane cekak'a,* of course he will come; *rǫṛ akat' khane,* if he has said.

—*re.*

341. As regards the meaning of *re* the reader is referred to para 87 (a). *Re* denotes 'in', 'inside', 'within', and refers to time and space, or (in a verb) to a concept as modified by an action.

When used with the verb reference is to the condition brought about, or to be brought about, by the verbal construction. According to the verbal suffix used it may be translated, 'when', 'while', 'during', 'in case', or with similar words.

In connection with certain suffixes we have to render *re* with a conditional conjunction. In these last named constructions it often has a *hõ*, also, added.

Special attention might be drawn to the use of *re* between the verbal suffix (if such is used) and *ge, baṅ* and *nạhĩ* (as in the Anterior with these particles, see paras 284 and 330).

Re may follow a fully equipped sentence (only without the finite *a*) or any verbal form.

Besides the examples given para 87 (a) the following will show the use :

sedaere ṭaka ạuri janamok're, formerly, before money came into use; *oṛak'reko duṛup' akan tahẽkanre,* while they were sitting in the house; *Asamteko sẹnlenre,* when (in case) they go to Assam (or, when they went or had gone, the meaning depending on the context); *ạpuñe gọc'enre Asamreñ tahẽkana,* I was in Assam when my father died; *ạpuñe gọc'lenre ọhọñ tahẽlena,* when my father dies (whenever that may happen) I shall certainly not remain; *kuṭạm ḍaṅgra boṅgak' dọ jọm simlenre sẹ manan jãhãnlere hoyok'a,* the bullock-felling-sacrifice is performed, when the *jọm sim* festival is held or when a vow of some sort is made;

menaere hõ sẹ bạnugic're họ baṅ cekak'a, it does not matter whether he is here or not; *emañre hõm,* even if you give it me;

dak'iñ ñũanrege, I must have a drink of water before anything else;

calak're, when going; *bik'cạrreko gọṛọaea,* they assist him in judging;

ñamkatere hõe karac' kurujok'a, even when he has got it he will grumble.

—te.

342. The postposition *te* may, when added to a noun, mean either movement towards (anything inanimate), or the instrumentality or cause, the attending circumstance, the means or manner. When added to a verbal construction the first mentioned meaning never occurs, as might be expected. It is always the other, and its use is analogous to what has been stated para 92 (c) with the restrictions naturally following the *te* being suffixed to a verbal construction. It denotes the cause, the instrumentality, or the attending circumstances.

We may translate it 'as', 'since', 'when', 'because' or with similar conjunctions, or simply with a participial construction.

This *te* is frequently used in descriptive narratives, the verb taking the *te* stating what took place before or during the happening of the finite verb.

E. g., *onkoko hec'ente iṅdoṅ chuṭiyena*, as they came I got free; *Asamreko seṭerente asulok' reak' bhabna cabayentakoa*, when they arrived in Assam their anxieties in connection with supporting themselves ceased; *adoko guric' ṭanḍiket'te holoṅteko khonḍket'a, ado gaiko agu sorkedete dak'ko chiṭkau-adea*, so they prepared a place plastering it with cowdung and made a magic circle with flour; thereupon they brought the cow near and sprinkled water on her;

hape hapete beret'enteye calaoena, getting up quietly he went away; *calak' calak'teye bindarena*, he fell down as he was walking along.

343. *Te* is very extensively used added to *ka* and *a*, forming the postpositions *kate* and *ate*. These have been dealt with previously. See paras 95 and 97 (b). They are here mentioned functioning as verbal postpositions.

(*a*) *Kate* being the Intentional Indeterminate suffix *ka* with *te* affixed cannot be added to anything else than the bare base-word, never to a verbal suffix. It is only used in participial constructions and not with a verb having a pronominal subject. By use it has apparently melted into one particle, so its composition is not felt.* It may thus have the postposition *re* added. See last example para 341.

The meaning conveyed is 'by doing' or something similar, or, very frequently, it may be translated 'having done', viz. what the base-word expresses.

---

* While it seems to be beyond question that *kate* is composed as stated, the form is in one respect different from what it should regularly be. *Ka* is the bare suffix of the Indeterminate Intentional; but when used as a suffix in connection with a word functioning as a verb it has always an infix following, a personal pronoun infix (for animates), an *ṅ* for inanimates, or if this is wanting, a genitive infix in its stead. Only in the Imperative the subject pronoun may be added to the bare *ka*. We have here apparently to do with a kind of neutral form, Active, but without any object infix. Cf. para 306 (b).

Kate may be added to all conjugational bases except the Performative. When added to the Repetitive base the meaning conveyed is the same as when the Intentional suffixes are affixed to this base, a frustrated or not fully performed attempt.

Kate is frequently used in narratives as a conjunction or an adverb in the meaning of 'this done', 'thereafter', always referring to a previous statement. Cf. the similar use of *khan* or *khange*. For other uses of *kate* see para 95.

E. g., jǫmkateko calak'a (- *calaoena*), having eaten they will go (or, went); *buj sujkate kạmipe*, work intelligently (thinking of what you are doing); *phạsiạrakateye hataoket'a*, he took it acting deceitfully; *gǫc'kate*, having died, after death; *gǫc' gǫc'kateye pharnaoena*, after having nearly died he recovered; *idiket'ako*; *kate ńẹl baṛaket'ako*, they took it away; thereupon they looked at it; *idi idikateye tahẽ ocoat'koa*, having made several attempts at taking them away he let them remain.

(*b*) *Kaete*, possibly a sideform to *kate* is heard in a few words, such as, *ḍherkaete* and *asǫkaete*, both meaning 'especially', 'particularly', 'as a rule'.

(*c*) *Ate* is a demonstrative *a* with *te* affixed, lit. 'this-with' or 'this-by'.

Ate is added to the bare base (in analogy with *kate*); when this is functioning as a verb it denotes a circumstance attending the performance of the word to which the word with *ate* is added. It may be translated 'with', or by the Present Participle of the verb to which it is affixed.

The relationship of *ante* and *ate* is observable. The first denotes possession of what the word denotes, *ate* only some attending circumstance.

Ate may be added to all conjugational bases except the Performative.

E. g., rak'ateye calaoena, she went away crying; *seren serenate*, singing; *hoṛateye calaoena*, he went accompanied by people (not alone); but *hoṛanteye calaoena*, he went taking people with him (who were expected to do something for him).

344. The verbal postpositions hitherto dealt with all presuppose the omission of the finite *a*. The language has one postposition that used in connection with a verb demands the finite *a*, viz. *mẹnte*.

Mẹnte has been dealt with under the Postpositions (see para 96 (d)). As there mentioned the literal meaning of this *mẹnte* is 'by saying'. When used in connection with a word functioning as a verb this literal meaning is generally discernible. As mentioned it is always preceded by the finite *a*, except, naturally, when the verb is in the Imperative.

Mẹnte is used in connection with both direct and oblique oration, following the quotation. When following more than one sentence or verb, the common way is to have *mẹnte* at the last verb and to omit the *a* in all verbs, except the last one immediately preceding the *mẹnte*.

The use of *mẹnte* to finish off a directly or indirectly reported speech is the old and apparently genuine way of the language. As already mentioned (see para 96 (d) footnote) many present day Santals have under the influence of Bengali or Hindi commenced in stead to use *je* or *jẹ*, corresponding to English *that*, introducing the sentence.

Otherwise a common way of introducing direct oration is to use *baṅma** before quoting the sentence, or, as is frequently the case, to do without anything either introductory or final; one has the bare quotation and nothing more. In ordinary colloquial language this is perhaps the common way.

E. g., *mẹn akawadeaṅ, ọkọe hŏ aloe lạiakoa mẹnte*, I have told him, that he must not tell anybody; *ọkọe hŏ bako rọṛlak'a, ẹm ruạṛkak'me mẹnte*, no one said, give it back.

---

* I have heard it said (not, however, by a Santal), that in certain parts of the country *baṅma* is used conveying a meaning of uncertainty or referring only to a hear-say statement.

Conditional particles used in connection with the verb.

345. The language has a number of conditional particles used in connection with the verb about what would have happened in certain circumstances or under certain conditions, which have not, however, taken place, as a result of which the consequence did not happen either.

These particles are: *honaṅ*, *hoṇeċ'*, *huneċ'*, *hoteċ'*, *huteċ'*, *hutạm*, *hutkeċ'* and *hutkạm*.*

The particle may be added to the verb either in the protasis or in the apodosis. The protasis is often only implied, not spoken.

There does not seem to be any difference in the use of these particles; they are used indiscriminately and may be translated by 'in that case', 'then' or some similar word, if the particle needs any translation at all.

E. g., *am alom heċ'lenkhan iṅ doko hoekiṅa honaṅ*, if you had not come they would have done for me; *noṇḍe hoteċ'em aṛea*, here you should have made the embankment; *nẹ hutạmle sẹnkoka*, we should have gone just now (if you had not stopped us); *alo huteċ'e calak'khan doe goċ'kok'a*, if he had not gone he would have died; *aloe hijuk'khan iṅ hutkạmiṅ ṅamkea*, if he should not come, I should get it.

The Infinitive and Participles.

346. The language has no special form or suffix to show the Infinitive. From what has been stated about the word-concepts ruling the language (see para 9) it will be understood that the Indeterminate or Future of any conjugational base in any voice and in any set of suffixses may function as an Infinitive. There is naturally no subject and no finite *a* (except

---

* I am inclined to suggest that these particles are forms of the verbal root *bhu*, to be, borrowed partly from Bengali, partly from Hindi, with a Santali final consonant or syllable.

when the 'Infinitive' is followed by *mẹnte*); but the 'Infinitive' may take direct and indirect object infixes and also possessive infixes.

Attention must, however, be drawn to what has been stated about the word-concept, that a bare word may stand for any form of speech, for an Infinitive, a Present Participle, a Perfect Participle of the Passive, and so on, there being nothing in the word itself to show, how it is to be understood. When the term Infinitive is used, it is because this term fits certain cases; but it will be understood that as used for Santali the term has a wider application than in our languages.

While any bare word may be used functioning, in accordance with our ideas, as an Infinitive, it should be borne in mind that in many cases the language will, to avoid misunderstanding, use the Performative, more especially to express our Active Infinitive, and in the case of words used in the Medium or the Passive, the base-word with the Indeterminate or Future Medium suffix *ok'* (*k'*) or the Passive Performative *ogok'* (- *gok'*).

A base-word in any of the forms mentioned above followed by *lạgit'* (*lagat'*) or *-a mẹnte* will in all cases be possible of being translated by an Infinitive. In many cases I am under the impression that what we call a Participle will often be nearer the concept of the Santal mind.*

The examples here following will show the use.

E. g., *jọmko metadea,* they told him to eat; *ọlọk' paṛhao dọñ baḍaegea,* I know to write and read; *eskar tahẹn dọ bañ bogea,* it is not good to live alone; *bạk'gi dọ alga dọ bañ kana,* it is not easy to leave off; *gujuk'e duṛup' akana,* he is sitting to die (is on his deathbed); *dadale chuṭạuka,* he will com-

---

* When Mr. Skrefsrud in his grammar states that the language has an Infinitive also for each tense, this was naturally a slip of the pen.

mence to strike; *hako sap'ko calaoena*, they have gone to catch fish; *hapekok'e mẹn akawadiṅa*, he has ordered me to wait; *dil akae tahẹnko uskurket'koa* they urged them to have courage; *calaoenako gitic'*, they went to lie down;

emań dọ bae rẹbẹnlena, he was unwilling to give me; *onko ąguko manakom*, forbid them to bring those;

laiapea mẹnteń hẹc'ena, I have come to inform you; *ọrụk'ko kiriṅko lạgit'*, to buy ploughing cattle.

347. Bearing in mind the reservation referred to in the previous para in connection with the word-concepts of the language, it may be said that any word functioning as a verb may also function as a kind of Participle; this applies to all conjugational bases in all voices and tenses, with direct or indirect object and possessive infixes. In other words, any verbal form without a shown subject and without the finite *a* may be said to function as a Participle. Sometimes one is tempted to classify it as a participial construction even when a subject pronoun is used. As will be seen, forms mentioned in para 346 functioning as an Infinitive may also without any alteration function as a Participle.

In the living language a Participle will generally be heard used either adjectively prefixed to another word or with a determinative suffix added, or having postposition added.

In the last case frequently only the subject is wanting to make it what might be called a subjunctive clause, possibly often it is really to be understood to be this.

E. g., dadal họṛ dọ nui, ar dal ocoyenic' dọ huni, the beater is this one and the one beaten is that one over there; *mọn dukok'ko dọko calaoena*, these who had grief are gone; *ńamkedeyic'* (or *ńamkede họṛ*) *dọe okayena*, what has become of the one who found him (or may also mean, who was found); *mẹrọm kiriṅkeko hoṛ dọ bạnuk'koa*, there is none wanting to buy the goats; *kạk'mi kan tahẹkanic'*, the one who was working; *ruą jaṛao akan hoṛ*, a person down with fever; *dag hilok'*, a day with rain: *noko kuṛi dọ dạṅguạko sẹ jăwăeko kanako?* are these girls spinsters or married ones (lit. husbanded ones)?

kulhi mucaṭ're biṭlaha hoṛ gola gamchawante loṭa dak' banar tite sepeń akat' joṛhat kateye teńgo akana, at the entrance to the village street the outcasted man is standing with a piece of cloth twisted round his neck holding a lota with water up on both his hands kept in the position of supplication;

edrelenkhan hopon se apa bare hõko jomkoa, if they (the witches) get angry they will eat even their child or their own father and brothers; *hijuk' khan ma hec' ocoaepe,* if he will come let him; *hijuk'te hõ hijuk'pe,* be sure to come;

khange aimaiko do riau jarwakate dhuti dahṛiyente ar luṭire merom up' laṭkaokate birte Marań buru ṭhenko mohṇḍayena, thereupon the women came together calling on one another, and having taken on men's loin-cloth and headwear and having fixed goat's hair to their lips they set out to go to the forest to Marań buru.

---

348. The language makes constant use of compound verbs, two or more base-words placed side by side, functioning as a conjugational base. In a few cases the base-words may stand on an equal footing; but as a rule one is the word taking the verbal suffixes and one word functions as a kind of participle, standing in relation to the other word as an apposition to the verbal subject or as the object of the constructed word, or as an apposition to the object.

We look here away from words that are formally double, concepts expressed by two words; of such there is a very large number in the language.

E. g., agu ruaṛket'koae, he brought them back (lit. bringing he brought them back); *ańjom roṛkedeań,* I heard him say (lit. I heard him saying); *ńel janamkedeań,* I saw him born (i. e., lived at the time of his birth); *ḍaṭa ḍhil ńũrentińa,* my teeth came out being loose; *asul goc'kedeako,* they kept and fed him until his death; *banako dal gitic'kedea,* they beat the bear so he fell down; *lai tiok'aeme,* reach him telling, i. e. let him (also) know; *ńel agukedeań,* I went and saw him and have brought knowledge back (I brought having seen him); *hoho agukom*, call them and bring them (calling bring); *ńel got'kat'koako*, they saw them off; *bań ńel dareako kana*, I am unable to see them; *bae hec' dareat'a*, he was unable to come (come he could not); *paiye koe aguket'koa*, he asked them for measures and brought these; but *paiye koe aguket'a*, he asked for and brought measures (in this case the object of both verbs is *pai*; in the preceding example the object of *koe* is the people he asked, and these are shown in the verb).

---

349. Some words used as the second part of a double word and of very frequent occurrence are mentioned here below, thus *tora*, *dara*, *bara*, *got'* and *hot'*.

(*a*) *Tora* and *dara* are in one respect used exactly in the same way, i. e. when they form the second part of a compound verb; both then denote 'along with', *tora* in going and *dara* in coming.* But while *dara* is used also as an independent verb, *tora* is not so used; on the other hand *tora* may be used as an adverbial postposition, which does not happen with *dara*.

(*b*) Used as the second word of a compound *dara* signifies, as stated, performing what the first word denotes coming along towards the subject or speaker. The verbal suffix is added to *dara*, always the suffix required by the first (i. e. the principal) word.

E. g., *agu darakom*, bring them when you come along; *jom dara akawanań*, I have brought having eaten with me, i. e., I had my food before I started; *hat khon mit'tec' nakic' kirin darawańme*, buy and bring me a comb from the market.

(*c*) *Dara* is, as mentioned, also used as an independent verb in the meaning of coming, to come. It is constructed as an impersonal verb with the (logical) subject as a direct object infix.

---

* As a curiosity it may be mentioned that the Mahles who linguistically are very closely related to the Santals, use the same words, but *dara* where the Santals use *tora*, and vice versa.

It occurs only in the Indeterminate and Future and in the Definite Present, only in the Active voice, and only with the 3rd pers. pr. object infix (with inanimates no infix). It further shows one peculiarity which it has in common with the Intentional Indeterminate and the Continuative *aka*, in as much as the singular object infix (*e*) is added to the final *a* without any euphonic semivowel (which is otherwise used).* The forms occurring are consequently :

darae (*a*), he comes, will come (not *darayea*) ;
dara (*wa*), it comes, will come (inanimate); *darae* is also used ;
darakin (*a*), they two come, will come;
darako (*a*), they come, will come ;
darae kan (*a*) he is coming (not *daraye kana*) ;
dara kan (*a*) it is coming (inanimate);
darakin kan (*a*), they two are coming :
darako kan (*a*) they are coming.

As regards the use of these forms without the finite *a* and as 'participles' there is no difference from the ordinary verb; used as a participle the determinative suffixes may be added.

E. g., *nonkan din darawa*, such days will come; *darae hapta*, the coming week; *darae kanic'*, the coming one.

(*d*) *Tora*, as second part of a compound, functions exactly like *dara*, doing what the first word denotes when going away. In constructions like this *tora* cannot be used with verbs that denote 'coming', just as *dara* cannot be used with a word denoting 'going away'.

E. g., *sen torayenae*, he went along (with others); *merome idi tora'et'kotakoa*, he took their goats away along with him (when he went); *peran hiri toraket'koa*, I visited the friends

*This peculiarity might possibly point to our here having a different word, viz. *dar*, constructed as a v. a. d. impers. This *dara* and the *dara* dealt with above have identical stress. If we had *dar* with indirect object the stress should regularly be on *dar*, which it is not. The inanimate form (*dara* or *darae*, not *darak'*, as might be expected) also is against this supposition.

as I passed on my way (with *dara* the same might have been said, only that he visited coming); *jọm toraket'ae*, he had his food as he went (before going).

(*e*) While *tora* is not, like *dara*, used as an independent verb, it is frequently used as an adverbial postposition conveying the meaning of 'just after', 'immediately after', 'off and away', or the like. Used in this way *tora* is mostly immediately following the bare verbal base, but may also be heard after a verbal suffix.

E. g., *hẹc' tora kạmiye ẹhọp'ket'a*, he commenced to work as soon as he came; *ńẹlket'ko torae dạṛket'a*, he ran away as soon as he saw them.

(*f*) *Tora* is further used added to a personal pronoun and to certain demonstratives and the word *ọkọń* (or *ọkọe*), conveying the idea of 'off and away'.

It should be noted that in these cases *tora* is only used when demonstration, pointing at something visible, is possible. It is not commonly used in this way with an inanimate demonstrative.

E. g., *jọmken, ńũken, hũi torae calaoena*, he had his fill of food and drink, then there he is off and away; *nũk'ũi torae calaoena*, this one here, there he is off; *pạhil reak' katha, hanẹ tora calaoena*, the former report, there you heard it passing; *iń tora lekan ḍher hoṛ menak'koa*, there are many people just like myself; *am torako hõ menak'koa*, there are also those like you (about age, status, etc.); *ale tora hoṛ dọ bale duṛup'a*, people like us will not sit down (e. g., in the presence of superiors); *ape tora dohaete*, by the blessing of you and yours; *enko toranko*, people like those;

ọkọń tora, just now, at once; *ọkọe tora* is used in the same way, but not by all, some saying that *ọkọe* is improperly employed in this manner.

(*g*) *Baṛa* is of constant occurrence. It is never used alone, but only as the second or last part of a compound conjugational base. The verbal suffixes are added to *baṛa* and are the suffixes needed for or demanded by the previous word or words, the only exception to this being when *baṛa* is used in the Performative; in this case the rules for this form of the verb are followed.

Baṛa otherwise follows the rules of a verb with single final vowel. It is frequent in the Performative (*babṛa* or *bak'ṛa*), both when the principal word is in the Performative and when it is unaltered. The reciprocal *bapaṛa* is also used.

The addition of *baṛa* conveys the meaning of being engaged in, occupied with, busy with, or repeatedly doing what the principal word denotes, often with a side-meaning of leisurely, desultorily or even inefficiently doing what is referred to. It may also imply that several perform the same act separately.

E. g., *jǫm baṛaket'ako*, they are done eating; *calak'e mẹn baṛaea*, he speaks about going (but is apparently not quite decided); *noakoreye dãṛã baṛae kana*, he is wandering about here; *gạchiko ńańam babṛa kana*, they are trying to get seedlings; *si bak'ṛa kanae*, he is occupied ploughing (leisurely); *hẹc' baṛayenako*, they have all come (one after the other); *dapal baṛayenako*, they had a fight; *rǫṛ baṛayet'ae*, he is talking (now and then, or here and there); *lạpại bapaṛayenako*, they have informed each other; *ńẹpẹl bapaṛayenako*, they have seen each other (these preliminaries to a marriage have been gone through).

(*h*) *Gǫt'* and *hǫt'* (with side-forms *gǫl* and *hǫl*) are used added to the verbal base, giving the meaning that an act is performed or to be performed quickly, rapidly, without delay, or suddenly. What was remarked as regards construction in connection with *baṛa* holds good for these words, only we have here two words with final chequed consonant, the rules of which are followed.

E. g., *Lại hǫdme*, tell it quickly; *hẹc' gǫl'enae*, he came quickly (or suddenly); *ạgu hǫt'ket'koae*, he brought them quickly; *ńẹl gǫt'*, lit. see suddenly (very frequently used about 'seeing off', 'saying good-by to').

350. The Santal verb is, as has been seen, astonishingly regular. We have not a number of so-called irregular verbs. This peculiarity is undoubtedly due to the agglutinating character of the language.

On the other hand the language has a few words that on account of their meaning can only be used in one tense, if tense it should be called.

These verbs are (besides the auxiliary *kan* and *tahẽkan* dealt with paras 225-230) three, *dukạn*, *menak'* and *bạnuk'*.

Dukạn.

351. *Dukạn* is constructed like an intransitive verb in the Indeterminate Active; it may take a possessive infix and certain postpositions. The word means 'went', but presupposes return; it consequently corresponds to the Anterior Past of *sẹn* (*sẹnlen*).*

E. g., *hola haṭtele dukạna*, we went yesterday to the market (but are here now); *Asumtele dukạnre noa oṛak' dǫ lǫyen-*

---

* What this *dukạn* is, it is only possible to conjecture. Three possibilities suggest themselves; one that it is *du* + *kan*, the Medium of the Intentional Simple Past (cp. *tahẽkan*); against this explanation may be objected that, except for the borrowed numeral, no word *du* is heard in the language; further that *kạn* has a resultant vowel which is not otherwise heard; this last objection may, however, be met by supposing that the form has melted into one word, its original composition being forgotten (like in *tahẽkan*). In support of this conjecture may be quoted Stieng *du* (go), Semang *do'* (*du'*) (run), Alak *du* (flee), Bahnar *kodu* (run away, also: back), Khmer *tou* (*dau*), go away. And a number of related dialects.

Another conjecture is that it is originally *duk* + *an*, i. e. *duk* with the suffix of the Medium Simple Past with indirect object. The same may be objected here; *duk* (except for the borrowed *duk*, grief) is not otherwise met with in the language and the resultant vowel will have to be explained. Here Boloven and Lave *dok* (go) might be quoted.

A third conjecture is that we have a word *dukạ* with the *n* suffix mentioned para 59.

Present-day Santals are apparently uncertain as to what the word really is; the writer has heard forms like *dukạnlenae*; but this is not deemed correct language.

talea, this house of ours was burnt down when we were away in Assam (we are here again); *phalna ṭhenem dukạnte cet'em jọsana*, what did you gain by going to so and so? *holako dukạntalea*, our people went yesterday (are back now).

352. *Menak'* and *bạnuk'* are both constructed in accordance with the manner of impersonal verbs, that is to say, verbs that have no subject, only an object, in the case of animates an infixed object pronoun. Before dealing with the two verbs mentioned a few words about this class of construction are called for.

The language has a number of words that are constructed impersonally. Thus all words that denote what is felt (the so-called verba sentiendi, not, however, the words that describe 'active' feeling), the effect of an external, not concretely fixed or demonstrated cause; further certain words that denote wish or pleasure.

This kind of construction naturally is met with only in the Active voice. Many of the words are capable of regular construction, when the Agent is known. In the Medium or the Passive regular construction is used, generally with a somewhat different meaning attached to the word.

We hear impersonal constructions with both direct and indirect object; certain constructions with indirect inanimate object and a following possessive infix are very common, more especially with women.

The following examples will show the constructions:

Tetañiña, I shall be thirsty (or, am constantly thirsty).
Rabañet'mea, you are feeling cold.
Sebelede kana, he thinks it is tasting well, he likes it.
Hasokedea bọhọk'ko, he felt a pain somewhere in the head.
Rẹṅgẹc'ledea, he felt hunger (but *rẹṅgẹc'enae*, he became poor).
Haṛhat' akadiña, I am feeling it bitter.
Sebelkepea, it may be sweet to you.
Sanakidiña, I wished, felt a desire for.

Ąuriyea, he is not come as yet; *ąuriataea,* he is not ready as yet; *bañatae kana,* he is quite unwilling; *bañ ąuatae kana* (a women's expression), she does not care a bit.

As is seen there is nothing irregular, except that a subject is wanting.

Menak' (*henak'*) and *bạnuk'*.

353. (*a*) These two verbs occur only in one tense due to their meaning; they denote existence and non-existence; they are both constructed as impersonal verbs without a subject, and with the logical subject as the grammatical object; in case this is animate, a personal pronoun is infixed, if inanimate, there is nothing.

As these two verbs in the singular show some irregularities (as distinct from all other Santal verbal constructions) the full forms are given here below.

(*b*) *Menak'*, exist (with a parallel form *henak'*).

Sing. 1st person animate	*menaña* (*menąña, minąña*). I am, exist.
„ 2nd „ „	*menama* or *menak'mea.* Thou art, existeth.
„ 3rd „ „	*menaea.* He, she is, exists.
„ „ „ inanimate	*menak'a.* It is, exists.
Dual 1st p. inclusive animate	*menak'laña.* I and thou, we two are.
„ „ p. exclusive „	*menak'liña.* I and he (she), we two are.
„ 2nd p. „	*menak'bena.* You two are.
„ 3rd p. „	*menak'kina.* They two are.
Plur. 1st p. inclusive „	*menak'boa* (*menak'bona*). I and you, we are.
„ 1st p. exclusive „	*menak'lea.* I and they, we are.
„ 2nd p. „	*menak'pea.* You are.
„ 3rd p. „	*menak'koa.* They are.

With inanimate subject there is only one form *menak'a,* the base *menak'* + the finite *a. Henak'* is comparatively rare, apparently being used by preference by certain individuals. Except for the initial sound it does not in any way differ from *menak'*.

(c) *Bạnuk'*, not exist, not be.

Sing.	1st pers.	animate	*bạnugiña.* I am not.
„	2nd „	„	*bạnuk'mea.* Thou art not.
„	3rd „	„	*bạnugic'a.* He is not.
„	„ „	inanim.	*bạnuk'a.* It is not.
Dual	1st pers. incl.	anim.	*bạnuk'laña.* I and thou, we two are not.
„	1st „ excl.	„	*bạnuk'liña.* I and he (she), we two are not.
„	2nd „	„	*bạnuk'bena.* You two are not.
„	3rd „	„	*bạnuk'kina.* They two are not.
Plur.	1st „ incl.	anim.	*bạnuk'boa* (*bạnuk'bona*). We, I and you are not.
„	1st „ excl.	„	*bạnuk'lea.* We, I and they are not.
„	2nd „	„	*bạnuk'pea.* You are not.
„	3rd „	„	*bạnuk'koa.* They are not.

With inanimate subject there is only one form, *bạnuk'a*, the base *bạnuk'* + *a*. See also para 335.

354. As is seen these verbs show in the singular some irregularities.

We shall first deal with *menak'*, leaving aside the forms *menạñ* and *minạñ*, due to the influence of the *i* in the *iñ* (see Mat. I. para 23). If one had not the comparatively rare *menak'me*, one might be tempted to suppose a base *mena* for the singular. The *k'* is, except as mentioned, always eliminated in the singular; the first and third person never show any trace of it. See footnote para 355.

Under the supposition that the pronominal infixes are object infixes, the pronominal infix for the 1st p. sing. is regular, verbs with final single vowel taking *ñ*. But both the 2nd and the 3rd p. sing. do not follow the ordinary rules for direct object infixes. In the 2nd pers. this is regularly *me* (occurring in *menak'me*), the only exception to this rule being the Intentional *ka* that may take only *m*. On the other hand the suffixed form of the same pronoun is after final single vowel, with few exceptions, *m*.

The 3rd pers. shows a similar peculiarity. When the object infix *e* is added to a verbal base with final single vowel, an euphonic *y* is employed. Here this *e* is added directly to the base forming a diphthong with the final vowel. An analogy is again found in the Intentional form, where the same object infix added to *ka* always becomes *kae* and not *kaye*, further in the Continuative, where the related *aka* with this infix always becomes *akae* and not *akaye*. The Indeterminate with indirect object (*-ae*) might also be mentioned.

355. With reference to *bạnuk'* there is only one peculiarity to point out, the infix of the 3rd p. sing. being regularly *ic'* in stead of *e*. A form *bạnugea* or *bạnugia* is now and then heard, especially with *an* (*bạnugian*), and is possibly coming into more common use than it has been. This might be thought to show that the present day Santals consider these two verbs as being impersonal verbs with direct object infix.

A similar use of *ic'* is heard in connection with *ạuri*; *e. g.*, *okoric' ho*? *ạuriyic'a*, why, where is he? he is late, not yet here; besides *ạuriyea*; cp. also the follwing, *joṇḍra beleyentapea*? *ạuriak'a*, is your Indian corn ripe? not yet. It seems to be clear that we have the determinative suffix, in other words here in the 3rd pers. sing. a word with the determinative suffix added plus the finite a. Whatever may be thought of the other forms, it does not seem possible to take this 3rd pers. sing. to be an impersonal verb with direct object infix.*

---

* It might be interesting to find out the real composition and consequently also the real construction of these words. We seem to have the roots *he* or *me* and *ba*, to which *nak̓* and *nuk̓* respectively are added. What *he* or *me* are, is doubtful; they may possibly be demonstrative roots As to *ba* there does not seem to be any need of doubt; it is the ordinary Santali negation. Muṇḍari and Ho here show similar forms; strangely enough we here meet with *baṅ* and *bano*, while the ordinary negation in both languages is *ka* (corresponding to Santali *ba*). One Muṇḍari dialect, however, also has *kanu* or *kano*.

The corresponding forms of the singular of these two verbs in Muṇḍari and Ho are: *menak̓iña* (Ho *menak̓iña*), *menak̓mea*, *menak̓ea*, and *bañiña* (Ho *bañiña*), *baṅmea*, *bañak̓ea*, and (inanim.) *banoak̓*.

It is of some interest here to compare what is met with in some of the languages spoken on the Malayan Peninsula and elsewhere in the East. There seems to be relationship.

Semang *moah* (be, become), Sakei *mo*, *moñ*, Senoi *beng*, Mon *mang* (remain), So *mi*, *maimi* (have), Khmer *mean* (be, have), Gondi *man* (remain) might be compared. For *henak̓* Mentera *ha*.

All who have written about Santali grammar have without exception and without putting any question taken these forms to be constructed, as also here supposed, as impersonal verbs with the logical subject as a direct object infix.

From what has been stated, it will be gathered that the forms, more especially in the singular, do not in all respects conform with what is regularly met with when a verb is constructed with a pronominal infix of the direct object. With the otherwise invariable regularity of these constructions one is tempted to doubt that we here have to do with an impersonal verb. This doubt is strengthened when we reflect that while the presupposed construction demands some kind of activity with the grammatical object as its goal, it does not seem very well possible here to discover any activity in any of the words, especially not in the word denoting non-existence.

One is tempted to ask whether we have not to do with a concept-word to which a suffixed, not an infixed, pronoun is added, in one case substituted by the animate determinative suffix (*banugic̓*).

One is instinctively reminded of the formation of the Imperative in the language. See para 286, footnote.

It might in this way be possible to explain the irregularities. This is, however, only hypothetical.

356. (*a*) All forms may take a possessive pronom. infix (*tiń*, *tam*, *tae*, etc.) immediately following the infixed 'subject' pronoun, or, in the case of the 'subject' being inanimate, following the *k'*.

(*b*) In stead of the finite *a* it is very common, especially in the 3rd p. sing. to hear *anẹc'* or *anań* used. For *bạnugic'a* one mostly hears *bạnugic'an*. See paras 151 and 335.

(*c*) The use of the finite *a* is not different from its use in the regular verb.

357. These verbs cannot, properly speaking, be said to belong to any verbal tense. They denote existence or presence, or non-existence or non-presence. The concept does not allow of any tense-variation. If a Future is wanted or a Past, other words have to be used, e. g. for the Future *hoyok'* (become), for the Past *tahẽkan* (was).

This does not, however, prevent these forms, more especially the inanimate form, from being treated as a derived concept. Such use is, however, very rare. I have heard expressions like this: *bạnugok' kan taea eṅgale, menak'tae tuluc'e mẹnel'a bạnuk'tiń*, it is becoming non-existence with him, by the mother; having he says I have not.

Tables of the Verbal Suffixes.

358. The following three tables of the verbal suffixes will show at a glance their use. The note at the bottom of Table I naturally applies to all three tables.

Table I. The General Form of the Verb with direct object.

Tense		Active	Medium and Passive
Indeterminate and Future	Base	(+anim. obj. infix)	*ok̇ (- k̇)*
Indefinite Present	,,	*et'* (+anim. obj. infix)	*ok̇ (- k̇) kan*
Definite Present	,,	*et'* (+anim. obj. infix) *kan*	
Indefinite Imperfect	,,	*et'* (+anim. obj. infix) *tahẽkan*	*ok̇ (- k̇) kan tahẽkan*
Definite Imperfect	,,	*et'* (+anim. obj. infix) *kan tahẽkan*	
Simple Past	,,	*ket'* (+anim. obj. infix)	*en*
Anterior Past	,,	*let'* (+anim. obj. infix)	*len*
Anterior Pluperfect	,,	*let'* (+anim. obj. infix) *tahẽkan*	*len tahẽkan*
Accidental Past	,,	—	*ken*
Optative	,,	*ke* (+anim. obj. infix)	*kok̇*
Anterior	,,	*le* (+anim. obj. infiix)	*len*

Note : (+anim. obj. infix) or (+ anim. or inanim. obj. infix) in parenthesis is intended to show the place of the obj. infix when such has to be used. Except in certain tenses of the form with indirect object and of the Intentional form there is no inanimate obj. infix. Intransitive verbs naturally have no obj. infix.

The optional possessive infix always follows the object infix, if any such is used. It may come immediately after the obj. infix or after *kan* or after *tahẽkan* in tenses where these occur. When no object infix has to be used the possessive infix may (but must not) stand where the obj. infix should have been.

Table II. The General Form of the Verb with indirect object.

Tense		Active	Medium
Indeterminate and Future	Basė	*a* (+anim. or inanim. obj. infix)	*joṅ*
Indefinite Present	,,	—	—
Definite Present	,,	*a* (+anim. or inanim. obj. infix) ***kan***	***joṅ kan***
Indefinite Imperfect	,,	—	—
Definite Imperfect	,,	*a* (+anim. or inanim. obj. infix) ***kan tahẽkan***	***joṅ kan tahẽkan***
Simple Past	,,	*at'* (+anim. obj. infix)	***an***
Anterior Past	,,	—	—
Anterior Pluperfect	,,	*at'* (+anim. obj. infix) ***tahẽkan***	***an tahẽkan***
Accidental Past	,,	—	—
Optative	,,	*ke* (+anim. obj. infix)	***kok'***
Anterior	,,	*le* (+anim. obj. infix)	***len***

Table III. The Intentional Form of the Verb.

Tense		Active	Medium and Passive	Indirect Medium (Reflexive)
Indeterminate and Future	Base	*ka*(+anim. or inanimate object infix)	*kok'*	*kok'*
Definite Present	,,	*ka*(+anim. or inanim. obj. infix) *kan*	*kok' kan*	*kok' kan*
Definite Imperfect	,,	*ka*(+anim. or inanim. obj. infix) *kan tahẽkan*	*kok' kan tahẽkan*	*kok kan tahẽkan*
Simple Past	,,	*kat'* (+anim. obj. infix)	*kan*	—
Anterior Past	,,	*lak'*	—	—
Anterior Pluperfect	,,	*kat'* (+anim. obj. infix) *tahẽkan*	—	—
Perfect with direct object	,,	*akat'* (+anim. obj. infix)	*akan*	—
,, with indirect obj.	,,	*akawat'* (+anim. obj. infix)	—	*akawan*
Pluperfect with direct obj.	,,	*akat'* (+anim. obj. infix) *tahẽkan*	*akan tahẽkan*	—
,, with indirect obj.	,,	*akawat'* (+anim. obj. infix) *tahẽkan*	—	*akawan tahẽkan*

Conjunctions, conjunctional Adverbs, Particles and Interjections.

Copulatives.

359. *Ar*, and, also, further, more.*

As a copulative conjunction *ar* is used to connect statements, sentences and single words, adding something fresh to what has been already stated. It corresponds as a conjunction entirely to our 'and'.

E. g., *apatṭet' ar uniren gidrạko*, the father and his children; *arak' ar poṇḍ*, red and white; *boge ar bạric'*, good and bad; *bar gẹl ar bar*, two-and-twenty (this is the old way; language 'civilized' by schools now-a-days omits the *ar*); *hoṛ ar hoṛ*, people and people (in Santali it may mean addition, something like masses upon masses of people, or it may mean, different kinds of people.

360. *Hõ* (or *hõ*), also, even, too.§

(*a*) This is not properly speaking a conjunction, but a postpositional particle; it has been called enclitic, but this is

**Ar* is probably a borrowed word (from Skr. *apara*); the Hindi form is *aur*, which in Santali should produce *ọr*, so the borrowing must have taken place where standard Hindi is not used. Bengali has *ar*, and so has Panjabi. Like in Hindi *ar* is also in Santali used as an adjective or as a noun, and even as a verb. We have *arak̕*, the rest; *arak̕ko dọ okor*, where is the rest? *arko*, the others; *ar arko*, the others; *ar arak̕*, the rest; *arlẹt'*, more, still more; *ar baṅ rọṛa*, I shallnot speak any more; *ar emaṅme mit' dhao*, give me once more; *ar dinre hapẹnbon jọma*, we shall eat (this) at another time; *ar betarre ọmọn mọkọṅena*, it all sprouted some time ago; *arhõ*, again, also, still; *arhõehẹlena*, he has come again; *ona chaḍa arhõe rọṛket'a*, besides that he also (or, again) said; *ar dọ*, so, further; *ar dọ bạnuk̕a*, so there is nothing; *ạgu nae aret'a*, *poesa nae idi akat'*, he will just not bring it; he has, you see, taken the money with him; *hẹc̕ nako arok̕ kana*, *dingeko kọyok̕ ocoyet'lea ọntẹ*, they are sure not come, they make us look that way (waiting) every day.

§ The origin of *hõ* is obscure. A *hũ* is found in Bihari, meaning 'also'; to this may be compared Bengali *o*. These are probably to be derived from Skr. *bhu*. The original meaning would then be 'being', 'existing', from which the present meaning may be derived. The affirmative particles *hã*, *hẽ*, *hũ* may also be compared.

scarcely correct. It has always to stand after the word to which it refers, but may have the stress.

Hǫ̃ is not added to finite sentences, but to words, single or modified by the addition of suffixes, postpositions, etc.

(*b*) The use of *hǫ̃* in connection with certain interrogative pronouns to render indefinite pronouns has been mentioned (see especially para 191 (b)).

E. g., am hǫ̃ń ńęllet'mea, I saw you also; *onko hǫ̃ lạiakom,* tell them also; *ęn hǫ̃e calaoena,* even then he went; *ęnre hǫ̃ko ạkrińkedea,* even in that case, still they sold (the goat); *dal hǫ̃ko dalkedea,* they also beat him;

sęn hǫ̃ bae sęnok'a, he will not even go; *sęn hǫ̃e sęnok'a,* he will even go.

(*c*) Two or more *hǫ̃* (*-hǫ̃ -hǫ̃*) are used as conjunctive conjunctions, conveying the meaning of 'both - and', 'as well - as also'. Santali simply repeats 'this also, that also'. With a negation we get what corresponds to 'neither - nor'.

E. g., iń hǫ̃ bań lạimea, am hǫ̃ bam lạiyińa, I shall not inform against you, nor shall you against me; *alc hǫ̃ ape hǫ̃,* both you and we; *dal hǫ̃ko dalkedea, jęręt' hǫ̃ ko jęręt'kedea,* they both beat him and set fire to his house.

Temporal conjunctions.

361. *Adǫ,* and, so, then, further, moreover; more.*

(*a*) As a conjunction it is used to connect sentences, not single words, and conveys the idea of thereupon, then, what is consecutive.

E. g., adǫe męnket'a, so he said; *adǫe gitic'ena,* thereupon he lay down.

(*b*) *Adǫ* is in narratives often combined with *khange,* either before or after. In the folktales *adǫ, khange adǫ,* or *adǫ khange* are most commonly heard, *ar* on the other hand not so often, i. e. to connect sentences.

---

* *Adǫ* is possibly a combination of the demonstrative *a* + *dǫ*; it may also be *ar* + *dǫ,* with elimination of *r.*

E. g., adọ khange onka hudis baṛakate atoren hoṛ then khon barea pạiye kọe ạguketʼa ; adọ onako pẹnẹ pạiye khadleketʼa ; khange adọe jolak̃ kana are ghanṭayetʼa, thereupon having thought this he asked the village people for three pai-measures and brought these ; so he put the three pai-measures into the cooking pot ; thereupon he makes a fire and stirs.

(*c*) *Adọ* may also be used adverbially in the meaning 'more' : *adọ cetʼem ńam kana,* what do you want more ? *adọ cetʼiń rọṛa,* what shall I say more ?

362. *Khan* and *khange,* with parallel forms *khacʼ* and *khacʼge,* then, thereupon.

(*a*) These two conjunctions have been mentioned before (see paras 98 and 340). *Khange* is *khan* + the emphatic particle *ge.*

There must always be a reference to something previously told or only implied, as *khan* really is a postposition. This is particularly shown in the compound conjunctions, where *khan* is joined to a demonstrative adverb that sums up the previous statement. We have *ẹnḍẹkhan* and *tọbẹkhan,* both used as a temporal conjunction and also, and perhaps more, as a conditional conjunction, introducing the apodosis.

Examples of the use of *khan* are found in paras 98, 340 and 361 (b).

E. g., uniye hẹcʼenkhan ẹnḍẹkhan (or *tọbẹkhan*) *ale dọle chuṭiyena,* when he came we became free, were released ; *ma ẹnḍẹkhan jọmme,* then please take your food ; *khange ko calaoena,* so they went.

(*b*) *E̱nkhan,*
 E̱nkhante,
 E̱nkhacʼ,
 E̱nkhacʼte, } then, in that case, then only, after that.

The demonstrative pronoun *ẹn* with *khan* (or its parallel form *khacʼ*) to which the postposition *te,* by, may be added. Lit. meaning, 'when that', or 'by when that', when that has happened, or by such and such a thing having happened.

Used to introduce a statement of what is done or to be done, when something has taken place; it is temporal, but also refers to the *conditio sine qua non* for an action.

E. g., enkhanin calak'a, in that case I shall go;
sari rorme, enkhante don goroama, speak the truth, then I shall help you;
herele jomlege, enkhante orak' hortet' due joma, when the man has first eaten, then only the wife will eat.

363. *Jãhãtisre*, whenever.

Jãhãtinre, whenever (during the day or night), at any hour.

Composed of *jãhã* and *tis*, or *tin*, and the postposition *re*.

Both words are really indefinite pronominal adverbs (see para 198), but are frequently used as conjunctions.

E. g., jãhãtisre desteko calak' iń hõ laiańpe, jemon iń hõń sen dareak', whenever they go to the low country tell also me that I also may go; *jãhãtinreye hijuk', sin se ńinda, ekkalte badae ocoñpe*, whenever he comes, be it during day-time or at night, let me know at once.

364. (*a*) *Auri* has also been called a temporal conjunction; this is not correct, and *auri* should not have been mentioned here, if it were not for the many mistakes made by beginners in its use. It suits us to say that it means 'not yet'; we may most conveniently translate the word in this way. There is, however, no negation included in the Santal word; but the convenient translation induces beginners, and I am afraid also more mature students, to construct as if *auri* contained a negation and to perpetrate such howlers as *auriye hec' akana*. Strangely enough, I have heard Hindi and Bengali speaking people, trying to express themselves in Santali, committing the same blunder.

Auri in Santali means 'afterwards', 'presently', and can consequently only be constructed with the Future. It is not a conjunction, but a concept-word, used sometimes as a noun, meaning delay, sometimes as an adjective meaning 'later', 'out of season', sometimes as a verb (constructed with the logical subject as a direct or indirect object infix), and mostly as an adverb.*

E. g., *ạuriko hijuk'a*, they have not yet come, lit. they will come delayed, afterwards; *marsal ạurireko sẹṭẹrena*, they arrived before day-light (while light was late); *iñ ạurire*, before my time; *ạurite dọ alope hijuk'a*, do not come before time (lit. by out of time); *ạuritẹt'geñ jọma noa dọ*, I have never as yet tasted this.

(*b*) It might in this connection be mentioned, that Santali makes use of this *ạuri* followed by a verb in the Future and one of the postpositions *dhạbic'* (or any of its equivalent forms *dhạric'*, *hạbic'* or *hạric'*), *re* and *te* (*ge*) to express a subordinate clause with the conjunction 'until' or 'before'.

It will be readily understood that *ạuri* is not here functioning as a conjunction, but as an adverb modifying the meaning of the verb, and that it is the postposition which gives what corresponds to our conjunction, the meaning of the postposition being specified by the prefixed *ạuri*.

E. g., *ạuriñ emam dhạbic' nọṇḍẹ durup' hatarok'me*, sit here in the meanwhile, until I give you (something or other), lit. later I give you - up to;

ạuriñ calak're disạwạñme, remind me, before I go (lit. later I shall go - within);

cando ạuriye hạsurok'tege birpe pargmok'a, you must pass the forest, before the sun sets (lit. the sun later he will set - by).

(*c*) To give the full use of *ạuri* the following examples may serve:

---

* Its use as a noun in Santali makes it probable to derive the word from Skr. *abela* of which, besides *aber*, the forms *aver* and *aberi* are met with in Hindi. It would be easy to explain the phonetic change from this to Santali *ạuri*. *Abela* means lit., what in Norwegian is called '*utid*', out of time or season; in Hindi the word means 'delay'. The Santal use of the word may be partly explained from the Hindi word's meaning; but to get all the meanings in Santali we need exactly the Skr. word. The examples will show the use.

jomket'am? ąuriu, have you had your food? not as yet; *jondra beleyentapea? ąuriak'a*, is your Indian corn ripe? not yet; *thora ąuriataea daka do*, her rice (food) is not quite ready as yet; *ape ąuripete do bale bilomoka*, we shall not be detained by your not being ready (we shall not wait for you); *onko ąurikore noabon sat hatara*, we shall finish this in the meanwhile, before they come; *okoric' ho? ąuriyic'a*, where is he (who should have been here)? he is not ready as yet.

Disjunctives.

365. *Sẹ*, or.*

(*a*) *Sẹ* is used like our 'or'.

E. g., *hoṛ sẹ deko*, a Santal or a Deko; *okoebon lahak'tabona, ape sẹ ale*, who shall start of us, you or we? *jinisem ẹmok'a sẹ ṭakam halawańa*, will you give goods (mustard seed), or will you pay me back the money? *ańjomket'am sẹm bańa*, did you hear or not?

(*b*) This *sẹ* is often used added to a verb or the negation *ba* (*bań*), corresponding to 'or how,' 'is it not so?'

E. g., *calaoenae, basẹ*, he is gone, is it not so? *hẹc' akanako sẹ*, they are come, or how?

366. (*a*) *Bańdo*, whether.

Bańdo introduces indirect questions; the verb of a sentence introduced by *bańdo* does not ordinarily take the finite *a*. Note, *bańdo* does not demand the suffix of the Anterior Past in past tenses.

As to composition see *bań* and *do*.

E. g., *nondẹ khon bańdoko ńẹl ńamok'*, will it be possible to see them from here? *bań baḍaea, bańdoe calaoen*, I do not know whether he has gone; *bańdo am sadherre hẹrẹl do menama*, are you the only man in the world (women's abuse).

---

* The origin of this *sẹ* is doubtful; one might compare it to the Hindi ablative suffix *se*, or to the demonstrative *se*. But it seems more likely to take it to be an original Santali word. It might be mentioned that Santali has several words sounding much like this *sẹ*, but of quite different meanings (*sẹ*, foam, *sẹ jel*, a certain kind of deer, *sẹ mãyãm iṛi*, a kind of millet, *sẽ*, onomat. about heavy breathing; *se*, a louse, *se uḍi*, that much).

(b) *Bańdo - bańdo*, whether - or.

E. g, *bańdoe calaoen, bańdo oṛak're menae, ɔhoń men daṛelea*, whether he is gone, or he is at home, I am unable to say ; *bańdoe ńel akat' bańdo bań, bań badaea*, I do not know, whether he has seen it or not;

bańdo hoṛ bańdo bonga, whether man or spirit.

(c) *Parlek - parlek*, whether — or.

367. - *hõ ba(ń)*, also not, nor, not - either, not even.

- *hõ ba(ń) - hõ ba(ń)*, neither - nor.

These conjunctive particles need no explanation; they are the above mentioned - *hõ* with the negation *bań* suffixed. *Hõ* being postpositional these are also the same. - *hõ bań* may be repeated ad libitum. The literal meaning is obvious. They are used both with single words and with compounds, but not with full sentences.*

E. g., *am hõ bań*, not you either ; *sen hõ bae senok'a*, he will not go either ; *roṛ hõ bań roṛ akat'a, ruhet' hõ bań ruhet' akadea*, neither have I spoken nor have I scolded him ; *bae kirih joma, sukri hõ bań merom hõ bań*, he will not buy, either pigs or goats ;

368. (a) *Hoe - hoe*, either - or.

Borrowed from Bengali; mostly used with sentences, about alternatives. Always prefixed.

E. g., *hoe mit' hoṛ thene jamaṛok', hoe mit' hoṛe kurudae*, he will either hold to one, or he will hate one.

(b) *Ek - ek*, } either - or.
ek do - ek do, }

The *ek* is borrowed from Bengali; used about alterna-

---

* - *hõ ba(ń)* added to an interrogative pronoun or adverb is used to denote the negative demonstrative pronouns and adverbs, the interrogative meaning being lost to the sense.

Cet' hõ bań, nothing ; *oka hõ bań*, nothing ; *okoe hõ bań*, no one ; *cele hõ bań*, no one ; *okare hõ bań*, nowhere ; *oka leka hõ bań*, in no wise ; *oka lekate hõ bań*, in no way at all ; *cet' leka hõ bań*, in no way ; *cet' lekate hõ bań*, in no possible way.

tives, always prefixed the word or the sentence to which it is attached.

E. g., *ẹk dọe huṇḍar kana, ẹk dọe tạrup' kana,* it is either a wolf or it is a leopard ; *okaren kombṛo cọko gẹt'ket'a, ẹk dọko Pạhạṛia kana, ẹk dọ Jọlha,* some thieves from somewhere have cut this ; that are either Paharias or Jolhas ; *gại ẹke ạguye, ẹke tahẽ ocoae,* he will either bring (the cow), or he will let it remain.

369. - *cọ(ṅ)* - *cọ(ṅ)*, either - or.

- *cọ(ṅ)* - *baṅ cọ(ṅ)*, whether - or not.

The particle *cọ(ṅ)* expresses uncertainty; *cọṅ* may also be used as an affirmative particle; see para 377 (c). When doubled it is used to express the subjective doubt as to which of two alternatives.

Cọṅ is always postpositional.

E. g., *ọkọe baḍae ? hẽ cọṅ baṅ cọṅ, ki jạni hẽge cọṅ,* who knows, it may be true or it may not be ; who knows (*ki jạni*, also heard pronounced *ki jạnic'*, is likely to be taken as third person for *ke jane,* the corresponding Bengali expression ; lit. it would mean 'what do I know ?'), it is possibly true (an answer once given to the writer when asking the opinion of a certain Santal on the guilt or otherwise of a person whose case they had before them); *hoṛo cọṅ joṇḍra cọko ạgu akat'a,* they have brought either paddy or maize (I do not know which) ; *lại cọe baṅ cọṅ,* (one cannot say) whether he will tell or not.

Adversatives.

370. (*a*) ***Mẹnkhan***, but.

Mẹnkhan is composed of *mẹn*, say, and *khan* (see para 340), the lit. meaning being, 'if (that) is said', or 'if (or, when) saying (so)'. With regard to the use of *mẹnkhan* as a conjunctional postposition in conditional sentences see para 340 (*b*).

Mẹnkhan is used both in connection with single words and with full sentences.

E. g., jọtọ hoṛe lại akawat'koa, mẹnkhan iń dọ bań; he has told all, but not me; *jãhãnak'ye kiriń ạguime, mẹnkhan mạric dọ alo*, buy and bring anything you can get, but not pepper; *kulạiyiń ńẹlledea, mẹnkhan bań sap' daṛeadea*, I saw a hare, but was unable to catch it; *nitok' dọ mit' leka bes menak'lea, mẹnkhan tayọm hilok' dọ cet' cọń hoyok'*, in one way it goes well with us now, but who knows how it will be afterwards.

(*b*) *Menek*, *Mẹnẹk*, } but; however.

Composed of *mẹn*, say, and *ẹk*, one. Word is used in rustic Bengali in the same sense.

It is used in the same way as *mẹnkhan*, but much more rarely than this in this meaning. *Mẹnẹk* is frequently used also in the meaning of 'however', 'as for that', etc.

E. g., calak'e mẹnlak'a, mẹnẹk bae sẹnlena, he intended to go, but he did not; *uduk'aeye mẹnlak'a, mẹnẹk bae uduk'adea*, he said he would show it to him, but he did not do so; *kạphạriạu jọkhẹc' menek bań tahẽkana*, I was not, however, present at the time of the quarrel.

(*c*) *Bickọm*, *Bickom*, } rather, but rather, on the contrary, preferably.

E. g., uni bańkate bickọm unigeń hataoea, I will rather take this one than that one; *nitok' dọ bickọm bań calak' kana, tayọmteń calak'a*, I prefer not to go now; I shall go later on.

(*d*) *Bọrọń*, *Bọrọń cọ(ń)*, *Bọr cọ(ń)*, } rather, preferably.

These particles (except *cọń*) are borrowed from Bengali; the last *bọr* is not so often heard. They are used very much like *bickọm*.

E. g., bọr cọń iń dọ bạń jọma, am baṛẹ jọmme, I shall preferably not eat; you eat please, *iń dọ bań calak'a, bọrọń cọń iń bọdọl amge calak'me*, I shall not go, better you go in my place; *hoṛ dọ ḍher dọ bako sẹnlena, bọrọń deko hạṛtige ko tahẽkana*, many Santals had not gone there, rather there were more Hindus.

(e) *Bañkhan,* } or else, otherwise, naturally, of course,
Bañkhac', } if not.

Composed of the negation *bañ* and the postposition *khan* with its parallel form *khac'* (see para 340). Lit. meaning, 'if not', or 'when not'.

E. g., onka dọ alom rọṛa, bañkhanlañ dalmea, don't speak in that way, else I shall beat you; *jọm bañkhane cekaea,* of course he will eat it (lit. eating if not (what) will he do); *ẹm bañkhac'e cekak'a,* naturally he will give (note, in such expressions *ceka* is given the same voice as the verb referred to would have; here it would have been *ẹmọk'a*);

ma bañkhac' amge calak'tabonme, you had better go for us; *ẹm akawadeam? bañkhac' dọ,* have you given it to him? Of course I have.

(f) *Ẹn hõ,* } even then, yet, still, nevertheless.
Ẹnre hõ, }

Lit. that also; or, in that also.

E. g., manakedeañ, ẹn họe calaoena, I forbade him (or warned him), yet he went; *bako ẹm akawadea, ẹn hõe kọkọe kana,* they have not given him, still he is asking;

un dhao dalem jọm akat'a, ẹnre hõ bam bạgiyet'a, so many times you have been punished (thrashed), yet you do not leave off; *jãhãtinạk'em emaere hõ, ẹnre hõ bae tirpitok' kana,* however much you give him, still he is not satisfied.

Causals.

371. *Ẹnte,* because, for, as.

Also used as an adverb (in postposition), by all means, all right, just so, of course, why, then.

Ẹnte is composed of the demonstrative *ẹn,* this, and the instrumental postposition *te,* by. When used as a conjunction, the sentence introduced by *ẹnte* gives the cause or reason of the previous statement, the cause being anticipated by *ẹnte.**

* A good many Santals, especially in the Northern parts of the country, in stead of *ẹnte* now use *cedak' je,* lit. why? that. This is a rendering of a Hindi expression. I cannot call to mind having heard an illiterate village Santal using the expression.

A side form *ẹntẹt'* is common, having the same meaning as *ẹnte.*

Ẹntẹt' is especially used, when answering a question something like 'just so, because'.†

E. g., alom bọtọrok'a ; ẹnte iń menańa, don't be afraid, for I am here ; *hẹc'enań ; ẹnte uniye metadiń tẹrọń,* I came because he told me to (it would have been more correct to have the finite *a* instead of *tẹrọń*, a postposition that conveys the same meaning as *ẹnte* ; the sentence is, however, as heard in the mouth of Santal) ;
bam ạgu daraledea bạhuttẹt' ; ẹntẹt' bape metadiń khan, you did not bring his wife with you ; because you did not tell me to do so ; *hat̤ khon hat̤ak' bam ạguadińa ; ẹntẹt' bam rọṛ gọt'adińa,* you did not bring me a winnowing fan from the market-place ; because you did not speak to me about it when I went.
ma ẹnte caluk'me, so please go then ; *hẽ ẹnte, noa dọń rọṛ akat'a,* why yes, this I have said (I confess to this) ; *uni ẹnteye rọṛ akat'a,* why, he has said so (this adverbial *ẹnte* often corresponds to the use of *altsaa* in Norwegian).

Conclusives.

372. (*a*) *Onate,* by that (cause or means), for that reason, therefore, thereby, so that.

The demonstrative pronoun *ona* with the instrumental postposition *te.*

Used as a conjunction introducing a consecutive clause to state the result of a previous statement, *onate* referring to this. See para 329.

E. g., onate dọ bae hạnok'a, he will not be hurt thereby ; *katha akawat'koale, onateko hẹc' gọdọk'a nãhãk',* we have sent them word, so they will come presently ; *onate bae kạmi daṛeak'a,* therefore he cannot work.

---

† *Ẹntẹt'* may be either *ẹn* + *tẹt'* (see para 41), or *ẹnte* + *t'*, a formation that has several parallels (as in *lagat'*, *lạgit'*, *cet'*, *cetat'* ; cf. also the verbal suffixes with final *t'* ; *tẹt'* is possibly *tẹ* + *t'*).

(*b*) *Ona iạte*, } on account of that, for that reason,
Ona tẹrọṅ, } therefore.
Ona karọnte, }

The demonstrative pronoun *ona* with the postpositions *iạte*, *tẹrọṅ* and *karọnte* (see paras 92 and 94).

All these are used in the same way, recapitulating a previous statement that gives the reason for what follows.

E. g., *ruạk' kan taẖẽkanań*, *ona iạte* (or *tẹrọṅ*, or *karọnte*) *bạń hẹc'lena*, I was ill; therefore I did not come.

It should be remarked, that although *ona* is most commonly used any other demonstrative may be employed when suitable or wanted (as *inạ*, *noa*, *hana*, etc.). However, only *onate* will convey the meaning of 'so that'.

(*c*) *Ẹṇḍẹkhan*, *ẹṇḍẹkhac'*, } then, thereupon, in that case.
Tọbẹkhan, *tọbẹkhac'*, }

Composed of the demonstr. adv. *ẹṇḍẹ* or the adverb *tọbẹ*, borrowed from Bengali, and *khan* or *khac'*.

The conjunction represents the previous statement, giving the temporal precedence and condition for what follows.

E. g., *ẹṇḍẹkhan amge calak'taboňme*, so then you please go for us; *tọbẹkhane dalkedea*, thereupon he struck him.

(*d*) The demonstrative adverb *ẹṇḍẹ* is used with one or the other of a number of postpositions to convey the meaning of 'then', 'in that case', the sense of locality (*ẹṇḍẹ*, lit. meaning 'there') having become changed into the idea of temporal condition. Besides the above mentioned *ẹṇḍẹkhan* we have the following:

ẹṇḍẹ anaṅ, - *anẹc'*, - *ẹrọṅ*, - *ẹnẹc'*, - *ena*, - *enaṅ*, all meaning 'then only'.

ẹṇḍẹte, in that case, then; thereupon; why.
 ,, with any of the above particles added having the same meaning as *ẹṇḍẹ anaṅ*, etc.

ẹṇḍẹtege, why, I have heard (when followed by past tense); then (when followed by Future).

ẹṇḍẹ nāhĩ, then only.

ẹnḍẹre, there, then, in that case, then only; why, I thought (with past tense).

ẹnḍẹre ma, ẹnḍẹre sẹ, do.

ẹnḍẹre anaṅ, - anẹc', - ẹrọṅ, -ẹnẹc', - ena, - enaṅ, with the same meaning as *ẹnḍẹ anaṅ*, etc.

ẹnḍẹrege, same as *ẹnḍẹtege*.

ẹnḍẹ rẹsẹt', then only.

ẹnḍẹ bapo, then only.

ẹnḍẹ mọtọ, then only.

The above mentioned 'conjunctions' are, as will be seen not conjunctions proper, but really adverbs.

Conjunctives.

373. Besides those mentioned under Copulatives (- *hõ* - *hõ*) should here be mentioned

ẹkẹn - dọ baṅ, mẹnkhan - hõ, not only -, but also;

- eskar dọ baṅ, mẹnkhan - hõ, not - alone, but also.

Both are used very much alike, the difference being that while *ẹkẹn* mostly refers to the whole expression, *eskar* especially refers to the immediately preceding word. For all practical purposes the two expressions are synonymous. When needed *alo* is used instead of *baṅ*.

E. g., *ẹkẹn gidrạko dọ baṅ, mẹnkhan sẽṛã họṛ hõ*, not only the children, but also grown up people; *phalna eskar dọ baṅ, mẹnkhan atoren sanam họṛ hõko calaoena*, not so and so alone, but all the villagers also went; *ẹkẹn sẽṛã họṛ dọ alope hijuk'a, mẹnkhan gidrạko hõ ạgu darakope*, don't come only you grown-up people, but bring also the children along.

Instead of *mẹnkhan - hõ* only *- ge* may be used.

E. g., *ẹkẹn am* (or *am eskar*) *dọ baṅ* (or *alo*), *jọtọkoge hijuk'-pe*, not only you, come all of you.

Conditionals.

374. The postposition *khan*, added to the protasis, has been mentioned (see para 340); *ẹnḍẹkhan* and *tọbẹkhan*, recapitulating the condition of the protasis, have also been mentioned (see paras 98, 372 (c) and 340.

Khạjuk, provided, if only.

Khạjuk is used to introduce the provision, the *sine qua non* for the statement of the apodosis. The verb is always without the finite *a*, and the negation used in connection with *khạjuk* is always *alo*.

Judi, if, in case, recently borrowed from Bengali. The verb does not take the finite *a*, but has frequently *khan* added.

E. g., *gapań calak'a, khạjuk aloe dag*, I shall go to-morrow, provided it does not rain; *dọhọmeań, khạjuk ińak' hukum lekam kạmi*, I shall keep you, provided you will work as you are ordered to; *judim calak', noa idi toraeme*, if you go take this along; *judi onkoko ńẹl akat'ko khan*, if those have seen them.

Comparatives.

375. The use of *khọn* to form comparative has been mentioned previously (see para 60).

To compare Santali has the postposition *leka*; this is very extensively used to form pronominal adjectives and adverbs of manner and quality (see paras 164 and 186).

As a postposition added to a word or a sentence it serves equal to 'like' or 'as'.

Added to the interrogative pronouns *cet'* or *oka* we get *cet' leka* or *oka leka* which are frequently used as conjunctions. They are always placed in front of the word or the clause to which they refer, and may be taken up in a following *onka leka* or similar word. By adding the instrumental *te* the words become more descriptive. See paras 186 and 329. *Re* may also be added.

E. g., *noa leka benaome*, make (it) like this; *baha leka daka, hako leka utu, sẹṅgẹl leka pạurạ, bala leka peṛa okarem ńamkoa*, where will find rice like flowers, curry like fish, liquor like fire, friends like a co-parent-in-law? (a Santal saying).

disạime, cet' leka takẹ̃kantama, remember, how you had it; *uduk'aeme, cet' lekateye kạmi*, show him in what way he is to work;

uduk'at'me leka (onka leka) tearme, prepare it as it was shown to you; *ṭhikem batlaoade leka akat'ae*, he has done just as you have instructed him;

cet' leka am iñ hõ onka lekage, as you so I also;

cet' lekam ñẹl oṭolet'le, onka leka menak'lea, we have it just as you saw us.

Finals.

376. To introduce final clauses the language makes use of *jãhã lekate* and *jẹmọn* (this last a fairly recent borrowing from Bengali), both corresponding to 'in order that', 'that'.

As to a similar use of the postposition *mẹnte* cf. paras 96 (d) and 344.

E. g., *lạiakom, jãhãlekate* (or *jẹmọn*) *aloko sorok'*, tell them that they must not go near.

Subservient particles.

377. Santali has a number of particles that serve to emphasize, to draw attention or to express doubt or mental reservation. They are always suffixed to a word; they have no separate existence, although they may get the stress, wherefore they cannot be called enclitic particles. They are the following:

(*a*) *ge*.

This is a generally not translatable particle emphasizing the word it is added to. *Ge* may be added to base-words, to suffixes and to postpositions.

If to be translated, it may be rendered by 'certainly', 'really', or similar words.

Some people have got into the habit of writing *gi*, this is due to mishearing (see Materials, I., para 4).

E. g., *ọkọe kanam? ińge*, who are you? I; *ac'geye rọṛ akat'a*, he has said it himself; *sạrige*, really, truly; *hẹc'-engeae*, he has come (really); *rọṛge bae rọṛet'*, he does not speak at all; *nuige* (or *nui kangeae*) *naṭer guru dọ*, this one is the mischiefmaker; *uniye hẹc'en khọnge noa katha dọ ań-jọmok' kana*, from the very time of his coming this is heard.

(*b*) *dọ*, as for, with reference to, concerning.

Generally not translated. This particle draws attention to; it might be said often to serve as a kind of spoken punctuation-mark.

Dọ is very frequently used attached to the subject, sometimes also to the object.

E. g., *iń dọ bań*, *amge*, not I, but you; *ḍạn dọ ale hoṛ họ-pọn reak' marań jala*, the witches are the great plague of us Santals; *nitok' dọ pẹ isi serma hoyok' kana*, it is now sixty years ago; *noko dọ ale leka dọ bako cọlọna*, as for these they do do not behave like we do; *cele oaris bạnuk'ko khan disomreu raje ńama dhọn dọ*, if there are no heirs the owner of the land (the zemindar) gets the property; *adọm lebṛa hoṛ dọ sẹnge bako sẹnok'a ọnḍẹ dọ, lajaote sẹ bọtọrte*, some covetous people do not go there at all, out of shame or out of fear; *ale dọ nọnḍẹle tahẽ hataṛok'a*, *ape dọ lahak'tabonpe*, we shall remain here for a while, you please go on in advance; *bana dọko gọc'kedea*, *khikṛi dọko phaskaokedea*, they killed the bear, they lost the fox.

(*c*) *cọ(ń)*, perhaps, who knows; why!

Cọń has been mentioned under the disjunctive conjunctions (see para 369).

It is used in a double way, on the one hand to express subjective doubt as to a statement, and on the other hand to meet the subjective doubt of another person, in which case it becomes an affirmative particle.

Cọń cannot be used with the finite *a*, if it in any way refers to the verb.

E. g., *ọkọe cọko calak' lạgit'*, somebody or other (not known to the speaker) will go; *ọkọe baḍae cọń*, who knows? *ac' cọe bae akat'*, why, he himself has put it aside; *nũk'ũi cọń*, why, here he is; *nȩk'ȩe cǫn*, why, here it is; *cet' cǫn*, what? (I did not catch it), or, whatever it may be, something who knows what.

(*d*) - *tȩt'* has been mentioned previously (see para 41) as a suffix and needs no further mention here.

(*e*) *tǫ*, *thǫ*, *thǫr*, } surely, as you know, then.

Tǫ is borrowed from Bengali. These particles are used to emphasize or put some stress on the word to which they are suffixed. Used after an Imperative it gives some stress, but would not convey any idea of respect. These particles are not generally translatable.

E. g., *hẽ thǫ*, yes, that's it; *khange thǫ*, thereupon; then you see; *amren kangeae tǫ*, he is thine to be sure (anyhow); *ma ñũime tǫ*, drink then; *duṛup'pe thǫr*, sit down then (don't stand).

Affirmative particles.

378. The language has several affirmative particles, likely borrowed from Hindi; the one most commonly used is

(*a*) *hẽ*, yes.*

Besides as a particle *hẽ* and its parallel forms are used as adjectives, verbs and nouns.

E. g., *hẹc'enae? hẽ, hẹc' akanae*, has he come? yes, he has come; *ona dǫ hẽ kangea*, yes, that is so; that is a fact; *hẽ sạrige*, yes, truly; *hẽ ẹnte*, yes, of course; *hẽ ẹnteń rǫṛ akat'a edretege*, yes, I have certainly said so in anger; *hẽ cǫń*, may be; *hẽge cǫń*, yes, likely, may be; *hẽ jạnic'*, yes probably; *hẽ pasẹt'*, yes perhaps; *hẽ ma hẽge*, that is quite so (but -); *hẽket'ae*, he said yes, agreed; *calak'e hẽket'a*, he agreed to go; *jãhãnak'geye rǫṛ hẽạtaeme*, say yes to whatever he says; *okaṭak'bon galmaraoket' ona dǫ hẽyena*, what we talked about was assented to; *hẽ hẽ inạk'ge*, yes, yes, that is enough.

* Through Hindi from Skr. root *bhu*, to be.

(*b*) *hẽk'*, yes.

This is a sideform to *hẽ*, more especially used as a verb.

E. g., *amem idi akat'a? hẽk', idi akat'aṅ*, have you taken it away? yes, I have;

alom hẽga, don't agree; *hẽk'ket'ae*, he admitted it; *hẽk'-ataeme*, consent to his proposal.

(*c*) *hã*, yes.

A side form to *hẽ*, but very seldom used; it is pure Hindi.

(*d*) *hẽ hũ*,

is not used as a particle, but as a verb in the sense of assenting to.

E. g., *enaṅ dọe hẽ hũket'a*, a while ago he assented; *hẽ hũadiṅae*, he said yes to me, promised; *hẽ hũipe*, say yes, assent; *bạṛic' suluk tạkina unkin haṛam buḍhi tikin dọ, hẽ-kak' hũkak' jãhãnak'ge koṛae mẽn kuṛi hõ inạge*, this husband and wife live in great peace with one another; whatever the man says the same also the wife says.

(*e*) *hạı*, yes.

This particle (that comes from the same root as *hẽ* and parallel forms) is used partly as an affirmative particle, partly as an interjection. Compare the use of *ja* in German (*thue es ja*, do it please).

E. g., *hijuk'me! hạı, calak'aṅ*, come! yes, I will;

calak'me hạı, do go, won't you; *alom lạia, hạı*, don't tell, please; *hạı tọbẽ emaṅme*, surely, then give me;

hạı hạı, ọnḍẽge hasoyediṅ kana, yes, yes, just there it pains me.

(*f*) *hạı ke bọṭẽ* (with parallel form *hạı ko bọṭẽ*), yes, certainly, quite so. *Hạı* + Beng. *ke bọṭẽ*.

E. g., *hạı ke bọṭẽṅ disạket'a*, that's it, now I remembered it; *hạı ke bọṭẽ, onageṅ mẽnlet'a*, certainly I did say that.

(*g*) *Họi*, yes, quite so, just so; will you, won't you, do. Of the same origin as *hạı* and used in the same way.

E. g., dẹn iṅ hõ bape imạṅa? họi, emamalaṅ, please, will you not give me also? just so, we two shall give you (i. e., certainly not); *ona dọpe kạmiket'a? họi, kạmitam lạgit'ko,* have you done that? you may be sure, they are on the point of doing it for you (i. e. not at all);

ẹ phalna! họi, o you so and so! yes, here I am;

calak'me, họi, go, won't you.

họi họi, onage cọṅ mẹnet', quite so, that is just what I say; *ma hẹc' hodọk'me! họi họi, calak' kanaṅ,* come quickly! yes, yes, I am coming;

(*h*) *họi ke bọṭẹ,* the same as *hạị ke bọṭẹ.*

E. g., họi ko bọṭẹ, noa kangea, undoubtedly, this is it; *họi ke bọṭẹ, jut utạrena,* quite so, it fits exactly.

Particles of negation.

379. The language has three particles of negation, one for the simple assertive negation, another for an emphatic negation and a third for prohibition, *baṅ, ọhọ* and *alo.*

(*a*) *Ba, baṅ,* no, not.

The bare word is *ba,* which is used when the subject pronoun is suffixed to the negation, although the full *baṅ* may also be used, more especially when the negation has some stress. *Ba* is further used in certain connections enclitically added to other words, especially interrogative pronouns, conveying the meaning of 'why', 'well', etc.

It should be noted, that when *ba(ṅ)* is used as an assertive negation, a verb having the Simple Past suffix cannot be used; the suffixes of the Anterior Past or any other tense may be used.

Baṅ may be used as a verb, and in compounds prefixed, corresponding to our *un* - or *in* - .

E. g., calaoenae? baṅ, bae sẹnlena (or *sẹn akana*), did he go? no, he did not (or is not gone); *lạiam sẹm baṅa,* will you tell or not; *baṅ ṅẹl ṅamok'a nọṇḍẹ khon,* it is not to be seen from here; *uni sọṅgẹtekhan dọ hẽge, baṅ khan baṅ-*

tẹt'ge, if together with him, I am willing, otherwise absolutely not; *bae hijuk'a*, he will not come; *bae emadea*, he did not give him;

bae hẹc'ena mẹnkhan, if he does not come; *oṛak're bako lạikel'a, baṅma, onka nonka?* did they not tell at home, viz. so and so? (note tense-suffix in these two last sentences, where *baṅ* is not an assertive negation);

baṅa sẹ, onka dọ baṅ kana, no, it is not so; *alom baṅaṅa*, don't refuse me;

okor ba, lit. where, no; no, don't you see; nowhere here;

ba sẹ, it is so, is it not; *cet' baṅ sẹ, ọhọm pạtiạulena*, you have no idea how it was, you would never believe it;

baṅ-gujuk' ọt, land on which crops will not die; *baṅ-ṅẹlogok'ak'*, what is invisible;

amem ranlekhan baṅ họnẹc'e phạriạkok'a? if you had given him medicine would he not likely have recovered?

(*b*) *Ọhọ*, no, not, not at all, certainly not.

Ọhọ is emphatic, assuring. It is, when connected with a verb, generally followed by the Anterior, but may also take the Future, the first conveying a general negation, the last a negation referring to the special case mentioned. Both *baṅ* and *ọhọ* may be emphasized by adding *ge, tẹt'* or *tẹt'ge*.

Ọhọ may also be used as a verb, especially with indirect object. *Ọhọ* may also take the Optative tense suffix (*ke*).

E. g., ọhọe hẹc'lena, he will certainly not come; *ọhọe gujuk'a*, he will surely not die (this time); *ọhọṅ mẹnlea*, I am unable to say; *alom bọtọrok'a, bae cek'kawa, ọhọa*, don't be afraid, he will not hurt (you), nothing of the kind; *ọhọa sẹ, ọnḍẹ dọ alo*, by no means, not at all there; *ọhọ tọko jãhã cekamea*, they will surely not do you anything;

ọhọtẹt'geṅ ẹmlena, I shall certainly not give; *ọhọgem hẹc' daṛelena*, you will surely not be able to come; *amem tahẽlenkhan ọhọtẹt'ge honaṅe cekakelea*, if you had been there he would certainly not have tried to do us anything;

bae ọhọea, he will not say no; *ọhọbon ọhọletaea*, we shall certainly not say any no to him; *tisre hõ bae ọhọ akawat'tiṅa nin din dọ*, he has never said no to any request of mine up to this; *nit bam calak'a? baṅ, ọhọatiṅ kana, enaṅre dọ cet' hõ bako mẹnlak'a*, won't you go now? no, I don't care to, a while ago they did not say anything; *jãhãtege qhoatiña*, I shall certainly not go anywhere.

(c) *Õhõk'* and *ũhũk'* will be found below among the interjections, where they rightly belong.

(d) *Alo*, no, don't.

It is tempting to compare *alo* with the negation found in a number of Semitic languages.

Alo is used as a prohibitive particle (the verb always in the Future, not in the Imperative), whether it be an order or a wish. It is also used in final clauses, and in conditional clauses with a condition *sine qua non*.

It may be augmented by repetition or by adding *ge*, *tet'*, *tet'ge*, *se*, *bare*; it may also be used as a verb.

E. g., *alom rora*, don't speak; *bes leka tolme*, *jemon alo rarak'*, tie it well, so it may not be loosened; *aloñ senlenkhan uni tuluc' do qhoñ ñepellena*, if I had not gone, I should not have met him; *ghotna alo bare hoyok'a*, may no accident happen; *alo bareye ñũrok' ma*, may he not fall down;

alo se onka do, please don't in that way; *alogem calak'a*, don't go; *alotet'em* (or *alotet'gem*) *emok'a*, do not give under any circumstances; *aloye lañgak' ma*, may he not be tired out; *alom senok'*, *ona boroñ bogege*, if you don't go, that will be the better course;

bae aloat'tiña, he did not forbid me; *aloatam ma*, may you be refused.

Interjections.

330. The language has a very large assortment of interjections to call attention, to warn, threaten, or encourage, to express admiration, surprise, joy, grief, sorrow, pain, and so on. Some are used by all, others only by men, and again others only by women, some only to men, others only to women.

Most of them are prefixed, some are added to another word or sentence. All of them may take a verbal suffix.

381. *To call attention.*

(*a*) *E*, o, oh ! hey !

E is used before names, titles, etc., when addressing, also before other interjections of calling, such as *ho*, *hǫ*, *ya*, *na*, etc. It should be noted, that *ẹ* is not obligatory when calling, as a matter of fact it is often omitted in addressing, especially when questioning, and during conversation.

E. g., *ẹ baba*, o father ! *ẹ gọ*, o mother ! *ẹ raj*, o king ! *ẹ Suną*, o Suna ! *ẹ Lela apat*, o father of L., *ẹ ho*, I say, oh !

It might be mentioned here that Santals do not use the proper name when addressing any one in a higher position (or what to a Santal amounts to the same, older) than oneself; the name may be used when speaking to children and inferiors, but is preferably avoided.

(*b*) *ẹa*, *ea*, } listen ! look here !

Composed of *ẹ*+*ya*, sometimes also written *ẹya* or *eya*.

This interjection is used in addressing younger and inferior male persons (not females), also rebuking or scolding. It is always initial, and may be used alone, or prefixed like *ẹ*.

E. g., *ea bạbu*, look here, boy ! *ea Pạṇḍu*, listen, Pandu ! *ẹa phąsiąrako*, you hypocrites ! *ẹa*, *onka dǫ alom rọṛa*, look here, don't speak in that way;
cet' iạtem ẹawadiña, why did you address me with *ẹa* ?

(*c*) *Ei*, look here ! listen ! hallo !

Used to call attention, and without any name or title, always standing in front. It is a familiar and somewhat vulgar interjection, especially used between boys and girls or companions, and never to superiors.

E. g., *ẹi*, *nǫtẹya bẹṅgẹdme*, hallo there, look this way, you fellow ! *ẹi ẹi*, *nǫtẹ hijuk'me sẹ*, listen ! come here !
ẹiań kanam, *ińak' sạgại dǫ bam baḍae kana*, you address me with *ẹi*, don't you know what relationship I stand in to you ?

(*d*) *E ho*, oh ! I say ! hallo ! listen !

Used by men to men, to call attention (see below *ho*); often used in answering or remonstrating in a mild way.

May be used addressing all, superiors and inferiors.

E. g., *e ho, pera hor*, I say, friend (addressing a stranger); *e ho, gorom*, I say, namesake ; *e ho, baba*, I say, sir ! *e ho, note ma hijuk'pe*, I say, please come here.

(*e*) *E ho*, oh ! I say ! listen !

Equivalent to *e ho*, but used by women to women, and sometimes to their husbands.

E g., *e ho, hatom*, I say, aunt.

(*f*) *Ia*, *Ia ho*, } I say.

This demonstrative (see para 193 (a)) may be used as an interjection, about equal to *e ho*.

E. g., *ia, do se calak'me*, I say, you, please go ; *ia hoñ metam kana*, I say you, what's your name, I tell you.

(*g*) *-ho*, oh ! listen ! I say ! you there !

This interjection is always added to another word or interjection. It is used by men calling upon other men, generally of the same age, especially also unknown or unseen persons ; it is used addressing a *mamot* (mother's brother), also a *teñat* (elder sister's husband) ; addressing a women it is used to one's *balat era* (the mother of the girl or boy with whom the speaker's son or daughter is married), not otherwise.

E. g., *henda ho*, I say, you there ; *okoe ho*, who is there ? *alom hoaña*, don't call to me using *ho*.

(*h*) *- ho*, listen ! I say !

This is equal to *ho*, only that it is used in this meaning by women to other women and to an *erceltet' kora* (husband's younger brother, in this case).

Ho used equivalent to *o* will be mentioned below.

E. g., henda hǫ, listen you! *hape hǫ, gońgo apat*, wait, you father of my nephew (said by *hilit* to *erveltęt' koṛa*); *ę hǫ*, listen!

(*i*) *Henda*, listen! look here! hey! I say!

Henda is used to call attention, especially also in questioning. It is used by all and to all, may stand alone, but is frequently followed by title, name or an other interjection, such as *- hǫ, - hǫ, - ya, - na*, etc.

E. g., henda bạbu, cet'em cekayet'a, look here, boy, what are you doing; *henda hǫ, gạiye at' akantińa, ńęl jãhãn akadeape*, I say, my cow has been lost, you have not by any chance seen her? *henda na, okatem dukạna*, listen, girl, where did you go? *hendaya, bam ańjǫma*, look here, boy, will you not hear?

(*j*). *- ya*, you boy, young man, you chap, fellow.

This interjection is always suffixed to a preceding word or another interjection (such as *ę ya, henda-ya*).

It is used by all to males younger than the speaker; it is a familiar expression; it would be considered an insult if addressed to one's superiors; used between boys it is a sign of intimacy.

E. g., calak̇meya, hǫhǫam kanako, go, fellow, they are calling you; *ea bạbuya, bam ańjǫmet'aya*, young chap, don't you hear; *hendaya, okateyam helaok' kanaya*, hey you fellow, where are you off to? *nui dǫya, oka lekan hǫṛ kan cǫe ya*, look here, old top, what kind of a man is this one? *ma ya, emaeme ya*, do, give him; *dela ya*, come along; *dę ya*, give it.

(*k*) *- na*, you girl.

Used like *- ya*, but to girls and women younger than the speaker.

E. g., ę na, hijuk̇me na, come, girl; *dę na, am na ạgui talańme*, you girl, please bring it for us; *okor na, bacǫń ńęl akade*, no, girl, I have not seen him at all; *ma na, bạṭiko ạguipe na*, do girls, bring the cups; *henda na*, look here, girl; *dela na, birte*, come along, girl, to the forest.

(*l*) - *yọi*, } hallo there! look out you there! have a
- *nọi*, } care!

These interjections are used like - *ya* and - *na*, added to a word or other interjection, - *yọi* to males and - *nọi* to females. It is a loud address, generally to a number of persons more or less distant; it often conveys a warning.

E. g., *mẹn yọi, hor khon ọcọgok'pe, hawa gạḍi dara kana*, look out you, get out of the way, a motor car is coming; *sọntọrok'pe nọi, bhalok' setae ṅir baṛae kana*, take care, girls, a mad dog is running about.

(*m*) *Hui*, }
Hui hui, } get off! away!

Used when it is dark or in forest thickets to warn or drive away those who may possibly be there.

E. g., *hui, nọtẹre cele cọṅ ṅẹllede*, get away, I saw some one hereabouts; *hui hui, cele cọṅ pasẹt' menak'pe*, get away, whoever may possibly be here; *ạḍi bạṛic'e huiadea*, he shouted many times at him (to drive him off).

(*n*) - *rẹ*, oh you!

An interjection of calling or of intensification. This *rẹ* is borrowed from Bengali. It is always postpositional. In Santali it does not convey the idea of contempt in calling, as it often does in Bengali, but it will intensify the idea conveyed by the word or the interjection to which it is added.

It might be noted that it is frequently used in Santal poetry as a 'padding'.

Examples of its use will be found in connection with other interjections.

E. g., *ẹ babarẹ*, oh! dear me! *bạburẹ*, do.

(*o*) *Ek'*, }
Ẹk', } er, ah! look!

This interjection is partly used as an expletive particle, often in enumerations (in this case preceding each thing mentioned), somewhat corresponding to the English er, ar, ah. It is also used in calling attention to something.

E. g., *ẹk' uni*, *ẹk' hunkin*, he or those two; *unre dọ ek' nonkatele sẹnlena*, then we followed - er - this road; *ẹk' ẹn ẹnḍẹ*, look just there; *ẹk' noko darako kana*, look there, those are coming; *ẹk' nitgeye jọskedea*, there, now he hit it.

This *ẹk'* seems to be the interjection *ẹ* with the inanimate *k'* added; *ẹ* may possibly be a demonstrative particle.

(*p*) *ẹk' ẹk' ẹk'*, oh!

Used to express alarm at something suddenly happening with one.

E. g., *ẹk' ẹk' ẹk'*, *ńurhạyenań*, *ńurhạyenań!* oh, oh! I am falling, I am falling!

382. In this connection the following with reference to the way in which the Santals address people may be noted.

A Santal will not address anybody by name, if the addressed person is not younger than the speaker, and even then the name is preferably avoided; the real name is generally not used, and the second name (nickname) is also avoided in address (see the writer's paper On Tabu and therewith connected customs among the Santals, J. A. S. B. Vol. LXVII, pt. III, No. 1 of 1898). In stead of the name an appellative, denoting title, sex, age, relationship to a child, relationship to speaker, etc., is used.

The names of relationship used will be found para 20.

E. g., *gọ*, *ayọ* (mother, or woman older than oneself), *baba* (father, sir), *ka*, *kaka*, *goṅgo*, *mama*, *kạki*, *hatọm*, etc. (uncles and aunts of sorts); *bạbu* (young man, boy, male child), *mạku* (young girl, especially a term of endearment), *pạku* (= *mạku*, a recent introduction), *mại*, *mũi* (young girl, woman younger than oneself), *ẹ Pạṇḍu apat*, o Pandu's father, *ẹ Nasọ eṅgat*, o Naso's mother; husband and wife address one another and speak of one another in this way; previous to getting children they will have the relationship to somebody else to use; to use the name is out of the question.

383. *Affirmative, and negative.*

These interjections have been partly mentioned before under the affirmative and negative particles; see para 378.

(*a*) *Hạ̣i*, *Họi*, *Hạ̣i hạ̣i*, *Họi họi*, — see para 378 (e) and (g).

(*b*) *Ọi*, *Ọi ọi*, — yes, what is it; take care!

This interjection is used in a double way, partly as a grunting acknowledgement, partly as a remonstrance.

E. g., *ọi, nọtẹre menaṅa*, yes, I am here on this side; *mit' dhaoe ọiket'a, adọe okayen cọṅ*, he answered once, then he disappeared somewhere; *ọi, cet'em cekayet'a*, take care, what are you doing? *ọi ọi, cet'em ṅam kana*, yes, yes, what do you want? *ọi ọi, cet'em cekayet'a*, be careful, what are you doing? *enaṅ khone ọi ọiok' kana, okore hijuk' kana*, he has been answering for a long while, why, he is not coming.

(*c*) *Ã*, how, what was it? eh!

Used when not hearing exactly, and wishing the speaker to repeat. Cf. rustic Norwegian *hæ?*

E. g., *dẹn aguime! ã?*, bring it, eh, is that what you are saying?

(*d*) *ẽhẽk'*, *ẽhẽk' ẽhẽk'*, *õhõk'*, *õhõk' õhõk'*, *ũhũk'*, *ũhũk' ũhũk'*, — no! not so! not at all! nothing of the kind!

These particles or interjections are all used to remonstrate and show dissent, something analogous to shaking one's head; especially *ũhũk'* is often accompanied by this; cf. para 384 (h) and (i).

E. g., *ẽhẽk', baṅ jutem batlaoae kana*, not so, you are not instructing him well; *ũhũk', baṅ disạyet'a*, no, I do not remember it; *õhõk', bam baḍaea ẹnḍẹkhan am dọ*, nothing of the kind, then you do not know this you; *ũhũk' ũhũk', ona katha dọ alom rọṛa*, no, not so! don't mention that matter; *ũhũk'et'ge dọe, bae ganok' kan dọ*, he is saying no, he is not willing.

384. *Of warning and remonstrance.*

(*a*) *Ạika,* } mind! I warn you; but, only, on the understanding.
Ạikhạ,

E. g., ạḍi ṭakań khọrọc akat'a, ạikạ niạ dhao dọ khub jut akana, I have spent a lot of money, but this time, however, it has succeeded exceedingly well; *sọṅgẹteń calak'a, alo ạikạm bạgiańa,* I shall go along with you, but mind, don't leave me; *dẹc' dọ dẹjok'me, ạikạ noa ḍạr dọ ṭhasahagea,* well, climb the tree, but I warn you, this branch is brittle; *sẹn dọń sẹnok'gea, bań ńamlekhan ạikạ alom ruhedińa,* I shall go, only if I do not find it don't scold me; *ma sabeme, ạikại gẹgẹra,* catch hold of it, but take care, it bites.

(*b*) *Iạ ạikạ,* } I say, but remember!
Iạ ạikhạ,

E. g., iạ ạikạ din hilok' hijuk'me, be sure to come daily; *iạ ạikạ alom raga, adọń idimea, bańkhan dọ bań,* remember you are not to cry, then I shall take you along, otherwise not; *iạ ạikạ ọhọń sẹnlena,* remember I cannot possibly go.

(*c*) *Hãhã,* } take care, beware, stop, hold, don't!
Hãhãk',

These interjections may possibly be connected with *hã*, a parallel form to *hẽ*; however, cf. also below (d), (e) and (f).

They are the call out generally used when a person tries to stop any misbehaviour or to drive people or animals away.

E. g., hã-hã, inạkak'me, stop, that is enough; *hã hã, alom dalea,* hold! don't strike him; *ọkọe hõ bako hãhãlak'a,* no one called out to stop (no one came to the rescue); *hãhã tuluc'gekin jọmket'a,* they ate although warned not to; *hãhãteak' jọmak' dọ bań hak'soa,* what is eaten (by animals) when they are driven away, does not give pain (the owner of the crops will not take notice when there was some one to drive the cattle away); *hãhãk' hõ bae mẹnlak'a thoṛa gan hõ,* he did not interfere in the least.

(*d*) *Ahak',* don't, take care, hold, stop!

Used like *hãhã*; cf. *ẽhẽk'* and *ũhũk'*.

E. g., ahak', alom dalea, stop, don't strike him; *ahak', ọntẹ dọ bań kana,* take care, it is not in that direction.

(*e*) *Aha*, } alas!
Aha aha,

This interjection is mostly used to express pleasure and joy, but is also heard to express regret. Cf. *hãhã*.

E. g., *aha, thoṛaṅ bacǫlket'a, baṅkhaniṅ jǫskea honaṅ*, it's a pity, I just missed it, otherwise I should have hit it.

(*f*) *Ahaha*, } don't, stop, hands off!
Aha haha,

Used of remonstrance and warning.

E. g., *ahaha, ǫntẹ dǫ alom calak'a*, stop, don't go in that direction; *aha haha, onka dǫ alom rǫṛa*, hold! don't speak in that way.

(*g*) *Mẹn*, mind, take care, beware, look out!

Used to warn, caution or admonish. Is very frequently followed by an other interjection.

E. g., *mẹn sǫntǫrok'pe*, be careful; *mẹn, alope lǫi baṛaea*, mind, don't tell; *mẹn mẹn, ape sẹc'e daṛet' kana*, look out, look out, he is running towards you;
mẹn baba, look out, sir; *mẹn gǫ* look out, mother; *mẹnya, mẹn na, mẹn yǫi, mẹn ho, mẹn bạbu, mẹn mại*.

(*h*) *Ẹhẹ*,
Ẹhẹ ẹhẹ, } hey there, be careful, keep off, hist!
Ẹhẹ ge,
Ẹhẹ rẹ,

These interjections are used to express remonstrance or warning, *ẹhẹ ge* being especially used towards girls, whilst *ẹhẹ rẹ* is used when the speaker wants to make the person addressed ashamed.

Ẹhẹ may be followed by other interjections. Cf. para 383 (d).

E g., *ẹhẹ, okatem calak' kana*, hey there, where are you going (you have no business to go there); *ẹhẹ, cet'em cekayet'a, ṅẹlet'megeaṅ*, hey there, what are you doing? I am seeing you (e. g. when a person is making off with something); *ẹhẹge, alo ǫntẹ dǫ*, hist, girl, not in that direction! *ẹhẹ ẹhẹ, cet'em idiyet'talea*, hallo there, what are you off with of ours? *ẹhẹre, cet'kom kạumạu baṛayet'a,* hey you, what are you making for noise there? *ẹhẹya,* hey there, you!

(*i*) *Oho,* take care!

Cf. 383 (d).

E. g., oho, nem bạṛija, take care, you are on the point of spoiling it.

385. (*a*) The Santals, like other oriental peoples, make use of the words for father or mother to express surprise, whether it be astonishment pure and simple, or annoyance or even anger. It is the appeal of infancy to the natural protector or nearest intimate friend which has become stereotyped.

The same words are also used to give vent to pain. The words used are *babare, ẹ baba, ẹ babare,* oh father! *baba gọ,* oh father mother! *ayọ, ayo, ayọge, ayọgọ, ayogo, ạyuguh,* o mother, o ma! o dear! dear me!

E. g., ayọ, ayọ, ayọgọ, ạḍi ãṭ hasoyediń kana, ẹ babare, bań jutiń ạikạuet'a, oh mother, o mother, o mother o ma! it pains me exceedingly, o father, I feel badly;

babarẹ, cet' hoe akantapea, o father, what has happened to you? *ẹ babarẹ, un marań dọ bạń ńẹl akal'koa,* o father, so big I have never seen them;

ayo, nitge nọṇḍẹye tahẽkana, strange, he was here just now; *ayọge, behal nitok' dọe ruḱhet' kanaya,* dear me, how awfully he is scolding now; *ayoge, bam añjọmet'a,* o mother, don't you hear?

(*b*) *Ạige,* hallo, dear me, what!

Probably a corruption of *ayoge,* if it is not Bengali *ai,* grandmother, that has been adopted.

It is used as an interjection of surprise, sometimes coupled with resentment.

E. g., ạige, nọtẹ dọ reaṛe họeyet'a, hallo, here there is a cold breeze; *ạige, nui họṛ dọ oka leka họe rọṛet'a,* hallo, how is this fellow speaking!

(*c*) *Ạiyo,* hallo, dear me!

Probably a corruption of *ayo.* Used as *ạige.*

E. g., ạiyo, enańre haṇḍeń ńẹllet'mea, tinre nọṇḍẹ dọm hẹc'ena, hallo, a while ago I saw you there, when did you come here? *ạiyo, bam bọtọrok' kana,* what, are you not afraid?

(*d*) *Ạijo,* what, is it possible, strange!

Possibly another form of *ạiyo.* Used to express surprise.

E. g., ạijo, okayena? what in the world has become of it? *ạijo, behal at' at'en dọ,* strange, how it could be lost.

(*e*) *Ạjjo,*
Ajjo, } used like *ạijo.*

386. *To express surprise.*

(*a*) *Durrẹ,* hallo, strange!

See below, where interjections of annoyance and vexation are mentioned.

E. g., durrẹ, cet' cọń ạḍi cọṭ jol rakap' gọt'ena, strange, something or other suddenly blazed high up.
In stead of *durrẹ* the form *durẹ* may also be heard.

(*b*) *Ẹh,*
Ẹh ẹh,
Ẹhrẹ, } o, what, indeed, really, my, o dear!

Interjections of surprise, or annoyance, mostly used by women. Same word is used in rustic Bengali.

E. g., ẹh, ạḍi jut ńẹlok' kana noa dọ, oh dear, this is looking very nice; *ẹh, ac' eskargeye dhẹjket'a,* o my, he managed it by himself alone; *ẹh, jọrọadińa,* o dear me, (water) trickled down on me; *ẹh ẹh, hasoyedińa,* dear me, it pains me, *ẹh ẹh, cet' leka ńẹlok' kana,* wonderful, how does it not look! *ẹh ẹh, nẹ nãhãk'e daleńa,* oh oh! presently he will beat me.

(*c*) *Eh,* another pronunciation of above word. Compare below.

This form is mostly used about pain or annoyance.

387. *To express annoyance, concern and pain.*

(*a*) *Eh,* oh, o my, dear me!

Besides (as mentioned above) to express surprise this is used to give expression to annoyance or disgust or the feeling of nuisance. Used mostly by women.

E. g., *eh, baric'geye losot'ket'a*, ugh, he has made it very dirty.

(*b*) *Ehe hehe he*,
Eh hehe hehe, } o dear dear, fie !

Gives expression to feeling of annoyance and disgust.

E. g., *ehe hehe he, gotae losot' akana*, fie, fie, he has become dirty all over ;

eh hehe hehe, nonde do alope aguyea, gotae maila akana, fie fie ! don't bring him here ; he has befouled himself all over.

(c) *Eh ehe*,
Ehe he, } oh, dear me, alas !
Ehe hehe

These interjections are used to give expression to the feelings of annoyance, concern or pain.

E. g, *ehe he, nonde hasoyediń kana*, oh ! oh ! it is paining me here ; *ehe he, nui hor do tibe adi bhabna curtiyentaea*, o dear, this man has thus got a great deal of increased trouble ; *eh ehe, bogete hasoyedińa gota hormo*, o dear dear, I have great pains all over my body.

(*d*) *Oh ho*,
Ohre, } alas, dear me, oh !
Oh hoho ho,

These interjections give expression to pain or regret.

E. g., *oh ho, thora bań josleda*, alas, it wanted only a little that I should hit ; *oh ho, nonkan hor kanae*, dear me, is he such a person ? *ohre, katha dobon kharapket'a*, o, dear me, we have spoilt the matter ; *ohre durre, cet' lekam ńelok' kan*, o dear, fie, how are you looking ? *oh hohoho, adi hasoyediń kana*, oh ! oh ! it pains me very much.

(*e*) *Oh*,
Oh oh, } oh, dear me, alas, what a pity !
Oh oho,

These interjections are used to express regret, annoyance and pain. Cf. *uh*. The last *ho* of *oh oho* may be repeated ad lib.

E. g., *oh, hani torań paskaokedea*, o ! there I let him get off ; *oh, adiń langat akana kicric' selet'*, dear me, my clothes are falling into rags; *oh, goc' gidiyenae,* alas, he died and is lost; *oh oh, noań hiriṅket'a,* o dear, this I have forgotten (to do); *oh oho, thora bań josledea,* what a pity, I just missed it; *oh oho hoho, neyiń barija,* o dear, it is going wrong for me.

(*f*) *Uh,* } alas, dear me, oh!
Uhre, }

Interjections of pain, sorrow or jealousy, also to express alarm at what might have happened.

E. g., uh, uniak' duk ńelte adi bhabnań aikauket'a, dear me, seeing his sufferings I felt great sorrow; *uh, neń bajaok'a,* oh, a little more and I should have hurt myself; *uh, khub bhageak'ko ńamket'a,* o dear, they have got very fine things; *uh, abon nondebon tahenkhan honań dhoragebon tenkok'a,* o dear, if we had been here we should certainly have got it over us;
uhre, katha dobon baric'ket'a, alas, we have spoilt the matter; *uhre, uni dobon kahil ocokedea,* what a pity, we have let him become dangerously ill.

(*g*) *Uhu,*
Uhu uhu,
U huhu, } alas, oh, dear!
U huhu huhu,
Uh huhuhu,

Interjections of regret.

E. g., uhu, thora bań sap'ledea, alas, it wanted just a little that I should have caught it (e. g. the fish); in stead of *uhu* any of the above might be used.

(*h*) *I,*
Ih, } oh, dear me, fie!
Ih ih,

Interjections of pain, annoyance or repugnance. *I* is a rarely used form.

E. g., ih, hirkhage sok' kana, fie, it smells abominably; *ih, bogete rabań kana,* o dear, it is very cold; *ih, janumiń rok'ena ho,* o dear, I have got a thorn (in my foot); *ih ih ih, gota hormo latkao akawadea,* o fie, fie, the child has got its whole body covered (with dirt);

(*i*) *Is*,
Is is, } oh, dear me, get away, fie!

Interjections used to express sudden annoyance, repugnance or pain.

E. g., *is, janumiń rok'ena*, o dear, I have got a thorn in (my foot); *is, hirkhage sok' kana*, fie, it is smelling abominably; *is, arisediń kanam*, get away, you are annoying me; *is is, alo sem jotediña*, fie, fie, don't touch me;

mit' dhaoe iskat'a, adoe thirena, he said *is* once; then he became quiet.

(*j*) *Aigu*, oh, o dear, dear me!

Interjection to express sudden pain, probably from *ayogo*, q. v.

E. g., *aigu, ackań beret' got'ena, nonde hiric' marte haso kidiña*, o dear, I arose suddenly, and then I felt a stinging pain here.

(*k*) *Aege*, hallo, dear me, oh, o dear!

Interjection to express surprise, pain or fear, probably from *ayoge*.

E. g., *aege, tiar got'ena*, hallo, it stretched itself out; *aege, botor got' ocokidińam*, o dear, you gave me a fright.

(*l*) *Au*,
Au au, } oh, ah, o dear!

To express fright, fear, pain or surprise (real or feigned).

These interjections are used by women, and mostly only among themselves.

E. g., *au de na, cet' katha coe metalań kana*, o dear, girl, listen, what it is he is saying to us; *au, nonde na haso got'kidiña*, oh, I got a sudden pain here; *au dela na, cele coń lebet'kede*, oh, come here, I have tread on some creeping thing;

au au, nonde nań tohot' hasoyena na, o dear, I stumbled here and it has given me pain.

(*m*) *O*, oh, well, alas!

This interjection is used to express understanding, defiance, anger, compassion.

E. g., o bachatiń, oh, my son! *o, sari ona do lań hiriń-ket'a*, oh, to be sure, that we have forgotten; *o, onam men-et'a*, oh, is it this that you mean; *o lań thapamea*, well, we shall slap you.

(*n*) *Ho*, well, oh!

This is used very much like *o* by both men and women.

The *ho* used by women to call attention has been noticed above.

E. g., ho, bań disayet'a, oh, I do not remember.

(*o*) *O hae,*
O hae hae, } oh, dear me, alas, to think!

These interjections are used by women to express surprise, astonishment, regret, sorrow, pain. Cf. *hae*.

E. g., o hae, goc'kedeae, dear me, he killed him; *o hae, bogete hasoyediń kana*, o dear me, it pains me very much; *o hae, cet'iń cekaea*, o dear, what am I to do?

o hae, nui gidra ńelepe, nonkae dar dareak', only think! look at this child, how it can run; *o hae, nui kanaye*, just think, it is him;

o hae hae, unak'e kostok' kana, o dear, so great a hardship she is suffering; *o hae hae, nunak' sud do bań badaelak'a*, o dear me, I had no idea that the interest would be so much.

O hae seems to be used by women to express anything and everything or nothing at all.

388. *To express pain, sorrow, pity.*

(*a*) *Hae,*
Hae hae,
Haere, } oh, alas, o dear, woe!
Haere hae,
Haere haere,

These interjections are used to express pain, sorrow, grief, regret. They are used especially also at lamentations and may give expression to the deepest sorrow and grief.

E. g., hae, cet'iń cekaea, o dear, what am I to do? *hae am do, cet'em cekayet'a*, woe unto you, what are you doing? *hae hopon tiń*, alas, my son!

hae hae, hoete aditet'e loksanket'a, alas, the wind has caused much loss;

hae hae, jalapurire, hae hae, nukin manewa, hae hae, busųṛ akankin, oh, oh! on the sea, oh, oh! these two human beings, oh, oh! have been born (from a traditional song);

haere, ohoń senlena iń do, o dear, I shall certainly not go (women's language);

haere, kopal bhaṅgatiń, woe is me, all is over with me;

haere haere, toa daretiń do, alas, alas, my milk tree (i. e. mother, lamentation at death);

haere hae, tinreń cekaea, o dear, when shall I do it;

haere hae, aditet'iń kostok' kana, o dear, o dear! I am in great straits.

(*b*) *Jare jare,* alas, woe!

Used by women, especially in lamentation at death.

E. g., Jare jare, ado ohoń ńamlea, alas, alas! I shall never find him hereafter.

(*c*) *Durre,*
Dure,
Durhak',
Dur kharak',
Dhurhak',
Dhur karak',
Dur karahak',
} oh, hallo, alas, woe is me, strange, fie!

These interjections, all being formed from Hindi *dur,* what is at a distance, are used to express surprise (see above), regret, annoyance, grief, admonition.

Dure is a common mispronunciation of *durre,* and *dhurhak'* is probably only an intensification of *durhak'*. Cf. Mat. I., para 74.

E. g., durre, adi baric'iń botorena, oh, I got thoroughly frightened; *durre, unak'ko hec' akana,* o wonder, so many have come together; *dure durre, ohobon sambṛao daṛelea,* oh, oh, we shall certainly not be able to keep this in check; *dhurhak', hiriṅket'ań,* alas, I have forgotten; *dhur karak', cedak' noarepe durup' akana,* dear me, why are you sitting here (whilst you might have a better place).

(*d*) *Dir,*
Dirrẹ,
Dirhak',
Dir karak',
Dhir,
Dhirrẹ,
Dhirhak', } oh, hallo, alas!

These interjections are used like *dur*, etc., and need no further mention.

(*e*) *Mor,*
Morhak',
Morrẹ,
Mor jala, } oh, alas, what a pity!

Interjections used to express regret and anxiety.

E. g., morem sẹnlenkhan boge hoekok'a, oh, if you would go it would be well;

morrẹ, ọnḍẹ baṛẹm tahẹn khan bes hoekok'a, oh, if you will stay there it will be good; *morhak', cak' cọm hẹc'en,* what a pity, what has brought you here?

mor jala, aloe sẹnlenkhan, what a pity, if he only would not go!

(*f*) *Dhiṭ,*
Dhiṭhak',
Dhuṭ
Dhuṭhak' } oh, fie!

Interjections used to express contempt or disapproval.*

E. g., dhuṭ, onka dọ alom rọṛa, fie, don't speak in that way; *dhuṭ, ọnḍẹ dọ ọhọń sẹnlena,* no, I am not going there;

dhiṭ, cak' cọń nonkaket', pity! why did I do this? *dhuṭhak', cedak' cọń rọṛ kạiket',* why in the world did I let myself speak in such a way?

As to the dot below the *ṭ* see Mat. I. para 74.

---

* These interjections are phonetically abnorm. They are pronounced as written. The language does not otherwise permit an initial dental *d* or *dh* to be followed in the same stress-unit by a cacuminal *ṭ*. The second aspirate is explained by the pronunciation which is *dhiṭ* (*dhuṭ*) *hak*, not *dhi*(*dhu*)-*ṭhak*. We have two words. One might be tempted to connect the *dhuṭ* with Hindi *dhut* (but in this case why should Santali have *dhuṭ*?) and *dhiṭ* with Hindi *ḍhiṭ* (but here why *dhiṭ*? *ḍhiṭ* is found in

389. *To express pleasure and joy.*

(*a*) *Ah*, *Ah ah*, *Aha*, *A haha*, *A haha haha*, } oh, ah, how pleasant!

These interjections are used to express pleasure, joy, a glad surprise. It should be noted that *ah* and *aha* is also used to express pain (see para 384 (e)).

E. g., *ah, nit utạr besiń bujhạuet'a*, oh, now only I feel well; *aha, bạric' jute hoeket'a nọtẹ khon*, oh, a most pleasant wind came from this side; *ah ah, ạdi jut reaṛiń ạikạuket'a*, ah, I feel it very cool and pleasant; *ah haha haha, nonkan rạṛ dọ ạdi mõńjiń bujhạuket'a*, oh, so pleasant, I think such a melody beautiful.

(*b*) *Hạlạ*, *Hạlạre*, } bravo, well done, hurrah!

Possibly to be derived from *bhala*, well.

This interjection is used to express praise and admiration. The *l* is often doubled or rather lengthened in pronunciation.

E. g., *hạlạ, jọsket'ań*, hurrah, I hit it; *hạlạ, teheń dọko sap'kedea*, bravo, to-day they caught it; *hạlạ bhại*, well done; *hạlạre, jitạuenam*, well done, you have won!

(*c*) *Bah*, *Bah bah*, *Bahwarẹ*, *Baoha*, *Baoharẹ*, } bravo, well done, excellent!*

These interjections are used very much like *hạlạ*, to express admiration. *Baoha* is likely a transposition of *bahwa*.

E. g., *bah, am do khub koṛa kanam*, well done, you are a fine boy; *bah bah baohare, nui koṛa dọe utrạu akana*, hurrah! well done, this young man has developed splendidly; *baohare, nui leka dọ bape khacaṛok' kana*, fine! you (others) are not so energetic as this one.

Santali as an ordinary base word).

* The Hindi (Arabic) *wāh*.

390. The language has a number of exhortative particles intending to *urge* the person addressed to act, to come along, to give, etc.

(*a*) *Do*, do, please!

Do is used prefixed to a verb in the Imperative or the Optive to urge. It may also be put after the verb.

E. g., *do, calak'pe*, do go; *doya, idi oṭokam*, please, my boy, take it away (to the place known and leave it); *do na, hirikom*, please, girl, pay them a visit; *do sẹ, sap'ko tabonme*, do, catch them for us.

(*b*) *Dẹ*, *Dẹn*, } do, please, here, let us, give!
Dini, } give him!
Dinkin, } give the two!
Dẹnko, } give those!

These particles are used to urge, exhort or entreat. The fundamental form is *dẹ*, and this is enlarged into *dẹn*.* When the particle is an exhortation to give an animate being, the suffixed personal pronoun for the third pers. is added. It is noteworthy that for the sing. *i* is used in stead of *e*, in analogy with the forms of the demonstrative pronouns. The question is, whether the pronom. element is to be taken as an object infix, or the whole as a formation in analogy with the demonstrative pronouns. The last seems most likely. They do not, however, take postpositions, but may take the personal pronouns with the genitive *ṭa* prefixed added.

E. g., *dẹ lạime*, do tell; *dẹ sẹ, ẹmọk'me*, do give; *dẹ ho, thamakur ẹmok'tabonme*, please, give us tobacco; *dẹbo jọma*, let us eat; *dẹn daka*, please bring the food; *dẹnya ạguime*, do bring it, you; *dinitiń kisni*, give me my maena; *dinkin kaḍa laga ạgukinme*, please bring the two buffaloes along; *dẹnko hako ạgukom*, please bring the fishes.

* Possibly to be connected with the Aryan root *da*.

(*c*) *sẹ*, do, please!

Santali makes use of a *sẹ* added to certain interjections, optative and prohibitive particles and to Imperatives, conveying the idea of emphasis or of incitement or encouragement.

This *sẹ* may possibly be connected with Hindi (or Bihari) *sa* (found in some dialects as *se*), used as an adverbial suffix in the meaning of 'very', 'intensely'. It is different form the disjunctive particle *sẹ*.

E. g., *dẹ sẹ ẹmọk'me*, do give; *dela sẹ*, do come along; *alo sẹpe raga*, please do not cry; *ma sẹ amge rọṛtalaṅme*, you please speak for us two;

cet' baṅ sẹ, nonkan sebel utu dọ tis hõ baṅ cakha ạikạu akat'a, you have no idea, such savoury food I have never tasted; *baṅ sẹ, onka dọ bako rọṛa*, no, so people do not speak; *dạṛe dạṛkeda sẹ*, he ran, you should have seen how he ran.

(*d*) *Ma*, do, please, let them!

Ma is used as an interjection to express exhortation, urging, permission, concession. This *ma* is prefixed.

For other uses of *ma*, partly in connection with the verb, see para 332.

E. g., *ma ạbukok'me*, do wash yourself; *ma duṛup'me*, please sit down; *ma sẹ hijuk'me*, do come; *ma ẹnte*, well then, please;

iṅ ma baṅ aṅjọm akat', I have not heard it (so I can say nothing);

hẽ ma hẹge, that is quite so, but -.

(*e*) *Mẹ*, do, come along, get!

This interjection is used to express urging to act.

It is possibly an attenuation of *ma*. It is always prefixed.

E. g., *mẹ ọcọgok'me*, get out of the way; *mẹya hijuk'me*, come now, young felow; *mẹ sẹ oḍokok'pe*, please get out; *mẹ na* (to girls); *mẹ bon calak'a*, come let us go; *mẹ dela*, come along; *mẹ delabon, nit bon calak'a*, come all of us, now we shall go.

To cats:

pusic', get off!
gunu gunu, come!

Cats are also very common with the Santals.

The Santals do not keep other animals as a rule. If they e. g. have a pony (now-a-days some more well-to-do Santals have), they address these as they have learnt from the other races.

Additions and Corrections.

p. 10, (end of para 9). The two additional examples here following will help to show the way in which the language works:

Jãwãe, son-in-law, husband; *jãwãetẹt'*, the son-in-law; *jãwãeyic'*, the married girl (lit. the husbanded one); *jãwãekedeako*, they married her; *jãwãeyenae*, she was married. It should be possible to translate the last two expressions 'they made him a son-in-law' and 'he became a son-in law'; these construction are not, however, used in this meaning.

Bạhu, daughter-in-law, bride, wife; *bạhukedeako*, they made her their daughter-in-law; *bạhuadeako*, they procured a wife for him.

One may in these two examples also see how the social laws or ideas influence the language.

p. 20-25. Add the following:

(after section *Gọrọm*) ***Buḍhiạ*** and *buḍhi ayo* may be used about a (still living) grand-mother.

Jiạ (*-ń*, *-m*, *-t*), (my, etc.) grandmother (rarely used alone); *jiạ* (*-ń*, *-m*, *-t*) *buḍhi*, do.; *bońga jiạ* (*-ń*, *-m*, *-t*), (my, etc.) paternal grandmother; ***hẹrẹ jiạ*** (*-ń*, *-m*, *-t*), (my, etc.) maternal grandmother.

Tata (*-ń*, *-m*, *-t*), (my, etc.) grandfather; *jiạ* (*-ń*, *-m*, *-t*) *tata* (*-ń*, *-m*, *-t*), (my, etc.) grandparents.

Nạti nạtkạr, grandchildren.

(after section *Goṅgo*) *Hoṃoṇ* (*-iṅ, -me, -tet'*), (my, etc.) elder brother's child, nephew; used only by a woman, by a man's younger sister about his children, but is not used by a man.

(after section *Hatom*) *Nana,* father's sister (in address only).

(after section *Bhagna*) Note, *bhagna* is used by a man about his sister's children, not by a woman, except that a man's wife will use it about her husband's sister's children.

p. 30, para 23 (b). Add: The following expression is heard: *bhitri do alom baeyea,* don't bury (him or her) deep, about the burying of the placenta after birth (*baea,* inanimate construction as would seem natural, is however, also heard).

p. 30, para 23 (e). Add: A star constellation may be constructed inanimate, when the name used ordinarily is inanimate and *ipil* is omitted. *Buḍhi parkom sidup'ena,* the Ursa major has got into an erect position.

p. 100, top line. 108 (the para number) has fallen out.

p. 113. Add at end of para 124: Any animate pronoun of the classes mentioned will, when attached to and preceding an inanimate word, have the meaning of a possessive pronoun. When preceding an animate word, it may do service as a possessive pr., but not necessarily so. *Ale oṛak',* our house; *onko oṛak',* their house; *okoe oṛak',* whose house; *ale haṛam,* our old man (housefather); *ale hoṛ,* we Santals; *okoe haṛam,* which old man; *onko koṛa,* those boys (but may also mean, their boy).

p. 135, l. 4 from below: para number 151 should be 152.

p. 150, top line. For 'possibly connected with *cet*' read 'to be connected with *ceta,* with *t* or *t'* suffixed'.

At the end of this section add: The language has an interrogative pronoun *ceta,* in this bare form heard preceded by *sẹ*, finishing off a question, and conveying the meaning of a remonstrating, reproving or simply wondering 'or what?', 'or how?' *E. g., calak'am sẹ ceta?* will you go or what? *nonkako rọṛa sẹ ceta?* they say so, don't they?

When *ceta* has not been noticed before, the cause is that it has always been taken to be *cet'a,* and not *ceta.* It has, however, the full, not the checked consonant.

This *ceta* (probably composed of *ce+ta*; cf. footnote p. 153) takes the suffixed personal pronouns (see para 111) *cetań, cetam* and *cetat,* lit. my, your, his what. *Cetań* is very rarely heard and many Santals will not acknowledge it to be a form used by them. *Cetam* is commonly used by women (rarely by men); a sideform *cetame,* also, but rarely heard, corresponding to forms like *mocame* (with long and stressed *a*), proves the explanation of the form given above. *Cetat* is very common. *Cetat'* may be explained in the same way as, e. g., *ẹntẹt'* for *ẹnte* (for, because). See para 371.

Cetam (and *cetame*) are used also as interrogative adverbs in the meaning of 'why', 'wherefore', more especially by women (rarely by men). The examples here following will show the use of these both as pronouns and as adverbs.

Cetań hǫ bańtiń, marań utạr oṛak'iń ẹhọp' akat'a, cetańte bhalań kạmi ocoea, I have absolutely nothing, I have commenced to build a very large house, what have I to pay people to work? *cetam hǫ bań tama, họṛ tuluc'em kạphạriạu baṛaea, mǫṛẽ họṛko sap'lem khan cetamem ẹma,* you have absolutely nothing, you are quarrelling with people, if the village council lays hold of you what have you to give (in fine)? *haṭtem calak' kana, thamakur ḍher ñõk' ạgu daraeme; cet'teñ kiriña? cetañteñ ạguia,* you are going to the market, bring a good quantity of tobacco with you; what shall I buy it with? what have I to get it? *bam hala daṛeak' khan cetamem ạgu baṛaea? nitok' dọm oko baṛae kana, cetamre cetam bañtam,* if you are unable to pay back, why are you borrowing? now you are hiding, you have absolutely nothing; *cetam·tem halawakoa,* what have you to pay them back with? *dam họ bạnuk'talea, cetameyem ạguale kana,* we have nothing to pay with, why are you bringing us this? (in this last example *cetame* is pronounced with stress on the lengthend *a*); *cetamre cetam dhẹj bañtama, itạ bae reak'; nitok' dọ itại ñam kana, cetamrem ñama,* you are quite unable to manage, even to lay aside some seed; now he is asking for seed, where have you anything from where to get it? All examples with *cetam* are women's scolding.

p. 153. A para 186 A should be added: Interrogative adverbs referring to cause or reason.

Cedak' (i. e. *cet'+ak'*, why, wherefore?

Cak' (possibly *ce+ak'* with elimination of *e*), why, wherefore?

Cetam (*cetame*), why? (with a reproving meaning; see above note ad p. 150).

Cedak'em dalkedea, why did you beat him? *cak'·em laiket'a,* why did you blab? (both *cak'* and *cedak'* have often a side-meaning of reproof, but are not considered abuse, as *cetam* often is).

p. 177. l. 3 from above: for 200 read 210.

p. 217. l. 10 from above 'caught hold of' has fallen out; it should be 'if he had not caught hold of my arm'.

p. 237. Para 311, 2nd line should be: 'The Medium and the Passive Voice.'

p. 246. l. 3 from above: omit 324.

p. 256. Part of l. 15 and 16 from above should read : 'with direct and indirect object.'

p. 270, para 345. The following particles, *bhaṭẹć*, *bhaṭić*, *bhaṭkạm*, *bhaṭkẹć*, *bhaṭkić* may also be used in the way mentioned. The *bh* goes to support the suggestion in the footnote p. 270.

p. 274, para 349. Add : Besides the words quoted the following should be mentioned, none of these having a seperate existence; they are always added to a verbal base :

oco, causative or permissive (see para 219) ;

oṭo, added to a verbal base denotes that the agent performs an act and departs. In the Active with direct object it is always followed by an Intentional verbal suffix, except in the Anterior Past, where no Intentional suffix is found.

Idi oṭokadeań, I took him there (and came away) ; *bạgi oṭoaeme*, leave it for him and come away.

bọṭẹc', always added to a verbal base, conveys the idea of what might, perhaps, possibly, likely happen. *Lại bọṭẹc'keae*, he may (might) possibly tell ; *ńẹl baṛalegeń, menak' bọṭẹc'a*, let me look for it first, it is possibly there ; *hẹc' bọṭẹc'kok'ae*, he might come ; *rọṛ bọṭẹc' akat'am*, you may likely have said so ; *dal bọṭẹc'kemae*, he may likely (or might) beat you.

p. 277, para 349 (g). Add : *baṛa* is very frequently added to words otherwise only adverbially used, to form a verb denoting performance or occurrense of what the main word denotes. The addition of *baṛa* often makes the use of an Active suffix possible. *Bhasań bhusuń baṛae kanae*, he is constantly going here and there.